MARTHA inc.

**THE
INCREDIBLE
STORY OF
MARTHA
STEWART
LIVING
OMNIMEDIA**

CHRISTOPHER BYRON

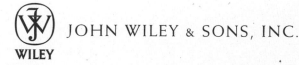

JOHN WILEY & SONS, INC.
WILEY

Published by John Wiley & Sons, Inc., New York.
Published simultaneously in Canada.

Wiley also publishes its books in a variety of electronic formats. Some content that appears in print may not be available in electronic books. For more information about Wiley products visit our Web site at www.wiley.com.

ISBN 0-471-12300-5 (cloth ed.)
ISBN 0-471-42958-9 (paper ed.)

Printed in the United States of America.

10 9 8 7 6 5 4 3 2 1

*Do not wish to be
anything but what
you are, and to be
that perfectly.*

—Saint Francis de Sales

CONTENTS

PROLOGUE   1

1   NANCY DREW AND THE CASE OF THE HIDDEN CHILDHOOD   33

2   A MODEL LIFE   47

3   TO WALL STREET   63

4   THE PAGE TURNS   75

5   A NASCENT EMPIRE: THE MARTHA MOMENT IS BORN   87

6   WHO'S AFRAID OF VIRGINIA WOOLF?   99

7   MAKING THE BEST-SELLER LIST   109

8   KMART CALLS   133

9   HOW TO NEGOTIATE A CONTRACT   155

10   STRATEGY: GET OTHERS TO PAY   173

11   CONTROLLING THE STRESS LINES   187

12   NO GOOD DEED GOES UNPUNISHED   203

13   TIME TAKES MARTHA   215

14   MARTHA TAKES TV   225

15 IN THE COMPANY OF WOMEN   243

16 SCHEMING TIMES   261

17 A TAXING SITUATION   273

18 TIME TAKES A LICKING   283

19 LABOR RELATIONS   297

20 WHEN BEING IN THE PUBLIC EYE IS NOT
    A GOOD THING   309

21 FROM WALL STREET TO MAIN STREET   337

22 TO THE ENDS OF THE EARTH   355

EPILOGUE   365

ACKNOWLEDGMENTS   391

SOURCE NOTES   393

INDEX   433

PROLOGUE

I t was 5:30 A.M. on a June morning in midtown Manhattan, and on Madison Avenue about the only signs of life came from a sanitation truck that slowly worked its way up the street. Every half-block or so the truck would stop, its brakes screeching in the damp air that clung to the pavement. Then two men at the back would hop off and begin collecting the plastic garbage bags that are the by-product of successful commerce on one of the world's fanciest shopping boulevards.

It can get hot in New York in June, really hot, as anyone who hasn't left already for the Shore (or the Hamptons, or upstate) will tell you. And in the predawn hours of this particular day in late June, one group of New Yorkers was feeling the heat already.

These were the 120 employees of the CBS television network who worked on the network's 7 A.M. to 9 A.M. program, known as *The Early Show*. The time-slot had been a problem for the network for years, and indeed even longer than that. Yet suddenly, and out of nowhere, a crisis had erupted that represented both an opportunity and a threat. Handled well, the situation could bring new life, vitality, and stability to a revolving door operation whose executive producer and star had both left the show only weeks earlier. Handled poorly and network officials could easily conclude that the show was unfixable and simply cancel it, turning the time-slot back to local affiliate stations to do with it what they wished—something they had done at least once in the past already.

In the spotlight and ready for her close-up: The show's affable and somewhat shell-shocked young co-anchor, Jane Clayson. As she settled into her dressing room chair for the airbrushed application of her makeup, no one had to remind her of the stakes involved, from the $30 million studio that CBS had built to showcase the talents of her recently departed boss and co-host to the obvious fact that her own job was now on the line as well. The latest in a long list of female co-hosts who had tried to make a name for themselves in what had come to be viewed as the CBS death slot, Clayson was about to square off in what promised to be the make-or-break interview of her career.

In fact, there seemed little doubt that the interview in question would be one of the toughest, most contentious, and possibly even vicious, that CBS had ever aired. Not only did the subject matter involve questions of a possible felony crime—always a dangerous area for a journalist to explore—but in this case there was something more . . . something that promised to push the looming encounter beyond normal journalism entirely. In this interview, Clayson would be facing off against nothing less than her show's most popular regular guest, Martha Stewart, arguably the best known and most widely admired woman in America—and network higher-ups, from her own boss, Michael Bass, up to the head of the entire CBS News Division, Andrew Heyward, had made it clear that she was to pull no punches.

No one at CBS wanted this to be happening—least of all in a way that put the spotlight on a chronically troubled programming time-slot that the network had spent millions trying to fix. But the crisis had ballooned into a challenge from which the network could not shrink. As far as the brass at CBS were concerned, there was simply no choice: Everything rode on Clayson's ability to rise to the moment and somehow get a woman widely regarded as the very paradigm of domestic virtue to say on television whether or not she was a thief and a liar.

The interview was no less significant to Martha Stewart, who dreaded the very thought of it, and had been fighting with every resource at her command to avoid it. At what appeared to be the peak of a 30-year career as the embodiment of all that that the American woman could and should be, Martha Stewart now found herself suddenly and astoundingly at the center of a Wall Street financial scandal that she seemed to be making bigger and more unmanageable with her every attempt to escape from it. For whatever reason, her legendary talent for successful self-promotion had deserted her at the moment she needed it most. In almost no time at all she had morphed into an object of scorn, derision, and even hilarity—America's new national joke.

How could something like this have happened? The whole of America seemed amazed and confounded by the spectacle—and no one more so than I. Three months earlier a book I had written on Martha Stewart had been published, and happily for me, it had done well, offering a portrait of a successful businesswoman and her hidden world of unfulfilled dreams and deep private torments. Then, scarcely had the book reached bookstores when Martha appeared to rush onstage with a performance of accelerated self-destruction—from the very hobgoblins of her past that stalked the pages of *Martha Inc.*

More than half a century of history lay behind this approaching moment for Martha Stewart and CBS alike, and both were now hurtling toward each other with a force and momentum that no one could have imagined even a few weeks earlier.

For the past three years, *The Early Show* had been broadcast from a street-level studio on Fifth Avenue at Fifty-ninth Street. The studio had been built to showcase the network's latest attempt to make the time-slot competitive against its network rivals NBC and ABC. Both had street-level studios of their own only a few blocks away, and CBS executives thought it only proper to offer their show's newly hired anchor, Bryant Gumbel, and his co-host, Jane Clayson, the same. (Also, if the show flopped, no executive wanted to take the blame for not having provided the same sort of set-up that had worked for their rivals. If nothing else, the studio on Fifty-ninth Street was thus, in the least, a $30 million lucky rabbit's foot.)

What's more, the new facility also represented a break with the network's many previous failed efforts to make a success of the morning time slot—all of which efforts had been broadcast from CBS's main studio facilities. The place was known as the CBS Broadcast Center, and it was located 10 blocks across town on West Fifty-seventh Street. The facility was cavernous and largely windowless, and at one point in its history had actually been a horse stable.

Yet for the past 40 years, the Broadcast Center had been the true heart of CBS. Eric Severeid had worked there, as had Walter Cronkite. And so did Dan Rather, now broadcasting from his anchor desk at the center of a massive two-story interior space known as Studio 47, which the network built for him in 1986 after he had replaced Walter Cronkite and ratings for the *CBS Evening News* had started to fall.

Predictably, construction of the new studio did nothing to lift the ratings of the *CBS Evening News.* But when the network's executives decided 15 years later to go all out in a last desperate effort at reviving the 7 A.M. to 9 A.M. time-slot by sticking Gumbel and Clayson in it, they instinctively built them a whole new studio, just as had been done for Rather—and this time with as much distance as possible between the new place and CBS's past.

Thus, it came to pass that on this early June morning of 2002, one of the most stunning news interviews in the history of CBS was about to take place, not under the watchful bronze gaze of Edward R. Murrow, whose bust greets all visitors in the lobby of the CBS Broadcast Center, but across town in the chrome and smoked glass surroundings of a studio that had been built by CBS executives in homage to the goddesses of pretence and illusion—the same two deities that the show's guest that morning wished just as desperately to claim as her own.

The overnight mist still clung to the streets when a limousine swung to the curbside on Madison Avenue, and eased to a halt. Its arrival was not unexpected, as evidenced by the reporters who were already beginning to gather.

The limo contained lawyers (how many no one counted), and one after the next they emerged—purposeful looking, with briefcases at the ready—and headed into the building. They had come for what all knew or doubtless suspected—to be the latest, and maybe last, "Mission Impossible" in a season overflowing with impossible missions already. Their assignment: To try, one last time, to pressure Clayson and her boss Michael Bass, the show's executive producer, into letting Martha control the terms under which she would appear on the show.

But it was hopeless, and they knew it, because more than two straight weeks of attempting to accomplish just that had gotten them nowhere. Instead, the network had stood firm, insisting just as adamantly that it, and it alone, would set the agenda for the interview. So, despite their best efforts, the weeks had dwindled to mere hours, and the moment was now at hand. In barely three hours' time, the central figure in a scandal that had consumed the nation—Martha Kostyra Stewart, the Queen of the American kitchen—would have to present herself, live and unrehearsed, before the unblinking stare of a CBS news camera, and somehow convince the world that she was neither a chiseler nor a fraud. And as all knew too well, it was going to be Hell.

The actual details of what had led to this moment were known only to a few. But the still-incomplete narrative—and the rumors and speculation that formed its missing, connective tissue—had already become, scarcely one week into the summer of 2002, possibly the biggest and most distracting obsession on earth. What Martha Stewart had done, or said (or not done, or not said . . . to whom, when, and why) on a certain day the previous December, had already ballooned into congressional hearings in Washington. Investigations were underway at the Securities & Exchange Commission and the Department of Justice. Her behavior had become the focus of nonstop chatter on cable TV, on network news shows, and on radio talk shows.

And it was no different abroad. In Britain, Martha Stewart had suddenly and astoundingly upstaged Princess Di as the preoccupation of Fleet Street. At the BBC, producers scoured the earth looking for people to put on the air and interview about her. She was making headlines from Pakistan to Brazil, from Canada to Sydney to Seoul. Wherever one looked, people wanted to know the same thing: What exactly had Martha done, why had she done it, and would she go to prison for it?

The focus of all this frenzy was a handwritten note on a single piece of paper in a secretary's phone log. The secretary worked for a well-known Manhattan business figure named Samuel Waksal, who headed a New York-based biotech company bearing the name Im-Clone Systems, Inc. The note itself disclosed little, revealing only that at shortly after 1:30 P.M. on the afternoon of December 27, 2001, a person identifying herself as Martha Stewart had placed a telephone call to Waksal's office, left a brief message, and asked that he return the call.

By a curious set of events that had begun that same month with a stalled government investigation in Washington, DC, the note had found its way from the secretary's desk into the hands of a talkative congressional press aide, as well as to investigators for the Securities & Exchange Commission and the FBI. Two months later, the existence of the note was leaked to the press, along with evidence that Martha had sold close to a quarter million dollars worth of ImClone stock at almost exactly the moment she was placing the call—and her life exploded in a firestorm of rumors and speculation.

It was the context of the note, more than its actual contents, that set the Martha Stewart story ablaze. Though Stewart and Waksal had occasionally been linked in the society pages, the nature of their relationship was almost never discussed. The two simply tended to appear together at summer social functions in the fashionable Long

Island village of East Hampton, where both owned homes, and that was about it.

But now came *The Note*, with its subtext of suggestion that their relationship operated on more than one level. And thanks to Sam Waksal's own collapsing image, the public perception of Martha took on a new and disturbing dimension.

Until lately, Waksal's company, ImClone Systems, Inc., had enjoyed a high-flying stock price fueled by excitement in the press that the company was on the verge of bringing to market a revolutionary new drug for the treatment of cancer. The drug, called Erbitux, had been under development for a decade, and though it had yet to make ImClone's shareholders a dime in profits, it had made Waksal both rich and famous, as he basked in his twin roles of humanitarian business leader on the one hand, and art connoisseur on the other.

But Waksal had secrets of his own to hide, and they were stranger and more menacing—to himself and those around him—than even the darkest of shadows from Martha's own past. Unknown to almost anyone, Waksal was a thief and had been one for years.

To maintain the lavish lifestyle that gave him entrée to a cache of celebrities and fast-lane friends, he stole freely, even wantonly, year after year—seemingly anywhere and anyhow he could. He stole from his own company, ImClone Systems, Inc., by taking out personal loans from the company treasury that he never paid back. He hid money in offshore shell companies that he maintained in Switzerland and the British Virgin Islands, also illegally. He stole from his banks by double-pledging the same collateral for separate loans. He cheated on his taxes, he chiseled his financial backers, he ripped off his own employees and business partners, and lately he'd even begun entangling members of his own family in his plots.

But he did it with such charm and finesse that no one seemed any the wiser—or at least no one seemed to care. So he had stayed at it, year after year, even as the sums grew larger, and the thievery more aggressive and obvious. And the more he stole, the more he spent—on homes, apartments, artwork, real estate—until, by the end of 2001, he was more than $70 million in debt, with the entire affair held together by a scaffolding of fraudulent bank loans, illegal stock sales, and worthless promissory notes.

As 2001 drew to a close, the facade covering Waksal's frauds at last started to crumble. The problems began late in December, when federal regulators at the U.S. Food & Drug Administration (FDA) ruled that ImClone's field testing of Erbitux had been so slipshod and flawed that they could not give approval for the drug to be sold to the public. If ImClone wanted to bring Erbitux to market, it would have to redo the field tests all over again—a process that could take years and would likely bankrupt the company.

No outsider yet knew the panic this unleashed in Waksal, who had already learned of the FDA's intentions through an ImClone lobbyist in Washington. But a clear sign of trouble came when, for no apparent reason—and on literally the eve of the FDA announcement—an avalanche of ImClone stock cascaded onto the market. It was an obvious case of insider selling, and as the winter of 2002 gave way to spring, suspicion began to center more and more on Waksal himself as the culprit.

Martha had fans by the millions, to be sure, and they adored her. But many people also disliked her, and some even loathed her. So, when the note of her December 27 phone call to Waksal surfaced on June 7, she was quickly dragged into the center of the scandal, as suspicion spread that she too had been illegally dumping ImClone stock in advance of bad news that would devastate ImClone stock.

The note simply read, "1:43 Martha Stewart something is going on with ImClone and she wants to know what She is on her way to Mexico and she is staying at Los Ventanos."

But those 28 words—jotted down punctuation-free and in haste by a secretary who had been fielding calls to her boss every few minutes since 10 o'clock that morning—began making headlines at the very moment when Waksal was being arrested on charges of insider trading, in the midst of an avalanche of CEO scandals and corporate fraud. In the process, Martha, who consistently denied having done anything wrong, morphed from Ultimate Homemaker into Ultimate Stock Market Swindler, poster gal for the CEO Crime Wave that had become Wall Street's legacy from the Great Bull Market of the 1990s.

The three weeks between June 7, when news of her phone call to Waksal first broke in the press, and her close-up before CBS's cameras on the morning of June 25, were simply unbelievable. On June 6, she took a seat as a member of the Board of Governors of the New York Stock Exchange (NYSE) in what should have been the crowning moment of her career as a businesswoman. The very next day the scandal exploded and cries instantly arose that NYSE governor Richard Grasso toss her off the board. The stock price of her company, Martha Stewart Living Omnimedia, Inc., collapsed. She became the target of just about every editorial cartoonist in the country. Crowds of reporters gathered at the driveways of every home she owned, pursuing her everywhere with shouted questions about her trading activities in ImClone's shares. And the more she ran from the questions, the more her behavior became its own unspoken answer. She was convicting herself in the court of public opinion before she'd been formally accused of anything.

Cocktail party gossips exclaimed that even her appearance was fraying. Martha spotters noted that she was putting on weight, that her hair often looked unwashed and unstyled. It seemed as though she had aged overnight, with her once golden face taking on a haggard look. At one point, she took to wearing a raincoat when she went outside whether it was raining or not.

Martha's behavior quickly swung the spotlight to CBS, where she had been doing weekly homemaking and cooking segments for the *The Early Show* since 1997. Though the program's format was largely entertainment-based, with lots of easy, back-and-forth banter between Gumbel and Clayson, the show itself was a property of the CBS News Division. And that, in turn, brought into play a whole new, and more stringent set of standards for accuracy and fairness than prevailed elsewhere at the network.

At CBS Entertainment, headed by Nancy Tellem, you could reenact events through invented dialogue and actors. You could use special effects to enhance the dramatic impact of a shooting or a plane crash. In the Entertainment Division, it was the theatrical impact of the show that counted.

By contrast, at the News Division it was still fairness and accuracy that counted for most. And that put the division—in fact, the whole network—on the spot when Martha, whose Tuesday morning segments were the show's single most popular feature, began more and more to act as if she had something to hide.

To be sure, the CEO Crime Wave had been a plenty big story before Martha came along. But now that she had popped up in the middle of it, the story had become a hundred times larger, as white collar crime on Wall Street spread from the business pages of broadsheet newspapers, to the covers of magazines that more typically chronicled Rosie O'Donnell's weight issues.

For CBS, the problem was acute—and that was especially so for Andrew Heyward, the head of the network's News Division. Under his predecessor, Eric Ober, the News Division had suffered a series of devastating setbacks, and when Ober was replaced by Heyward in early 1996, the division's fortunes continued to sag while its ratings just kept slumping.

The 7 A.M. to 9 A.M. time-slot was the biggest problem of all, as it had been for a generation. It seemed that nothing could dislodge the *Today* show for long from its permanent position as Number One. And after the *Today* show came *Good Morning America* at ABC.

Heyward tried everything he could think of, including a 1997 raid on NBC, from which he lured away Martha Stewart to become a CBS "lifestyle correspondent" for the morning slot. Yet after a momentary burst in the ratings, the viewers drifted away and the situation reverted to lackluster.

Next, Heyward turned to Bryant Gumbel, who had earlier stepped aside as host of the *Today* show and taken up a life of early retirement as a nonstop golfer. Luring him back to work with a $5 million annual contract, Heyward made him host of a TV news-magazine called *Public Eye*. But the show quickly proved a flop and was cancelled. So Heyward next set him to work on a series of profiles, but they wound up rendering his new $5-million-a-year man almost invisible, both inside the company and out.

Finally, in late 1999, faced with poor ratings and an expensive news celebrity who wasn't doing much, Heyward tried his last, most desperate shot. He convinced Gumbel to return to morning television as the foundering show's new anchor. Its oft-changed name was changed yet again—from *This Morning* to *The Early Show*. Clayson was lured away from ABC, the obligatory new studio was constructed, and the new show went on the air—almost literally a clone of the the *Today* show formula.

Now, less than three years later, here was Heyward in this impossible mess, with the very first person he had brought to the morning time-slot, Martha Stewart, having long since established herself as the show's most popular and durable personality, now dragging the entire corporation into a fiasco of her own creation—one that she kept making worse every day by her bizarre and inexplicable behavior.

Harvard-educated Heyward had spent nearly his entire adult life at CBS News, beginning as a news writer for the network's local New York station, WCBS-TV, in 1976 and moving up from there, typically by playing to his strengths as a consensus builder who avoided confrontation whenever possible. Some of his colleagues thus viewed him as weak, and said he had let Nancy Tellem's predecessor in the Entertainment Division, Les Moonves, gain the upper hand in the relentless power struggles that had gone on for generations between the network's News and Entertainment Divisions.

In 1998, Moonves was elevated from head of the Entertainment Division to head of all of CBS Television, with his successor, Tellem, and Heyward, now officially both reporting to him. Meanwhile, the memory of Heyward's own failed struggles with Moonves lingered on, underscoring a sense within the News Division that the Entertainment Division was still calling the shots.

Unfortunately for Heyward, it was a view that put him on the spot, for having lured Martha away from NBC, he could hardly now permit her to continue with her weekly appearances on *The Early Show* without confirming the belief that the entertainment value of a media personality like Martha Stewart was more important to CBS than the journalistic principles of the News Division itself.

Much as he might have wished it otherwise, the question was thus ultimately quite simple: Who was really in charge of CBS News, Heyward or Martha Stewart? How could CBS News ever cover any scandal in the future if one of the network's own top on-air talents could stir up a global scandal about herself, and then refuse to answer questions about it even for her own CBS viewers?

No one on *The Early Show* doubted that Martha Stewart was a valuable asset. Granted, her contribution to the show's ratings was modest, in part because she normally appeared only during the last half hour segment, from 8:30 A.M. to 9 A.M. During this period, viewership dropped precipitously anyway, typically totaling no more than about two million as compared with more than five million for the *Today* show, and four million for *Good Morning America*. But Martha gave the show something more than mere ratings, she gave it prestige and a sense of stability among advertisers who didn't like the feeling of constant turmoil that seemed to envelop the show.

For the show's staffers, it was all rather ironic, because up-close and off-camera, Martha had been a one-woman storm of turmoil from the moment she walked onto the set. Her segments aired regularly each Tuesday, and she typically arrived with an entourage who prepared her segments, cooked all the actual food, and handled the set-ups for handicraft activities.

To the show's cameramen and floor technicians, her demeanor seemed arrogant and imperious from day one, and they soon took to regaling one another with stories of her abusive behavior, much of which seemed to fall on a member of her entourage who went simply by the name of "Ski." His job seemed basically to follow her around, making himself constantly at the ready to answer any question or execute some command.

"I don't know how to do this!" she would bark, holding up a seashell for a crafts segment on the decoration of picture frames, and Ski would leap forward to show her.

Still more of her abuse fell on a waif-like creature whose name most of the crew never learned. But all would observe her with a mixture of fascination and horror as week after week she'd arrive as a member of the entourage—almost anorexic in appearance—and week after week be subjected to ritual tongue lashings from Martha for one perceived failing or another. By the end of the morning, she'd typically leave shaking, but the next week she'd be back, and the week after that.

Oblivious to those around her, Martha put on performances of such encompassing self-absorption that crew members eventually began swapping their stories back and forth as if they were trading baseball cards. She complained constantly that her kitchen set— specially designed to her specifications by the show's set designer, was sneakily being used in her absence by CBS staffers who habitually failed to clean up after themselves and left the place a dirty and unsanitary mess. Eventually Post-it notes began appearing everywhere. "Keep Out!" read the warnings, and "Wash Your Hands!" and "This Means You!"

So the news spread like wildfire one morning when one of the floor crew happened to wander into the kitchen, only to find Martha seated on a countertop, her bare feet on the counter in front of her, with a member of her entourage hunched over them in concentration, giving, as one staffer put it, milady a pedicure.

Only the show's anchor, Bryant Gumbel, seemed to be able to handle Martha, which he did by mastering a kind of "yessum" demeanor, as if he were a combination of cowed son and kitchen help. The staff thought this hilarious because Gumbel had a temper of his own, and no one could be sure which of the two would blow up at some luckless staffer first, after which the couple would revert to their schtick as CBS News' off-camera "Bryant & Mom Show."

But Gumbel had been gone from the show for more than a month by now, and in the vacuum created by his departure, Martha's presence grew larger and more overbearing than ever—magnified by the escalating headlines concerning her involvement with Waksal.

As a result, and perhaps not surprisingly, whenever Martha was not around, the floor crew acted as if they were grade school children whose teacher had just left the room. Two of the crew were always in the thick of it, making jokes about her size ("Martha's getting LAARGER . . . !") and passing around whatever cartoons of her had been clipped that morning from the papers. Then Martha would walk onto the set and all cartoons would instantly disappear, leaving only the sound of the occasional, stifled snicker from one or the other of them still lingering in the air: "I wonder what colors she's going to use in her cell?"

The show's surviving star, Jane Clayson, understood the need for the crew to let off tension. But as cruel as Martha had been to them, and even to her own staff, Clayson seemed to feel a certain sympathy for the woman, and she would sometimes confide her feelings to others.

"Jane viewed Martha as a troubled and lonely woman," said one. "And she felt that deep within her there was a basic decency that had somehow gotten warped and destroyed. What a life she must have had, to have put up a wall of such hostility and defense!"

The source paused for a moment and then, remembering something Clayson had once said, continued: "Jane told me that Martha once gave a Mother's Day present to Jane's mother—a handmade craft gift of some sort. And Jane was really touched, and her mother was, too, because neither one had expected anything of the sort."

The source shrugged, then added, "It seemed so out of character to Jane for Martha to have done that, especially in light of how she'd dealt with those around her on the show. Jane talked to me about it afterward . . . not once but several times. She just could never quite figure out what was at the core of Martha Stewart."

Clayson had not asked for the role that fate had now assigned her. But anyone who thought she'd be a pushover for the parboiled Martha Stewart, didn't know the toughness that lurked beneath her Noxema Girl good looks.

Blonde and trim, with piercing blue eyes and a ready smile, Clayson looked like a college coed barely old enough to vote. The first time he met her, the network's official living legend, Mike Wallace, came completely apart. The occasion was an editorial meeting in the CBS Broadcast Center on Fifty-seventh Street, and a source in the room later reported seeing Wallace slipping Clayson notes as the meeting progressed. Later the word got around that the notes contained advice from Wallace regarding how to handle an interview Clayson had set up for the following day with then-presidential-candidate George W. Bush Jr.

Said Wallace's colleague, Andy Rooney, when he subsequently met her, "Oh my God, I'm in love."

What neither man knew was that behind Clayson's charm and ingénue looks was a 34-year-old woman of extraordinary toughness and courage. Though no one would have guessed it without reading her clip-file, Clayson belonged to a rare breed of women indeed—the female war correspondent—and as a network reporter based out of Los Angeles for ABC News, she had covered everything from the fighting in Bosnia and Kosovo to street rioting in Jakarta, Indonesia.

Now she would need all the toughness, determination—and at the same time diplomacy and tact—she could call on to draw forth from Martha Stewart the truth that Stewart seemed just as determined to refrain from sharing. Negotiations over the interview had gone on for more than a week, but mostly the two sides wound up talking past each other. Martha's people wanted to control the content of the questioning, whereas CBS wanted only to offer her the best and most relaxed setting possible so she'd feel more at ease with what was going to be an excruciating segment to say the least.

But the Stewart side rejected everything, up to and including the suggestion of the executive producer, Michael Bass, that the interview take place in the most dignified setting the show could offer: the same sofa and backdrop that was used for interviews with presidents and visiting heads of state. But the Stewart team rejected it. Martha would feel more comfortable in her kitchen, they insisted. And so the curtain rose on one of the most astonishing interviews in CBS history—made all the more memorable, and even surreal, by the setting Martha had insisted on: her TV show kitchen, because there, it was felt, she could be most herself.

By the time Martha arrived at the set, her advance party of lawyers had already retreated in defeat. One had gotten as far as an actual face-to-face with Michael Bass. The lawyer had wanted to make one last plea to set the agenda for the interview—that is, to spell out specifically what Martha should be asked and what Clayson should steer clear of. But his arguments were by now familiar and not only unconvincing, but downright irrelevant. It simply made no difference whether the subject was under investigation by the Feds, by Congress, by anyone. So what if Martha had been told not to talk, on advice of her counsel? Martha's lawyers had one agenda, but CBS had another—the public interest—and whether she answered Clayson's questions or not, Clayson was going to ask them.

Martha's segment was not scheduled to air until the 8:40 A.M. time-slot. But she arrived early, and flanked by assistants, headed straight for an empty desk. Undeterred by the failure of her lawyers to sway Bass in the Control Room, she commandeered the desk's computer and began furiously typing away. Moments later, she snatched up a printout of her work and headed for the Control Room to show it to Bass. It was a script of the questions she wanted Clayson to ask her—to each one of which she had written out the very answer she had already memorized and now intended to provide.

But this was the same basic plea her lawyers had already made unsuccessfully that morning . . . the same approach her legal team and PR aides had been futilely pressuring CBS to agree to all week . . . the same approach, in fact, that now seemed to define what so much of TV itself had become, with its fake spontaneity and scripted sincerity: an exercise in the witchcraft of illusion.

Yet here she was, confronting the most volatile and dangerous moment of her career, when she needed more than ever to take control, not of the circumstance but of herself—in short, to calm down and dial back the rage that was consuming her. Instead, minute-by-minute she was cranking up the heat and making herself angrier, as she struggled furiously and in vain to seize control of the interview—right up until mere minutes before it was to air.

"You could have heard a pin drop when she walked onto the set," said one floor crew member, recalling her angry red face and twitching jaw muscles. "The tension was just unbelievable."

Moments later, Clayson walked onto the floor as well and headed for the kitchen set. As she stepped around the counter and took her position at Martha's side, one of the cameramen muttered, "Here we go."

Clayson turned to Martha and smiled as she always did at the start of their segments. But Martha, who normally responded in kind, did not look or smile back. Instead she stared motionless, as if in a trance, at the countertop before her . . . and at the carving knife gripped in her hand.

What Clayson must have thought as she began interviewing a clearly angry woman with a carving knife in her hand isn't known to this day, but one can well imagine, as eight feet away and next to Camera One, the floor director began counting down the seconds and flicking out his fingers, "Five . . . four . . . three . . . two . . . one . . ." and then jabbed his forefinger at Clayson . . .

. . . and in two million homes across America, people looked up from whatever they were doing to see the familiar and attractive face of *The Early Show* co-host smile at them and say, just as natural as you please, and without even an introduction:

"As we've reported, our good friend Martha Stewart has been in the headlines lately, fighting allegations of insider stock trading stemming from her sale of shares in a company called ImClone.

"The investigation into Martha's transaction comes in the wake of the arrest of her friend, ImClone CEO Sam Waksal, who was charged with sharing negative information about the company before it became public. Martha did sell her shares one day before the announcement that an experimental cancer drug the company was working on was rejected by the FDA.

"But she said in a statement that her stock sale was, quote, 'proper and lawful' and that she was cooperating fully with authorities . . ."

There is a moment in the 1990 psycho-thriller *Misery* when the hefty-framed Kathy Bates, playing an outwardly sweet but secretly tormented woman named Annie Wilkes, begins to go through what develops during the course of the movie into one of the most horrifying transformations ever captured on film. At the beginning of the movie, she is seen rescuing a successful novelist, played by James Caan, whom she discovers near death in a snow bank after his car runs off the highway in a snowstorm. She hauls him back to her cabin and nurses him back to health. But as the movie progresses and he regains his strength and prepares to leave, she prevents him from doing so, eventually morphing into a maniac who breaks his legs with a sledge hammer to prevent him from leaving.

And in its way, something oddly reminiscent of that now began to unfold on the *The Early Show* set, as off to one side—and from a distance that seemed far but also near—Clayson could hear something . . . a strange sound . . . that she couldn't place . . .

She continued to speak, saying, "To further complicate matters, late last week the stockbroker who sold Martha's shares was suspended by Merrill Lynch for what it called 'factual issues regarding a client transaction.' . . ."

And the sound continued, growing louder. She hadn't heard it before . . . on the show . . . or anywhere . . . It was distracting . . . . methodical . . . metronome-like . . .

She pushed on: "The investigation into the matter is far from over. In the midst of all of this . . ." But the sound grew louder still, as if someone had crept onto the set and begun to hammer a nail.

whack . . . whack . . . thump . . . thump . . .

"Martha is here this morning for her weekly turn on *The Early Show* . . ."

louder and louder, whack thump, whack thump

"Martha, it's good to see you," and Clayson turned to welcome her guest . . . at which point she almost shrieked, for staring back at her in a rage, with her jaw muscles clenching to the beat of the whacking, and her eyes afire with fury, was the Queen of the American Home rhythmically smacking her carving knife against the mutilated mush of what had once been a head of cabbage . . . which Clayson knew was not cabbage at all, but so far as Martha was concerned, was actually Clayson's pretty blonde head.

And things went downhill from there.

"Hi," said Martha, as her whacking continued . . . "Well, we're going to make salad, but . . ."

Clayson cut her off. "We are," she said, "but first let me ask you a few things about all this. You . . . you've released a statement saying that you were not involved in any insider trading, but you haven't public . . . publicly commented on this. What . . . what do you say about the allegations here?"

Martha stared back furiously. "Well, you . . . as you understand, I'm involved in an investigation that has very s . . . serious implications. I . . . the investigation really centers around ImClone and its drug called Erbitux . . ." She began groping and stumbling, then recovered herself and continued, saying, ". . . I'm just not at liberty at this time to make any comments whatsoever, and I certainly hope that the matter is resolved in the very near future."

Clayson, referring next to Waksal, asked, "Are you worried that what he did might further complicate matters for you?"

Martha's responses now grew discordant and strange, as she answered, "Well, again, I have nothing to say on the matter. I'm . . . I'm really not at liberty to say . . ." Then, delivering the first of the two lines that were destined for sound-bite immortality, she said, "I think this will all be resolved in the very near future, and I will be exonerated of any ridiculousness."

Exonerated? Ridiculousness? *Wha . . . ?* Clayson was agog.

"I know that . . . I know that image is . . . is so important to you," she said, searching for the right words to convey the moment's surrealism, as the image-obsessed Martha Stewart pulled the pin on one image-shattering hand grenade after the next.

And then came the clincher—the second of Martha's comments that were headed for sound-bite stardom on the evening news—as she said, echoing the last incoherent ravings of Richard Nixon's goodbye speech to his White House staff, "Well, we have been the center of media—you know . . . I'm in the media business . . . that's why our company is called Martha Stewart Living Omnimedia. And I have been the subject of very favorable reporting . . . and very unfavorable reporting and . . . throughout the years . . . This is not new to me . . . And I choose to go ahead with my work . . . I go ahead to concentrate on the good work that our company does . . . My employees and I are hard at work at making our company the best omnimedia company in the world, Jane . . . And we will continue to do that, and . . ." as the whacking and slashing now began again, more furiously than ever, "I want to focus on my salad . . ."

Clayson tried to interrupt, but Martha shoved her aside.

"*. . . because that's why we're here.*"

It was? Even to the end, Martha never seemed to get the point of what the interview had been all about. Determined at all costs to avoid being questioned about her relationship to Waksal and what had transpired between them on December 27, she failed to realize, until it was too late, that the questions were ultimately unavoidable. As a result, she ignored exploiting what little of benefit might have been found for herself in the situation, and wound up coming across instead as imperious and angry at the thought of having to undergo any questioning at all.

Worse still, when Martha insisted, through her handlers and advisers, that the interview take place on the *The Early Show* kitchen set because it was there that she would feel most relaxed and able to "be herself," she made a spectacular blunder. Instead of choosing a setting that somehow emphasized the very "unfairness" of what was happening to her, she chose exactly the opposite, underscoring the very message she did not want to convey: Martha Stewart in her natural surroundings, knife in hand and sputtering incoherently at the forces arrayed against her.

Having remained adamant from the start that she was not going to answer any questions regarding the scandal, Martha at least might have tried to deflect responsibility for the stonewalling, pushing blame for her silence away from herself and onto others. For example, she might have tried insisting that while she herself was eager to answer Clayson's questions, it was her lawyers who wouldn't let her.

In short, she needed one way or another to present herself sympathetically to viewers as the situation's victim. But incredibly, she emerged instead as furious at the thought that some annoying nobody from CBS News should be interrupting her with questions about crime on Wall Street when she was trying to focus instead on the far weightier matter of how to chop up a head of cabbage.

As for Clayson, the *The Early Show* co-host had handled the situation perfectly, asking her questions nonconfrontationally but seriously, then artfully stepping back to let the "real" Martha Stewart show through: snarling, resentful, and in deep denial over what her life had now become.

The fallout from the interview proved catastrophic. By the end of the day, the price of her company's stock, Martha Stewart Living Omnimedia, Inc., had tumbled by more than 25 percent, and by the next morning nearly every major media outlet in the country had turned against her. "Martha Can't Hack Questions on TV" headlined the tabloid *Daily News* of New York, "Knives Out as Stewart Minces Words, Cabbage." Or, from the *Orlando Sentinel:* "Martha Chops Salad— Anchor Adds Pepper." Or, from *USA Today*, the sound-bite headline that seemed to say it all: "Stewart: I Want to Focus on My Salad."

I n researching and writing *Martha Inc.* it had seemed to me as if Martha Stewart's life had all along been a kind of high-wire act, as she moved forward by constantly seeking a balance between the call of greatness and even genius, and the pull of some darker energy that forever threatened to consume her from within. In the summer of 2002, she finally seemed to lose that balance, and all forward movement stopped as she wobbled precariously above the abyss. And as the year drew to a close with her fate still unresolved and in doubt, it was hard to imagine her ever again regaining the kind of effortless poise that had brought her applause from around the world for simply showing women how to fold a dinner napkin or prepare capered salmon on toast points for 75.

But it also seemed worth remembering that the applause had been real and heartfelt, and for much of her life it had been deafening, as Martha Stewart, during a 40-year career in the spotlight of public acclaim, enjoyed greater fame and adulation than any businesswoman had ever before known.

It was simply stunning to reflect on how quickly it had all changed—and how dramatically, and how much even my most recent memories of Martha now seem part of another age. I think sometimes now of one moment in particular, one of the last times I saw Martha Stewart, up close and personal, before the storm broke. It was for Sunday brunch at a restaurant in Connecticut, and so much has happened since then, for both of us. It was another time, really, and already now history, disappearing into the past that eventually becomes us all.

I still remember that Sunday brunch even now. The restaurant bore the name *Paci*.

It was a sparely decorated place, occupying what used to be the waiting room in an abandoned train station on the MetroNorth rail line in the fancy-pants village of Southport, Connecticut, home to celebrities like Phil Donahue and his wife, Marlo Thomas, and radio personality Don Imus.

I arrived a few minutes early, sat down, glanced at the menu, and began to imagine how the breakfast would go. Would she turn out to be arrogant and snooty, as folks in town claimed she was? Or would Westport's wealthiest resident turn out to be a nice down-to-earth babe? But the answer was obvious. If she were the imperious witch described by so many, why would she be agreeing to have breakfast with me? What was in it for her? Actually nothing. Martha Stewart was on the verge of becoming a billionaire, and I was just some guy from around town who'd said something nice about her in print. So she'd agreed to have breakfast with me to thank me in person. Who couldn't like a person like that?

I picked up a roll from the breadbasket and squeezed to see if it was fresh. Crisp on the outside . . . nice and soft on the inside. Like Martha, I fantasized. I stared at the wall and imagined her sweeping elegantly into the restaurant, like Loretta Young in the movies, "Chris, my darling . . . it's been so long . . ." as we hurried to the limo for the night flight to Saint-Tropez.

Tick, tick, tick . . .

And then suddenly there she was, in the doorway, dressed in jeans and a T-shirt, and looking half my age—and I was younger than she. It was too much: The perfect entrance . . . Martha Stewart Everyday. She was grand.

She sat down, placed her cell phone beside her—very "Martha" I supposed—and we ordered breakfast and began to chat. We talked about her stock offering on Wall Street and the strange ways in which our lives had overlapped through the years. She was charming, she was real, and she was smooth, effortlessly pirouetting the conversation from herself to the life and career of the reporter sitting opposite her.

It was a virtuoso performance, and when I looked back on that breakfast years later, I saw no sign that she hadn't meant every word she said—not least because she delivered on everything she offered to do. I told her I hosted a daily radio show for MSNBC and asked her if she'd like to be a guest on it one day. She said sure, and six months later, she was. I told her I was interested in starting a separate, syndicated radio show like the TV thing she'd put together, but that I didn't know how to go about it, and she said, "Call my lawyer, Allen Grubman. He'll handle everything for you." The next day, an e-mail arrived from Martha to let me know she'd spoken to Grubman and he was waiting for my call. I told her I was writing a book on stock market investing, and she said, "Great," and offered to have me as a guest on her show to promote it when it was published. Eighteen months later, she put me on her show, and in a matter of hours my book began rocketing up the Amazon.com rankings.

It was remarkable. I'd been in the woman's life for half an hour and the ideas were pouring out of her—ideas for how to advance my career along with offers to help. I'd heard all these stories about how busy she was, how every waking minute of her day was booked and committed to something. Yet in the middle of all that, she'd somehow found the time and interest to involve herself in my life at a level that seemed astonishing. Who could not be grateful for that? It was a Sunday morning in the 'burbs, and there I sat at breakfast with a person soon to become one of the wealthiest women on earth—good-looking, captivating, and interested only in me.

Toward the end of the conversation, she turned to me and volunteered a piece of information. It wasn't about her dogs, or her housekeeper, or anything from the world of a woman in a T-shirt and jeans on a Westport Sunday morning. It was news from another world altogether, of mansions bought from the estate of Edsel Ford, and chartered jets and autumn hikes up the slopes of Kilimanjaro and boat rides up the Amazon.

She said, "I'm leaving tomorrow for bird-watching in Tierra del Fuego, you know . . ."

Only later, when the puzzle pieces of her life began to snap into place—when I learned, for instance, that 20 years earlier her husband, Andy, had left her alone over Christmas in the big house on Turkey Hill, and had himself gone to Tierra del Fuego in search of whatever lost parts of his soul he may have hoped to find there—only then did I realize the question I should have asked at that moment. It was not about Andy or any of that part of her past, but about the emptiness she, too, seemed to be trying to fill by journeying to the ends of the earth. I should have responded, "Sounds like fun, Martha, are you going alone?"

But instead, she started talking about her properties and a fishpond she was stocking with carp, about her neighbors in East Hampton, and about her growing accumulation of acreage in nearby Fairfield.

Finally, the conversation ground almost to a halt, so I decided to play a few rounds of "do you know." I mentioned a neighbor of mine who, like Martha, had been a student at Barnard and had gone on to become a best-selling author in her own right. I asked, "Hey, do you know Erica Jong?"

Well, let me say that Martha Stewart's reaction would have been no different if I had asked, "Would you mind if I just leaned over and spit in your Eggs Benedict?" Her face reddened, her jaw muscles began to twitch, a vein on her neck popped out, and her eyes narrowed to slits as she said, "That god-damned woman ruined my life!"

What do you do in a situation like that? Do you respond, "Geez, sorry to hear it"? Do you say, "Hey, my life sucks, too"? What I thought was, "Well, let's not go *there*!" and I said, "I'll get the check."

Before I started this book, I had no firm ideas about the two faces of Martha Stewart—the person who could be warm and accommodating in one instant, and furious and hateful in the next. Was one the "real" Martha, or were they both?

I had known Martha in a casual way for years—decades even—because we were neighbors. I had seen her in stores around town, I had said hello to her once in a parking lot . . . things like that. I frankly didn't even know who she was; and for most of that time she wasn't much of a somebody anyway . . . just another good-looking blonde in Westport, Connecticut, a town that seemed to be overflowing with them.

When I finally began writing this book, I discovered that we had actually been leading parallel lives. We had lived within a two minute walk of each other on Manhattan's West Side, then had moved at almost the same moment to the suburbs, settling not more than ten minutes away from each other. For thirty years, we had both remained in that same chichi community in Fairfield County, Connecticut.

Our families seemed almost clones of each other. Martha's husband, Andy, had gone to Yale and become a lawyer. I, too, had gone to Yale and become a lawyer. The Stewarts were parents to an only child, a daughter named Alexis. Our first child was a daughter as well, and we had given her the nearly identical name of Janalexis.

The Stewarts had bought the "fixer-upper" farmhouse that they renovated and eventually made famous—at 48 Turkey Hill Road, in the town of Westport, Connecticut—because it was basically the only home they could afford. Remarkably, my wife, Maria, and I had actually been shown the same home several months earlier by a real estate agent and decided to pass on it because of its deteriorated condition. So the house remained on the market, eventually the Stewarts bought it, and through the combined energies of the two, the house had made Martha famous.

Meanwhile, Maria and I wound up buying a fixer-upper ten minutes away and, like the Stewarts, we spent the next twenty years fixing it up; the house didn't make us famous, of course; it had simply helped us raise a family. We had sent our daughter to the same country day school where the Stewarts had sent theirs, and after that, to the same college: Barnard. Martha and I both had worked for a time for the same employer—Time Inc.—in the same line of work (magazine publishing) and had even been exercising daily in the same local health club.

When our lives finally intersected, Martha became a friend, though never what you'd call a best friend. But from the first moment I met her, I found her to be a likable, decent person, which certainly didn't square up with the opinion of many local residents. At least half the people I knew thought she was a witch—and were ready to say so to anyone. The other half thought she was a saint and were equally vocal about it.

It was odd, for the inhabitants of Westport—like those of Beverly Hills or perhaps East Hampton—had long since mastered the art of simply ignoring the celebrities living in their midst. From Scott and Zelda Fitzgerald to Paul Newman and Joanne Woodward, the history of Westport has been a story of tolerance and acceptance and the granting of personal space to the lives of its public figures . . . partly, one may say, because everybody's property values improve when the real estate agent can take clients through a house and casually let drop, "Oh, and Keith Richards from The Rolling Stones lives at the end of the block, but they like to keep to themselves. . ." or ". . . that house we passed at the corner? That belongs to Robert Redford . . ."

With Martha Stewart, it was different. By the time I got to know her, Martha Stewart was not only the most famous—and wealthiest—person in town, but also the most notorious. On a strictly public image basis, the mere mention of her name could polarize any group of people and start an argument that would quickly escalate to surreal dimensions.

It wasn't simply that people either loved her or hated her, it was the intensity of their feelings that seemed so remarkable. She had built an astonishingly successful business by marketing herself to the world, among other things, as the very epitome of womanly self-expression in the home. Yet this had turned her into a lightning rod for every conceivable opinion about what "being a woman" really meant.

Wherever her name was mentioned, half the women within earshot would pronounce her the living ratification of their worth as human beings. The other half would say they wanted to throw up at the thought of her. Many said they adored her for her example in their lives; many others said they despised her because she made them feel guilty for what they could not accomplish for themselves.

It was no different with the men. Half would turn accusingly to their wives and say, "Why can't *I* get dinners like *she* serves!" The other half seemed to feel threatened by all that she had become. How many of *them* had begun with a farmhouse fixer-upper, and ended up with a ten-digit net worth?

But Martha Stewart was more than just the final triumph of the American homemaker. She was the ultimate female handyman, the ultimate businesswoman, the ultimate adventurer—each of these roles sparked whole new sets of arguments about what Martha was, and what she was not . . . and whether the rest of America needed to be judged by her standards.

And beyond all that came something that was, for her Westport neighbors, the most dislocating perspective of all. Not only did they know Martha as she appeared in her books and magazine pages, and on TV specials and over the radio . . . they also knew Martha as she appeared in real life, at least in Westport, Connecticut.

To the world at large—or at any rate, to her army of fans and followers—Martha Stewart was earnest, charming, and diligent. She was a mother, and though now divorced, someone who honored traditions and family values. But many of the stories and gossip about Martha that flew around Westport portrayed no such woman.

Neighbors on Turkey Hill Road told of instances in which children playing in the street would accidentally throw a ball onto Martha's lawn and she'd come running out, "screaming like a maniac." One shop in town—Westport Camera Arts—actually placed a bulletin board in the store where locals could post venting messages about Martha and her behavior after she published an open letter in the *New York Times* complaining that her neighbors were no longer friendly to her. Soon the bulletin board was festooned with notes: Of the time Martha had cut to the head of the line at a tag sale, . . . had spoken rudely to a local merchant, . . . had failed to pay a bill.

But on the other hand, many people seemed to benefit by being associated with Martha in the briefest and most casual ways. A working-class housewife from Yonkers, New York, sends a letter to Martha offering to teach her how to make Italian tomato paste, Martha puts her on her show, and within days the woman is fielding six-figure book contracts from eager publishers. In Vermont, a dairy farmer makes a brief appearance on her show and his mail-order cheese business explodes overnight.

One time I ran into Martha at a Christmas party in New York. I saw her standing alone (Martha is not a good mixer at parties) and went over to say hi. I told her I'd seen her a few days earlier on a very low-rent program on Westport's public access cable TV station and asked her why she bothered with such a thing. She looked at me somewhat perplexed and answered, "They're nice people. They need help. Why shouldn't I?"

That was the Martha I knew: Busy, sometimes distracted, but a clear thinker, a good talker, and a follow-through person on her word. Someone who seemed to have no trouble sharing her success with others.

Yet in researching and writing this book, I learned more—a lot more—about Martha than just that . . . more, in fact, in both business and personal terms, than I could possibly have imagined. I discovered the astonishing backstory to the growth of Martha's company—an achievement for which she herself deserves most of the credit. During the "new media" 1990s, while the world went mad over worthless dot.com stocks and the World Wide Web, this one-time Connecticut housewife was busy putting together a largely "old media" business of such stupefying growth prospects and cash-flow profitability that executives from the largely male-dominated world of "big media" fell all over themselves in an attempt to copy her formula for success. They all failed, even as Martha took many of them to the cleaners in business deals over and over and over again, until she was very nearly dragging them by their noses through the streets of midtown Manhattan. As Muhammad Ali said of Sonny Liston in the 1964 heavyweight championship fight: Martha whupped 'em good.

But I learned something else about Martha that rarely crept into her public performances as Martha Stewart, America's Everything Gal. Just offstage, I found another infinitely more complicated Martha lurking in the wings.

Time and again, things in Martha's past turned out to be different from what Martha had claimed. They ranged from trivial matters such as conflicting accounts of her first visit to Europe to more substantial concerns such as the difficulty she seemed to have in managing the everyday details of her life—the mastery of which was one of the core elements in her public image. And one could also not help but be struck by the toll that the tension between her public and private worlds seemed to be taking on her personally as the frenzied pace of her professional schedule escalated.

The story of Martha Stewart is the story of an extraordinary woman, who had the brains to recognize opportunities when they dropped in her lap . . . and who had the drive, energy, and determination to turn them into unprecedented success in business and on Wall Street, not least by gathering around her—and often ruthlessly exploiting—the talents, and sometimes even the loyalty, of many people.

The less visible story is the "how" and ultimately the "why" all this happened: the secret world of Martha Stewart and her dreams. That is our story here—the story of a little girl who never got over what life never gave her and wound up inventing for herself a past she had never known—a hologram of life so powerful that it not only convinced her personally but mesmerized the world. In this way, the quiet little girl from the house on Elm Place became, in time, the richest self-made businesswoman in America—by selling the world all her missing parts. This is the story of what was missing, why it was missing, and how she turned it into a billion dollars.

Nancy drew and the case of the hidden childhood

Martha Stewart was born in New Jersey in August 1941, the second of six children. Her father was a self-absorbed narcissist named Edward Kostyra, who escaped the draft, and, blaming the world for never allowing him to live up to his own expectations of himself, wound up a high school gym coach and after that a salesman. Nonetheless, he had the artistic sensibility of an aesthete, and that—combined with the mercurial temper of a bad drinker—made him the most powerful force in Martha's life, setting standards of excellence and intolerance that became in time dominant characteristics of her own personality as well.

Those who knew Eddie Kostyra recall him as a braggart and a bully, who couldn't hold a job, who drank too much, and who would stagger around the house yelling at anyone who came near him. He puts one in mind of the character in the rhyme by Hilaire Belloc:

> *Godolphin Horne was nobly born,*
> *He held the human race in scorn.*

"My father was super critical," said Martha's oldest brother, Eric, now a dentist living in Buffalo, New York. "And Martha is very demanding. It's the family curse."

By contrast, Martha's mother, for whom she was named, was a coldly disengaged housewife, whose family was shocked and upset when she married Eddie because both families were Catholic and the marriage was the end result of an unintended pregnancy. Together, the two made a perfect couple for a lifetime of abuse: Eddie, the aggressive, stern husband angry at the world and ever on the lookout for a dog to kick . . . and Martha Sr., the resentful, sullen peasantlike wife, willing to suffer the abuse, mixed with sudden rages in which she'd shriek back in anger—in Polish.

There are early pictures of Martha Sr. that hint at happier moments. There is a yellowing black-and-white photograph, snapped, one would imagine, by Eddie. It shows his wife and daughter—the two Marthas—in the bow of a rowboat on what appears to be Central Park Lake. They are wearing coats and bonnets, which suggests that the picture was taken in the spring. Because the child appears to be between three and four years of age, the outing might have been on Easter Sunday of 1945.

The face of the child shows a pouty expression, but the mother seems relaxed and is smiling, as if enjoying herself on an afternoon in New York. Perhaps the family had come over from New Jersey for the Easter Day parade and decided to take a boat ride on Central Park Lake.

Eddie is not visible, presumably because he was behind the camera in the stern of the rowboat, snapping the picture. But one telltale clue hints at what lay ahead for all of them—if it wasn't part of their lives already: Sitting on the deck of the rowboat, with a Dixie cup atop it, can be seen what looks to be an opened bottle of either beer or wine.

As evoked through the haze of her memories, Martha Jr.'s childhood unfolded straight from the pages of *I Remember Mama*. The memories came complete with the happy chirping of children at holiday time while Mama Kostyra (that would be Martha Sr.) shooed them from underfoot as she went about the eternal rituals of preparing kielbasa and dumplings. All of it has been recalled by Martha Jr. in loving detail on her TV shows, with Mama standing next to her on the set, flour covering the front of her sweater, demonstrating the long-lost art of making hand-rolled pastries.

Yet there was another side to being the mother of six in a working-class neighborhood in northern New Jersey; and this side, too, comes to us through the recollections of Martha . . . though only in bits and pieces, over many years. It trickles forth, a detail at a time, in her newspaper and magazine columns. It is the life the Kostyras really lived—day in and day out—as a working-class family in New Jersey, in the 1940s and 1950s. Shorn of the lace and filigree, Martha Sr. appears not as her daughter would want us to see her, but instead as almost any such person from that era and demographic slice of life would appear—a woman who spent most of her time cooking, washing, and cleaning for a family of eight. And when she wasn't doing that, she seems often to have been found sitting at the kitchen table in a housedress with her girl-friends . . . smoking cigarettes, playing cards, gossiping, and drinking beer.

The Kostyra family seems to have inhabited a rather joyless world revolving around Eddie, the father, in a seeming state of perpetual anger at his wife for placing the limitations of parenthood on his life. There was fighting, quarreling, and relentless bickering over money, of which there was apparently never enough. At the end of such scenes we may imagine Eddie retreating to the basement, where he'd rigged up a photographer's darkroom, to spend hour after hour studying photographs he'd taken, while dreaming about a life more fulfilling than the one he was living upstairs.

Rather than the syrupy, escapist world of the early 1950s TV comedy-drama, *Mama*, which Martha would watch avidly each Friday evening when it came on CBS with the words: "I remember the big white house on Elm Street . . ." life in the Kostyra household seems to have been more like something out of *A Streetcar Named Desire*, with the brutish Stanley Kowalski presiding over the trembling inhabitants of Elysian Fields.

The first three years of Martha's life (from August 1941 to autumn 1944) were spent in the walk-up second-floor apartment of a two-family row house in Jersey City, New Jersey, where Eddie's father ran a bar. During this period, Eddie managed to dodge the draft by holding down a job in a shipyard. The job, plus a down payment from his mother, helped him swing a mortgage on a $7,500 "moving up" home of his own in nearby Nutley, an ethnically mixed (Italians, Poles) working-class town not far from Newark.

The Kostyra home, at 86 Elm Place, was small, on a 45-by-178-foot lot a half block from a commercial through street to downtown. The home's 2,000 square feet of living space were divided into a front parlor, a kitchen, three bedrooms, and a semifinished "sewing room." The house had a single full bath, and two washrooms—one in the basement and the other off the kitchen, where Eddie would shave and relieve himself during mealtimes whether his family liked it or not, suggesting a life for the Kostyras that in retrospect must have seemed rather like growing up next to an economy class washroom on an airplane.

Eventually, eight people occupied the dwelling, meaning there was almost never a time when someone wasn't in someone else's way. There was no room in the house where a footstep taken—or a word spoken—could not be heard in every other room. A fight in the kitchen would reverberate from the attic to the basement.

In the little house on Elm Place, there was simply no escaping the domineering, controlling presence of Eddie. In Martha's columns and remembrances, seldom does her father "ask" for something; he "orders" or "instructs" instead. Eventually, the controlling presence of Dad reached the point at which he rigged up an actual, working intercom system, and began barking orders into it like a bizarre Captain Queeg, ordering the family members to rise for the day, or whatever. Once assembled in the kitchen for breakfast, the Kostyras would encounter yet more of Dad, as Eddie would emerge from the bathroom that was five feet from the kitchen table, tucking in his shirt while directing the members of his family never to "slice" English muffins but always to "tear" them. Food wasn't simply placed before the children, they were served the food and "forced" to eat it. There is a subtext of aggression and control—authority and submission—in almost every such scene and remembrance. It is not intentional, but it is there nonetheless, unmistakable and strong.

In her columns, Martha has tried to portray these moments as providing her with a lifetime of priceless, warm memories. But on a deeper level, the associations often look to have been hideous. Indeed, the recollections of seeing her mother begin her days from breakfast onward in a housedress—the functional equivalent of appearing in a bathrobe and curlers—seem to have brought Martha such pain that, as an adult, she is said to have banned anyone from wearing a housedress in her house. From Eddie's command, "Don't slice the English muffins" we get Martha's order, "There'll be no housedresses in *my* home!"

This is how Martha Stewart appears to have begun her life, against a backdrop of parental tension and ugliness that would still be pounding in her ears each morning when, at 7:45 A.M., she would step from the front door of her home on Elm Place, turn left at the sidewalk, and take a five-minute walk, often with her cousin from down the street, to her third-grade class at Yantacaw Elementary School.

It was certainly a different time. In those days, at the start of the 1950s, young children could walk without adult supervision to school in Nutley, New Jersey—or indeed almost anywhere else—without parental qualms of any sort. Some fifty-three children of various ages lived on Elm Place when Martha was growing up, and they played in the street and in each other's yards without the slightest fear of the stranger who might be lurking at the corner.

Nevertheless, the Kostyra parents seem to have been ultracasual with their children's well-being in at least one respect. When she was as young as nine years old, Martha traveled by train—alone—to visit her mother's parents in Buffalo, New York, a six-hour journey on the New York Central Railroad.

But by the winter of 1950, the main topic on everyone's lips in Nutley, New Jersey, wasn't crime or even communism (though it was much in the news that winter as the espionage trial of Alger Hiss reached its climax). The focus instead was on technology. Marvels seemed to be raining down on the American people in a deluge of unending progress. In New York City, surgeons brought a man back to life on the operating table by massaging his heart after it stopped beating. It seemed a miracle. Indeed, it seemed only slightly less miraculous when, in Detroit that winter, the Cadillac division of General Motors Corporation introduced the world's first passenger car with a wraparound, one-piece windshield of curved glass. Meanwhile in New York, the RCA Corporation introduced the world's first commercially produced color television set. People everywhere gasped in wonder as the company's chairman, David Sarnoff, proclaimed the arrival of "a new era in television—the era of color."

In the Kostyra house, they didn't have a Cadillac. In fact, they didn't yet even own a car. And they didn't have a TV either—black-and-white *or* color until the end of 1950—the last family on Elm Place to acquire one. Martha would be attending Barnard College before her family upgraded to color.

According to Martha, when her father finally broke down and bought a television, he positioned it in the parlor at an angle so that he personally had the best view—from his favorite chair, at one end of the room—whereas the other family members had to squint and strain to see the screen.

Though Eddie had promised his wife to modernize the kitchen at the first opportunity when they bought their house on Elm

Place in 1944, it took twelve full years before he could scrape together enough money to put down a new linoleum floor and add some new cabinets. On the other hand, he never seemed to have trouble coming up with money for expensive clothes for himself or for his own hobbies and pursuits, such as his mysterious basement world of amateur photography. From time to time, he would try to improve conditions around the house through various do-it-yourself projects, but they almost always turned out badly—which Martha would not hesitate to bring to the attention of the world decades later.

You could see her resentment peeking out from her "Remembering" columns in *Martha Stewart Living* a half century later, when time and again, she'd refer to one aspect or another of her family's "meager" circumstances. In one column, she finds a way to bring up a family in the neighborhood known as the "Richies." They were said to be the wealthiest folks on Elm Place and thus enjoyed the services of a maid—which, of course, the Kostyras did not. In another column, she tells of standing in front of her closet Cinderella-like and crying because all the clothes in it were handmade and she lacked suitable jewelry to attend her first real New Year's Eve party. In yet another column, written in 1996, she complains, "When I was growing up, I wasn't one of the lucky ones whose every meal was accompanied by a fine damask napkin in a silver napkin ring. Nor was I fortunate enough to receive a trousseau of heirloom table and bed linens when I married."

On still another occasion, Martha recounted her family's trips to the Jersey Shore for crabbing in the summers—not failing to slip in stiletto-like digs at her father (by then dead for a decade) for not having earned enough money for the family to rent a house at the Shore like the other families had.

The overcompensation in reaction to all this eventually reached the point at which Martha was collecting houses the way the Romanovs collected palaces. A frequent weekend guest at her Westport,

Connecticut, farmhouse estate—Turkey Hill—took to referring to a barn on the property as the "Winter Palace." And Martha herself would often refer to a nearby chicken coop as the "Palais des Poulets" (Palace of the Chickens).

Eventually her search for grandeur reached the point at which she bought an antique Polish nobleman's carriage, which she used to squire herself around the countryside like the ghostly wife of King Popiel the Heartless, who was said to covet everything he saw. According to Polish legend, the dreaded king would shoot arrows at his own servants; he insisted that all food on his table be cooked and spiced to perfection—and would fly into horrifying, uncontrollable rages when it was not. The queen was said to be even worse.

The fact of the matter was that the Kostyras were working-class poor, and the man in the hot seat was Eddie. His family blamed him for failing to lift them from poverty, and in the perfect circularity for a lifetime of abuse, he blamed them for dragging him into poverty in the first place.

In later years, Martha recalled her father as a man of great artistic talent, who taught her about gardening and decorating as well as the value of being a perfectionist in one's pursuits. But on a deeper level, she also found him to be "disappointed in his life" and "not so satisfied with his lot in life." In fact, Eddie Kostyra blamed those around him—most notably his wife and children—for somehow holding him back, and he was constantly at war within himself over his natural feelings of parental love on the one hand, and his resentful feelings toward those around him on the other.

One thus never knew, with Eddie Kostyra, which face of Janus was in control at any moment, which meant that no one could ever be sure when a pleasant family activity or outing would suddenly veer into a scolding, belittling lecture from Eddie—a put-down from Dad for the perceived failings of his family members to achieve the levels of perfection he had failed to achieve in himself. In time, it became a pattern that would manifest itself over and over again in Martha's own life and relationships. As the years went by, she simply read more and more from the first "relationship script" she had ever learned—the one in which the authority figure maintains control by yelling the loudest and oppressing the most harshly, while insisting on undifferentiated and blind obedience as the expression of true love.

By the time Martha graduated from Nutley High School in 1959, powerful forces were at work to change, irreversibly, the structure and culture of the American family. The focus of that change was American youth, who were cleaved into two worlds by a chasm that ran straight through the class of 1959. Those who came before grew old before their time; those who came after had trouble growing up at all. Eventually, Martha found the message that resonated with them all: Never mind politics, forget about culture—just do what Big Sister says.

When Martha was growing up, everybody's young brother and sister had already developed the secret language that defined pop culture. DAs weren't District Attorneys, they were Duck's Ass haircuts; JDs weren't Juris Doctor degrees from law schools, they were juvenile delinquents. When you "chopped" a car, you didn't turn it into liver pâté, you turned it into a hot rod. In this world, Martha Stewart was the emissary from authority-land—that mythic place where the parents still ruled and a voice on the radio could send the nation marching off to war.

Martha and her high school contemporaries were only three years older than the oldest of the baby boomers who were born at the end of World War II, but they actually had little in common. The Class of 1959—Martha's class—was, in many respects, the last reinforcement from the land of the past, as if the social changes that were sweeping through American life hadn't yet discovered the ordinary little working-class backwater just outside Newark.

Martha's world still validated the role of the American housewife with an ideology of domesticity; and a heavy contribution to that faith was an inventor named Earl Tupper. In the 1940s, he had created Tupperware—a plastic, molded dishware with airtight lids. By the 1950s, Tupperware had developed into an entire subeconomy in the United States, with a moral value system that infiltrated countless households at "Tupperware parties."

Tupperware was big in the Kostyra household, where Martha Sr. would fill several of the plastic bowls with macaroni salad and potato salad, cookies, and maybe even a layer cake, then snap the airtight lids shut, place them in a picnic hamper, place the hamper in the trunk of the car, and the family would head for Asbury Park or Sandy Hook, or some other nearby shoreline, for a summer outing. The children would drink lemonade and iced tea; Eddie would be well-stocked with his personal stash of beer, from which Martha Sr. would eventually begin sipping as well.

Earl Tupper not only invented the most famous food storage system of the twentieth century but almost the entire toolbox of the post-war domestic female: His inventions included a flour sifter, dish rack, tampon case, easy-to-clip-on garter hooks, eyebrow dyeing shields, egg-peeling clamps, color-coordinated knitting needles, and much more.

In 1950, an impoverished Detroit housewife and single mother, Brownie Wise, hit on a way to make some badly needed money out of all this: She'd invite some friends over and see if she could sell them some of Mr. Tupper's plastic dishware. It was the first Tupperware party, and by 1954 she was on the cover of *Business Week* magazine as the emblem of the new world of womanhood. Alas for Brownie Wise, who eventually became Tupperware's vice president for home marketing and wound up presiding over an enterprise that many thought would soon eclipse even Sears Roebuck, she eventually tiptoed beyond the barrier of the kitchen door and published her autobiography. Like an early Martha Stewart, she filled her book with syrupy recollections of her grandparents and held

forth her life as an example of how far women could go by capital-
izing on "feminine knowledge." Earl Tupper was furious and instantly fired her.

These were the circumstances in which Martha and her classmates
grew up, becoming in a way, a transgenerational age group with
their feet planted in two worlds—the received value system and authority structures of prewar Americans, and the self-expressive,
youth-centered world that began to emerge after the war's end.

Looking back on the class of 1959 from the perspective of a new
century, only a few of its members seem to have sensed the opportunities that awaited them. Most—Martha included—present themselves to us uncertainly, clinging to the worlds of their parents as if
the received wisdom of prewar America were driftwood from a ship-
wrecked culture.

"We were a close-knit group," recalls Vinny Cina, one of Martha's
classmates, whose favorite pastime was watching the TV series 77 Sun-
set Strip. "Not a lot of the outside world had touched us yet. There were
drugs and alcohol out there somewhere, but we didn't know about it.
We were just naive, you could say. We were focused on our studies."

The girls in Martha's class all seemed to be frozen in aspic from
an earlier time, when their mothers were themselves young women.
In their high-school yearbook, a surprising number listed gardening,
cooking, and homemaking—the skills that Martha would later turn
into a billion-dollar business—as their main interests in life.

Strikingly, the girls of the Class of 1959 looked old before their
years, like late adolescent 35-year-olds, with serious expressions and
tightly curled and rolled permanents. Mostly they were Catholics—
Irish, Polish, Italian. For their graduation photographs, each and
every one of them wore personality-suppressing sweaters and neck-
laces of pearls—even Linda Jackson, Marion Butler, and Olivia
Flemming, the only three Black girls in the class of 276 students
(which also included just two Black males).

Most of the faces showed neither joy nor even mischievousness, as if the girls knew full well what the future held: more of what had happened so far. Of them all, only a handful looked distinctive in any way. Eleanor Adam wore her hair in a ponytail (one of only three girls in the class to do so), offering a kind of interested, curious smile that seemed to say, "Don't worry, world, I'm getting out of this place real soon." Pamela Hayford had a similar expression. So did Joyce Menegus, one of just two faces in the class that might readily be pronounced authentically beautiful. The other belonged to Beverly Otis, under whose dazzling, wide smile and large almond eyes is written "Desire is to live in Greenwich Village."

Though you wouldn't have known it from her photograph in the senior class yearbook (in which she too wore pearls, a sweater, and a forced smile), Martha had by now grown so detached from the life of the school that she had wrangled herself a job as a clothing model at Bonwit Teller's department store on Fifth Avenue, and would often leave school early to catch the bus into New York.

Martha belonged to the Nutley High School Honor Society, the Art Committee, and various other committees and groups. But most appear to have been Hamburger Helper to pad out her resume for getting into college. As far as actual impact on her peers was concerned, her presence was hardly felt at all. She wasn't voted "cutest" or "best looking" or "most talented" or "wittiest" or "most athletic" or "friendliest" or "nicest smile" or "most likely to succeed." She was just there, on one committee after the next, staring straight at the camera with a purposeful look in a large and serious face framed by tight bangs and curls that reeked of motherly approval.

In various "Remembering" columns that she pens monthly in her magazine, *Martha Stewart Living*, Martha has sometimes claimed to have been an avid reader of the literary classics as a child, but her friends in Nutley have said her favorite reading also included the Nancy Drew detective series. The Nancy Drew character is quoted in the original edition as being "ingenious, alert . . . the daughter of a famous criminal lawyer, and she herself is deeply interested in his mystery cases. Her interest involves her often in some very dangerous and exciting situations." The *Women's Almanac* describes Nancy as "one in a long line of motherless girls. Her handsome, romantic father treats her more like his wife than his daughter. She is spunky and independent. . . . She flew an airplane, drove her roadster, competed in a golf tournament, fixed her own car, and made her own decisions. She was incredibly superior to everyone around her."

The sentiment under Martha's senior class picture in her high-school yearbook could have been penned by precisely such a person. It reads: "I do what I please, and I do it with ease." She returned to that theme more than thirty years later during an interview with television personality Oprah Winfrey when she declared, "I can almost bend steel with my mind. I can bend anything if I try hard enough. I can make myself do almost anything."

Thus, in the fullness of time, the mantle of notoriety, if not actual greatness, passed over the students voted "most likely to succeed," "cutest," and "most athletic," to fall, instead, on the Nancy Drew-like Martha Stewart.

2

A MODEL LIFE

A lot can happen to a person when a lifetime of pent-up frustration bursts forth beyond the suffocating confines of one's home—and with Martha Stewart, it all seemed to happen at once, the very moment she left for college. Technically, she didn't really leave at all—at least not initially. She simply became a day student at Barnard College for Women in New York, commuting daily from her home in Nutley to Manhattan's upper West Side, where Barnard is part of the Columbia University campus.

Yet, almost overnight her part-time modeling work for Bonwit Teller ballooned into a full-fledged modeling career. Within three months of beginning her classes, she had moved out of her parents' house entirely and found a place to live in New York. Three months after that, she was deeply involved with the scion of what looked to be a family of Wall Street millionaires. A year later, she was selected a "Best Dressed College Girl" of 1961 by one of the nation's leading fashion magazines. Gone were the sweaters and afternoon pearls. Gone as well were the tightly permed curls, and in their place were the looser and longer locks of a *Glamour* fashion model.

It was the start of the lifestyle for which she would become famous—the blur of the Do Everything achiever, living at warp speed—and it began the second she got out of the house and began living life on her own. No more playing surrogate parent to her

brothers and sisters, no more ducking bullets in the crossfire between mom and dad. She was now Martha Kostyra, college girl, on
her own in New York.

It had all been waiting there for her, just a 20-minute bus ride
from Nutley. You'd swing right at the corner, turn onto Kingsland
Street, and 15 minutes later you'd be heading into the Holland Tun-
nel. A minute under the Hudson River, and then up you'd pop . . . in
the Land of Oz, with its skyscrapers and restaurants and millions of
people going everywhere fast.

It was the start of the 1960s, and a sense of anticipation hung in
the air. A New York advertising agency was soon to unfurl a slogan
for New York's Chemical Bank that would frame and define the
emerging role of women in this era. It would show a sleek, well-
dressed, executive-looking young woman, framed against the New
York skyline, checking her wristwatch on the way to an upcoming
appointment. The voice-over would say, "The New York woman
. . . when her needs are financial, her reaction is Chemical!" Martha
was not the model for that ad, but the message it conveyed was the
sort of Martha Moment young Ms. Kostyra was living every day of
her life.

Martha's transformation from Nutley High School's girl in the
corner to the first person in the class of 1959 to be known beyond
Nutley is a story of Rashomon-like complexity. Martha has
claimed in her magazine columns that a neighborhood girlfriend
introduced her to a modeling agency while she was still in high
school. But according to her brother Frank, this would only have
been after she had spent many hours being photographed by her
father, Eddie, who appears to have been the driving force in putting his teenage daughter to work. Apparently, he wanted the
money—or at least let us say, he wanted Martha to begin paying
her own way.

As it happened, Martha's camera-friendly good looks had captured the attention of an obscure New York booking agency—the
Foster-Ferguson Group—which landed her a job on Saturdays during

high school as a floor model for Bonwit Teller on Fifth Avenue, and thereafter, a 30-second bit with a voice-dub (at this early age, she hadn't yet shed her "Joisey" accent) in a commercial for Lever Brothers' Lifebuoy soap.

"She sat right in front of me in homeroom," recalls her classmate at Nutley High, Joyce Menegus, "and regular as clockwork she'd get up every day at 2:30 P.M. and leave for New York. She was very nice and friendly, and everybody liked her, but she clearly had other interests on her mind."

It had been her Honor Society academics (and her aggressively packed resume) that had gotten Martha accepted into Barnard, one of the prestigious Seven Sisters colleges for women that were regarded then (and even now) as a kind of distaff Ivy League. But it was the modeling work—and the money it generated—that enabled her actually to attend classes. As a day student, she avoided the room-and-board fees that would otherwise have put the price of such an education beyond the reach of even the entire Kostyra family.

Children who grow up playing the stretch-role of parent for younger brothers and sisters often develop lifelong control habits rooted in the learned experience of filling authority vacuums and discharging tasks for which they are not yet equipped, simply to get the jobs done—and in this Martha was no different from many others. Throughout her career, she has been accused of being a "control freak" who micromanages everything, but it was in college when she first discovered that micromanagement of one's life can be more than a survival skill in a dysfunctional family—it can actually get you ahead in life.

It took Martha exactly one freshman semester of commuting from Nutley to Manhattan before she closed the door permanently on the suffocating world of Elm Place. Through the Barnard undergraduate placement office, she landed a job as a live-in domestic for two spinsters on Fifth Avenue, cleaning, cooking, and running errands in return for room, meals, and a weekly stipend. Later in her career, she looked back on the job and recalled the experience as having been ". . . kind of fun, but depressing." And there can be little doubt as to the reason for the conflicted feelings. There she was, having escaped Nutley only to land, of all places, on New York's Street of Dreams—Fifth Avenue—but as nothing more than a live-in domestic, trading off the very skill-set of homemaking chores she'd fled from Nutley to escape. Yet still they stuck with her, like gum to her shoe, from Elm Place to Fifth Avenue. Was she destined forever to be cleaning up after others?

Such were the circumstances of Martha's life when she met, in the spring of her freshman year by way of a blind date, the man destined to become her husband for the next two decades. His name was Andy Stewart, a handsome six-footer in his second year at Yale Law School; he came from a family of Wall Street jet-setters whose lives seemed impossibly glamorous by the standards of Nutley, New Jersey, and the Kostyras. Martha snagged this fluke grounder on the short hop and was soon spending weekends with him in New Haven. Midway through her sophomore year, she was engaged to him, and by the following July—1961—they were married.

Martha thought she was marrying her way into money, though it seems clear that the two were also in love. Yet there was less to the Stewarts than met the eye, and the disappointments that soon began unfolding from that fact wound up eating like an acid at their relationship until Martha was treating Andy in exactly the same way that Eddie Kostyra had abused and mistreated Martha Sr.

To begin with, the name "Stewart" sounded Presbyterian, which meant a step up to WASP-land for a Polish-Catholic Kostyra. But George Stewart, Andy's father, was actually the son of Russian immigrant Jews—so marrying up for Martha soon turned out to be marrying down. And behind the disappointed illusions of social standing was the grim truth of the Stewart bank account. George had held a seat on the New York Stock Exchange but had been forced to give it up in the 1957 market downturn, becoming thereafter a promoter and private investor in penny stocks. In the Stewart household, one could never be certain whether the family would be spending the summer in Newport or pinching pennies to cover daily expenses. Only after she and Andy were married did Martha discover that the Stewarts, who at one point occupied an apartment in New York's Ritz Towers, were actually far less well-off than they may have seemed.

Andy's mother, Ethel—recalled by some as bossy, domineering woman with fierce red lipstick that made her mouth look like an open wound—seemed to maintain order in these circumstances by throwing herself into decorating binges, then bizarrely commanding that visitors neither touch nor sit on anything. "One time I went to the Stewart apartment and Ethel had just had the parquet floor ripped up and replaced with glass tiles on which no one was allowed to walk," recalled one of Andy's friends. "It was strange—to cross a room you had to tiptoe around the outside of it."

But others recall Ethel more fondly. One friend of the era remembers her as a slim, gracious woman with devoutly religious beliefs as a Christian Scientist, who dressed like a 1920s era flapper with her hair in a bob, and always seemed to be "praying" for something, which she'd do quite publicly. "She wanted everything in the world to be right and perfect," says the source, "and she got really agitated and concerned at the thought that someone somewhere might be suffering over something. I liked her very much."

How all this affected Martha can well be imagined. Mistakenly believing Andy to be from a family of eccentric stock market millionaires, Martha likely saw in him a way to bring affluence and security to a lifestyle she had by now begun almost completely to provide on her own. Andy was handsome, he was a Yalie, his parents were rich. Anyway you cut it, he beat that whole crowd back in Nutley, who by now were fast fading from her world anyway.

At around this time, with the couple by then engaged though not yet married, Martha got a break that became, in effect, a kind of personal career-dowry—a new entry on her resume that she could point to as further proof that if you wanted to get something done, you needed to do it yourself. In later years, this lesson was simply reinforced as, one by one, the hopes and expectations she had invested in her husband were dashed. The triumph? In the spring of 1961, Martha was selected by *Glamour* magazine as one of America's ten "Best Dressed College Girls" of the year. For someone who aspired to a career in modeling and was already turning up occasionally in magazine product ads, it was not unlike being able to add "Superstar in the Making" to her resume.

Martha got the award on her own, by sheer hustle, submitting an entry packet that consisted of fashion shots of herself wearing clothes she had borrowed from friends or had sewn herself from patterns the way her mother had taught her. Realizing, no doubt, that her chances for success would not have been helped by acknowledging that she was about to become a married woman, she simply left that part off her entry application, and as she had hoped, she was selected by the magazine's editors as one of the ten winners.

One obvious reason for choosing her was that Martha looked very much like the magazine's best known winner from the previous year—an attractive young coed named Norma Collier. After being named one of *Glamour's* "ten best" for 1960, Norma had been quickly deluged with international fashion modeling assignments and offers. Picking someone who could repeat that success would be a coup for *Glamour*, and Martha seemed to fit the bill. Both Martha and Norma were blonde, photogenic college coeds with serious-sounding majors (philosophy for Norma, art history for Martha), and Martha already had her toe in the modeling world door. This suggested that she might be able to recreate the career success of Norma, who by the spring of 1961 was already appearing nearly monthly in the pages of *Vogue, Marie Claire,* and *Harper's Bazaar.* So successful had Norma become that she seemed almost to represent the look of the times—the woman that even Jackie Kennedy, new to the White House and already the most photographed woman on earth, seemed somehow to be mimicking.

Glamour's editors clearly hoped to clone Martha into another Norma. Thus, Norma became a strong influence in Martha's life and fledgling career before the two girls had even met. To get press coverage pointed in the right direction, the magazine assigned Norma to chaperone Martha and Andy around New York when Martha received the award that spring—not realizing that Martha and Andy were more than just friends and were in fact about to be married.

But married they became. And being married when one spouse is an undergraduate in one city, and the other is attending law school in a city seventy-five miles away means that somebody has to make a sacrifice. And considering that the time in question was the start of the 1960s, there was little doubt about which party would be doing the sacrificing. Martha had no choice but to put her own career—and education—on hold for a year and move to New Haven as Andy finished his third year of studies at Yale Law School and took his degree.

Martha has written almost nothing about the year they spent together in New Haven, suggesting perhaps that she would just as soon forget their first year of life together as newlyweds. One can easily enough imagine the first seeds of resentment taking root in the relationship as Martha found herself having to put her most singular and direct personal achievement—her modeling career—on hold to serve the career ambitions of her new husband.

After all, what person would not wake up in the morning at least slightly frustrated at hearing the clock tick on a career that promised glamour and fame yet might be over before it could gather momentum? Then, couple that fear to the assertive personality of a creative, self-centered, strong-willed young woman who had been fleeing her own childhood from the moment she left home, only to keep making choices that caused her to collide with the past over and over again. In that volatile circumstance, it is easy to imagine the person thinking to herself, "Well, I'm doing *my* part in this deal, so you'd better be doing *yours!*"

Andy graduated at the end of that school year, in June 1962. Shortly thereafter—just as the Soviet Union began to secretly ship nuclear missiles into Cuba, setting the stage for what would become the Cuban missile crisis and by general agreement the start of the Swinging Sixties—the Stewarts returned to New York. They unpacked their bags and boxes in a cramped, roach-infested apartment a block from the Barnard campus, where they lived a hand-to-mouth existence for the following two semesters while Martha resumed her education and Andy took a postgraduate course at the Columbia University School of Law.

Eventually Andy landed a job as an associate at a midtown firm—Webster, Sheffield—and the Stewarts moved into somewhat more spacious digs on Riverside Drive, overlooking the Hudson. By then, Martha had to wonder whatever happened to that Wall Street fortune of her eccentric stockbroker in-laws. At one point things got so desperate that Martha and Andy actually had to take the bus out to Nutley to get a square meal. Once there, they would sit down across the kitchen table from the scowling eyes of Eddie, who made it known that he didn't welcome having his son-in-law come around to eat his food.

What's worse, as the sixties gathered steam, the WASPy, all-American look of women like Martha Stewart began to be eclipsed by the increasingly exaggerated extremes of models like Twiggy and Jean Shrimpton. Said Richard Avedon of Twiggy, "Women move in certain ways that convey an air of the time they live in, and Twiggy, when she is in front of lights, is bringing her generation in front of the camera." About Martha, Richard Avedon said nothing at all.

And let us not forget the exotic and sexually charged Countess Vera Gottlieb von Lehndorff (aka Veruschka).* She reminded the

---

* Vera Gottlieb von Lehndorff was born in East Prussia, in a region that is now part of Poland. Her name-change to Veruschka came in New York in a surprising way. Norma Collier's modeling agent, Barbara Thorbahn, was also the agent for Vera, and Norma says she was present when Barbara and Vera were discussing the name "Vera" as a moniker for her career. During the conversation, Barbara simply invented the name "Veruschka" because it sounded "more exotic" than "Vera" and seemed to fit better with the model's smoldering good looks.

world that there was a whole other way for Polish women to appear in public than wearing trumpet-flared waistcoats and clutching alligator handbags—say, for example, when Veruschka appeared as herself, wearing nothing at all, in Antonioni's groundbreaking 1966 film, *Blow Up*. By comparison, Martha Stewart—the "other" Polish model in mid-1960s New York—was listed in November 1962 at a second-tier day rate of $40 per hour. She could be found under her maiden name, Martha Kostyra, in the client face book of the *Plaza Five* modeling agency, with only two magazine credits (*Glamour* and *Mademoiselle*) to her name. Norma Collier, quoted at a higher day rate in the same face book, shows credits for the same publications listed for Martha, plus appearances in *Vogue, Seventeen,* and *Harper's Bazaar*. Was Martha's career dead already, a casualty of her husband's need to get that law degree that had forced her into the slow lane up in New Haven for an entire year?

Then something happened. In the middle of a revived career that was having trouble gaining traction, Martha Stewart became pregnant—a development that overnight changed everything, beginning with the importance of the phone that wouldn't ring. It is impossible to assay the personal chemistry between Andrew Stewart and his wife that led to the birth of their one and only child, Alexis, in September 1965. But little before or since would have given observers reason to believe that a child was something Martha Stewart wanted or had room for in her life.

Of all the many observations, both pro and con, that people have offered about Martha Stewart over the years, the one comment you simply don't hear is that she was warm or nurturing to her child. Andy himself has said exactly that about them both: They simply weren't good parents, or even very interested parents. In the end, they just didn't care. Martha eventually ended all possibility of more childbearing when—whether to deal with menstrual problems or to avoid getting pregnant again—she submitted to a hysterectomy.

Decades later in 1996, however, she said in an interview that not having more children had been a mistake.

At just about this time—with Martha still a new mother, gamely schlepping herself, Alexis, and an armload of baby gear to fashion modeling cattle calls—the second of the many women destined to play major supporting roles in her career entered Martha's life.

The woman who followed in Norma's footsteps was an attractive young photographer's assistant named Kathy Tatlock. Like Martha, she was young and just married, and for them both, the earth was new and life was exciting.

Kathy's office studio was in the Flatiron district of Manhattan, and decades later she could still remember her daily routine as if she had repeated it only that morning. She'd exit the subway at Fourteenth Street and Union Square, proceed past the fruit and vegetable stands and the flower racks, then head around the corner and continue until she reached the granite and brownstone loft office where she worked: the Paul Elfenbein Studio. It lingered in her mind in a kind of beckoning haze, beyond the shimmering heat waves of forty summers come and gone. Who could not be grateful to be present at the dawn of all our tomorrows . . . to be living in New York, free and full of promise, at the start of the 1960s? Does it get any better than this?

Kathy could remember the Chock Full o' Nuts where she'd stop for her morning coffee. At the corner was the newsstand where she'd sometimes get a newspaper; she'd started reading the *New York Post* at around that time. She liked its smart-alecky new columnist, Pete Hamill, who seemed so urgent and concerned, and had such a way with words.

The points of intersect in their lives were astonishing. Like Martha Stewart, Kathy Tatlock was the daughter of Eastern European immigrants. Martha's parents were Poles, who settled in Nutley, New Jersey. Kathy's parents were Hungarians, who settled in Chicago. Martha had gone to Barnard College and become a fashion model. Kathy had attended the Sorbonne and become a fashion photographer's assistant. Martha had married a young lawyer from Yale, who was working in midtown. Kathy as well had married a young lawyer from Yale, who was also working in midtown.

The two couples had taken apartments within a five-minute's walk of each other on the Upper West Side, and had been living their parallel lives, oblivious to each other and what fate held in store. Then one day in the spring of 1966, Kathy was sitting at her desk, searching for a model for a mother-and-baby advertising shoot she'd been preparing for Johnson & Johnson's (J&J) baby powder, when she turned the page of an agency's face book, and four parallel lives began to converge.

"This is it," she said, holding up the book to her boss. "Isn't she what we're looking for?"

It was the face of a young fashion model she'd seen several times in magazines. It was a clean, fresh, alluring face that evoked a time before life grew angry and bloodshot and it stopped being cool to look like you grew up in New Canaan, Connecticut. The name under the picture read "Martha Stewart," and Kathy thought, "I wonder if she has a baby . . ." and reached for the phone.

Thus it came to pass that Martha Stewart picked up the phone in her apartment on Riverside Drive and heard a female voice on the other end say, "This is the Elfenbein Studio. May I please speak to Martha Stewart?" The speaker was Kathy Tatlock, hoping against hope that Martha might just be a mom, with a baby she'd be willing to pose with for a mother-and-daughter spread in an upcoming J&J shoot. Could that possibly be the case?

"She said yes," Kathy told me, recalling the moment almost forty years later as if it had happened only yesterday. "She seemed so happy and eager, and I felt exactly the same way. I knew I was going to like Martha from that very first moment. I could just tell it in her voice."

Kathy Tatlock was eager, all right. Maybe just a touch too eager. Because Martha had Alexis, Kathy offered to come to her apartment to help her collect her things and bring them to the studio. Martha graciously said no, that she could manage on her own. They set a time, and at the appointed moment, Martha stepped from the elevator at the Elfenbein Studio, Lexi in her arms—and there at the elevator to greet her stood Kathy, smiling and helpful.

There are some people you just know you're going to be friends with from the moment you meet them. And that was how Kathy Tatlock felt about Martha. Perhaps it was how Martha smiled back so openly and easily, how she held herself so confidently and moved with such effortless grace and poise, even with an infant in her arms.

"Let me help you," Kathy said, and reached for Lexi. She began nuzzling the baby's nose as Martha handed her over. "Oh, my, thank you," said Martha, and the three went inside.

Kathy had lived in New York in a world of men—her husband, Chris', friends . . . her boss, Paul's friends. She worked in a world of men, she socialized with men. Wherever she went, she found herself surrounded by men and their male friends. She liked the attention they showered on her, to be sure. "What can I say," she said years later, "I liked being a babe." But there was a void in her life—she didn't know one woman she could truly call a friend.

Martha Stewart became Kathy Tatlock's first true girlfriend as an adult in New York. She was swept away by Martha's charisma and charm, her energy and self-confidence. The J&J shoot went well enough, though Kathy knew before it was over that Lexi lacked the kind of happy, white-bread sterility that Johnson & Johnson looked for in its babies. She was dark-haired, not blonde, with exotic deep eyes. The baby looked like she had a lifetime's story to tell already, and she was barely six months old.

But Kathy wasn't about to let that stand in her way. When the ad agency called from J&J a few days later with the turndown, Kathy called Martha with the news and, without missing a beat, asked, "Look, would you and your husband like to come over for dinner?"

It was a fabulous evening. The men hit it off instantly, and before anyone knew it, all four were talking at once. They had so much in common. It was like looking in a mirror and seeing yourself reflected back four ways. Their immigrant backgrounds from Eastern Europe, their lawyer-husbands. And as far as Kathy was concerned, the best part of the evening was that it had all occurred because of her. She had been the catalyst that had found common ground and friend•ship in the worlds of two couples who might otherwise not have known each other at all.

In the months that followed, Kathy Tatlock felt herself being swept up and away by Martha's energy and self-confidence. Martha had been a "Best Dressed" *Glamour* girl in 1961, and Kathy was astonished to learn that Martha made—or at least claimed to have made—a lot of her own clothes, by hand. "We'd go all over New York together, looking for just the right patterns and fabrics," said Kathy. "Then Martha would hand-sew them into beautiful dresses that just blew me away. The stitching was so perfect you could wear them inside out. It was amazing. I had never met anyone like that in my life."

Both sensed that Martha's career as a fashion model had peaked. But that didn't seem to faze Martha at all. "She knew modeling had become a dead end for her," Kathy said later on. But it didn't slow her down at all. She had bigger enterprises in mind—new projects, whole new worlds of ideas. She talked of opening an antique shop—a string of antique shops . . . of starting a floral business. "She wanted to be famous," said Kathy. "It was as simple as that."

In all human relationships, there is a dominant personality and a submissive personality, and from Day One it was clear who the alpha dog was in the Martha and Kathy story. "We would make plans for dinner," says Kathy. "And I'd spend the day cooking; we were all experimenting with food by then, and I'd be trying new cuisines and dishes that would sometimes take hours to prepare." Then Martha would phone, an hour before dinner, to say that she and Andy couldn't make it because she was sick or Andy was working late or some other similar excuse . . . and there would go an afternoon's work, right into the trash.

But Kathy kept coming back for more . . . and the more she came back for, the more of it she got. "What can I say," recalled

Kathy, as a note of fatalism and surrender crept into her voice. "I just liked her. She was my friend. My best friend. I let her get away with things I probably should not have. I suppose you could say that I trained her to mistreat me."

What Kathy did not realize at the time was that Martha did not reciprocate Kathy's feelings. Kathy was a friend, to be sure . . . but not a terribly important one, and one that she certainly would not have gone out of her way to include on the A-List list of her relationships. In many respects, Kathy Tatlock was just fill-in-the-dance-card material for when Martha needed, or wanted, someone to accompany her somewhere on an errand . . . or for company when Martha and Andy weren't throwing a party, or hadn't been invited to one themselves. If something better came up, Kathy got the brush-off.

In her books and remembrances, Martha writes of parties she had begun throwing at around this time—big extravagant affairs at her place on Riverside Drive, with as many as eighty or ninety people coming for cocktails and even dinner. There were people in the arts, the media, professors from Columbia and Barnard, as Martha and Andy worked to get themselves established in the world of New York's fast-tracking young power people. Kathy and Chris Tatlock were never invited to such parties, and in fact did not even know of them until years later, when Kathy began reading about the occasions in the pages of Martha's books and magazines. They were events for which she and Chris had not qualified to make the cut.

Meanwhile, within months of meeting Martha and Andy, Kathy herself became pregnant. Had Martha's ability to juggle her career and mothering roles with such supermom aplomb given Kathy confidence to become a mom? No, says Kathy, not at all. Quite the contrary, if there was one thing that had disturbed her about Martha even then, it was the distance and disengagement she seemed to have from her child, Lexi. "There was just so little affection there," said Kathy nearly four decades later. In the intervening years, Kathy raised not one but two children; one of them went on to become an honors student at Yale, and the other to become an educational consultant.

"I really wanted children," she said, looking back on those days. "I didn't care if they vomited in my lap and did all the disgusting things that babies do. I just wanted to get my hands on them and hold them . . ." and she reached out her hands and began squeezing her fingers, as if seeking to draw love from the very air about her. "I just wanted to be a mother. I don't think Martha ever did." Was there any evidence to support that belief, evidence beyond a woman's mere intuition? "Sure," said Kathy. "After Lexi began to walk, Martha gave me her carriage. She said, 'I won't be needing *this* anymore.' And she certainly never did."

Kathy Tatlock's husband, Chris, had been working as a young associate at a white-shoe law firm in Rockefeller Center— Winthrop Stimson Putnam and Roberts. It was not far, in fact, from where Andy Stewart had been working at Webster, Sheffield, a politically well-connected firm (then Congressman John V. Lindsay had been a partner). But neither man's career was proving satisfying, and Chris was the first to take action. From a friend, he learned of an opportunity as a lawyer in the U.S. State Department's Aid for International Development program in Bogotá, Colombia, and he jumped at the chance. "We'll see the world," he told Kathy, "it'll be great." They'd be part of the legacy of John Kennedy and the New Frontier and its Alliance for Progress in Latin America. The world was erupting in the energy of sixties politics; everything was changing. Here was how to stay with it, be hip, stay aware.

Kathy welcomed the idea. On the one hand, she had her new baby, Alison, and her circles of friends—at the center of which stood Martha. But the lure of a cosmopolitan life appealed to her, and Chris seemed attracted to it as well, and it was pretty much at that point that any debate over alternatives simply shut down in her mind.

To celebrate the new page that was about to turn in their lives, she and Chris invited the Stewarts to dinner. As always, they brought Lexi; Martha placed her in front of the TV while Ali slept in a crib in Kathy and Chris' bedroom, and the evening began. It was pleasant, though touched perhaps with a tinge of nostalgia at what, for Kathy at least, had been the best year of her life. She'd prepared coq-au-vin from a Julia Child cookbook, which both women were by now working their way through, recipe by recipe. And the wine flowed, and the reminiscences poured out, and the hours passed by as they talked of what had been and what was coming, and all the things that you form into the personal history of your life, to call on a half century later when most of life is gone.

And then suddenly, in the late evening hours, as the conversation drifted to a murmur and silence began spreading between the sentences, the bloodcurdling scream of a child split the air. For a second, no one moved, as Kathy's eyes fell first on the TV and the pillow cushion where Lexi was no longer seated . . . then darted in the direction of the darkened bedroom, where the door that had been closed all evening now had swung open on its hinges.

Leaping to her feet, Kathy raced to the bedroom with the most horrific visions that a mother can have flashing through her mind. And as she entered, she beheld a scene she'd never forget: Two-year-old Lexi had climbed up on the rails of the sleeping baby's crib, and to get the attention of Martha and Andy, who had not spoken a word to her all evening, had leaned forward with her face toward the baby and let out an ear-splitting scream that was still reverberating through the apartment as Kathy entered the room. It was Lexi's way of getting the attention of parents who sometimes acted as if she weren't even alive.

To Wall Street

In the spring of 1968, as Kathy and Chris Tatlock were packing their bags and heading for the U.S. State Department in Bogotá, Martha Stewart at last abandoned her struggle to reestablish herself as a New York fashion model, and decided to try something else. Considering that it was the 1960s, and that the energies of the time had already begun to gather on Wall Street, it is hardly surprising that Martha would have decided—without what appears to have been a whole lot of thought—to become a stockbroker.

Exactly when the revelation came to her that her best hope for fulfillment was to be found on Wall Street isn't known, and her own conflicting remembrances make her a poor source. But the evidence suggests that as 1967 drew to a close and the nation began to separate into two armed camps over Vietnam, along with all the social and cultural issues for which it had become a metaphor and a lightning rod, Martha decided to cast her lot with the haves instead of the have-nots.

Getting her hands on money—ultimately a lot of money—had already become a major subplot in Martha's life. As time passed and it became increasingly apparent that Andy's income was not living up to her aspirations, it was almost inevitable that she'd sooner or later succumb to the tug of stocks and bonds. In New York, it is one of the strongest tidal forces there is.

Martha lasted on Wall Street for five years—from the late summer of 1968 to roughly midyear 1973. And though she has sought to portray the period as a time of challenge and opportunity, the reality of the work she was entangled in, combined with the stresses of family life, sent her fleeing from the scene, leading to what one of her close friends from the era says was the functional equivalent of a nervous breakdown.

Martha had interviewed at a number of brokerage firms, but had been turned down by all but one, a small, obscure start-up firm bearing the name Perlberg, Monness, Williams & Sidel. It had, in fact, been Andy who had opened the door for her. With her job search hitting one dead end after the next, she had turned to her husband for help, and Andy, at the suggestion of a young associate at his firm named Michael Pantelioni, had made contact with a fellow named Davis Weinstock, who in turn was a friend of young Andy Monness, one of the partners in the upstart brokerage firm.

It was the spring of 1968, with the market so hot that firms were hiring people almost literally off the street, when Andy Monness walked into Ed Perlberg's office with some news—news that, almost overnight, would change the firm's fortunes dramatically for the better, turning what had previously been not much more than the tinkle of coins falling into a cup into a late-bull-market crescendo of wealth that drowned out the footfalls of approaching doom.

The news? That Andy had just interviewed a woman who'd been sent to him by the husband [Michael Pantelioni] of one of his clients, who worked at a midtown law firm named Webster Sheffield, where one of Pantelioni's colleagues [that would have been Andy Stewart] had a stunning-looking wife named Martha who had been working as a model but was apparently interested in a career change.

Monness explained that he had gone ahead and interviewed the woman, who was not only good-looking but eager for money. "This gal is smart," explained Monness. "She'd be good in sales."

Perlberg thought about it for a minute. Female stockbrokers were almost unheard of at that time on Wall Street. Bache & Company had hired one a few years earlier—a young woman named Muriel Siebert, who had made a name for herself in aviation stocks. Known around the Street as "Mickie," she'd recently left Bache to start up her own firm—Muriel Siebert & Company—and was now the only female to hold a seat on the New York Stock Exchange. But being a pioneer, Mickie had controversy swirling all around her, and the new "women's lib" movement of people like Betty Friedan and Gloria Steinem were already gathering about her as their newest cause. Did Ed Perlberg need any of that in his life? Besides, as Monness explained things, this Stewart woman apparently had no training whatsoever in finance, and hadn't yet even taken her broker's examination.

On the other hand, the notion of having a good-looking dame in the company's sales operation appealed to him. As the Greek philosopher Aristotle observed nearly 2,400 years ago in a trenchant bit of wisdom that has certainly stood the test of time, "Personal beauty is a greater recommendation than any letter of reference." Said Perlberg of his reasoning in an explanation that was at once sexist and obvious, "I told Andy to go for it. I figured, what the hell, people would probably enjoy working with a woman more than they would a man."

So Martha took a brokerage course at the New York Institute of Finance, and on August 14, 1968, was licensed to conduct securities transactions with the public as a member of the New York Stock Exchange. Her timing was spectacularly unfortunate as within weeks the stock market topped out and the bull market of the 1960s began its long slide into the long bear market of the 1970s.

No one disputes that Martha did her job well as a member of the firm, even as the business eventually began to crumble around her. In fact, the evidence suggests that she did it so well she probably saved the firm from collapse. The only question is whether the job that she did was something worth doing, and what the real reason was for the disillusionment that drove her from Wall Street when she discovered it was not. Whose neck was she really trying to save—her clients' or her own?

She, as well as the man who hired her, Andy Monness—and even the firm's original senior partner, Edward Perlberg—have all subsequently tried to characterize the company as one of the fast-tracking investment boutiques of the go-go sixties. But the main activity of the firm was actually to sell overpriced stocks to customers during the final, blowout phase of the 1960s bull market. In the early days of its brief and little-noticed life, the firm didn't even have offices of its own but operated on a catch-as-catch-can basis by renting desks and phones in the offices of other, more established firms. It ultimately went bankrupt in the seventies bear market.

In a 1999 biography of Martha entitled, *Martha Stewart, America's Lifestyle Expert*, the author, Sara McIntosh Wooten, writes, "From the start, Martha was on the company's fast track. She threw herself into her new job with enthusiasm. Within two years she was one of the firm's top salespeople."

The fact is, the firm had little obvious purpose in life other than to peddle whatever was hot at the moment, and if possible to make it even hotter. Martha acknowledged as much when she said, in a 1991 interview, "The movie *Wall Street* had nothing on this firm," referring to the 1987 Oliver Stone financial thriller in which Michael Douglas plays a corrupt stock swindler named Gordon Gekko, who boasts, "Greed is good."

More importantly, to describe her as "one of the firm's top salespeople," doesn't present the full picture. In reality, Martha, along with her colleague Sandy Greene, and actor Brian Dennehy—who had been hired almost literally off-the-street because of his commanding voice—were just about the only salesforce the firm had. One of Martha's colleagues at the firm—a young Yale man named Greg Gilbert—recalls that even at its zenith, the firm never had more than twenty employees, and for most of its history the total never reached anywhere near that.

A good measure of just how obscure and unimportant the firm really was can be gleaned from the fact that Martha claimed, in her top year as a salesperson at the firm, to have netted barely

$135,000—certainly a respectable enough income, but hardly much for one of the firm's "top producers" to be boasting about at the peak of the 1960s bull market. Perlberg himself has said that when Martha arrived, the firm was grossing no more than about $250,000 per year—a good indication of just how much the firm's fortunes coincided with her arrival. Prior to that, the firm had been dogged by such basic matters as how to pay the rent.

What was Martha's job? The same job any good-looking young woman got in the 1960s in a world dominated by men: Walk into the room, sit down, and cross her legs.

When it came to closing a deal—which is to say, getting the client to sign the check and *buy* the stock—well, the general view at the office was, Martha wasn't very good at that. So, when it came time to clinch the sale, her boss, Andy Monness—recalled by those who knew him at the time as having a fondness for loud shirts and wraparound mirrored sunglasses—would appear and take over. And it always worked because no client seemed able to resist buying the stock simply to get Martha to come back.

But what junk they were selling: wireless phone stocks before there was wireless telephony . . . tire retread companies . . . and the one that wound up effectively finishing off the firm completely: Levitz Furniture. When Andy Monness was asked, thirty years later, what was the worst investment decision of his life, he answered without hesitation: Levitz Furniture. When Frank Williams, who wrote the original research for the firm's report on the stock, was likewise asked many years later which investment he most regretted, he, too, answered Levitz Furniture. It's not surprising why. Levitz Furniture was not only one of the most spectacular and widely chronicled financial flops of the early 1970s, it was also a huge scandal, with allegations of kickbacks, market rigging, and organized crime involvement swirling about the stock for more than a year. And, said Greg Gilbert ruefully, "Levitz Furniture was the firm's biggest investment."

The Levitz promotion was typical of not just the stocks that Martha's firm was pumping up, but of the deals in which nearly all of

Wall Street was becoming entangled as the bull market of the 1960s approached its inevitable end. Levitz operated a regional chain of discount furniture outlets in the East, and its stock soared to astronomical heights on nothing more than a stampede of follow-the-leader buying by late cycle speculators. What none of them knew was that the company had become entangled with organized crime through undisclosed ties to elements in the Teamsters Union, even as institutional investors and brokerage firms all over New York were blindly piling into the stock and driving it skyward.

This situation, more than anything else, appears in retrospect to have sent Martha Stewart fleeing from Wall Street as suddenly as she'd arrived. Like nearly all novice investors who arrive at the end of an extended bull market, Martha had seemed to believe that stock prices would only keep rising since that's what they'd been doing for as long as she or anyone else her age could remember. So, when prices began dropping during 1969 and into the first quarter of 1970, she drew comfort from the men in the office, who told her not to worry and that each dip was actually a buying opportunity for her clients.

And as the spring of 1970 gave way to the summer, and prices began to recover, their wisdom seemed confirmed. Apparently the bull market was still intact and poised for that next upward advance after all. Now Martha began steering her clients—among them friends such as Norma Collier and a college professor named George McCully—back into the market with a vengeance. The hot stock of the day? . . . Levitz Furniture.

But trouble soon began to dog the stock. In January 1972, *Barron's* newspaper published an article questioning the trading activities of Levitz's management in the shares, and the overpriced stock—then trading at close to $60—tumbled nearly 10 percent in a single morning. A few days later, the Securities and Exchange Commission (SEC), the New York Stock Exchange, and the New York State Attorney General's office all announced the opening of probes into trading in the company's shares.

Experienced investors would have known it was time to get out immediately—no matter how bad the seeming loss at the moment— because, with regulators and law enforcement officials now circling the shares, they had nowhere to go but down. But the young and inexperienced crew at what was now known as Monness, Williams & Sidel hung tough, and continued to push the shares as aggressively as ever.

Andy Stewart—timid by nature and cautious by training— hadn't been comfortable with what Martha had been doing from Day One at the firm, and for more than a year he had repeatedly cautioned her not to make promises to her clients or get carried away in her sales presentations. He particularly didn't like how close the firm's partners seemed to be getting to the companies in whose shares they were trading, and as a lawyer he worried about the legal implications of those entanglements. But Martha stuck with it, and continued to sell the shares of a company that had disaster written all over it.

And the situation grew worse every day—with one story after the next, until the declining fortunes of the company, and deepening scandal surrounding its shares, were becoming almost daily fodder in papers like the *New York Times* and the *Wall Street Journal.*

Soon the news took an ominous turn, shifting from the activities of the company itself to the behavior of the investment firms and brokerages involved in the stock. In June 1972, the SEC suspended all trading in the stock. This was followed by an SEC lawsuit against the company for securities fraud, including an order barring the company from selling further stock to the public.

For Martha and the others at her firm, Levitz Furniture had become the news story from hell, as every week brought more—and increasingly serious—revelations regarding an apparent conspiracy on the part of some brokerages and their clients to rig the market in the company's shares. To add to the anxiety, the stories never named actual names, but instead dripped with leaked hints from investigators as to which firms had been involved.

For Norma Collier, as well as other friends to whom Martha had sold the stock, the situation was awkward to say the least. And the situation took an unpleasant turn when Norma found herself chatting one day with Frank Williams' wife in front of the Manhattan preschool where both couples had their children: "Frank is very upset," Norma recalled being told by Frank's wife, "The firm is in some sort of trouble. I don't know what it is, but there may be indictments."

For Martha, the final straw came in February 1973, almost a full year to the day from the time when the scandal first broke. The news? Published reports that New York State Attorney General Louis Lefkowitz was charging "unidentified stock brokerage firms and institutional investors" with having taken kickbacks from Levitz Furniture in return for issuing favorable and "bullish" investment reports on the company.

Martha was never implicated in any aspect of the scandal, and neither for that matter was her firm. Yet not long after, she resigned and left the business. Thereafter, the firm itself went bankrupt. By the start of the 1990s, Martha appeared to have repressed the Levitz Furniture fiasco into little more than a fading bad memory, and when the subject of her final days on Wall Street came up in an interview with a *New York* magazine reporter, she dismissed her firm's antics as "totally juvenile" while nonetheless acknowledging that, by the end, she had become "a nervous wreck" who couldn't sleep and "woke up with hives."

Meanwhile, trouble dogged the Levitz operation like a shadow. As pressure intensified from various government probes, the company's president dropped dead of a heart attack. In the vacuum that followed, the Levitz family fell to fighting among themselves over control. Proxy fights further weakened the organization, and eventually Levitz collapsed as well in bankruptcy. Adding a mordant note to the proceedings, Gary Levitz, the son of Leon Levitz, one of the company's cofounder brothers, was arrested and eventually

convicted and sentenced to prison for income tax fraud and investing money that he knew came from a drug ring involving two race
car drivers on the Indianapolis 500 circuit. In the wake of all this,
Gary's uncle—Ralph Levitz, the other cofounder—dropped dead of
a heart attack too. Ralph's wife, Jacqueline, then moved from Palm
Beach, Florida, to Vicksburg, Mississippi, and built herself a southern mansion where she planned to live out her widowed years in an-
tebellum grandeur. Shortly thereafter, she was murdered in a
homicide case that has never been solved.

As for Monness, Williams & Sidel, it too was raked by the after-
shocks of the Levitz disaster. During the five years Martha had
worked there, the firm underwent numerous name changes and
changes of address; in the wake of the Levitz debacle, the partners
wound up fighting in a New York state court over who was responsible for paying the rent on the vacated premises where Martha had
actually interviewed for her job.*

When the firm finally collapsed in the 1974/1975 recession, not
all of those who climbed from the rubble went on to good things.
One of the firm's partners at the time—Larry H. Friend—had come
to the Perlberg, Monness operation by way of another, larger, though
controversial firm (Bear Stearns & Co.)—and that's where he returned
after Martha departed and the business collapsed. He was thereafter
fined and censured by the SEC for excessive trading in the accounts

---

*The trial judge in the case was the Hon. Hortense Gabel, a much-liked New York
judge whose career—and reputation—went up in smoke not long afterward when she
became entangled in bribery allegations swirling around Bess Myerson, winner of
1945's Miss America beauty pageant. Myerson had gone on to become New York City's
cultural affairs commissioner, and then became involved in a much-publicized love affair with a city contractor named Andrew Capasso, who was married. The matter eventually wound up in a divorce case before Judge Gabel. Gabel, in turn, was drawn into
the scandal when Myerson attempted to influence her to enter a ruling in favor of Capasso, by giving Judge Gabel's daughter, Sucreet, a job on the New York City payroll as
an assistant in the Cultural Affairs office.

of his Bear Stearns clients. He subsequently left and launched his own firm, where he was fined for an illegal, market manipulating practice called "free riding." He died of prostate cancer at the age of 62 in 1998.

Andy Monness was soon back in business with a wealthy new partner named Neil Crespi, and by the end of the 1970s, he was heading what he calls an "institutional boutique" named Monness, Crespi, Hardt & Co. This bunch, too, soon ran afoul of the law, and in the nineties had to pay over $2 million in disgorgement and fines for price-gouging its own customers by illegally marking up the shares of penny stocks before delivering them to the firm's clients.

Ed Perlberg, the founding partner of the firm, also became a broker with a past. Almost immediately after leaving Perlberg, Monness, he signed on as chairman of a firm controlled by a mob-linked corporate raider named Asher Edelman. With Perlberg at the helm, the Edelman operation promoted the IPO of a Puerto Rican airline; the SEC subsequently halted trading of the shares when it turned out that the company was bankrupt and operating fraudulently.

Ed left the Edelman operation in 1973, and a year later the firm itself ceased trading and was soon out of business. By then, Ed had resurfaced in yet another Edelman-controlled operation—Arbitrage Management Company—following which he joined a notorious penny stock bucket shop named D.H. Blair & Company. More recently, he was involved in some ugly squabbling with his sister over the diminished estate of their mother, Gertrude. When Gertrude died in 1999, Ed's sister was horrified to discover that the estate, which she believed to have totaled $15 million, was substantially smaller, and she filed suit against her brother claiming that he abused his power of attorney. The suit continues to work its way through Florida's courts.

As for Martha—who was undoubtedly more responsible than any other single person at the firm for keeping it alive—well, those partners who are still around talk of her almost reverentially to this day. Says Andrew Monness, "She was the most competent single person I ever met." But, seemingly anxious not to incur her disfavor, he declined to provide details, especially regarding the reasons for her hasty departure. "If Martha says it's okay to talk with you, I will," he said. He never called back.

But others who knew her at the time were not so shy. One such person was George McCully, the Columbia University history professor who'd fallen into her orbit and become a fixture at her parties. After Martha left Wall Street and the Stewarts were attempting to reinvent themselves as pre-Yuppie farmers in Connecticut (about as close to the counterculture as Martha was ever to get), McCully's own marriage fell apart and he became a regular—and solo—weekend houseguest at the Stewart home. The position afforded him an up-close-and-personal view of Martha's deepening turmoil, which he recalled in an interview in Boston a quarter-century later.

Virtually every biography and magazine profile in which Martha has cooperated has stated her reason for leaving Wall Street as being that by the summer of 1973 the market was tanking in earnest, and her commission income had dwindled to the point that there was simply no reason to continue as a stockbroker. There surely is an element of truth to that since thousands of brokers like her left the business at around the same time.

But as far as George McCully was concerned, such explanations, at their core level, were largely bunk. As George saw things, the reason Martha had quit Wall Street had been a combination of fear and flight: fear of what was happening to her reputation now that nearly every person she called a friend had lost money—in some cases, a lot of money—as a result of following her advice . . . and flight in the sense of fleeing a bad world she'd milked too well. "She was afraid she'd lost every friend she had on earth," said McCully. "The pain was too much to bear and she simply ran away."

THE PAGE TURNS

Two years before leaving Wall Street, Martha and Andy moved from New York City to the suburbs of Connecticut, setting in motion a series of events that would eventually astound and confound some of the most powerful men in American business. But it was not an auspicious beginning as, on a spring day in 1971, Andy and Martha Stewart stepped from the car of an elderly, chain-smoking real estate broker named Daphne Bayles to behold an abandoned six-room farmhouse at 48 Turkey Hill Road South in Westport. It was the house that was destined to change their lives—giving Martha the raw materials to begin refashioning herself from a stockbroker at a failing firm into, first, a suburban caterer in the hearth-and-home 1970s, followed by best-selling author in the 1980s, and ultimately, media impresario and businesswoman in the 1990s. But the house also became the battleground on which she and her husband engaged in the struggle that destroyed their marriage.

In her columns and remembrances, Martha has been oddly circumspect about the reasons underpinning the couple's move to Connecticut. It is strange because the Stewarts' home on Turkey Hill Road would develop into far more than just the residence where the Stewarts lived. In time, the house would emerge as almost a character in their lives—a kind of late twentieth-century Cézanne landscape, lifted from the gardens of Aix-en-Provence, with hens and sheep and beehives, and the air thick with the fragrances and colors of irises and impatiens . . . through which Martha would stroll, like a character out of a Bo Widerberg movie. You can almost hear Geza Anda and the Berlin Philharmonic in the background, as she returns to the cottage, her giant wicker basket filled with freshly picked strawberries, to the dying notes of Mozart's 21st Piano Concerto in C-Major.

Her most specific statement about their move to Turkey Hill appears in her 1982 best-seller, *Entertaining*, when the house was already beginning to take on mythic proportions in the iconography of her life. In the book, she says that by the start of the 1970s the couple's apartment on Riverside Drive had filled up—apparently as if by some primordial, earthly yearning on Martha's part—with plants, flowers, potted herbs, pets, and whatnot, and concludes, "[O]ne day we took stock, read all the signs of our restlessness, and moved to a house in Connecticut."

Not quite. In reality, they moved out of New York City because of Andy. Succumbing to incessant needling by Martha that he wasn't making enough money, Andy began looking for a better job than his perch as an associate at Webster, Sheffield. By and by, he found one—or at least a better paying one—as part of the in-house legal team at a New York-based multinational mining conglomerate called Bangor Punta Corporation.

Andy took the job at the start of 1970; yet scarcely had he begun working than he learned that the firm was planning to relocate from Manhattan to lower cost offices in Greenwich, Connecticut, thirty miles north of New York. A colleague in the legal department—Stan Atwood—who happened to live in Westport, told him about a house in his neighborhood that was on the market for a cheap price if anyone wanted to take on the headache of fixing the place up. So, looking around for a real estate broker, they hooked up with Daphne Bayles, and paid a visit to the residence at 48 Turkey Hill Road South.

The scene that confronted them as they stepped from Daphne's car must have been a shock, for the house was little more than a hovel—a blight on an otherwise attractive neighborhood of two-acre lots and middle-class homes. The place hadn't been painted in years, maybe decades. The floorboards were warped and separated, the roof leaked, and there was no central heating. In the two bathrooms, the plumbing was antiquated; most of the walls lacked insulation and the electrical wiring was frayed and hazardous and lacked circuit breakers. There was no garage on the property, and the grounds themselves were overgrown and weed infested, with junk and clutter scattered about. The only thing missing to complete the picture would have been a mongrel dog tied by a chain to a pickup truck with no tires.

On the other hand, even a rock-bottom price of $33,750 was expensive for the Stewarts, who were already feeling financial strain from the collapsing stock market. So, realizing that this was about as good as they'd be able to do, Andy approached his company and arranged for a short-term $13,000 loan for a down payment, then approached a local bank in Westport and took out a 25-year, $50,000 mortgage on the property. With the proceeds, Andy repaid the $13,000 loan to Bangor Punta Corporation, paid the remaining $20,750 on the purchase price, and, once legal fees and closing costs were taken care of, wound up with about $15,000 cash to finance the renovations.

This was a woefully inadequate amount for the magnitude of the work that needed to be done and it meant that the Stewarts would be embarking on the stressful and exhausting business of renovating the home with their own hands because they couldn't afford the labor of others.

In time, a visit to the Stewarts became not much different from dropping in on the world of the Kostyras two decades earlier, with Martha in the role of the tyrannical Eddie, who had long been known throughout the neighborhood back in Nutley for his authoritarian, angry parenting. He was constantly ordering family members about on "projects" that ranged from weeding and hoeing in a squatter's garden he'd created in a nearby vacant lot to constructing a barbecue pit in the backyard. That was a project Martha tried to dodge as often as possible, though Eddie invariably spotted her shirking and pressed her back into service.

"He was a real disciplinarian, I'll tell you that," said the Kostyras' next-door neighbor, Tommy Allegri. "Everything was real regimented in that house. It's how Mr. Kostyra ran things."

Twenty years later, this was translated by Martha into the expectation that Turkey Hill visitors and weekend houseguests would lend a hand with the innumerable projects that were always underway. Such a guest arrived one afternoon and was directed by Martha to weed a flower bed. "Are you serious?" asked the visitor incredulously and promptly got in her car and left, never to return.

George McCully, the Columbia University professor who was a frequent houseguest of the Stewarts during the 1970s, told similar stories. So did Norma Collier, who had moved to the neighboring town of New Canaan at about the same time that Martha and Andy had moved to Westport, and who had also become a frequent visitor to the house. Yet more stories came by way of Kathy Tatlock, who likewise visited the Stewarts from time to time. Many eventually stopped dropping by as a visit to the Stewarts became not much different from volunteering for stoop labor on a farm.

The house also became, in a sense, an objectification of the tension that was developing between Martha and Andy, bringing to the surface the latent resentments that Martha seemed to feel toward her husband—resentments that were rooted in his perceived failure to provide for her any better than Eddie Kostyra had provided for his own family.

People live their lives on the basis of their learned experiences, and Martha appeared to be no exception. Fixing up the "house on Turkey Hill" became, in some ways, the reinvention of all that she disliked most from her own childhood. Reading from the script of domineering and controlling criticism that she had learned from her father, she had already begun blaming and belittling her husband for failing in his presumed role of being the family's breadwinner. "It was awful and embarrassing," recalled Norma Collier, years later. "She would put him down for everything—and I mean *everything*."

Moreover, once the pattern had been established, and Martha had become what amounted to the alpha male in the relationship, Andy slipped easily into the role of Martha's submissive and co-dependent partner. The arrangement recalled the tortured relationship between her own parents, as Martha seemed to be reliving, over and over again, the emotional trials of her childhood. Never once did she seem to grasp that her migraines, insomnia, hives, and rashes—and what Andy eventually claimed were her occasional suicide threats—were most likely the price she was paying for treating her husband the way she had watched her own father treat his wife. It was, in effect, the toll that life was extracting from her, every minute of the day . . . every time she gazed into the mirror of her past and saw reflected back, not the lovely and dutiful young person remembered by her childhood friends, but the twisted and domineering image of the one person who wound up controlling her, even from the grave: Eddie Kostyra.

Of all the people who knew Martha and Andy Stewart during their years in New York—or indeed, earlier—none ever recalled the couple as being anything other than happily married during that period. None of her friends, neighbors, or acquaintances from her childhood and teenage years in Nutley, had anything unkind to say of Martha at all. Most described her with words like "nice," "focused," "a good student," "really hard working," and "smart." Many professed bewilderment and genuine anger at press profiles that portrayed her as a shrew and a witch. The Kostyras' next-door neighbor, Thomas Allegri, spoke for many when he said, "If you want negative comments about Martha Stewart, you've come to the wrong place. She was a wonderful person. That's all I'll say."

It was the same on Wall Street. "I'm not going to say anything negative about Martha," said her brokerage firm boss, Andy Monness. "She was the hardest working, most competent person I ever worked with."

Perhaps Martha functioned well on Wall Street because she had been surrounded in her work by men with strong and forceful personalities—in effect, a world of alpha males—and she found among them a routine, and a pecking order, in which she could function. In her columns and remembrances, she has recalled those times as both satisfying professionally and personally rewarding, and in a sense they no doubt were.

Only later, when she moved to Westport and began to "take control" in her relationship with her accommodating and malleable husband, did the "Other Martha" begin to make her appearance, presumably guided by the ghosts of her childhood. Years later, the Stewarts' frequent house guest, George McCully, could still recall scenes of Martha attacking Andy for not being a good provider, for not working hard enough around the house—just the sorts of indictable offenses that had orbited around, or emanated from, her own father as Martha was growing up.

"She would curse and swear at him for almost anything," said McCully. "It just wasn't normal."

From Manhattan to Westport, things had changed—a page had turned. And there, for the turning of the page, once again, was Kathy Tatlock.

Three months before Martha Stewart made her fateful decision to look for a job on Wall Street, Kathy and Chris Tatlock had taken their fateful step into government service. One road led to the palaces and bank accounts of a billionaire, the other to a family racked by financial stress and pain. Though neither woman yet seemed to realize it, both were living through the incipient stages of crumbling marriages. It was by then the start of the 1970s, and history had already taken one of those vast, hairpin turns that can betray a person's expectations for a lifetime. Martha was adapting, Kathy was not.

Naively, Kathy had thought that the opportunity for Chris to join the Johnson Administration as a member of the State Department's Alliance for Progress program meant a chance to make the world a better place. It is not hard to see how an idealistic young woman who'd been educated at the Sorbonne would have felt the call to "make a difference"—especially when doing so promised an opportunity to travel abroad and see other cultures.

Nor did the turmoil that was spreading across the country dampen her enthusiasm, at least at the outset. Kathy and Chris—like Martha and Andy—had come of age before the assassination of John Kennedy in Dallas, and had thus never really tuned in to the cynical and shrill chorus of the antiwar movement that "public service" was just a synonym for "murder machine."

Kathy knew nothing of the shadows that moved behind the half-lit scrim of the State Department's Alliance for Progress program in Latin America. She did not know, for example, that the eight-year-old program—set forth by John Kennedy within weeks of his inauguration—had long since been entombed in the CIA-controlled Agency for International Development, which was using it for covert action programs in the very station where Chris had been assigned: Bogotá, Colombia.

She only knew that Chris had been accepted into the program, and that they were heading for Washington for a total immersion training program in the Spanish language and the cultures of Latin America. Then it would be off to Bogotá, where Chris would be serving as the USAID program legal counsel for Colombia and Ecuador.

It sounded so exciting and urgent, and above all, so worthwhile.

Kathy and Martha shared many of the same interests—in food, clothing, and the womanly arts of homemaking. But whereas Martha turned those interests to her own purposes and transformed them into a business, Kathy took the same interests and transformed them into a charity. Thus it wasn't long before Kathy had found a school in a Bogotá barrio that was desperately in need of money and support. The conditions were wretched, and in no time Kathy began fund-raising efforts for the school. However, neither the other embassy wives nor her husband seemed particularly enthusiastic about her efforts beyond social functions that might arise from fund-raising activities.

Then one day, a letter arrived. It was from Martha—a kind of note in a bottle. Kathy read the letter, and as she did, waves of nostalgia washed over her . . . for the evenings they had spent with Chris and Andy on food excursions through the restaurants of Greenwich Village, for the afternoons of antiquing, and for the dreamy talks about "the future" and "our lives." And the best part of the letter was its purpose. In the inimitable, take-control manner that Kathy had found both admirable and, at times, slightly intimidating in her friend, the letter read, "We ought to come and see you soon, don't you think?"

And so, for the second time, the lives and paths of Martha and Kathy crossed. The Stewarts were coming for vacation, and Kathy was ecstatic as she meticulously planned an itinerary that she was certain would tap all Martha's interests . . . the museums, the street markets, the mountain villages like Girardot, where they sold earthenware, and to other villages as well, where they sold intricately worked silver bracelets and buckles. She planned a trip to the school to see the work that was being done from her fund-raising efforts . . . then a trip to the "hot country" in the plains below Bogotá . . . then a separate trip to the coffee country and the Mt. Ruiz volcano to the west . . . to anything and everything that would bring the country and its people alive for her friend.

Chris didn't like it. He was fond of Andy Stewart, to be sure. But he didn't much care for Martha, and the thought of being stuck with her for a week in the Colombian backcountry made him edgy. He still remembered the times when Kathy had prepared dinner parties for the four of them back in New York and Martha had phoned at the last minute to cancel on some phony excuse. One time she just never showed up at all. "She's a user," he'd tell Kathy, "I just don't trust her."

But Kathy wasn't listening, and her excitement was at a fever pitch when the Stewarts' plane touched down at Bogotá International Airport and she could see the towering figure of Andy coming through Customs, with Martha at his side and Alexis next to them.

Yet something was wrong. And the closer they came, the more worrisome Andy looked. He was walking slowly, and his shirt was soaked through with sweat. A few steps closer still and Kathy's jaw dropped. His face was covered, neck to forehead, with . . . with hideous green welts and sores. My God, she thought, what happened!

But Martha answered before Kathy had even asked the question, announcing, without even a glance in Andy's direction—and in a voice that dripped of sarcasm and anger, "He's sick. He's got the green meanies . . ." and things went downhill from there.

It seemed that Andy had gotten sick while waiting in the departure lounge at Kennedy Airport. He'd eaten something . . . or someone had sneezed in his face, or . . . well, however it had happened, he'd gotten sick with something hideous, and by the time they'd gotten off the plane in Bogotá, he was running a fever, he was drenched in sweat, and he'd begun to break out in hives. It was a wonder they'd let him enter the country at all. But there he now stood, helpless and barely able to stand upright. And next to him stood his wife, scarcely able to control herself at the temerity of the man who'd managed to infect himself with . . . with what? What had he caught, *leprosy?*

"Well, you're not going to ruin *my* vacation," she said, "let's go," and began looking around for an exit to the street.

Kathy was agog, and as they headed for the car, she sneaked a sideways glance at Chris, whose eyes seemed to answer back, "I told you so!"

Back at the house, Kathy called a doctor, and everyone tried to make small talk as they waited for him to arrive. But the tension was almost unbearable, and at one point Kathy turned to Martha and said, "I know how disappointed you are, but look, Martha, he's *really* sick . . ." and gestured toward the guest room where Andy was lying down.

"Oh, he'll get over it," she replied, and flicked her wrist as if shooing away a housefly.

Later that afternoon, the doctor arrived, pronounced him to have become infected with a staph bug, and gave him a shot of penicillin large enough to fill a turkey baster. "I don't think you'd better be going on any trips into the country," the doctor said, "you're pretty sick." But Martha wouldn't hear of it. "He's ruining our vacation!" she cried. "It's not fair!"

The next day they left. Having arranged for Alison and Alexis to remain with the Tatlocks' two young mother's helpers, the group piled into Chris' car, with Chris and Martha in the front seat, and Andy in the back with Kathy. It was the start of a four-day, 300-mile journey in which, for the first two days, Andy would simply be left at whatever hotel they'd checked into while Chris and Kathy followed Martha as she strode from one shop and museum to the next, her research and guidebooks at the ready.

"This is wonderful," she'd say, and hold up something from a store shelf, and Kathy would take a picture of the item, with Martha examining it. It would be Martha with an ashtray, Martha examining a poncho, Martha holding some coffee beans in her hand.

"Don't you think we'd better get back and see how Andy is?" Kathy would ask, and Martha would ignore her and turn her attention to something else.

Toward the end of the trip, Andy's health improved. The welts and sores went away, he was able to shave again, and by the time they reached Mt. Ruiz on the last day of the trip, he was fine. "I told you he'd be fine," joked Martha at one point, but Kathy hadn't thought the remark very funny.

"Why don't you two get over there and I'll take a picture of you," said Kathy, gesturing toward a boulder in a lava flow at the base of the mountain. Kathy watched as the couple walked over to the rock and studied it briefly. Then without discussing the matter in any way, they instinctively assumed the pose that seemed to define the whole trip—indeed, the emerging new relationship between them in which so much was changing: Andy leaned against the side of the rock, shoulders hunched forward, looking at his feet . . . Martha stood above him on the rock, oblivious to his presence, her eyes locked on the far horizon, focused on something that apparently only she could see.

Chris turned to his wife and said, "I'm going back to the car, I need a drink," and walked off.

Kathy watched him leave, then turned back to Martha and Andy, who were now heading for the car also, and she thought, what in the world is going on here? Martha had always had a selfish side to her, to be sure. And though the two had never been especially close or affectionate—at least in the presence of others—they had certainly been civil. But a chill now seemed to have settled over them like an autumn frost. Kathy watched as they approached, neither once touching or even acknowledging the other—no holding of the hands, or opening of the car door, nor any of the other tender gestures by which men and women grow together instead of choosing to grow apart—and she thought, "Maybe Chris was right." She just wondered whether he should be drinking quite so much.

There were moments on the vacation when time stood still, and Martha's infectious laugh echoed back through the years, and the four of them were once again in New York, laughing giddily and running down the sidewalk from the Yale Club late at night, headed to who knew where. But they were freeze-frame moments in a movie that Kathy wasn't sure she ever wanted to sit through again.

Thus, as Martha and Andy's relationship congealed around the rituals of abuse and submission, Martha turned her negative energies increasingly toward her husband, and her positive energies toward herself, beginning the process that would transform her home into a palace . . . and herself into its queen.

5

A NASCENT EMPIRE: THE MARTHA MOMENT IS BORN

Even as Kathy Tatlock was beginning what would become a decade-long absence from Martha's life, Norma Collier, Martha's college-era friend, was orbiting back onstage for the second of her major appearances as a supporting actor in the Martha Stewart drama: the person who got Martha started in business.

The trails of Norma and Martha had been crossing regularly over the years as Norma's star had risen higher and higher in the world of international fashion modeling. Eventually, Norma had become a friend to the aging Coco Chanel in Paris, even as Martha's career as a model had stalled out altogether.

When the two couples moved to Connecticut at the start of the 1970s—Martha and Andy to Westport and Norma and her husband, Wolf, to nearby New Canaan—Norma and Martha continued to see each other. Their visits became more frequent after Martha left Wall Street in early 1973, despite Norma's losses on Levitz Furniture.

Andy Stewart remembers Martha as having fallen into a deepening depression after the Levitz debacle and her departure from Wall Street. Her problem: What should she do next; how could she reconstruct the shattered elements of her career? Under such circumstances, many women absorb themselves in the lives of their children, but Martha seemed more concerned with her own plight than with her daughter, Alexis—and for that matter so did Andy. Scarcely had the couple moved to the country than they found enough money to dump the child in a fancy country day school a mile from Turkey Hill, and left her to fend for herself.

In fact, when Kathy Tatlock looped back into Martha's life for one final, tumultuous time in the late 1980s, she asked Martha why she had left Wall Street. Martha pointed the finger not at the firm's deepening troubles and her desire to escape before being tarred with them herself, but at her own daughter, Alexis. Said Martha to Kathy, "Lexi was a mess, and the school said I had to stop commuting and spend more time with her." Martha did the former, but not the latter.

Freed from the daily grind of commuting to New York, Martha cast about for what to do next with her life. Andy remembers that she took a real estate course but never actually became a broker, becoming diverted instead with increasingly elaborate and time-consuming renovation projects around the house. She threw herself into them with a kind of hyperactivity that grew more and more extreme.

One day in early 1974, Norma Collier dropped by for a visit to Martha's house and found her up on a ladder, painting. Norma mentioned the headlines that day in the newspapers, and Martha looked down at her and said, matter-of-factly, "What are you talking about? I don't even know what Watergate is about!" Absorbed as she was in the immediate and limited challenges of painting her house, weeding her garden, refinishing her floors, and a thousand other handyman chores, she had remained almost totally oblivious to the multiplying dimensions of the gravest political scandal in U.S. history.

I n that, Martha Stewart was not much different from many Americans, for the end of the 1960s marked more than just the turn of a decade; it also marked a change in the way Americans viewed themselves and the world about them. On Wall Street, people got poor instead of rich; in politics the nation's leaders turned out to be crooks and peanut farmers. Why watch the news at all!

With the passing of the sixties went the sense of newness and possibility that had defined the era, leaving nothing but a bizarre kind of cultural mopping up exercise as the seventies began. One after the next, the stories rolled in: The dynamite-packed New York City townhouse of a radical terrorist group, thought to be the Weather Underground, blows up by mistake, killing three members of the organization; the Beatles break up; National Guardsmen kill four students during campus protests at Kent State University; fugitive Black Panther radical, Angela Davis, is captured by the FBI. It was as if the seventh and final wave of historical inevitability had surged up the beach, to erase—once and for all—whatever footprints still survived from a decade that ultimately had led to nothing.

So it was hardly surprising that for Martha and Andy—and for many other Americans of that time—life in the 1970s became more localized and self-contained. As the Watergate scandal gave way to the self-absorbed preoccupations of the Ford and Carter years, the broader interests and political energies of the 1960s became increasingly ratcheted down to local friendships and one's immediate circle of friends. People stopped reading the *New Republic* and began discussing stories about woodstoves and composting from the pages of *Mother Earth News*.

The friends with whom Martha and Andy socialized tended, in the main, to be Martha's friends—many of whom turned out to be people Martha had met on the train during her daily commute into New York before leaving Wall Street. There was a book reviewer for the *New York Times*, Anatole Broyard, who seemed forever on the lookout for good-looking blondes and was notorious around Westport for his serial affairs. There was a medium-well-known writer named Jill Robinson, who enjoyed a local fame of sorts because her father, Dore Schary, had been a movie producer in Hollywood.

Martha and Andy also soon befriended a local writer named Erica Jong, who, like Martha, had gone to Barnard and thereafter moved to Connecticut after hitting it big with a fictionalized sexual memoir entitled *Fear of Flying*. Erica was then married to one of her many husbands, Jonathan Fast, son of a left-leaning writer from the 1940s named Howard Fast. She maintained a salon of sorts in her home in nearby Weston, and people were forever stopping by on the weekends to see who might be loitering in or about the hot tub overlooking the woods.

But of them all, the one friendship to which Martha seemed instinctively to be drawn was Norma Collier's. It was as if Martha saw in her former mentor—by now herself retired from modeling and in search of a way to relaunch her career—a person who could show her how to rebuild her life from a perch in the 'burbs . . . or if not that, then at least someone with whom she could share her frustrations.

The two would meet weekly—and from time to time, even daily—to embark on the time-wasting pursuits that Martha had engaged in with Kathy Tatlock years earlier in New York. They'd visit antique shops and tag sales, they'd shop for fresh produce from local farms and dairies and orchards. And wherever they went, whatever they were doing, it wouldn't be long before the conversation would swing to the same familiar refrain: We can do this! Why don't *we* start a business? We need to do *something!* We're *dying* out here!

No one can say for certain which of the two women came up with the idea first, or exactly how it was articulated. But one day, sitting in Martha's kitchen, lamenting their fate in the ongoing pity-party that seemed to be taking over their lives, one or the other of them tossed out an idea that Martha would grab and eventually turn into a billion-dollar business for herself. The idea: To start a local catering service.

In her 1982 book, *Entertaining*, which began to establish her as a new personality for the American kitchen, Martha offers a fictionalized version of how the service came about that grants no role to Norma Collier and does not even mention her name, though Martha later autographed a copy of the book for Norma, acknowledging that Norma was indeed her 50/50 partner in the business.

Several local women were exploring similar home-catering ideas at the time. Mikki Durshkin, who ran a dance school for girls almost literally around the corner from Martha's home on Turkey Hill, was already running a catering service part time out of the dance studio, where Martha's daughter, Alexis, was by then enrolled for classes, as for that matter was Erica Jong's daughter, Molly. A mile down the street in the opposite direction, a housewife named Patricia Orr—the wife of a vice president at Pan Am Airways—had also just opened a catering service; she, too, had enrolled one of her children in Mikki Durshkin's dance school and was seeing with her own eyes the developing demand for such a service.

There was no doubt that commercial home catering was an opportunity whose time had arrived. By the mid-1970s, rising oil prices, soaring inflation, and growing unemployment had reversed nearly all the economic gains of the 1960s, and families everywhere were discovering that to make ends meet, wives and mothers simply had to go back to work.

So, for the first time since the 1940s, when women had been called on to help the economy during World War II, women by the millions streamed back into the labor force. This time, it was not to answer the patriot's bugle call but simply to help pay the mortgage and put food on the table. It was the start of a whole new turn in American domestic relations, as these women encountered, for the first time, the conflicts inherent in *having* to do something (return to work), while actually *wanting* the independence and fulfillment that careers seemed to promise. In a sense, they were coming face-to-face with the same conflicts that were contributing to Martha's marriage problems with Andy. The desire to find fulfillment in the workplace (a message that had been part of the background hum of feminism for as long as anyone had been listening), was now alloyed with resentment at having no choice in the matter but to get out there and earn some money.

Into this turmoil stepped Norma and Martha, offering a service that instantly set them apart from every other catering business in town. Every successful marketing plan needs what is referred to in business school as a "unique selling point," and Norma's and Martha's was this: a catering service set up so as to look as if the woman of the house did all the work herself!

They called it, appropriately enough, "The Uncatered Affair," and it worked like this. Say you wanted to have a dinner party for twelve, and you wanted it to look as if you had done all the work yourself. The Uncatered Affair would show up the day before and take away enough of your cookware, casserole dishes, and whatnot, to prepare the meal off-site. Then they'd return at the appointed hour, set up your dinner table and theme decorations, place the pre-cooked food in your oven, bring in a waitress and other help, and begin serving the dinner—to guests who'd think that you had prepared the entire thing yourself.

It was brilliant, for here was a service that played directly into the guilt-ridden needs of the American supermom of the 1970s—the sort of woman who wanted to do everything, but was still not yet entirely confident of her ability to do anything . . . and was more than willing to fake her way through it in the meantime. It was, in a word, the birth of the Martha Moment: showmanship and make-believe, all the way from the surface to the core. Westport ate it up.

Norma and Martha formed a 50/50 partnership for the business. The agreement even included what amounted to exclusive marketing territories: Westport belonged to Martha; New Canaan belonged to Norma. Both would be permitted to develop business on their own, but the proceeds would have to be shared equally between them.

In *Entertaining,* Martha described her first job as a "wedding for three hundred" in which everything that could go wrong, did go wrong: glazed eggs that melted in their aspic . . . a basket-weave cake that collapsed . . . all the sorts of "you had to be there" moments that are less and less hilarious the more you retell them. Yet

Martha claimed she knew she was "hooked" from the instant the party began. In short, she had found her calling.

Norma says the incident is in fact an amalgam of perhaps a half dozen different jobs—all of which she and Martha catered jointly—and that Martha's decision to compress them all into one dramatic moment in a reach for comic relief is nothing but an inventive imagination at work, and that no such incident ever occurred.

There was something else that Martha chose not to discuss regarding The Uncatered Affair: the reason the partnership broke up, which happened in early 1975, scarcely six months after it had been formed. The collapse came about because Martha, realizing she had a winner on her hands, began increasingly to push Norma aside. She did it with the same needling, belittling asides that Eddie Kostyra had used to claim territory in his struggle to dominate Martha Sr.—the same approach that Martha Jr. witnessed as a child, and by now was using to dominate and control Andy.

The pattern was always the same: The more that the target of her abuse would retreat, the more she'd advance, and the more aggressive and hurtful would become her attacks.

"We'd be holding a cooking class in my kitchen for women from the area," said Norma, "and Martha would constantly interrupt what I'd be saying and announce that I wasn't doing something right or some put-down like that. And I'd just stand there dumbstruck at her rudeness, and the class would come to an end, and she'd sweep up her things and leave."

The final straw came one day when Norma walked in unexpectedly on a conversation between Martha and Andy in the kitchen at Turkey Hill. The two women had been preparing for an enormous party, with maybe two hundred guests, when Norma entered the room unannounced. Her shocking discovery? That Martha had been booking jobs and banking the proceeds, without telling Norma. "I was flabbergasted," said Norma later. "And frankly, I felt like a fool. I mean, I'd been hurt by her financially once already, when she'd lost all my money in Levitz Furniture and never told me that she'd bailed out from her own personal investment in the stock months earlier. And now here I was discovering that she was ripping me off all over again."

And it only made Norma all the more furious to listen to the malleable and weak Andy agreeing with Martha that what she was doing was only fair, even as Norma strode into the kitchen and the two fell silent in embarrassed surprise. "I've had it with you," Norma announced, summoning a tone of steely rage borne of months of slights and abuse. "I'll finish out the party with you tonight, but that's it. After that this partnership is over. We're finished. . . ." And she turned and strode from the room.

But Martha had a Get Even card to play, and she used it a week or so later when she telephoned Norma and asked her to drive to New York and meet her at the boutique that Andy's sister owned and ran on Madison Avenue. The purpose of the meeting? For Norma to collect various odds and ends of hers that had come into Martha's possession during the course of the partnership. Martha would be there with them, waiting.

At the appointed hour, Norma arrived, apprehensive but determined to be civil. When she entered the shop, Martha strode from behind a curtain and directed her to go back outside and wait.

It was cold outside and a drizzly autumn rain had soaked the streets. People hurried past with their collars pulled about them as Norma waited for Martha to reappear. Momentarily, the door opened a crack, and Martha's eye peered through. Then in an instant the door swung open the rest of the way and onto the sidewalk tumbled a torrent of bundles, bags, and parcels—Norma's "things" from the partnership. Then, even as the shocked Norma stopped to collect them as people hurried past, the door slammed shut and Martha Stewart was gone from her life.

It would be nearly fifteen years before Norma and Martha would reconnect—and then only briefly—for a kind of bury-the-hatchet birthday luncheon that Norma arranged and at which both women seemed to feel distinctly uncomfortable. By that time,

Norma's career as a high fashion model had long since faded, and along with it had gone any vestigial interest of Martha in her one-time friend and mentor.

Widowed and with little but some yellowing newspaper clippings to remind her of the world she once inhabited, Norma these days works as an organic gardener in Connecticut, having little to say that is nice about the billionaire businesswoman who was once her best friend: "I hope I never hear that woman's name again in my life," says Norma. "She's a sociopath and a horrible woman, and I never want to encounter her again or think about her as long as I live." What such a comment docs not reveal is the ultimate reason for the bitterness—that Martha had the smarts to see the opportunities presented by Norma—whereas Norma failed to recognize the dangers lurking in Martha. Norma Collier may have been the first person to make that mistake about Martha, but she would not be the last.

Having split with Norma, Martha promptly set about building her catering business on her own. A clothing shop for a newly emerging fashion retailer named Ralph Lauren—a designer with a talent for self-promotion—had opened in Westport next to a bro-kerage firm for Shearson & Company in a trendy collection of shops known as "The Common Market." Martha saw an opportunity to do some retailing herself and talked the owners of the store into letting her sell homemade pies and cakes from a table by the door. The arrangement foreshadowed a business strategy that would emerge twenty years later when the Starbucks, Inc., coffee chain began opening shops in Barnes & Noble bookstores around the country to catch the foot traffic of browsers looking for a place to rest and thumb a magazine or book.

But in the mid-1970s, when Martha opened her little business—which she named "The Market Basket"—the new buzzword in re-tailing was "quality," and affluent pre-Yuppie consumers in suburbs like Westport were just developing a taste for BMWs and alligator belts. One clothing shop, Ed Mitchell's, was already discovering that in a town like Westport you could move the goods by simply marking up the price. Martha—whose life was beginning to suggest nothing less than a mood ring for American pop culture—quickly took a page from that book.

One local resident, a newly retired corporate CEO named Miles Pennybacker, spoke for many when he described how he went shopping one Saturday for a necktie, only to emerge from The Common Market bearing a daintily wrapped pie instead, muttering in bewilderment to no one in particular, "I can't believe I just paid $20 for this!" But he had—and for the reason Martha had known he would: It hadn't been the pie that had enticed him—it had been the good-looking blonde who'd sold it to him, at an out-of-sight price that all by itself seemed to say, "I'm expensive because I'm so good."

The Market Basket was an instant, huge success, and word quickly spread through Westport that a clever young lady who catered parties around town had set up shop in the store off Main Street and was selling many of the dishes, desserts, and condiments she presented at her "uncatered" affairs. Demand grew so rapidly that she was almost overwhelmed. Lacking large enough pots to cook food in bulk, she went to a local delicatessen around the corner from the shop and asked the proprietor, a Greek man named Lee Papageorge, if she could borrow one from his kitchen. Lee said sure, but only if she promised to return it, which she readily agreed to do, but never actually did.

That oversight was probably because Martha already had bigger concerns on her mind. Realizing no doubt that it wasn't the product itself that was inherently that "good," but rather the illusion of quality embedded in the high price that made the product desirable—Martha quickly hit on a way to increase her sales: Boost pie output! To do that, she decided to subcontract the cooking work and began running ads in the local newspaper, the *Westport News*, seeking Westport housewives willing to bake pies and cookies and whatnot in their homes, then bring them to Martha, who would sell them as "home cooking" from her little table in The Common Market.

But this was really forcing the envelope concerning what was meant by home cooking. In fact, the food was home cooked only in the sense that it was cooked in someone's home—under conditions that presumably Martha and certainly her customers knew nothing about. Were the kitchens sanitary? Were the pots, pans, and other utensils washed in the proper scalding temperatures before use? Or were teenage boys wandering through the kitchen after school, shouting, "Hey, Mom, what's this . . . ?" and sticking their filthy fingers into the apple pie filling on the stove, or the lemon icing for the poppy seed bread?

Nor did anyone have the slightest idea how the food was being transported from the home kitchens around town to Martha's little table in the Common Market store. Were the cookie tins simply covered with plastic wrap and placed in the back seats of station wagons previously occupied by flea-infested basset hounds? It was one thing for a cottage operation like the Uncatered Affair to prepare food for sale out of an unlicensed, uninspected, noncommercial kitchen (namely Martha's) when the food was going to be distributed to houseguests in someone else's private residence (the client's). But it was another matter entirely to be selling food to the public without a license, in a commercial establishment, which is what The Market Basket was actually doing. Eventually, Martha opened her own shop, and the Westport Health District inspectors began making inquiries, forcing Martha and her landlord to install a commercial kitchen on the premises. But by then, Martha had turned day-to-day operation of the business over to a waiflike young Bennington College graduate named Vicky Negrin who had answered one of her ads.

Increasingly, Martha began to bask in the local fame that the business was bringing her. Had she opened her Market Basket and catering operations in any other town than Westport, she might never have emerged as a media star at all. But Westporters—accustomed to living among the celebrities in their midst, and ever on the lookout for a fresh face—quickly spotted Martha as a babe on the rise and were soon mentioning her to their friends. Since the town also had a sizable population of magazine and newspaper editors and writers who were always looking for something or someone to write about, it wasn't long before Martha was turning up in the pages of publications like *Family Circle* and *Cuisine* and even the *New York Times*.

Meanwhile, Martha had incorporated herself as a business, and on January 1, 1977, began conducting her affairs under the business moniker of Martha Stewart, Inc., based out of the home on Turkey Hill. It was the start of Martha's rise in business, as well as the beginning of the final descent into ignominy for Andy: Just at the moment when the kiss of good fortune set his own career on fire, he wound up on his wife's payroll, schlepping food to her catering affairs and eventually orchestrating the book deal that would make her famous . . . while he himself wound up with cancer.

WHO'S AFRAID OF
VIRGINIA WOOLF?

As Martha's career as a caterer gained momentum, Andy's own career began to brighten as well. Yet simultaneously as their stars were rising, Martha and Andy slid further into their personal domestic hell—deeper and deeper into the roles that fed the worst and most destructive impulses in each other. In her's, Martha played the dominating shrew, seeking success more and more aggressively in her newfound business pursuit as a caterer—all in a seeming desire to settle some deep, hidden score with her father. In the process, she transferred whatever resentments she harbored for Eddie Kostyra toward Andy, instead. Andy, meanwhile, had become her spinelessly accommodating husband, never able to speak up for himself, while throwing fuel on the blaze with each appeasing response.

In time, the couple's friends from their days in New York began to peel away, repelled by the tension and awkwardness that quickly enveloped any gathering at which the two were present. One such person was Sandy Greene, one of Martha's old colleagues from the Perlberg, Monness brokerage firm.

During the firm's salad days, Sandy and Martha had been a powerhouse marketing team on Wall Street—Martha as the traffic-stopping blonde who would sweep into the client's office in her hot pants and tights and bring all conversation to a halt, and Sandy as Mister Research who trailed in behind settling into a chair at her elbow, his briefcase at the ready, primed to answer any question imaginable on the investment they were about to pitch. It was a deadly combo.

The two were inseparable, lunching together with clients at places like Le Mistral and Pietro's, where they were regulars. On weekends, Andy and Martha would sometimes drive up to Sandy's place in New Hampshire to visit, and Martha would dazzle everyone with her active mind and ability to discuss—or at least show interest in—almost any topic. She seemed particularly fascinated by cookbooks, and on one visit brought a volume by Julia Child that she proceeded to read cover to cover before the weekend was over. Sandy thought it odd and asked her what was so absorbing about it, and she answered, seemingly unable to put precisely into words what was so captivating, "Oh, these are just the greatest books."

But after Martha left the firm, Sandy noticed a change begin to come over her relationship with Andy. For a time, he continued to invite the couple to New Hampshire for weekends, but the tension between Martha and Andy began to dominate the get-togethers. Martha did not directly attack and abuse Andy in front of others (the relationship had not yet deteriorated to that point), but she found ways to needle him with hurtful little digs and asides. For Sandy, it became less and less pleasant to have them around, and eventually he stopped socializing with them altogether. Years later, he summed it up this way: "On Wall Street she had a healthy competitiveness, but eventually it turned nasty. She became very demanding, without any thought for how the other person might feel." And Andy was first in the line of fire.

Others from the couple's New York days noticed the change as well. Norma Collier had attended several of Martha's and Andy's holiday gatherings when the couple still lived in New York, and though Martha had never seemed terribly warm or affectionate toward her husband, she had certainly been civil. Yet by the time she and Martha had set up their partnership in The Uncatered Affair, Martha's relationship with Andy had deteriorated to the point that she'd angrily attack and abuse him for the most inconsequential of perceived failings. At one of the couple's early Christmas parties at Turkey Hill, Martha prepared a bean casserole and began berating Andy in front of the guests when the beans wouldn't cook and the meal was an hour late being served.

George McCully, another of the couple's friends from New York, was horrified to witness, while visiting Turkey Hill one weekend, Martha berate Andy for how "fucking stupid" he was for stacking firewood the wrong way. Of course, that was not just Martha attacking Andy; it was a replay of Eddie Kostyra—railing down through the years—attacking Martha (and everyone else in the Kostyra home) for some alleged failure or other.

Andy seemed to sense that he was the lightning rod for Martha's unresolved issues with her father, and he would try to befriend Eddie by making small talk when they were together. But the gestures never got very far and always seemed to end sooner or later with Eddie somehow having the last word. Andy viewed him as a Willy Loman figure, stumbling downhill in his life from one failure to the next, papering over his shortcomings with incessant bragging and compulsive drinking. Dragging behind him was the smoldering fuse of a brutal nature toward his wife and children that seemed forever ready to flare up and explode.

Other visitors to the Stewart home recall a level of such constant tension between the couple as to have turned the kitchen of Turkey Hill—where most socializing took place—into a Torquemada's Theater of Tortures. Only instead of the auto-da-fé, the spectacle featured random provocations and ricocheting counterpunches reminiscent of Who's Afraid of Virginia Woolf?, with the audience unsure from moment to moment what the central character's husband might do (or not do) to send this real-life Martha into a rage.

Meanwhile, Andy caught his break. Not long after having joined Bangor Punta as its assistant in-house counsel at the start of the 1970s—a prestige-free job of utterly room-emptying tedium—Andy came to work one day to discover that his boss was being seduced away to become general counsel for the Times Mirror Company's magazine and book publishing operations. In the move, Andy was able to grab his boss' coattails and land at the company as the legal department's second-in-command.

Not long afterward, difficulties developed between the company and one of its division heads, a bilious octogenarian named Harry Abrams, who published a line of four-color, coffee-table art books. Abrams was legendary in publishing circles for his irascible manner and indeed was known in the Westport area for his equally charmless sister, Faith, who paraded around town with a miniature poodle named Renoir.*

True to his reputation, Abrams soon quit in a huff, creating an immediate succession problem for Times Mirror. As a result, Andy was given the job as the Abrams imprint new president and CEO, a promotion that overnight made him a *macher* in publishing circles.

Andy became quickly immersed in the business of publishing expensive, high-quality art books, developing an understanding of every aspect of the business, from its economics to its production processes, from its deal making to its marketing and distribution systems. It was this knowledge base, and these skills, that Martha tapped at the start of the 1980s, when she came to the attention of executives at Crown Publishing Company. With her husband's help, she convinced them to publish her first book, *Entertaining*—a kind of coffee-table cookbook that would lift her to a whole new level of recognition and fame in the world of domestic arts.

In book publishing, as in other creative endeavors in which luck plays a part, by the late 1970s Andy was viewed as holding a "hot

---

*Faith was the stepmother of nightclub comic and TV actor Richard Belzer, yet another local Westporter.

hand"—a reputation he had acquired almost from the moment he took over as the head of Abrams Publishing and brought forth a surprise bestseller entitled *Gnomes*.

The book was actually little more than a gimmick—a coffee-table art book with illustrations and text purporting to document the secret life of gnomes—Germanic creatures supposedly inhabiting the forests and enjoying life spans that stretched for centuries. The publication of *Gnomes* by Harry Abrams Publishing, Inc.—a company known for lavishly illustrated, high-priced titles like its *Library of Great Painters* series—seemed to make the book both respectable as well as cute, like putting a jukebox in a den filled with Queen Anne period pieces.

The success of *Gnomes* was a total fluke, and no one was more surprised than Andy, who had been pitched the book by a Dutch publishing company that had already brought it out in Europe and was now looking for an American publisher to translate it into English and bring out a U.S. edition. Andy liked the illustrations—suggestive, in a way, of the work these days of Thomas Kinkade—and figured, what the hell, he'd go for it. The company needed someone to do the text calligraphy for the book, so Andy asked Martha for the name of the person who'd been doing her hand-lettered menus and labels at The Market Basket, and paid her $100 to do the lettering for the book. Day-to-day editing was given to a 71-year-old editor at the office named Ruth Eisenstein, and the book was added to Abrams' autumn 1977 catalog with little fanfare.

Meanwhile, Andy struggled not only with his deteriorating relationship with Martha but with the sudden and shattering news, in the spring of 1977, that he had been stricken with cancer, confronting him with months of debilitating—though ultimately successful—radiation and chemotherapy treatments.

In the Stewart social circle, Andy was one of the lucky ones, for cancer hovered like a black cloud over the lives of several of the couple's similarly stressed friends—and even the husband of Martha's youngest sister, Laura.

There were Kathy and Chris Tatlock, for example, whose own marriage had come apart at just about the time Martha was establishing herself in the Common Market in Westport. In August 1976, Kathy had finally gathered her children and walked out on Chris, whose drinking and abusive behavior had become unbearable; not long afterward, Chris was diagnosed with cancer, dying in January 1977, scarcely three months before Andy was stricken. And there was Norma Collier, whose marriage had also ended in divorce, followed by the death from cancer of her ex-husband, Wolf.

Friends of Martha and Andy say they believe that the stress of the Stewarts' dysfunctional family environment—which had begun to crumble on all fronts—contributed to Andy's illness. And there was certainly plenty to be stressed about. Back in Nutley, life in the Kostyra home seemed to be going from bad to worse. In fact, scarcely had Martha and Andy moved to Connecticut than Martha's youngest sister, Laura, had fled the Kostyra home and moved in with them, spending her sophomore year as a student at Staples High School in Westport before returning to Nutley.*

Thereafter, another of the Kostyra children—George—fled Elm Place as well, and at Martha's urging became a fixture at Turkey Hill, where he did carpentry and handyman jobs . . . by which time Laura had returned to live with the Stewarts again. Meanwhile, Martha and Andy's daughter, Alexis, had left the house and, after a boarding school year at Choate in nearby Wallingford, Connecticut, had retreated still further from Turkey Hill, to become a student at Andy's old prep school in Vermont. When she returned to Turkey Hill thereafter, it was often with a boyfriend in tow to stay weekends in a separate studio apartment that Martha's brother, George, had built in the back of the house.

And where was Eddie through all this—the man whose controlling, negative energies seemed to have been steering Martha from

---

*Laura proceeded through a series of failed relationships of her own—one of which ended ironically, and tragically, when her second husband, to whom she was happily married, an actor named Kim Herbert, died of cancer.

the start on her uncertain course toward fame and glory? By the late 1970s, his own faltering career was finished, and much of his time was now being spent in a drunken stupor . . . a situation into which Martha might have intervened in a way to have helped them both . . . or at least, let us say, to have helped her come to terms with her conflicted feelings about her father. But it was not to be.

Instead, she turned him into something approximating—almost literally—a lawn ornament for her increasingly extravagant gardens at Turkey Hill. In that role Eddie made an appearance, unexpectedly, at a tour of Martha's house and grounds she had organized for the Westport Garden Club, and it foreshadowed the much remarked upon—and often uncomfortable—moments many years later when Martha would invite her aged mother, Martha Sr., to appear with her on her TV show to demonstrate cooking recipes where she served as a similar kind of stage prop.

The house and grounds had been manicured to hospital bed-corner tidiness for the tour, and a route had been laid out through the house and surrounding gardens, which by now had spread to an adjoining lot, which the couple had lately acquired for $47,000. There were beds of sunflowers that had grown as tall as hemlocks. There were irises, nasturtiums, snapdragons, and begonias. Rose bushes were everywhere, along with the stacked boxes of working beehives. Nearby stood a chicken coop the size of a Cotswold cottage, and a small penned-in area for goats. It was a gardening extravaganza, like something out of a child's fantasy—only bigger even than life itself.

Slowly and humbly, the ladies of the Garden Club wandered through, murmuring in suitably low tones at the grandeur of it all, for this was obviously the grandest garden on the entire tour, topping anything they had seen before . . . and, they all agreed, anything they would likely see thereafter.

One of the ladies on the tour that afternoon was a woman named Cary Pierce. Cary did not have a grand house, and in fact was not even a member of the Westport Garden Club. But she'd gotten herself on the tour after she'd learned whose house would be among those on it.

Cary did not know Martha from The Uncatered Affair. Nor for that matter had she ever bought a $20 Market Basket pie. Rather, Cary's connection with Martha Stewart reached back much further than that—back and back, as the years peeled away, to when Cary was growing up as a little girl at the end of World War II.

There is a moment in the 1961 movie, *One-Eyed Jacks*, when Marlon Brando, playing a desperado wanted by the police in Mexico, encounters the sidekick (played by Karl Malden) who had abandoned him years earlier in a gunfight with the police. Now, Malden has undergone an amazing transformation and is the sheriff of a town. Encountering him, the seething Brando says, in one of the great takedown lines of the cinema, "You may be a one-eyed Jack, but I've seen your other side."

Cary Pierce had come to Martha's house on the Garden Club tour, if not to say those words, then perhaps at least to think them, for Cary knew the face of Martha Stewart that was now hidden behind the black-eyed susans and the daylilies. Cary, like Martha, had grown up on Elm Place, in the working-class, blue-collar town of Nutley, New Jersey, only a few doors down the street from where the Kostyras had lived.

Cary knew all the stories of the tyrannical Eddie Kostyra. But nothing could have prepared Cary for what she saw next, when, gazing in the direction of the goat shed, she beheld a man, dressed in what appeared to be the pressed and creased uniform of an attendant, standing strictly at attention with a shovel at his side as the ladies passed. The man had been told to stand there obviously to play the role of a kind of field-hand mannequin, and as Cary moved closer she could see who he was—Eddie Kostyra, Martha's father—assigned to stand in sweating attention in the summer sun, like a lawn statue, to impress on the ladies of the local Garden Club that Martha had arrived . . . a point she no doubt intended to make, on some level or other, to Eddie as well.

Thereafter, Eddie died, after which Martha arranged for her mother, Martha Sr., to move to Westport to join the rest of the Elm Place clan. There is no doubt that Martha was making a noble and supportive gesture in gathering her family together under her protective wing. But on another level, what she had also done is uproot the dysfunctional world of her childhood and move it from Nutley, New Jersey, to Westport, Connecticut . . . with the singular and notable difference that Eddie was no longer calling the shots, Martha now was.

Meanwile, *Gnomes* had become an overnight, smash sensation, like nothing Harry Abrams Publishing had every experienced before, and Andy rode the wave as the whole country went gnomes mad. Licensing deals were struck for a *Gnomes* cartoon series for television. There were *Gnomes* calendars, *Gnomes* posters, *Gnomes* T-shirts and turtlenecks. There were *Gnomes* clocks and wristwatches, *Gnomes* Christmas tree ornaments, *Gnomes* bath soap, and ballpoint pens. By the end of the 1970s, it was all *Gnomes*, all the time, as sales of the book topped 750,000 copies while ad men worked overtime to crank out promotional lines like "There's no place like gnome."

It should have been Andy's finest hour. From a corporate lawyer nobody, he had emerged as one of the biggest and most influential figures in all of book publishing, the man with the golden touch, who could turn an obscure Dutch book about fantasy creatures into the top-grossing book on the *New York Times* best-seller list, ahead of James Fixx's *The Complete Book of Running*, James Herriot's *All Things Wise and Wonderful*, and many other titles destined to become household names at the start of the 1980s. In fact, it was to mark the beginning—and the end—of Andy's moment in the sun, as *Gnomes* was quickly overshadowed by the book he helped create for his wife— and, of course, she wound up with all the credit as Andy simply became known as "Martha Stewart's husband."

MAKING THE
BEST-SELLER LIST

E ven as the success of *Entertaining* marked Martha's emergence as an independent personality in publishing circles, it also brought the further eclipse of the man who had made it possible in the first place: her husband Andy. There is evidence to suggest that Andy coped with the problem by entangling himself with another woman. Although this is rarely if ever the right thing to do, it is something to which people are all too prone to fall victim when feeling rejected or overshadowed by those closest to them. The suspicions if not the reality added fuel to a separation that made a mockery of the storybook Stewart lifestyle, and likely made the eventual divorce far bloodier and more painful than anyone might have imagined at the time.

It was, in fact, at the launch party for *Gnomes*, which Martha catered, that she slipstreamed into publishing behind her husband's success. Ever since Andy had moved from Bangor Punta Corporation to Abrams Publishing, he and Martha had been talking about publishing a cookbook of some sort. And with the publication of *Gnomes* in 1977, Andy had learned the intricacies of such an undertaking— the publication of a "profusely illustrated book," as he put it.

Andy's reputation in the book publishing business initially encouraged Crown Publishing to go ahead with *Entertaining*. The catalyst turned out to be the head of Crown Publishing, Alan Mirken—a kind of *Schmendrick* figure who reminded some in publishing circles of a gnome in his own right. While attending the *Gnomes* launch party, Mirken, munching on an hors d'oeuvre, turned to Andy and declared in so many words, "These are great! Who made them?" Andy answered, "Here, meet my wife . . ." and Martha met the man who would become the publisher of *Entertaining*.

From this meeting evolved a proposal and through it a contract that Andy negotiated on behalf of his wife. Martha received a $25,000 advance, which was respectable enough in the Crown Publishing scheme of things—at least at the Clarkson Potter imprint where she was to be published. Yet it hardly put her in the same league with, say, Alexandra Penney, who was soon to be signed up at Clarkson Potter, with a $75,000 advance—the largest in the company's history—for an irresistibly playful book entitled *How to Make Love to a Man*.

Andy did much of the picture editing and laying out of the pages for *Entertaining*—many of which contained photos that he had taken of his wife and their lives at Turkey Hill. On a personal level, the book is notable for two things: (1) the lack of credit, in the original edition, to its actual writer, Betsy Weinstock, and (2) the thirteen separate photos of Martha, the mere three photos of Alexis (one with her back to the camera), and the single, poorly lighted snapshot of Andy.

On a larger, public level, *Entertaining* was a publishing phenomenon, the first cookbook since Julia Child's and Simone Beck's *Mastering the Art of French Cooking*, two decades earlier, to gain a truly mass-market audience beyond the kitchen. There was plenty of follow-on sniping by culinary critics and chefs with a pipeline to the media, who complained that the recipes had been filched from other cookbooks and often listed the wrong mix of ingredients for the intended result. A number of reviewers noted, for example, that several of her recipes seemed to have been lifted from Julia Child's book itself.

But the carping missed the whole point of what *Entertaining* was really all about. It wasn't actually a cookbook at all, but a celebration of a certain kind of tinselly, nouveau-grandeur that was seeping into American life as the 1980s began. Martha herself was already riding the wave, and by the time she incorporated her little home-based business as "Martha Stewart, Inc." at the start of 1977, she had begun turning her catering assignments into increasingly elaborate, "theme" type events. By the start of the 1980s, they were evolving into the food world equivalents of Busby Berkeley musicals.

"I prefer big parties," she told a reporter for the *New York Times*, and she wasn't kidding. At the same time that thousands of anti-communist protestors in Poland were gathering under the banner of a union leader named Lech Walesa to demand organizing rights throughout the country, Martha was putting the finishing touches on what amounted to a statement of her own 5,000 miles away in New York: a catered dinner for 1,500 guests of the American Museum of Folk Art at a pier on Manhattan's West Side.

Gone was the "did-it-myself" facade that had been her original selling point back in the days of Norma Collier and The Uncatered Affair, and in its place had now emerged an elaborately staged presentation that had taken five full months to plan and choreograph. Trees had been trucked in and planted throughout the cavernous pier, an entire industrial kitchen had been assembled, including institutional warming ovens, griddles, and place settings for 1,500. It had been an organizational effort worthy of the Pentagon, and it had been put together entirely by Martha and a couple of helpers in a cubby hole office out of which she was now running her business in a low-rent commercial neighborhood in Westport.

This was the scale to which her undertakings had grown, and *Entertaining* was intended to celebrate their majesty . . . at the center of which was beginning to emerge—into sharper and sharper focus—the maestro herself, Martha. The book itself was not written by Martha at all but rather by the ghostwriter wife of a New York Public Relations man, Davis Weinstock—the same Davis Weinstock who had steered Martha toward a job at the Perlberg, Monness brokerage firm on Wall Street more than a decade earlier. Now, his wife, Betsy, took on the task of interviewing Martha for the cookbook that Crown, at Andy's urging, had agreed to publish.

Martha herself seemed to have little clear idea how to write a book—or even to be interviewed for one—and seems to have continually meandered into embellished reminiscences of her childhood in Nutley, and her edited recollections of married life with Andy. Exhausted from trying to keep her focused and on point, Betsy eventually gave up and simply began copying down Martha's recollections, then writing them up afterward in a way that she thought might show Martha in her best light.

Yet when coupled with page after page of photographs of life around Turkey Hill, along with extravagantly presented table settings and photos of various dishes and foods, the effect was electrifying. More than half the book was devoted to recipes of one sort or another, but this was no cookbook. It was still two years before the airwaves would erupt with Ronald Reagan's 1984 reelection imagery of "morning in America," but in the pages of *Entertaining* it was already morning in the American kitchen, as families were invited to awaken to a whole new world that for most people had never existed.

In this world, dad no longer came downstairs to breakfast, zipping up his fly and yelling at mom for splitting the English muffins with a knife instead of a fork. Gone was everybody grabbing at once for the last slice of raisin bread. On this breakfast table sat nothing with lettering on it at all: no boxes of cornflakes, no jars of Tang. In this world, no one rose from the table and exited farting, or opened the fridge and drank from the milk carton. Gone was everybody talking at once—or, alternatively, staring sullenly at each other and saying nothing at all.

Instead of real life in the exhausted two-income households of the stagflation seventies, *Entertaining* offered a fantasy world of grandiloquent leisure—from breakfast onward, straight through the day . . . a world of fresh-cut flowers on every table, with parsley and capers garnishing every dish. In this world, children didn't fight and throw food: They came to the table in starched linen Sunday clothes and sat without a sound, like porcelain figurines. It was a world of utter neatness and airbrushed perfection, unfolding page after page in the aromatic and dew-drenched gardens of Turkey Hill, or against the richly burnished hues of the home's interiors. Here is "an intimate family Christmas Eve dinner . . ." with the Empire Regency armchair nestled cozily by the fire. Here is champagne for two, served in cut-glass goblets on a sterling silver serving tray with Hepplewhite feet.

But this was more than mere escapism, it was fantasy empowerment for a generation of American womanhood—the imperial kitchen of the supermom czarina. On page 25 readers can learn the secrets of "cocktails for twenty-five." A few pages farther on and it becomes "cocktails for fifty . . ." followed by "cocktails for two hundred." There are directions for preparing an "omelet brunch for eight to ten," or a "midnight omelet supper for thirty" or for sixty. There are clambakes for thirty, and buffets for forty, and dinners for fifty, and even a "sit-down country luncheon for one hundred seventy-five."

A reviewer for *Newsweek* took one look at the book and pronounced it "the art of showing off." Which the reviewer didn't seem to understand was pretty much the whole point. As the first copies of *Entertaining* were rolling off the press, America itself was embarking on a fit of showing off. After a decade of gas lines and hostages, and a President who'd pitifully pulled a cardigan about him as he went on TV to declare that the way to beat the Ayatollah was to turn down the thermostat and tie a yellow ribbon around something, Americans had had it—especially the women. As a result, the book and the country nestled together like two spoons.

The women were the ones who, like their mothers a quarter century earlier, had made survival possible at a time of national crisis. In fact, women accounted ultimately for the bulk of the growth in the economy as a whole, filling two-thirds of all 17 million jobs created in the United States during the decade. Just as Rosie's rivets had bolted together the war machine that had defeated the Axis in the 1940s, the second incomes of American women who had entered the workplace in the 1970s had tipped the balance in favor of survival for families who could no longer make ends meet on the income of a single breadwinner.

By the 1970s, the early liberal feminism of Betty Friedan had moved beyond the inclusive impulses of the National Organization for Women and Title VII of the 1964 Civil Rights Act, which prohibited sexual discrimination in employment. Instead, the organization was now beginning to press the broader, and more divisive, agenda of the Equal Rights Amendment. In the process, the movement had morphed into an array of more than 500 increasingly shrill special interest groups, with a thousand different issues and arenas for action.

A sign of what lay ahead came in the middle of the Watergate crisis, when even as Martha Stewart was painting her house and having coffee klatches with Norma Collier, the rest of America became momentarily mesmerized over whether an aging tennis world figure named Bobby Riggs—by then pushing 60—could beat the reigning champion of women's tennis: Billie Jean King. When King trounced Riggs in straight sets, in what had been billed as "The Battle of the Sexes," women's rights advocates quickly seized on it as the latest proof in an accumulating body of presumed evidence that women could do anything men could—from running corporations to fighting in the Armed Forces.

But was this what women really wanted in the first place? Many women were simply turned off by the movement as it splintered, at the margins, into groups like the "Women's International Terrorist Conspiracy from Hell" (WITCH), which staged guerrilla theater events that included bursting into society weddings and letting mice loose amidst the proceedings. Most women had neither the time nor much patience for such stunts—especially when many would have preferred to be walking down the aisle in society weddings of their own. Instead, they had found themselves "freed" by the movement to become the functional equivalent of pack mules in the struggling economy, engaged year after year in the heavy lifting that was delivering the economy a one-time free shot of growth-stimulating productivity—a windfall that was staving off national economic collapse in the face of soaring inflation, rising unemployment, and slowing growth.

As the decade progressed, an increasingly noisy feminist backlash began to take shape around individuals like Phyllis Schlafly, who attracted followers by pronouncing issues like the Equal Rights Amendment a federal government power grab to control all of domestic relations and set the agenda of American family life. Wrote one social critic of the era, Bruce J. Schulman, "It was not just the prospect of shared bathrooms and homosexual marriages that frightened anti-feminists. . . . Rather, ERA opponents worried that the amendment would eliminate all legal and traditional protections for married women."

The ERA amendment went down in defeat, buried under an avalanche of opposition from what would soon be known as the Reagan Democrats—working-class men and women who had supported Democratic candidates since the New Deal, but by now had grown so disenchanted with the Carter seventies and its perceived lack of follow-through, that they were ready to do the unthinkable and vote for a right-wing Republican candidate for President.

Hollywood sensed that a backlash was building and by the start of the 1980s had dusted off a character not seen in feature films in a quarter century: the female lead who has had it with a life as the functional equivalent of a man, and yearns for nothing so much as to become a woman again. *Arthur*, released in 1981, celebrated the triumph of a working-class girl with street smarts (Liza Minnelli), who lands a boozy millionaire (Dudley Moore)—a plot that echoed the theme of a movie twenty years earlier by Liza Minnelli's director-father, Vincente: *Bells Are Ringing*, starring

Judy Holliday and Dean Martin. Or what about *An Officer and a Gentleman,* released in 1981, in which a Naval officer rescues a working-class girl.

Even "women's lib" movies like *Nine to Five* (1980) in which a sexist boss (Dabney Coleman) is outsmarted by his female subordinates, couldn't escape the underlying tension that seemed to be gripping women everywhere: Great numbers of them just didn't like the life that liberation had made possible. They wanted to feel empowered, to be sure—with minds, rights, and authority of their own. But not a whole lot of them seemed terribly eager to become actual men.

These were the women whom Martha Stewart reached with *Entertaining.* They were destined to form the core of an audience that would expand and spread out in the years that followed, into columns in more than 200 newspapers . . . into syndicated radio programming on stations across the country . . . into TV shows, magazines, and brand-name marketing through the store shelves of the nation's second largest discount retailer.

They were Martha's readers: the women who came home exhausted from jobs they didn't really want, to confront equally exhausted husbands and resentful latchkey children . . . women who had to fend off Dabney Coleman at the office, only to return home to cook dinner and wonder why the man knocking back the Budweisers in the den couldn't at least have been a millionaire like Dudley Moore.

These were the women who picked up a copy of *Entertaining* and were instantly transported into the make-believe world where they'd always wanted to be—where the sun shone brightly through the panes of streak-free windows . . . where fresh fruits and flowers sat next to pitchers of iced tea . . . where men came to lawn parties dressed in suits and ties, and the women could prepare a lobster dinner for fifty and never break a sweat. It was the world of Martha Stewart that she herself had yearned for as a child—and when she invented it in the pages of *Entertaining*, she could have had no idea where it would take her.

The publication of *Entertaining* eventually eclipsed the publication of *Gnomes* as a runaway bestseller, and suddenly Andy was back in the shadows again. How he dealt with it personally isn't known for certain, but there is at least some evidence—much of it from Martha herself—that at this point he may have begun involving himself with another woman. Considering what Andy and Martha had been doing to each other, it might be surprising if *both* weren't by then sneaking around on each other.

Some years later, when the marriage finally fell apart and Andy filed for a divorce that dragged on for two years—after all the heartache and recrimination, the accusations and the court-issued restraining orders, and the fighting over Lexi and the estate—after all that, one would have thought that both parties would have wanted to let bygones be bygones and just get on with their lives.

But for Martha, it wasn't quite like that—and neither, for that matter, was it for Andy. In both cases, their attention seemed to focus on a single person: their neighbor, and writer, Erica Jong . . . who had been a student at Barnard College a year or two behind Martha.

Erica's reputation in town—particularly among men—was considerable, for here was a clever female writer who seemed, at least through her writings, to celebrate and flaunt a life of commitment-free sexual adventure. Her best-known book, *Fear of Flying*, had presented a character of memorable licentiousness—Isadora Wing—who was fun to read about, to say nothing of the glee that men took in speculating among themselves about the author who had created Isadora Wing.

How Andy and Erica met is not entirely clear, though they certainly became more than mere acquaintances. Not long after the publication of *Entertaining*, Erica wound up as Andy's handpicked author to write one of the follow-ups to *Gnomes*, entitled *Witches*, which she did eventually undertake.

Erica claims that she was introduced to Andy through writer Jill Robinson, who had been a mutual friend of both as part of Andy's and Martha's early circle of Westport chums. Be that as it may, George McCully, the Stewarts' regular weekend houseguest during the 1970s, says that he, Martha, and Andy visited Erica's house occasionally for parties, which often included actors and other celebrities who could be found lounging in Erica's *Boogie Nights*-style hot tub. McCully recalls that Erica sometimes seemed overtly flirtatious toward Andy at such moments—a fact that others commented on as well.

I'd already heard Martha blame Erica for breaking up her marriage, and though it seemed a bit far-fetched, I decided to ask Erica. But the answer I got back was less of a denial than a counterpunch at Martha, as Erica said, "She's been bad-mouthing me to people for years, and I just don't pay any attention to it anymore . . ." then proceeded to bad-mouth Martha right back.

If Erica did have an affair with Andy, she may not have been the only woman he had been involved with. When Andy finally filed for divorce, court papers that Martha thought had been filed under seal, but weren't, accused him of being an adulterer. Andy himself declined to comment on the matter for this book, saying that he didn't want to indulge in gossip. When the subject came up between himself and Kathy Tatlock, he was equally coy. Kathy asked him, "Did you have an affair with Erica Jong," and Andy sprouted an impish grin but said nothing.

Within a year of publishing *Entertaining*, Martha delivered a follow-up: *Quick Cook* (1983). In 1984 came a third title (*Hors D'Oeuvres*), then a fourth title in 1985 (*Pies & Tarts*), and a fifth in 1987 (*Weddings*). The outpourings turned Martha into, far and away, the most important writer at Crown Publishing's Clarkson

Potter imprint, overshadowing Alexandra Penney (*How to Make Love to a Man*) and every other writer on its list.

And the books also did something else: They launched Martha on her way to becoming America's preeminent marketer of day-dreams and fantasies for women. It was the beginning of Martha's autobiography, served up a coffee spoon at a time, of her life as Nancy Drew, with Martha herself as the ultimate daydream believer. The five books thus amount to a kind of "Early Martha" period in her remembered and augmented past—the base layer of a record that was destined to grow more fanciful, entertaining, and mar-ketable, though less and less accurate, with each successive retelling.

Like *Entertaining*, Martha's follow-on books relied heavily on rem-iniscences of her childhood and married life. And as the new books rolled off the press, the dim outlines of a life began to emerge—not the life Martha had actually lived, but a life adorned with the first subtle embellishments of life as she may have always wanted it to be . . . a life of rustic and homey warmth around wood-fired kitchen stoves, with sweet-faced grannies returning from the henhouse with their aprons full of fresh eggs, to give one last stir to the savory stew that simmered in the iron kettle over the aromatic hickory logs in the fireplace.

Did anyone actually live like that, particularly in fashionable and affluent Westport, Connecticut, at the start of the Reaganaut 1980s? Something about the picture just didn't seem to fit—like one of those questions on an IQ test that displays a drawing of a hammer, a nail . . . and a bicycle, and asks, "Which of these doesn't belong?"

That's what Martha and Andy's life seemed to look like in the pages of *Martha Stewart's Quick Cook: Two Hundred Easy and Elegant Recipes*—too many bicycles mixed in with the hammers and nails. Here was a couple in which the wife was a best-selling author and New York caterer, and the husband was one of the country's best known book publishers—and the couple's daughter was pursuing her education in various swanky and expensive New England prep schools. And in the midst of all that, *Quick Cook* purported to draw back the curtain on the private lives of a couple who seemed to be alternatively shoveling out the henhouse, then dashing off for a weekend of fun, sun, and antiquing in the hills of Tuscany.

Yet improbably enough, that is what Martha's and Andy's life had by this time become, as the two had increasingly developed into forty-something jet-setters even as renovations on the Turkey Hill property had turned the dwelling into an almost perfect museum piece from a Currier & Ives print. Nearly all the renovations were the doing of Martha herself, who had become so obsessed with preserving the original features of the home that much of the dwelling remained unheated except by fireplaces, making the guest rooms almost unbearably cold in the winter.

As for the property and gardens, Martha threw herself into farm work with an energy that astounded everyone. By 1985, she and Andy had planted 122 trees on the grounds, which by then included an adjoining two-acre lot, and Andy had been assigned the chore of keeping each and every tree pruned to perfect neatness.

Andy's mother had been nagging Martha for years to rein in her excesses—in particular, to get rid of the chicken coop and the livestock, which had become a nonstop demand on not just Martha's time but Andy's as well (to say nothing of unlucky weekend houseguests who wound up being dragooned into chicken-feeding duty). But Martha seemed oblivious to the pleas and simply redoubled her efforts, assigning her brother George to build a barn in the back, while hiring helpers to tend a series of vegetable and flower gardens that had long since become the talk of Westport for their elegance and extravagance.

By the start of the 1980s, her Market Basket business had closed, partly because of disputes with the owners of the store and partly, it would appear, because the shopping center had been converted to other uses. But Martha hardly missed it because her catering business had taken on a life of its own, with Martha and three employees cranking out twelve to twenty catered affairs per month—some as small as house parties for eighteen, others as large as corporate affairs for 700—from the kitchen on Turkey Hill. She was catering affairs for Tiffany's in New York; for Betsy Gimbel, the heiress to the Gimbel fortune, in Greenwich; for Sotheby's; for Paul Newman and his actress wife, Joanne Woodward—and each such assignment led to even more as word-of-mouth spread.

A lot of these events came by way of Andy, who was routinely throwing lavish book-publishing parties for Abrams authors, and was thus in a position to swing business toward his wife. Typical of the extravaganzas she put together: a midnight omelet supper for 1,000 at the U.S. Customs House in lower Manhattan, to celebrate the launch of *Faeries*, which Andy had positioned as a follow-up to *Gnomes*.

When *Entertaining* came out and instantly vaulted to best-seller status, Martha's reputation took another quantum leap upward as she became *the* caterer to hire. Soon, the fact that a dinner was being catered by Martha Stewart carried almost as much news value as any celebrity guests who might be attending the affair.

Martha reveled in it and quickly began to extend her "brand" in any direction she could. "I'll do anything to get my name in the papers," she once had told Norma Collier, and she began to show what she meant. She had already been featured in *Bon Appetit* and *House & Garden*, and now nailed down a deal as a freelance writer for *House & Garden's* arch rival publication, *House Beautiful*. Meanwhile, she had begun giving lectures on cooking all over Connecticut, and was soon making appearances in Washington, D.C., as well.

As Martha's fame grew, and she became increasingly absorbed in making it grow still more, she seemed to have less and less time available for her personal relationships—not just with Andy and Alexis, but with her employees, her neighbors, and anyone else she might encounter day to day. A brusque efficiency began to take over her conversations. People remarked on how Martha would end conversations by simply walking away, or by hanging up the telephone without even saying goodbye. "She was very efficient and businesslike, but not very warm," recalled a New Canaan interior decorator named Pamela Barnett, who worked with her on a 1980s renovation project. "She's not the sort of person whom I for one would want to have as a friend."

Having learned from watching her father manage the Kostyra household that the way she could get people to do what she wanted was by simply asserting authority over them, Martha had an abundance of militarylike "command and control" techniques at her disposal for the management of the world around her. She had learned from modeling how to walk into a room and cause every head in the place to swivel in her direction. She had learned to say "Hello" in a throaty, cool timbre that would cause everyone within earshot to stop talking and start listening. She had learned how to fix a person with a stare that would cause frost to form on the windows. In short, she had learned how to charm people and scare them all at once, and it enabled her to control people who really didn't want to be controlled at all.

Like a general commanding troops on the battlefield—which in some ways seemed a perfect metaphor for how she seemed to approach her life—she organized huge undertakings with the finely geared precision of a military drill team. This skill, which had already become the standout feature of her catering business, allowed her to manage the increasingly complex world of Turkey Hill as well as her ever more overloaded life.

But having never really developed the "people skills" needed to organize her colleagues' work in collaborative, nonauthoritative ways, she wound up coming across to them as "bossy" and "arrogant"—two words that were being applied to her with increasing frequency by friends and neighbors as well as her employees, who gossiped incessantly behind her back. They felt themselves viewed by her—rightly, in fact—as not much more than stage props in the Martha Stewart Story . . . the lifelong drama in which she played the starring role. At one point, at the very pinnacle of her success years later, when her company, Martha Stewart Living Omnimedia, had been taken public on Wall Street and her employee rolls had ballooned to more than 500 people, she walked down a corridor of her office, a pet dog in tow on a leash, then stopped and watched as the dog squatted on the carpet and pooped. Said Martha as she turned to an assistant at her elbow, "I just wish I could get my employees to do that when I say." Which may say just as much about Martha's concessions to her pets (or her lack of interest in dog-training skills) as it does about her desire for compliant employees.

After the publication of *Entertaining*—when Martha began to see the potential of what she could become, if only she could get those around her to do what she wanted—she began to impose her world-view not just on her own family but on the world beyond her front door. This approach to human relations eventually led *New York Times* columnist Maureen Dowd to describe Martha as being "scary . . . like Big Nurse with a pastry bag."

The first people to complain of her openly were her neighbors on Turkey Hill. Angry at the delivery truck traffic streaming in and out of her house everyday—and undoubtedly resentful, as well, at her emerging success as an entrepreneur—neighbors began to complain that the Stewarts were running an illegal home-based catering business in a residential zone. Stories began to appear in the press. Instead of trying to ease the bruised feelings of her jealous and angry neighbors, Martha dug in her heels and said she would sue the town of Westport to have the zoning rules overturned. In the end, she had to capitulate and relocate the business to rented space in a commercial district across town, but her retreat merely polarized relations with her neighbors into an angry standoff.

Local businesspeople complained as well. An elderly portrait photographer named Robert Satter—regarded as the dean of Westport area wedding photographers—encountered Martha at the wedding of the daughter of an area CEO—and fifteen years later was still griping at how she'd managed to position her own photographer at the ceremony in a way that blocked him from taking shots. When Satter complained, Martha retorted, according to Satter, "Do you know who I am? I'm Martha Stewart, and I cater for royalty. Now get out of my way."

Since Andy was the one most directly in her line of fire, he caught the brunt of her abusiveness. The two had so far managed to preserve a front of domestic tranquility, but the veneer was beginning to crack. Not yet accustomed to handling themselves in press interviews, the two inadvertently said a bit more than they should have when a reporter for *People* arrived to do an April 1980 feature on publishing's new power couple.

Seven more years were to pass before Andy would finally walk out on Martha. But the *People* reporter, Kristin McMurran, was closer to the hidden truth of their relationship than she might have realized when, toward the end of the profile—after celebrating their "Swiss Family Robinson" lifestyle and the emerging mythology of Martha's glamour gal career in New York—she described Andy as an "easygoing" person who "tries to be agreeable at home." The story quoted Martha as responding, seemingly out of the blue, "We have never even come close to getting divorced."

In fact, Andy was growing exhausted not only of Martha but of his entire life. He had already threatened to quit Abrams Publishing once over budget cut disputes, and in the wake of the *People* profile, he finally did so, and with a few colleagues, launched a new publishing company.

In December 1981, he took Alexis on a skiing trip to Utah in an attempt to rekindle his relationship with her, which had never been much to begin with; Martha stayed home to finish up work on the manuscript for *Entertaining*. Feeling alone and abandoned, Martha was unable to accomplish anything, and wound up crying constantly while eating food straight from containers in front of the fridge, just like the old days in Nutley. It was an experience she swore to her readers that she'd never repeat: Never, ever was she going to let herself be alone again for the holidays.

But the following December, when *Entertaining* had leaped to the best-seller list, sending Martha on a national author's tour, Andy abandoned his wife a second time, as if to say, "Not another holiday with *that* woman"—perhaps his own little counterpunch dig at a person whom he knew would be wounded by the gesture. And this time it wasn't just Utah. Surveying a map of the earth, he chose to spend Christmas as far away from Turkey Hill—and all that it was coming to represent to him—as he could get. The astonishing destination? A Christmas holiday on a bird-watching expedition to Tierra del Fuego.

When Martha learned of it, she flipped out, and phoning up a local reporter for the Connecticut Sunday edition of the *New York Times*, she planted a story that amounted to a dig at her husband's calculated cruelty. She was "pouting," she told the reporter, because her husband had gone on vacation without her. And what would Martha be doing in his absence? Well, that was the problem, Martha explained. It was now December 19—a week before Christmas—and no one had phoned up to invite her anywhere. So it looked like she'd be spending Christmas alone again. The story ended with what seemed to be a desperate plea to someone—indeed anyone—to come and visit her, so she wouldn't have to be home alone again. She said, "Consider this an SOS to friends."

In fact, though the Stewarts' "public" friendships were visible and increasingly numerous, fewer and fewer people wanted to involve themselves in Martha and Andy's private lives at all, since doing so meant bearing witness to the awkward and increasingly intense rituals through which publishing's new "fun couple" picked at each other's emotional scabs. As a result, the day-to-day deterioration in their relationship was actually seen by only a handful of people, none of whom seemed to enjoy what they were witnessing, though they wound up being drawn moth-like to it nonetheless.

One personal friend was a Turkey Hill neighbor named Mariana Pasternak, who lived with her husband Bart, a local doctor, in a house around the corner from Martha and Andy's at the top of the hill.

How it came to pass that Rumanian-born Mariana, an exotic and flirtatious woman with a fondness for tight jeans and spiked heels, wound up in the inner circle of Martha's personal relationships, is itself a story with twists and turns. But the result was to set in motion a series of events destined two decades later to cause much unwanted publicity and heartache for all concerned, as Bart and Mariana found themselves suddenly catapulted, in the summer of 2002, into the middle of Martha's insider trading woes over ImClone Systems, Inc. As each was thus destined to learn the hard way, navigating life's byways in search of wealth and fame is tougher than it seems when the journey's most perilous road hazards appear on no map.

Mariana, who seemed to wear an "I'm Available" sign on her back wherever she went, had come to the United States as an au-pair girl, taken some nursing-related courses, and wound up working at a hospital in the nearby town of Norwalk. It was there that she caught the eye of her future husband, Bart, a vascular surgeon at the hospital. Bart was living alone in Westport at the time, as a single man in a house around the corner from the Stewarts, on Clapboard Hill Road.

As it happened, Bart had already befriended Andy and Martha, whom he had met as a result of Martha's daily dog-walking strolls through the neighborhood. Thus, when Mariana and Bart became an item, Bart introduced Mariana to Andy and Martha, and the two couples became friends. By the time Bart and Mariana married, they had become the Fred and Ethel Mertzes for Martha and Andy's "Lucy and Ricky"—forever darting in and out of each other's front door unannounced for one thing or another.

But beneath the sitcom facade of life in the suburbs, Bart and Mariana's own marriage eventually ran into trouble, and those who knew the Pasternaks socially at the time recall an undercurrent of bickering that developed between the two. What's more, as time passed and Martha's success as an author gave her at least the appearance of wealth if not its reality, people began to detect in Mariana the same sort of anger toward Bart that Martha had by now sharpened to a scalpel's edge against Andy. In the rituals of their crumbling marriage, Martha had long since indicted, tried, and convicted her husband for being no better a breadwinner than her father, Eddie, had been. And now Mariana seemed to be leveling a similar type charge at Bart.

So it is perhaps not surprising that as the marriages of the two couples slipped further and further into decline, Martha and Mariana began comforting each other with gossip about the shortcomings of their husbands. One friend of all four people recalls Martha confiding at one point, "Can you believe it? Bart doesn't even *touch* Mariana, and look at her! How awful!"

As Mariana's relationship with Bart decayed, she seemed to turn increasingly to Martha as a source of the very comfort and understanding that she could not find in her husband. And as Martha's name began to turn up more and more in the press—first locally as a caterer and then more broadly with the success of *Entertaining*— Mariana's attentions became increasingly solicitous and even clinging. Eventually this reached the point where Martha would simply slam the door on Andy and head over to the Pasternaks, where she'd collect Mariana in her car and the two women would go to a late night movie and rage to each other about their terrible, cold husbands.

Oddly, Bart hardly seemed to mind, and to the degree that he complained at all, it was usually to confide in a friend that he wasn't able to earn enough money to satisfy his wife. A local Westporter who was part of their circle at the time recalls him confessing at one point, "I just can't make enough money at what I'm doing. I should have gone into plastic surgery or something." Not long afterward, the source says Bart announced quite excitedly that he'd gotten a tip on a new startup company in biotech that was going to make him rich.

The stock was ImClone Systems, and the tipster was the company's founder and chairman, Sam Waksal, who had lately begun turning up at Turkey Hill, where he charmed Martha and anyone else who would listen as he enthused over the future of the company.

Only a couple of other people had an unrestricted view of the private life of Martha and Andy and their relationship. And of them, none had a better perspective on the matter than a talented young New York illustrator named J. C. Suares. He too arrived at Turkey Hill through a series of twists and turns. But unlike Mariana, J. C. got out while the getting was still good—mainly because his entrée to Martha's life began and ended with Andy's access to it as well.

For Suares, the door to Turkey Hill swung open by a fluke. Having achieved fame of sorts in the 1970s as author of a 1976 book entitled *The Illustrated Cat,* Suares had not yet enjoyed another big hit. And that, in turn, made him just the sort of author publishers wanted: young, market-tested, and successful—but not yet priced out of reach by too much of success itself.

So, when Suares, then holding down a day job as art director for *New York* magazine, approached Andy with a collection of freelance photographs that he proposed to edit into a kind of personalized "J. C. Suares take" on life in New York, Andy jumped at it, hoping to grab hold of a rising young star who could bring him hits for many years to come.

Of course, life does not always fulfill one's expectations for what the future may hold. And rarely are the clues so obvious as to be recognized without the value of hindsight. So it was only many years later, when Suares mused over lunch in a midtown Manhattan restaurant as to how he had been drawn into the gravitational pull of Martha and Andy in the first place, that he recalled something odd about his first encounter with the man destined to become his publisher.

J. C. had brought Andy a portfolio of photos to review, and he laid them out on an art table as they talked. The photos—outtakes of a year's worth of photo assignments for *New York* by dozens of different freelance photographers—caught the city in its most up-beat, confident, rippled-muscles mood, from its sun-dappled sky-scrapers to the presumed heroism and glamour of its everyday workers.

It was Ronald Reagan's "shining city on a hill . . ."—urban America at its Hollywood grandest—and Andy liked what he saw. But it was also well past noon and, glancing at his watch, he suggested that they continue over lunch.

This was a good sign, thought J. C., who'd come for a half hour office meeting that was already ballooning into a luncheon affair that promised to take up half the day. Already he could hear that sweetest of all phrases to an author on the prowl ("Then it's a deal. . . ?"), ringing in his ears —and the two men weren't even yet out the door. So they headed into the street, making small talk, when J. C.—looking back on the moment many years later—figured he must have said something wrong . . . something that suddenly sent Andy careening off in a new and unexpected direction. "It was *bizarre*," recalled J. C., as he tried to remember what exactly he had said. But he couldn't. More than 20 years had by then passed, and though he could still remember the scenes, he could no longer recall all the exact dialogue.

But the moment certainly endured . . . and the feeling . . . and the anger and hurt that seemed to flash adder-like in his companion's eyes. At first, the two were talking about publishing, and books, and life in New York at the start of the 1980s. Like middle-aged versions of 15-year-old boys meeting for the first time, they were playing New York publishing's favorite get-acquainted game ("do you know . . . ?), spiced with momentary pirouettes into the business's next-favorite courting ritual (*"not*-name-dropping") . . . when suddenly, and out of no where, Andy rounded on him and snarled, "Would you like to know what a piece of shit my wife is . . . ?" and thereupon launched into a block-long diatribe about the woman, whose name was apparently Martha, and who lorded over some-place called "Turkey Hill" that was apparently quite important to them both, and who had wanted him to do something that morning (or not do . . .) or clean up (. . . or put away) . . . or "feed" or "water" or "wash" or "comb . . ." or . . .

And then, suddenly, it was over. They were at the restaurant, the rain had stopped, and the storm had passed. They went inside and ate, and J. C. Suares became an author of Andy's for nearly the whole of the decade that followed.

In the process, he discovered what the man had been talking about on the way to the restaurant that day—even as he saw, up close and personal, how Andy's enabling behavior fed the fires of animosity and rage that eventually consumed Andy and Martha alike. J. C. saw all this as he and his wife Nina were drawn, through Andy, into the orbit of Martha as well, whose loneliness seemed to grow more acute and desperate the more that her hunger for fame, and rage against Andy, lifted her higher and higher into the firmament of acclaim—until J. C. and Nina became two of the most intimate friends Martha had.

From this dress-circle seat, they watched as Martha, increasingly estranged from her husband, began to relive the disappointed Prince Charming fantasies of her college years through her daughter Lexi, encouraging the young woman—by now a vulnerable and somewhat frightened coed at her mother's alma mater of Barnard College—to forget workaday failures like her father and seek out only rich, socially well-connected friends . . . a message repeated over and over until Lexi was running with what was known at the time as the Euro-trash crowd—the spoiled children of Spanish merchants, Italian bankers, and Greek shipowners . . . all drenched with go-away money from absentee parents who'd struck it rich in the post-war affluence that had swept across Europe.

From this pressure, there eventually arrived in Martha's life a handsome young man named Peter Bacanovic, who had an even better credential than Euro-trash parents: a socially well-connected family of actual New Yorkers. He was a senior at Columbia College when Lexis was entering her freshman year at Barnard, the sister college of Columbia, which face each other across the street on upper Broadway. J. C. could not help but remark on the easy-going charm of Bacanovic when the two met for the first time at a weekend party at Turkey Hill, and he thought, "Well, I'll bet *he's* going places!"

And J. C. and Nina beheld as well the arrival on stage—as if on cue—of a Svengali-like character named Samuel Waksal, a man twenty years Lexi's senior, whose radar for vulnerable young women had somehow picked out Lexi from the crowd at a Manhattan discothèque, apparently spotting in her just the ticket to gain access to the *La Dolce Vita* life (and money) of her Euro-trash friends.

They watched as Waksal, who eventually hired Bacanovic to work for him at the start of the 1990s, seduced Lexi as well with money, paying the rent on the Madison Avenue apartment that Martha had leased for her while she was still in college, even as Martha herself seemed more charmed by Waksal than Lexi herself ever did. "Lexi called him 'Mister Waste Your Money,'" they remembered years later, even as Martha herself seemed to regard Sam's spending as image-bolstering money well spent. And when Lexi at last dumped Waksal, and Martha took up with him, neither J. C. nor Nina was terribly surprised. "Sam was Martha's dark side," said J. C. later on. "He appealed to every demon in her soul, and in the end he destroyed her."

As a waiter cleared away our plates, I asked Suares to recall the last time he'd seen Lexi Stewart, and he thought for a moment, then recounted the occasion. It had been a chance encounter, in 1992, at a gym on Ninety-second Street on Manhattan's upper East Side. Lexi had come up to him and said hello, and the two had chatted about this and that. And then, just as she was leaving, the young woman, by then approaching thirty, turned to him and muttered a lament that seemed to sum up everything J. C. knew—and everything he had ever witnessed—about Martha and Andy and the child who had grown into adulthood battered by their rage.

It was a lament that seemed to come from somewhere deep within her, and it came out of the blue that morning, echoing her own her father's anger at his wife, over whatever slight, real or imagined, that had tortured them both over the years.

What had caused it? What had provoked such rage and resentment as to cause a successful New York publisher, at the top of his game in a world where everyone's best advice boils down to the granite-chiseled commandment, "never let them see you sweat . . ." to turn to a man he'd known for all of two hours, and ask of him, "Would you like to know what a piece of shit my wife is?"

Martha Stewart had committed no murder, nor robbed a bank, nor even run off with another man. Whatever she had done—or he had *thought* she had done—had been trivial in the extreme, or he certainly would have been able to explain it in a way that his companion might have understood and remembered.

But as with all failing marriages, and all doomed relationships, the intensity of one's passion can be felt as strongly on the way out, as it had been on the way in. And often times the entrance and exit doors beckon for the same trivial reasons—so that without growth during the journey in between there can be little hope of not walking through both.

In any case, Andy's question is one for which I at least do not have an answer, even to this day . . . anymore than I know why, a decade later, Andy's daughter turned to J. C. in a Ninety-second Street gym and declared, out of no where, in answer to a question that had never been asked, "Everything would be okay . . . if I could only get rid of my mother."

KMART CALLS

In *The Great Gatsby,* F. Scott Fitzgerald commented that in the end, the life of his hero, Jay Gatsby, amounted to a collection of successful gestures. And the same may be said of Martha Stewart, who perhaps more than any other woman of her time, has seized opportunities as they have come her way.

Martha has said more than once that she never set out with any sort of grand design for her life, and that when it has come to her career and her fame, things somehow "just happened." Yet, of all the things that "just happened" to Martha, none gave her a stronger boost upward toward fashioning a global media business than the chain of events that was set in motion in the winter of 1984. The catalyst was a fast-rising Kmart Corporation executive named Joseph Antonini, who attended a marketing speech given in Detroit by a woman named Barbara Loren-Snyder and commented, "You know what, that woman is smart!"

After the meeting, Antonini approached Barbara and invited her to come to his office at Kmart, in nearby Troy, Michigan. "I have a few questions to ask you about us," he explained. "Will you answer them?"

"Will you shut the door?" answered Barbara without missing a beat. It was her way of saying, "Whatever you ask me, I'll tell it like it is. I'm a very honest person . . . I tell it like it is."

Barbara, herself, soon forgot the topic of the meeting, but she made an indelible impression on Antonini. She was smart, quick on her feet, and didn't mince words. Once she left the room, Antonini turned to a colleague and said, "If I ever become president of this company, I'd like to get somebody like that."

Barbara Loren-Snyder tended to affect people that way, especially men in business, who liked cut-through thinking without a lot of beating around the bush. Talking with Barbara was like having a conversation with a well-composed executive memo—crisp, insightful, and results-oriented.

The head of retail marketing for a Detroit TV station, Barbara could look back on a career that spanned almost thirty years in marketing and had made her something of a local legend in Midwest media marketing circles. While still in her twenties, she had invented the "Wendy Ward" character that had become a marketing icon for the salad days of the Montgomery Ward retailing chain in the 1960s. By the 1970s, when she turned forty, she was running her own advertising agency, and by the early 1980s she was supervising retail marketing for the ABC television network's local affiliate TV station, WXYZ-TV.

Then one day in the summer of 1986, the phone rang and on the other end was an assistant to Joe Antonini, the Kmart executive who had invited her to a behind-closed-doors talk on the future of Kmart at his office two years earlier. The message: Antonini was not just a Kmart executive on the make, he was about to be appointed president of the entire company—and once again, he wanted to pick Barbara's brain on a matter of importance to him: How he could go about revitalizing Kmart's cheesy image and flagging sales.

Antonini, a first-generation Italian American with the excitable energy of a visionary, was married and the father of two. He was short and stocky, with oversized glasses, graying hair, and a capacity to throw himself into projects with such enthusiasm that everything else around him seemed to fade into a blur. He loved golf and was crazy about his kids. The new boss was also smitten by the value of celebrities and had already helped bring TV actress Jaclyn Smith of *Charlie's Angels* fame to Kmart to jazz up the frumpy image of its women's clothing line. Now he wanted to try something grander.

When Barbara got to his office, he sat her down and got right to the point. He said, "Barbara, nobody knows this, but I'm going to be made president of this company in two weeks." He leaned forward for effect, and with his eyes locked on hers, he explained that he was forming a committee composed of two Kmart insiders and two outsiders. Their task would be to evaluate every department in the company and devise a strategy for making the company attractive to consumers. The question: Would Barbara join?

Barbara agreed almost instantly—and why not! Here was a chance to become involved from the inside in developing a top-to-bottom makeover for Kmart. The project, in a sense, would be the capstone to a career that had begun on a much smaller scale twenty years earlier at Montgomery Ward.

The committee was officially formed on August 26, 1986, with Loren-Snyder and Pat Kelly, a marketing professor at Wayne University, serving as the outsiders and Antonini and Mike Wellman the company's vice president for corporate planning, representing Kmart from the inside. Wellman was more serious than Antonini; quieter, and more reserved. He was a family man who loved to cook. He and his wife had remodeled their kitchen with top-of-the-line appliances and amenities that any serious chef would envy. Yet, he was down-to-earth, realistic, with a sense of quality and value. If Kmart wanted to move upmarket without losing its core customers, Mike Wellman was the sort of man the company should be wanting to attract. Barbara realized it immediately, and as the work of the committee began to gel, she turned to Mike often for his thoughts and input.

The committee spent its first few months poking through Kmart's various departments, looking for areas of most pronounced weakness. It wasn't long before everyone agreed that they needed to look no farther than the cookware area, known as Kmart's "Kitchen

Korner," which was filled to overflowing with tacky products that had not seemed to change much from fifties-era can openers and Aunt Jemima aprons.

As a first step, the committee spied a bit on the competition, to see how rival discount retailers like Target and Wal-Mart were handling cookware in their own stores. They made a January 1987 trip to Nashville, Tennessee, a nice, heartland city that was home to outlets of every major Kmart rival, and spent nearly a week exploring stores, taking notes, and conducting focus groups.

On January 18, just a few days after returning from Nashville, Barbara sent a memo to Mike Wellman. It was meant to be a teaser—to get him asking for more. She knew if she could win over Mike, the most levelheaded and straight-ahead person on the team, she'd have the whole committee. In the memo, she said she had a great idea for Kmart—something that might even sound a little crazy. She said that she'd let them all in on her secret at the next committee meeting.

Barbara spent the next three weeks mentally preparing for the meeting. She wanted the members to focus on a problem that should have been obvious to them all by now: Kmart stores were full of goods that appealed to 50-year-old Kmart merchandise managers and nobody else. How could the company possibly hope to catch the heart and soul of America that way? Kmart needed a spokesperson, in the housewares division, who could somehow promote its merchandise beyond its core customer base. What she wanted was a Ralph Lauren for the kitchen . . . somebody who could appeal to the dreams and aspirations of shoppers, not simply their needs.

So she set out for the local bookstore, looking for faces. And in the homemaking section, she kept encountering pictures of the same beautiful, wholesome-looking blonde author. Who was this Martha Stewart person anyway? That's what Barbara wanted to know.

The books were irresistible; there were four of them on the shelves by now, and the portrait they painted of their author was captivating. Martha Stewart, the housewife to die for, with one foot in America's past of hearth and family values, and the other in the elegance of the Virginia horse country. A dinner for eighty? No problem. Can your own preserves? No problem. Tempura from scratch in ten minutes? No problem.

This wasn't the Kmart customer rushing for the Blue Light Special in aisle six, with her impatient 12-year-old son dragging along behind, moaning, "Come on Mom, can't we go now?" and his sister rolling her eyes and saying, "Mommy, will you puleese tell Brad to shut up!"

No, Martha Stewart was the woman all these women secretly wanted to be, standing in the morning breeze by the open windows, with the fragrance of jasmine filling the house, as the soft breathing of the George Peppard look-alike husband, ornamental and asleep, whispered forth from the bed. Martha was Barbara's gal, she knew it instinctively . . . someone who could not only represent Kmart's kitchen department but maybe even move into other areas. Kmart had already been successful with Jaclyn Smith, who had been Joe Antonini's pet project, as spokeswoman for the company's apparel line. Now maybe Joe could be persuaded to see Martha Stewart as a kind of super Jaclyn Smith . . . a kitchenwares-plus person.

From the photos alone, Barbara could see that she'd be perfect for the job: She had style, grace, good looks. And the details were too much! The elegant fantasy farm life in Connecticut? It was pure gold. She was everything your average Kmart shopper was not . . . everything such a person secretly wanted to be. She wasn't a "role model," she was a *dream model.* Barbara wanted to get her so bad she could taste it.

After taking some notes from the books, Barbara went home and started calling newspapers around the country. She called ten lifestyle editors and reporters, and only one had even heard of the Westport beauty. Good, thought Barbara, some name recognition but clearly not a big, national star; she'd be able to get her for cheap.

It was a day in February 1987 when Barbara picked up the phone and called Westport, Connecticut, information. She assumed Martha's number would be private and unpublished, but to her surprise, it was public. She thought, well, either this woman is a total nobody or a very self-confident lady. Her curiosity grew as she dialed the number. She knew exactly what she'd say either way, because Barbara was a self-confident woman herself, and she'd made similar such calls to strangers for more than twenty years.

Martha answered and Barbara got right to the point. She said, "Martha, you do not know me. You have no reason to know me. But I can make you a multimillionaire and a star and it won't cost you a penny."

There was silence for an instant on the other end, and Barbara felt the first glimmerings that she just might have hooked her. There would be a long struggle ahead to reel her in, that was for sure. But Barbara had been trolling for a mere thirty seconds, and already she'd felt that telltale little tug announcing that the fish had risen to the bait. She had found Martha's sweet tooth: Money. In fact, she'd seen it already in many of her books—in the photos of her enormous storybook-size garden with its eight-foot-tall sunflowers . . . in her celadon-green china settings for "afternoon tea" . . . in the gracious lawns, the cut glass and the crystal champagne goblets, the buffet settings for fifty. This was a woman who loved money . . . or at least loved the illusions you could create with money. When you say to such a person, "I can make you a multimillionaire . . . and it won't cost you a penny . . ." and the person doesn't immediately retort, "We don't need any of that around here" and slam down the phone, you know you've got her number.

Barbara proceeded matter-of-factly, though without divulging what firm she represented—partly because she hadn't yet even cleared the idea with the Kmart committee. In that sense, she was like the guy who tries to hustle up the ingredients for breakfast by approaching total strangers ("If I had some ham, we could have some ham and eggs . . . if I had some eggs."). If she could get Martha to agree to become a Kmart spokesperson, then get Kmart to agree to hire her . . . well, then, she could have breakfast.

A day or so later, Barbara sent Martha a letter, confirming their conversation. In it, she reiterated her intention to make Martha a star, but once again made no mention of the company she represented, simply saying she worked for a leading national company and her current assignment could lead to Martha becoming its spokesperson. She wanted a meeting, face-to-face. She knew if she got it, Martha would be hers.

Barbara hadn't yet mentioned her plan to Kmart and certainly wasn't authorized to be calling people on behalf of the company, let alone setting dates with a prospective spokeswoman. But she hadn't divulged enough information to get her in trouble, and she figured, well, why not, she'd go for it. So she let another week pass, then phoned Martha again, and as she had hoped (and by now half expected), Martha agreed to a meeting. They set a date two weeks hence—the week following the next meeting of the committee. As far as Barbara was concerned, the date would work perfectly; she'd broach her idea at the committee meeting, and if the others didn't go for it—particularly, Mike Wellman—she'd just drop the whole thing and cancel her trip to Connecticut to meet with Martha.

In her career of making business pitches, Barbara had learned at least one important thing: Never walk into a meeting without a backup plan. She figured if she were going to propose that Kmart attach a celebrity to its kitchen line, she'd better have a couple of fallback candidates in case no one liked the Martha Stewart idea. What if Mike Wellman's wife had already tried her recipes and found that the soufflés never rose, or that the tomato fettuccine with snow peas Alfredo came out all clumpy and kept you heading back and forth to the bathroom all night?

As a fallback, Barbara's first choice was a lady named Jennifer Lang, the cookbook author and wife of the owner of the fashionable Manhattan restaurant, Café Des Artistes. Gorgeous and personable, Ms. Lang was one of the main attractions and helped her husband run the restaurant, which drew a nightly before-and-after dinner crowd from New York opera and ballet performances around the corner at Lincoln Center. Loren-Snyder even went so far as to meet with Lang and sound her out. She found the chef to be receptive to the idea, expressing no qualms about becoming a pitchwoman for a down-market discount retail chain. But not wanting to get her hopes up, Barbara told her at least one other person was in the running as well—not telling her that it was Martha Stewart.

Yet Barbara knew that, in a sense, Jennifer Lang's greatest appeal to the committee would be to make Martha Stewart look better as a candidate. Jennifer Lang was even less of a household name than Martha herself, which meant that using her as a spokesperson would require a lot of identity-establishment for Jennifer in the ads. Instead of spending money to promote Kmart, the company would wind up spending its ad dollars to promote its own spokesperson . . . the same problem that Ragú Spaghetti Sauce ran into when it hired a somewhat obscure singer named Enzo Stuarti to promote the sauce in TV commercials.

But Barbara left her on the list anyway. She knew the committee would welcome the idea of a spokesperson since Kmart had already enjoyed success with Jaclyn Smith. And she certainly expected Joe Antonini to jump on the idea if the candidate were a good-looking female celebrity. But what if the committee somehow found Martha Stewart to be a bit *too* obscure? There can be few things more embarrassing than to say, "How'd you like to meet the world-famous . . ." and then unfurl a name that is greeted with nothing but blank stares.

So Barbara figured, well, if something like that were to happen, she'd wheel out the name Jennifer Lang as a fallback and suddenly Martha Stewart would seem as famous as Princess Di by comparison.

For a second fallback, Barbara decided on the famous Jill St. John. This woman, too, had negatives that enhanced Martha's appeal. St. John had had her moment in the sun in the 1960s, eventually playing opposite Frank Sinatra in a couple of his rat pack era movies, and finally she had vaulted to the role of female lead opposite Sean Connery in *Diamonds Are Forever*, the eighth in the James Bond series (1971). But her image was muddled. Was she a sexpot?

She'd toured for a time with Bob Hope in his Vietnam-era USO show for the troops, but she'd logged plenty of miles since then, and trying to pitch her as a sex symbol for the 1990s might come off as almost comical . . . like talking up the oomph in Tina Louise thirty years after *Gilligan's Island.*

And there was also a question of Jill St. John's reputation. Vague though the details were, her past wasn't exactly convent white. She'd been married three times, and in between times had been romantically linked with a range of celebs from Sinatra to Henry Kissinger. By now she'd begun turning up as the ding-a-ling arm-piece for Hollywood pretty boy Robert Wagner, which suggested that she still had plenty of energy left in her. Hiring this woman as Kmart's spokesperson could wind up emptying the aisles of every Kmart store in the Midwest. So Barbara figured that if the committee meeting careened totally out of control, she could always toss in Ms. St. John's name as a candidate. If that didn't make Martha Stewart look appealing, what would?

The day before the meeting, Barbara called Mike Wellman to drop yet another teaser. "Mike, have you ever heard of Martha Stewart?" she asked.

Wellman knew who she was immediately. A food connoisseur and avid cook, he had even recommended that some of Martha's recipes be used for a recent corporate affair at Kmart's Troy, Michigan, headquarters. This was a good sign. Barbara could sense that her proposal would go over well.

It was February 27, 1987, when she finally walked into a conference room at Kmart's Michigan headquarters. It was 8 A.M. By 10:00 A.M., everyone had said his piece except for Barbara. She cleared her throat and began.

"I have what I think you need," she said, and proceeded to walk the others through her plan, outlining her proposal for finding another personality to attach to Kmart's products. She reminded the group how well things were working with Jaclyn Smith. They seemed interested, and she got to her core point: "You need to differentiate yourself," she said, repeating what she had been saying to herself for the past few weeks. "So, why don't we get Martha Stewart? This woman can upgrade the whole kitchen line just by being attached to it, and the entire rest of the company will benefit."

As she had suspected, no one but Mike Wellman even seemed to know who Martha Stewart was. So Barbara laid Martha's books out on the conference table and shoved them around to the other committee members. Watching Joe Antonini's eyes light up at the lovely dust jacket face before him, Barbara knew he, too, was now hooked, so she quickly cut to the chase, explaining Martha's appeal and suggesting that the company eventually introduce an entire line of Martha Stewart products into Kmart's 2,300 retail stores.

Antonini, who had been listening intently, turned to Loren-Snyder and said, "Go for it. You can spend $250,000 . . ." and abruptly as the meeting had started, it was over; Antonini rose from his chair, thanked everyone, and exited the room. For Barbara Loren-Snyder, it was a home run—a base-clearer that soared right out of Yankee Stadium and into the Bronx. And though neither woman knew it yet, for Martha it was an even bigger grand slam that would put her squarely on the track to becoming one of the wealthiest and best-known women on earth.

All Barbara had to do now was actually close the deal. Somehow, she had to convince this elegant lady from the Connecticut suburbs to lend her name to a discount retailer in fly-over America, where the store shelves were full of cheesy merchandise made in China, and typical shoppers were men who arrived unshaven in pickup trucks, accompanied by women with huge rear ends packed into Lycra Spandex tights.

Would Martha Stewart really agree to *that*? In fact, it would prove an easier sell than Barbara would ever have guessed.

The great thing about life is that everyone is always the star of his own movie, which means that people are constantly playing supporting roles in the dramas of others. Thus, when Barbara Loren-Snyder picked up the phone in her home in Boca Raton, Florida, that February day in 1987 and dialed Martha Stewart's home in Westport, Connecticut, she had no way of knowing just how she'd be fitting in with the drama unfolding at 48 Turkey Hill Road—or indeed whether she'd be invited to fit in at all. Lots of movies were going on in that house when Barbara placed her call, and not all of them had room for a walk-on character from out of town.

By the time Barbara placed her call, relations between Martha and Andy had all but reached the breaking point, meaning that the phone could possibly have rung at exactly the moment when the happy couple were glowering at each other as they passed silently in and out of the kitchen. How would Martha have received Barbara's offer under *those* conditions? Would she have said, "I'm busy now, call back later . . ." in her special, frosty way? Would Barbara have thought, "Well, I guess we can forget about *her* . . ." and moved on down the list to Jennifer Lang?

And there were other possibilities. Andy might have taken the call and forgotten to pass the message along to his wife. In only a few more months, Martha would be accusing Andy of carrying on a secret affair with Martha's personal assistant, Robyn Fairclough, an attractive brunette twenty years Martha's junior—something Andy has denied though he eventually went on to marry Ms. Fairclough. She was floating in and out of the house constantly by this time, and might possibly have grabbed the ringing phone in the absence of anyone else. Would she have passed on the message—to the wife of the man she was secretly sleeping with, if Martha is to be believed?

And yet another person was living in Turkey Hill at the time, who also might have fielded the call and forgotten to pass the information along: After an absence of more than a decade, Kathy Tatlock had unexpectedly looped back into Martha's life. In their doomed relationship, Kathy would become the dog that Martha would kick in anger after Andy packed up and left.

Farther in the background were other characters. The Stewarts' daughter, Alexis, who was by now in her senior year in college (her mother's alma mater, Barnard, Class of 1987), had been floating in and out of the house on the weekends with her latest boyfriend in tow, the increasingly familiar Sam Waksal, who was nearly twenty years her senior. Martha's mother, Martha Sr., was now living in the neighborhood as well, along with Martha's younger sister, Laura. And George, her brother, had now moved to the area also. In short, most of the supporting cast of the Nutley, New Jersey, household of Martha's youth, once again were shuffling up and down the backstairs of her private life, which still clanked behind her—like Banquo's ghost—all the way into ripening middle age.

The oddest character of them all—and certainly the one destined to have the most dramatic impact on Martha's own life—was Waksal. The eldest of two sons of World War II Holocaust survivors, Waksal grew up in Dayton, Ohio, where his father ran a scrap metal business.

Both Sam and his younger brother Harlan were steeped from an early age in competitive family values that stressed education and intellectual achievement. But somehow they both seemed to miss out on one of life's most basic lessons: the importance of obeying the law. By the time they reached adulthood, this powerful, but incomplete, value structure had had a particularly profound and damaging effect on Sam, warping him into an acceptance-obsessed social and intellectual poseur who seemed more concerned with the appearance of success than with the reality of actually achieving it.

Unable to afford the high-priced ticket of an Ivy League education for his eldest, Sam's father, Jack Waksal, sent the boy to Ohio State University, where he graduated with a doctorate in immunobiology. But reports of faked research soon began to dog young Sam as he raced up the career ladder as a researcher in microbiology, only to find himself shown the door, first, from Stanford University (1974) and next from the National Cancer Institute (1977) after questions arose regarding his research.

Thereafter Sam headed for Tufts Medical School where he landed a job as head of the university's cancer research center. Thereafter, his younger brother, Harlan, arrived on campus as well, to begin a residency in medicine, leading to a bizarre incident involving the two. This occurred when Harlan was unable to make his patient rounds on the ward—a regular duty of doctors completing their residency requirements—and Sam donned a white coat and hung a stethoscope from his neck, and made the ward rounds pretending to be Harlan.

Meanwhile, Harlan began developing a past of his own, and in 1981 was caught and convicted of attempting to smuggle two pounds of cocaine into the United States via Ft. Lauderdale International Airport. The conviction was eventually overturned on appeal when Harlan argued that his luggage had been searched illegally. But the combined effect of all this wound up getting Sam dismissed from Tufts as well.

Sam next turned up at Mount Sinai School of Medicine in New York where he was hired to run yet another research project. Once again he ran into trouble and wound up leaving under a cloud three years later, in 1985, amidst rumors that he had falsified research data. At that point, he founded ImClone Systems, based in a loft on Manhattan's lower West Side, and quickly spotted an opportunity for himself in Martha and Andy's alienated daughter, Alexis, who began bringing him home on weekends.

All these people and more had now gathered around Martha and were going about their intertwined lives when the phone rang at Turkey Hill that fateful February afternoon and Martha had the good fortune to answer it before anyone else. The message Barbara delivered was certainly intended to capture Martha's attention. But not knowing what was happening at that moment in the personal life-drama in which Martha was starring, Barbara had no idea what a head-turning business proposition she was actually making to her listener.

As Martha was reaching for the phone, the book that had started her rocket ride to fame—*Entertaining*—was about to go into its fifteenth printing. With something approaching 340,000 copies by now in print, it had become one of the best-selling cookbooks of all time. *Quick Cook* had gone into a second printing as well, as had *Pies & Tarts*. Her fifth book, *Weddings*, had just been released to awestruck reviews, and she was at that very moment gearing up for a national tour for the book that had been set up by her publisher's capable young public relations assistant, Susan Magrino.

Wherever Martha was appearing—at shopping mall book signings, at radio stations, at newspaper offices and TV stations for local interviews—huge crowds of women were gathering. They wanted to talk to her, touch her, somehow just communicate with her. They would bring her samples of bridal lace and ask her opinion, they'd tell her stories about their weddings, about the weddings of their daughters. They'd ask her about "Lexi," and about "Andy."

It had to be exhilarating, overwhelming, almost frightening: The doors were swinging open on the private life of 48 Turkey Hill Road, and women all over America suddenly wanted to walk right in and share it. Martha had wanted to be famous, and now it was starting to happen. The Butterball turkey company had sponsored a Thanksgiving "celebrity phone-in" for cooking tips that autumn, and the person the callers wanted to talk to was Martha.

It was the autumn of 1986, and the whole "turkey" thing had brought Martha to the attention of Public Broadcasting's Boston affiliate, WGBH, and the station had sent a film crew to Westport to put together a Thanksgiving program that it proposed to entitle "Holiday Entertaining with Martha Stewart."

And, on top of all that, a total stranger calls up and says, "I can make you a multimillionaire, and it won't cost you a penny." It would seem safe to say that anyone who doesn't feel his head swell just a little bit under such circumstances isn't really being honest with himself.

The WGBH project alone seemed to signal that Martha had at last arrived. At nearly the half-century point in her life—with her personal life in the same torment that had dogged her periodically since childhood—things were suddenly changing. Not only had her professional life at last caught fire, but it had given birth to a myth she had fostered in the very pages of her cookbooks—that gracious hearth-and-home living was what life in the Stewart household was all about. Now that myth was about to be immortalized on TV as a celebration of her actual, *real* life, and it promised to become as much an American tradition as gathering up the family to watch Perry Como's Christmas special or *Miracle on 34th Street*.

The show featured Martha's preparations for an elegant and homey Thanksgiving buffet for fourteen—an intimate gathering by Martha's standards. There was cold pumpkin soup, roast pheasant, root vegetable salad, and, of course, the centerpiece presentation of a puff pastry roasted turkey. The whole thing had the feel of casual and gracious warmth, with smiling guests murmuring graciously to one another as the camera panned lovingly from the buffet to the wainscot-paneled rooms and fine china breakfronts.

In reality, the whole affair was staged. The meal had been presented as something that Martha had whipped up in a day. In fact, the banquet had taken four days and ten people to prepare. The passing of the soup and the hum of pleasant conversation was all for the camera.

Stomachs began to growl, but the guests were not allowed to eat what they had placed on their plates because, over and over again, they had to get up from the table, empty their plates in the kitchen, then load up with food from the buffet all over again. They did this repeatedly, hour after hour, until the camera shots were just right.

Once seated, the guests then had to act as if they were engaged in courteous, subdued conversation with each other. These scenes, too, were shot over and over until the banter finally was editable into something that seemed spontaneous and warm.

A month or so later—after the Thanksgiving special had aired on PBS but before Barbara had called with her "make-you-a-millionaire" offer—Martha picked up the phone and called one of her friends from actual, real life: Kathy Tatlock. She had a proposal for Kathy, who was living in Brookline, Massachusetts, working as a freelance filmmaker to support herself and her two daughters: Would Kathy like to come to Turkey Hill and work for Martha on a special project she was developing?

The years that had passed for Kathy Tatlock had not been easy, to say the least. After the return from Bogotá, her husband Chris' drinking had gotten worse. He had left the government, stumbled through a series of failed job opportunities, and grown increasingly abusive of his wife and children, at one point threatening her in a drunken rage. Kathy had scooped up her children and walked out on him, and several months later he was dead.

So in early middle age, she had begun her life again, a middle-aged divorcee with two young children, no money, and no real prospects. But she had the sensibilities of a visual artist, and a background in photography. And since she had few choices, she taught herself filmmaking and wound up by-and-by with an increasingly successful career as an independent filmmaker in Boston. She became a cofounder of "Women in Film & Video, New England," and was invited to Robert Redford's prestigious Sundance Institute to develop her first feature film, *Everyday Dreams*, in 1984.

From that perch, Kathy had watched as her friend, Martha, had climbed higher and higher in the firmament of media world fame, alternately intrigued and bemused at each new success. And when she finally read in the Boston newspapers that Martha would be shooting a Thanksgiving holiday entertainment special for Boston's WGBH, Kathy picked up the phone and, on impulse more than anything else, called Westport to congratulate her. Martha responded immediately and graciously, inviting her to Turkey Hill to participate in the actual filming, with the result that Kathy sat through the entire buffet dinner scene—the oldest friend of Martha's in the room—watching in bemusement as the people all around her pretended to be the merry-making, lifelong friends they were not.

The trip to Westport had put Kathy back on Martha's radar screen. And when the visit was followed up a month or so later by Martha's invitation to come to Westport yet again—this time for that mysterious-sounding "special project"—Kathy was both flattered and intrigued.

Martha explained that she had obtained tentative approval and funding from Crown Publishers as well as a California wine distributor, Sterling Vineyards, to produce a home entertainment video. Martha said that she had talked to New York producers and to the WGBH folks in Boston as well about the project, but that everyone she approached had wanted 50 percent of the profits. "If I have to give up 50 percent of my share, I want to give it to a friend," said Martha. "I think you'd be perfect for the job. Do you think you can handle it?"

Kathy tried to stay calm, but her head was swimming. Here was her old friend, Martha Stewart, roaring back into her life with an offer to split the profits 50/50 on a video for which she'd already lined up backers. "Of course," said Kathy. "Absolutely."

Martha explained that the videos would focus on food preparation as it related to entertaining, along with tips for successful hosting. Martha's excitement was contagious, and when she asked what part of the production Kathy thought she could handle, it was all Kathy could do to keep from answering, "All of it!"

Reining in her enthusiasm, Kathy paused for a moment, then answered that she'd be comfortable writing, producing, and directing the shoots. Martha told her that WGBH had estimated that the project would cost Martha about $125,000. Always looking to save, Martha asked Kathy if she thought she could do it for less. "I think I can raise $100,000," said Martha. "Can you do it for that much?"

Kathy said she'd have to put together some numbers, but that $100,000 certainly seemed reasonable. The two agreed to meet and work out a contract in the coming weeks.

After she hung up the phone, Kathy reflected on what she'd heard. She recalled the times back in New York when Martha had invited the Tatlocks to dinner, then begged off at the last minute when, as Kathy sensed things, something better had come up. And with the publication of Entertaining, Kathy had also been surprised to read that Martha claimed to have thrown huge Christmas season parties at the Stewarts' apartment on Riverside Drive, which had been literally around the corner from the Tatlocks' apartment. If the Stewarts had indeed been throwing such parties, it was news to Kathy, who remembered Martha's and Andy's place as being relatively small and cramped. Nor could she recall having attended a single such party there—Christmas or otherwise. Perhaps the Tatlocks hadn't been on the Stewarts' A-list (or even B-list) at all.

Kathy's two daughters, by now in their late teens, had heard Kathy reminisce about Martha and Andy Stewart over the years—especially about the time when the Stewarts had come to Bogotá, and how Martha had treated Andy. So, when Kathy told them that evening about Martha's proposal, both expressed misgivings.

"Mom," one of them said, "You've told us about Martha. Be careful."

But Kathy wasn't listening, for her thoughts had taken flight—back to a time before her kids were born, when she was young and free and living in New York, and life was just beginning. Now, twenty years later, it seemed that the relationship between Kathy and her friend would evolve into what they had talked about so long ago—a perfect business partnership.

Opportunity was also about to rain down on Martha. After Barbara Loren-Snyder got the go-ahead from Joe Antonini, she called Martha again, to confirm the meeting. By now, Barbara had grown a bit nervous about how exposed she was really becoming in the matter. If Martha had misunderstood what she'd said in their original phone conversation, what then? Or suppose Martha chose, for whatever reason, to misquote her later on. Barbara could wind up looking as if she had misrepresented what she could really do for Martha. Things could get uncomfortable, even ugly.

Under the circumstances, Barbara figured the best, and safest, course of action was to have the meeting take place in the presence of Martha's lawyer. There would then be no possibility of who said what to whom later on. But Barbara didn't realize that Martha's lawyer was actually Andy Stewart, and that relations between the two had congealed into an icy civility that was guaranteed to cast a pall over any meeting the two attended. So blithely she plowed ahead.

"Martha, where's your lawyer's office?" Barbara asked as the arrangements proceeded.

"In the city, why?" Martha sounded wary.

Barbara didn't know why Martha was annoyed, but she stood her ground. "Because I'd like to meet you at your lawyer's office."

"We can have a meeting at my home," Martha snapped.

But Barbara insisted, not yet understanding why the woman on the other end had suddenly turned hostile. It was as if a whole other Martha had abruptly emerged . . . contentious and quick tempered. Why? It would be a while longer before Barbara would realize that the Other Martha seemed to surface whenever Andy's name came up.

Eventually, Martha agreed to meet Barbara at Andy's office at Stewart, Tabori and Chang in Manhattan, but by the time the two hung up the phone, it was obvious that Martha was going to walk into the room with an attitude.

As Barbara expected, Martha turned up at the meeting cold, crisp, and unfriendly, whereas Andy proved to be both warm and polite.

Even as Barbara entered the room, she still had not yet told Martha what company she actually represented, and considering the frosty atmosphere that now prevailed, she wondered whether it might be better to hold back for yet another meeting before popping the news. On the other hand, Barbara also realized that she might not actually get another shot at making her pitch, and that it was going to be now or never.

On her left wrist, she had written the three words she wanted to stress—"Multimillionaire," "Star," and "Kmart"—and taking them in order, she began to toss her chum in the water.

She stressed how the opportunity she was prepared to offer could make millions for Martha. She explained how much fame it would bring her. There'd be a national network advertising campaign, she'd be in the pages of *Better Homes & Gardens* and *Family Circle* month after month. She would, in short, become one of the best known personalities in America. Barbara could do all this for Martha, and more.

How?

At that point, she sprang the news. Her client was Kmart Corporation, the second largest discount retailer in America, and Kmart wanted Martha to become its spokesperson.

Barbara could feel the air being sucked from the room even as she spoke the words. Kmart? The tackiest, downmarket retailer this side of J.C. Penney?

Martha's face was a blank, expressionless stare.

By contrast, Andy seemed interested and began asking questions about the specifics of the deal. But Martha stayed silent. Barbara kept glancing at her from the corner of her eye and she hadn't budged—her face impenetrable and cold.

Finally, Martha spoke. She asked,

"How much money am I going to get?" and to herself Barbara thought, "Thank God . . ." the meeting was back on track.

Barbara began to reel in her fish. She said, "I'm authorized to pay you $50,000," knowing full well she had another $200,000 with which to work.

"What?" shrieked Martha. "That is disgraceful. I'm not going to do it."

"Well, Martha, what did you expect?" asked Barbara, sinking the hook deeper.

"I expected at least $200,000 a year," responded Martha, not realizing that Barbara had just reeled her in and was now watching her flop on the dock.

"You know what?" said Barbara, getting up to leave. "I think we can work this out. You can make millions. I'll have the lawyers get in touch with you." With that, Barbara headed for the door and the airport, destination: Detroit. Six weeks earlier, she'd been staring at an empty breakfast plate with the hope of hustling up a ham-and-eggs breakfast at Kmart's expense. Now, by persistence, guile, and sheer business street smarts, she had set herself up for a gourmet dinner of Martha under Glass.

Disembarking in Detroit, Barbara headed straight for Kmart's headquarters in Troy, where she briefed Joe Antonini on what had transpired, then set up a meeting for the Kmart biggie to get together with Martha. Arrangements were made for the three to have lunch at the Bloomfield Country Club, not far from Kmart's Michigan headquarters. Joe had no idea what to expect, knowing nothing of Martha except what Barbara had told him—not counting, of course, the lovely face of the woman, which he had already seen adorning the dust jackets of her books when he'd given Barbara the go-ahead.

The meeting, which amounted to little more than a relationship get-together, went well; and Joe seemed instantly charmed by the woman sitting next to him. Then, right in the middle of lunch, something happened. Abruptly, Joe stopped talking, his fork suspended in midair. Barbara looked at him, then followed the course of his gaze. It ended at Martha's hands.

Finally, Joe spoke.

"Martha," he said, "what happened to your hands?"

Barbara looked at them as well, noticing immediately what Antonini meant. Martha's hands were covered from the wrists down in sores, scratches, and bruises. The fingernails were broken, there were calluses on the knuckles. These weren't the hands of a TV star, they were the hands of a field laborer.

Though neither Joe nor Barbara yet realized it, they were the best evidence possible of the tough core of determination and guts that smoldered inside their guest. Beneath the veneer of Greenwich-like gentility, beyond the rolling lawns and the staged holiday buffets, was a woman willing to get up at dawn, feed 120 chickens and goats, double-spade the flower beds, spread out 500 pounds of pine bark and peat moss, and not come back inside until everything in sight looked exactly and perfectly like it ought to look. Behind the pretty face lurked the soul of a Polish farmworker. She was as focused and determined as the Ohio State football team, which Woody Hayes had said was prepared to grind out the yardage, three yards at a time, *and never quit.* And from her alabaster arms hung the brutalized hands that were the proof. Joe was impressed. If Martha worked as hard for Kmart as she worked on her gardens, Jaclyn Smith would be eating her dust in no time.

How to negotiate
a contract

I n the weeks that followed, Kmart's lawyers and Andy hammered out the terms of Martha's deal. The contract was negotiated to include $200,000 a year for five years as a Kmart "consultant," with an additional $3,000 paid to her for each of the 30 days she was obligated to attend Kmart-related events, either in stores or on company-sponsored occasions elsewhere.

But Martha kept zeroing in on details that no one else had apparently thought of. She wanted to make sure, for example, that she would get a piece of any sales of her books and tapes through Kmart and not have to share any of her royalties with them. It also soon became obvious that although she wasn't much interested in what she could do for Kmart, she was very interested in nailing down exactly what Kmart was going to do for her. "How much publicity will I get, and will it be favorable?" she asked, over and over again.

Finally, Martha pronounced herself pleased with the terms, and on July 6, 1987, she at last signed the contract . . . on the eve of which she had brought up one final little item: She wanted the press release announcing the deal to be worded so that it sounded as if she were being paid millions for her services. She didn't want the

$200,000 figure discussed at all; it seemed too chintzy and small. She was more interested in the public knowing the cumulative total of what Kmart would be paying her.

It was, in effect, time for Martha to pick up her change. Barbara had repeatedly assured her she'd be making millions from the deal, right? All that free publicity . . . the television and magazine ads, the newspaper inserts? Well, as Martha figured things, Kmart should just add it all up now and announce the number as being what the company was actually paying her. So what if it made the company look like squanderlust fools. That was Kmart's problem, not hers. The more money they seemed to be spending on her, the higher would rise her own market value for the next deal to come along.

The company set August for their launch of the Martha Stewart campaign, in which Martha quickly became a nonstop kibitzer. "Last year Martha Stewart had 42,569 people to dinner" read one of the first magazine ads, which ran in *Family Circle, Better Homes & Gardens,* and *House Beautiful,* with a striking picture of Martha surrounded by beautiful foods and flowers.

Announcement of Kmart's big catch was scheduled for August 6 at a press conference in New York. Barbara sent out more than 100 invitations to the event, each printed on a white chef's hat and apron, and asking the question: "What's Kmart cooking up now? Find out on August 6, 1987, at an 8:30 breakfast."

The event was at the "21" Club in midtown and received as much press as Barbara could have hoped for. Unfortunately, the comments were not as enthusiastic as Kmart might have wanted. One reporter who attended the affair filed a story that began:

> Many strange combinations have come out of American kitchens in the 80s, but Kmart may have served up the pièce de résistance with its recent announcement that entertainment guru Martha Stewart has signed a five-year contract to be its national spokeswoman and a consultant for home fashions. For many who are familiar with Mrs. Stewart's brand of stylish party giving, conveyed in five lavishly illustrated books, the link with the nation's largest discount retailer might have

seemed an odd combination—but then, people once laughed at goat cheese pizza, too.

Following the press conference, Martha returned to Westport, and Barbara headed back to Detroit. The two were set to meet again a week or so later in Troy, where Barbara had made arrangements for Martha to appear in an in-house video for Kmart's employees. Barbara wanted every store to be able to see who exactly Martha Stewart was, and to watch her in action, cooking up food in a real kitchen, alongside Kmart's man in charge, Joe Antonini.

But Martha already had grander plans than the starring role in a mere in-house video, and a few days before she was due in Troy, she phoned Barbara and sprang them on her. She wanted to make videotapes of herself that celebrated one aspect or another of the Martha Stewart lifestyle—tapes that Kmart would help her produce—which Martha would then sell in Kmart's stores. And she had a specific project in mind for the first tape.

It is said that the effective executive is the person who can compartmentalize the issues that make demands on his or her time, so that the challenges of one set of problems don't seep into and complicate the management of other and competing issues. By that standard, Martha Stewart was learning fast—though compartmentalizing her personal and professional lives was becoming increasingly difficult and awkward. For starters, the crisis of her private life threatened to erupt into full public view at any minute, risking her deal with Kmart, undermining the launch of *Weddings*, and making a mockery of her image as queen of the American homestead. The person who got caught in the crossfire of her rage: Kathy Tatlock.

By the time Kathy had reentered Martha's life in the waning months of 1986, Martha had already begun to see herself broadening from books and magazine articles into the dynamic and celebrity-rich world of television and the electronic media. The PBS

Thanksgiving special with WGBH had whetted her appetite, and she was soon approaching them with an idea for a videotape series she proposed to call *Martha Stewart's Tips for Entertaining.*

Meanwhile, yet another opportunity suggested electronic media possibilities. Five minutes from Martha's home on Turkey Hill Road stood a dilapidated farmhouse occupied by an elderly spinster named Ruth Adams. The house was of the same Federal architectural period as Martha's and Andy's home and in many ways suggested exactly what the house on Turkey Hill had looked like fifteen years earlier.

Like the original Turkey Hill structure, much of the Adams house lacked insulation and heating, with no running water or plumbing. Renovating and restoring the dwelling would be like revisiting the restoration of Turkey Hill itself. If Martha could parlay her growing fame into a bargaining chip to get local tradespeople and craftsmen to work on the project for little or no wages, she could videotape the transformation, and then she could probably sell the series for enough to recoup her purchase and renovation costs, and make a bundle in the process. In fact, there were probably hundreds of thousands of avid Martha groupies by now who would buy the tapes just to see their heroine in action.

Such were the prevailing conditions in her erupting business life when Martha decided to involve Kathy Tatlock in her WGBH pursuits, which amounted to yet a whole different videotape scheme. The basic idea: Turn the WGBH concept for a series of how-to tapes on entertaining into a project that Martha would handle with Kathy instead.

For Kathy, it was Martha at her finest—or at least her most "Martha," for so far as Kathy could make out, what Martha was really saying boiled down to this: "WGBH gave me this great idea. So now that I have it, who needs WGBH!" It was just another glimpse of the woman that Kathy found alternately so fascinating yet somehow unsettling. Energy and ideas seemed to fly out of her in all directions, just as they had two decades earlier in New York . . . it was simply that, as Kathy seemed to sense, you could never be sure when the ideas would ricochet off something (or someone) and knock you flat.

But Kathy had already made up her mind—she was signing on for the ride, and she began brainstorming ideas for various camera crews with whom she could work. Before long, she came up with an idea for a title for the series as well: *Martha Stewart's Secrets for Entertaining* (producer, director, and writer: Kathy Tatlock).

Shortly after the first of the year, Kathy began making regular weekly trips to Westport to discuss the project with Martha and begin putting things into gear. There was so much to do, and so little time. Kathy became a blur of energy as she raced back and forth from Boston to Westport to hammer out details. A crew had to be hired, treatments had to be drafted and approved, scripts had to be written.

Kathy had been aware from the start of how cold and fickle Martha could sometimes be, but on these trips she found her warm and engaging as they mixed gossip from the olden days with finalizing plans for the videos. As the weeks flew past, things were working out exactly as she had hoped they would, absorbing her more each day in the challenges of pulling together a videotape series for her long-time friend, Martha. She simply couldn't believe her luck and good fortune. It was electrifying.

As the winter of 1987 turned to spring, a similar excitement was spreading through all of the media. Deal making was in the air, and its contagion was touching everyone. Between the time of Martha's Thanksgiving special and the following April, the stock market soared 25 percent as each new merger spawned excitement of the next merger to come. Not even the first glimmerings of a widening insider trading scandal on Wall Street could chill the mood, as the moneymen of high finance simply brushed aside reports that financier Ivan Boesky had spilled the beans on corruption that reached into every corner of the junk bond market.

Who cared! Junk bonds had already built the business empires of media biggies ranging from Ted Turner, of CNN fame, to Steve Ross, the chairman of Warner Communications. It was a gold rush that was making megamillionaires out of people most folks had barely heard of five years earlier. Now they were the new heroes of American pop culture.

Martha Stewart was listening. At one point, she turned to Kathy and declared, "I will soon be a millionaire . . . and you will soon follow."

Yet behind the closed doors on Turkey Hill, the atmosphere was so charged that it seemed as if lightning would fork between Andy and Martha at any minute. The house itself was cold and drafty, with sections of it still unheated, adding to the chill and sense of foreboding. The feeling of somehow walking on eggshells was intensified by Martha's insistence that all visitors remove their shoes on entering so as not to scratch or mar her hand-stenciled floors.

One morning Kathy came downstairs for breakfast and found Andy at the stove, cooking frittatas. Kathy watched as Martha entered the room, looked at no one in particular, and said "Good morning, dear . . ." in a way that turned the word dear into something approaching a verbal ice pick. Andy gave it right back to her: "Good morning, dear . . ." without turning to look.

Occasionally, Kathy would ask Martha how things were going with Andy. "Oh, we have our issues," she would say, and that's as far as it went.

After several visits, Kathy finished up a formal treatment on her old Macintosh word processor and presented it to Martha. "You're brilliant," Martha exclaimed after reading the script, and she began introducing her to friends and visitors as "my brilliant director." By now, Kathy was driving back and forth from Boston twice and sometimes three times a week, so Martha suggested she simply move in at Turkey Hill and stay in Alexis' apartment in the back. The place had its own kitchenette and bathroom, and since Alexis wasn't coming around much at the moment, what was the harm?

At first, Kathy was overwhelmed by Martha's hospitality. Fresh flowers appeared as if by magic at her bedside daily. She fell asleep in more freshly fluffed pillows than she knew what to do with. She awakened each morning to baskets billowing with soft bath towels in her new home away from home. Kathy would spend three or four nights at Turkey Hill and then head back to Boston only to return the next week. This went on for months, through the winter and into the spring of 1987.

One reason Kathy was getting the royal treatment was that, Andy notwithstanding, Martha seemed to be feeling pretty good about things in general at the moment. Though Kathy knew nothing of it, Martha had by now been contacted by Barbara Loren-Snyder and was deeply immersed in negotiations that were supposed to make her a multimillionaire in no time at all—just the thing to be in the spring of 1987. So deeply involved in her Kmart talks had Martha become that by imperceptible degrees, Kathy Tatlock seemed to slip from her view, as her friend from Boston became increasingly just another walk-on player in the ever more spectacular drama of Martha's own life.

One result was that Kathy found herself working without the contract that Martha had promised her. She mentioned the matter to Martha once or twice, and at one point actually offered to draft one herself.

After several months, Kathy began to sense that Martha had other things on her mind. What's more, Martha began heaping more and more make-work chores on her—like running errands for the house—and they were starting to wear her down. But Martha was her friend, Kathy thought, and she obviously needed the support Kathy could provide. Besides, why complain when there was seemingly so much to lose?

Before Kathy could really get going on the actual shooting of any film, she needed a crew—namely, an associate producer, a director of photography, and an editor—and was already involved in interviewing candidates when Andy and Martha began raving about a local filmmaker named Dick Roberts, who lived in a waterfront home in Greenwich. They described him as a Renaissance man, who had invited the Stewarts to dinner recently and had not only prepared a drop-dead meal all by himself—a real test of accomplishment in Martha's book—but had finished off the evening by entertaining his guests at the piano, which had endeared him to Andy.

The Stewarts explained to Kathy that Dick had worked on several interesting documentary projects already. He was creative, they said, and had a background in advertising, which was also a plus. He had a state-of-the-art editing studio right in his home with all the equipment a professional director would need. What's more, he was willing to work for the Stewarts for a pretty good price.

Kathy had been expecting to handle the editing at a studio she used in Boston and had already mentioned that to Martha. But now it seemed Martha had other things in mind. Yet once Kathy met Dick Roberts, she found him to be all that Andy and Martha had said, and promptly agreed to work with him.

As Kathy understood things, Dick was to be her second in command with both of them working as freelance contractors—an arrangement the two settled into easily and quickly.

Thus, when Martha opened her house for her annual garden party, on a day in late June, Dick and Kathy set up their cameras and filmed the scene as women strolled through the grounds, admiring the flowers and bushes. And more than just garden club members were there as well.

Martha's sister, Laura, was present and accounted for—exhausted from a day of cooking food that now lay spread out on tables for the guests . . . the food that Martha was claiming to have prepared herself. Martha's brother, George—the Turkey Hill carpenter/handyman—was also there, bickering with Martha over this and that. In and out of the scene shuffled Martha's mother, silent and dowdy in one of the housedresses that Martha had loathed from her childhood and later banned from Turkey Hill. The cast of characters even featured Robyn Fairclough, Martha's winsome young assistant and Andy's future wife, now living in yet another apartment on the premises. In short, the entire gang of Martha's hobgoblins passed by in a Fellini-like parade, as Kathy and Dick panned the landscapes in search of the perfect "Martha Moment" to begin their video.

When the test videos were complete, Martha would send them off to her publisher in New York. Kathy never had any contact with the publisher, only receiving whatever feedback Martha chose to relay to her. Yet the messages were uniformly positive, with rave reviews—according to Martha—coming from none other than Alan Mirken, the head of Crown Publishing.

The praise inspired Kathy to intensify her efforts, and she wrote a formal proposal to Martha, suggesting that it would be a good idea to break up the videos into three separate tapes. There would be an antipasto feast, a formal dinner, and an outdoor summer buffet. Martha thought it was great, and reported back a few days later that the people at Crown agreed, saying the publisher had bumped up the budget to a cool $250,000. They had gone from $100,000 for one video to $250,000 for three. Kathy was thrilled.

There was just one nagging little problem, which had begun to taunt and torment her until finally she couldn't stand it anymore. She'd been doing all this great work for her friend, and the budget for the project had nearly tripled as a result. So how come, despite all that, Martha just couldn't make herself sit down and write up a contract for Kathy? With the news that Crown Publishing was increasing the budget to $250,000, Kathy decided to force the issue and ask for what was only right. She wanted a contract.

On a June day in 1987, Kathy finally got what she'd been asking for: a contract for the work she'd been doing for Martha for the previous six months. Martha had been paying her a day rate and covering her expenses, but Kathy still wanted a contract that set down in writing exactly what Martha had promised her: 50 percent of any eventual profits. Yet Martha had become so preoccupied with the Kmart deal that Kathy and the videotape projects had begun to seem like distractions that Martha wished could somehow just go away.

Then, suddenly, on a June afternoon when Kathy had returned briefly to Brookline, Massachusetts, on some personal errands, the phone rang and it was Martha on the other end asking her to hurry back down to Westport for her contract. Kathy was startled. After all the months of foot-dragging and delay, why had the contract subject abruptly become Topic A on Martha's to-do list?

Kathy didn't ask, and Martha certainly didn't volunteer any information. But as Kathy was heading for her car and pointing it westward on the Massachusetts Turnpike for the two-and-a-half-hour trip down to Westport, the evidence strongly suggests that Martha and Andy had gone into a kind of desperate, damage control mode in hopes of preventing their lives from becoming any more convulsed than they were about to get.

Though Kathy had yet to know it, Andy had by now reached a fateful decision and had dumped it on his wife: After twenty-five years of marriage, he was leaving. Tidying up the contract issue with Kathy thus seems to have been little more than an eleventh-hour effort—inspired by either Andy or Martha—to put some order into at least one relatively easily rectified aspect of their business affairs.

In fact, a contract for Kathy was the least of the problems the Stewarts needed to sort out, for contrary to their public image, the manner in which Martha and Andy had entangled their public and private lives had turned both into a spaghetti plate of loose ends. Since the start of 1979, Andy had actually been one of Martha's employees, and had been making tax-deferred contributions into the Martha Stewart company retirement plan. Those contributions now approached $150,000 and belonged to Andy but were under the control of Martha. That was something that needed to be addressed, as did the ownership of the couple's personal assets. Nearly all of them had long since become stage props for Martha's career, which arguably made them assets for her business. But Andy was arguably her biggest stage prop of all, so how did he figure into the division of spoils? It was all so complicated.

An even bigger potential complication was looming up in the form of the so-called Adams House. The ramshackle farmhouse, a scant five-minute drive from the Stewart front door, had intrigued Martha for years, suggesting a renovation project in which she could make some money by selling videotapes and books of the project to her fans. Martha had been coveting the property since she'd first learned the year before that it might be for sale. Result: No sooner had she finalized the terms of her consulting deal with Kmart, in April 1987, than she made an offer to buy the property. Her offer of $535,000 was accepted, and a closing date of July 1, 1987, was now looming, which meant that the house would be added to the assets the two would doubtless soon be fighting over. What's more, this was an asset that Andy was helping pay for even as Martha was planning to use it for her business. What a mess!

And on top of all that, both Andy and Martha had to contend with the contracts for Kathy Tatlock and Dick Roberts. Kathy had been wandering in and out of the house since January on a project in which she'd been promised a 50/50 split by Martha, but had been stonewalled by Martha on a contract from the get-go. These two freelancers could soon be making problems for the Stewarts if their situations weren't clarified. To the outside world, the lives of Andy and Martha Stewart may have seemed like paradigms of dust-free tidiness. But behind the drawn curtains at 48 Turkey Hill Road, it seemed as if something approaching small business pandemonium reigned.

Such was the backdrop—about which Kathy knew almost nothing at the time—when Martha summoned her to Westport and, on her arrival, ushered her into the kitchen for her contract. The date was June 19, 1987, with May flies and pollen floating in the sunshine beyond the kitchen window as Kathy entered the room to find Andy and Dick Roberts already seated and waiting. The mood was somber, even cold, and a chill ran through her. What was this all about?

Kathy and Martha drew up chairs and sat down, and the four people began to stare at each other, one person on each side of the rectangular-shaped worn wooden table. From the sheaf of papers lying in front of Andy, he handed one set of pages to Kathy and another to Dick Roberts. "Here," said Andy. "Your contracts."

Kathy began skimming her copy, but Andy interrupted and began going over each page with them, line by line. A sense of foreboding and dread began to spread through her. Something was wrong. But Kathy couldn't quite put her finger on what it was. And then suddenly there was the answer, on page three. Her eyes locked numbly on the words, as Andy's voice seemed to trail off to a great distance, saying, ". . . and you'll each get 10 percent."

Kathy could feel an emptiness spread through her, as she reeled to get her bearings . . . back through the weeks and months, as summer retreated into winter again, and she was seated at her Macintosh, batting out the scripts and treatments that she would capture in the rushes sent to Crown Publishers, that would bring back, by way of Martha, the second-hand praise from Alan Mirken. And not even there did it stop, as the calendar pages flew back to the endgame troubles with her husband Chris and then raising her children alone, always struggling financially—back and back, faster and faster, until she was once again in Bogotá, and Andy's voice was drowned out by the words of her dead husband, Chris, as they waited in the airport for Andy and Martha to clear Customs.

"I don't trust her," Chris was saying, "she's a user."

Kathy looked at Martha, then at Andy and Dick Roberts, who was also getting only 10 percent. That alone astounded Kathy because she thought that Dick was a contract worker, and she, Kathy, hadn't promised him a percentage of anything, just a fee. So she looked back at Martha.

"There's something wrong here," she said. "You promised 50 percent."

Martha stared back at her. "I never said anything like that," she replied.

Kathy started quoting Martha's words back to her—the very words when she'd explained that if she were to have to give 50 percent of the deal to somebody, she'd prefer it was a friend . . . etcetera, etcetera. But Martha just looked at her and said nothing.

Kathy turned to Andy, whom she had always believed to be an ally and a friend.

"Andy," she said, "what do you know about this?"

Andy answered vaguely, then looked away: "Well, Kathy, all I can tell you is that this is all I knew."

Tears welled in her eyes as she struggled to figure out which of her friends had betrayed her, and what to do next. Should she sign the contract or walk away and never again have the opportunities that were in front of her? But she had dug the hole so deep by now, what choice did she have? All those months of driving back and forth from Brookline, of passing up other opportunities to remain focused on this one. She'd been promised 50 percent of any profits, and had invested the only assets she had—her time and her skill—in the speculative bet that there'd be something to divvy up in the end. But in an instant, the 50 percent had been snatched from her, and her take had been slashed to 10 percent—and if she didn't take the 10 percent, she'd be throwing away the possibility of anything at all. It was one of the worst moments of her life . . . not just the betrayal by the person she admired and had trusted most, but in a sense, the betrayal of a lifetime built on trust and openness. She felt raped in an instant by a rich woman's exploitation of a friend's vulnerabilities.

Reluctantly, almost robotically, she picked up a pen and signed. At that point, Andy abruptly rose from the table and, with an uncharacteristic chill in his voice, said, "Congratulations. Excuse me, I have to go . . ." and turned to leave.

"I'll walk out with you," said Kathy, as she, too, stood.

She caught up with him in the driveway.

"Andy, what is going on here?" Kathy started.

"I don't know what to tell you, Kathy," he said. His voice was low and even, without malice or even shame, just matter-of-fact. "You can quit if you want. But I'm out of here. This is my last day with Martha."

Kathy turned to him.

"Jesus Christ," she said. "Are you really doing it?"

"I am," said Andy. "This is it. I've had it."

"Does Martha know?"

"Yes."

And with that, he shut the car door, said goodbye, and headed down the driveway and out of view.

Kathy watched him drive away, and she thought: "He's leaving and I have no recourse, and back inside that house is a monster."

The following hours went by in a blur, as Kathy walked back inside and began puttering about aimlessly in her room. Should she pack up and leave? Should she stay and try to reason with Martha again? It was all so impossible. In the CIA, they had called this sort of crisis an "AOS" moment, meaning "All Options Stink." But Kathy knew it now as something else. She had felt for herself the hard core of cruelty and control that lurked in the heart of her friend. She had experienced the ultimate bad "Martha Moment."

By and by, she found herself talking with Martha in the kitchen, listening as Martha muttered—as if to reassure herself as much as Kathy, "He's not going to be gone long, he's done this before. He'll come back." It was eerie, even frightening. She felt locked, trapped, paralyzed from moving, while the person in front of her acted out her own self-absorbed personal drama, oblivious to the pain she had just caused in her audience of one.

Kathy remained at the house, and in the days that followed, Martha's desperation intensified. Unknown to Kathy, an entire subplot involving the Adams House was coming to boil. Barely two weeks after Andy walked out, Martha and Andy were scheduled to close on the purchase of the house, and Martha could not cancel without alerting the world—especially Kmart—to the breach between herself and her husband. What's worse, five days after the Adams House closing, Martha was scheduled to sign her contract with Kmart, which had been kept totally in the dark about the turmoil reigning in the life of its star. In other words, she had to buy a house with a man who had just walked out on her while misleading her new partners that everything in her life was hunky-dory lest they walk out on her, too. Wherever she looked, whichever way she turned, it was AOS for her too.

Martha began calling Andy on the phone, trying to lure him back. But Andy would have none of it. By now, he had convinced himself he had hated living in Turkey Hill all along, with its cold, drafty rooms and museumlike feel . . . a house where you couldn't touch anything, or even walk on the floor with your shoes on. To seduce him back, Martha at one point even offered to move the two of them from the main house to the barn apartment in the back which had always appealed to Andy as a place to live. The structure had mammoth windows, gorgeous views, and plenty of light. But this didn't work either, for Andy had simply had it. For all that she had been able to control and manipulate the world around her, she had finally lost control of the person she needed to manipulate and control the most: her own husband.

In the process, Kathy became the whipping boy for her ire. Soon after Andy left, Kathy found that her fluffy pillows had been taken away. The baskets of soft towels became a single washcloth. Her in-room refrigerator, where Kathy kept coffee, juice, leftovers, and snacks, was unplugged. "I'm spending too much on electricity," Martha announced as she yanked the plug from the wall.

Next, Martha began heaping household chores on her: Water the garden, let the dogs out. Prior to Andy's departure, Kathy had eaten dinner often with the couple in local restaurants—particularly a Chinese restaurant not far from Turkey Hill. Now Martha began eating alone. At one point, Kathy suggested that the two go out to dinner together. Martha said she had other plans and waved her away impatiently. "Just eat with Mom," she said. The maître d' at the Chinese restaurant, a fellow named Gary, recalled Martha coming in, alone and without a reservation, at around this time, and demanding a table. A group of diners stood in the lounge area, ahead of her, awaiting tables as well.

"There'll be a wait," said Gary, "about thirty minutes. We've gotten backed up."

Martha cut him off. "Do you know who I am?" she demanded.

Gary looked at her. He knew full well who she was. By now, Martha Stewart was one of the best-known celebrities in Westport. And her imperious manner was also widely known—an arrogance that, in the wake of Andy's departure, she now seemed to carry around like a chip on her shoulder.

Gary put down his pen. "I know exactly who you are," he said. "And I don't give a fuck. You want to eat here, you wait, like everyone else." Martha turned on her heel and left.

Meanwhile, her physical appearance began to deteriorate. She wasn't sleeping, she looked tired, and she was constantly angry. Her hair often seemed unwashed. She stopped wearing makeup. As filming continued for the videotape project, Kathy began using a diffusion lens on the camera to soften Martha's features enough to make her look presentable and hide her weariness. Kathy suggested that Martha hire a wardrobe consultant, a makeup artist, and a hair stylist. But Martha dismissed these suggestions, waving her hand at Kathy. "No, no, no," she would say.

Kathy and Dick Roberts finally finished shooting the videos in early August, around the time that Martha and Kmart were announcing their deal to the world at the "21" Club breakfast press conference. When Kathy and Dick began editing the footage at Dick's studio in Greenwich, Martha would promise to come up and help with the editing, but typically she would show up and fall asleep, or not show up at all. On one occasion, Martha sat down in a chair in the studio, just behind Kathy and Dick, to observe as the editing progressed. As Kathy worked through a scene, a thought oc-curred to her, and over her shoulder she asked for Martha's input. But there was no reply. Kathy asked again. Still no reply. Turning to look, she beheld a scene she'd now come almost to expect: Martha Stewart, fast sleep, with her head back on the chair and her mouth half open.

By late autumn, Kathy had edited one out of the three videos and submitted a $30,000 invoice for her fees and expenses, and Martha paid her. But when she submitted invoices for the second and third videos a week or so later, she heard nothing.

Strategy: get
others to pay

On November 10, 1987, nearly an entire year after Kathy had first gone to work on the project, Martha told her to come with her to a meeting that had been planned with some Kmart people in New York. Martha said she wanted to recommend Kathy to Kmart as a possible director for some additional videotapes she was planning—a series that would memorialize and chronicle renovations on the Adams House, which had begun a few months earlier.

Kathy, meanwhile, had heard almost nothing about the business backstory to Martha's activities with Kmart. Thus, she had no way of knowing that behind the public facade of a happy relationship, Martha had orchestrated a power play of breathtaking audacity. Through what plainly looks to have been misleading information to Barbara Loren-Snyder—the Kmart consultant who had brought her to the retailer in the first place—Martha was in the process of maneuvering Kmart into lending her what would eventually total $400,000 (75 percent of which was interest free) so she could pursue her project on the Adams House.

Martha's ploy—as audacious and risky a move as she had ever attempted, and one that she seems unlikely to have risked had she not been so convulsed by the turmoil in her private life—traced back to the previous August and the immediate aftermath of the Kmart press conference at "21." A month earlier still, on July 1, she and Andy had closed on the Adams House purchase, for $535,000, and taken possession of the dwelling. Ten days later, on July 11, she'd sent Kathy to inspect the premises for videotaping possibilities.

Now Martha wanted to get Kmart to pick up the tab. Was there a way to do that without opening the door on the Stewart couple's entire Closet of Horribles?

Well, yes, there was—but the maneuver had to be handled deftly. She somehow needed to convince her new business partners to help her buy the Adams House as a business project without letting them sense that they might be investing in a property that could easily develop into the focus of a vicious struggle in divorce court. Somehow, she had to get Kmart *into* the project now that Andy was bowing *out of* it. In other words, Kmart had to become Martha's new Andy Stewart.

Thus in late August, not long after the press conference at "21," Martha sprang her plan on Barbara Loren-Snyder, saying, "I want to buy a house—the Adams House—because it is the same era as mine but it's for sale and I've always wanted that house. The house is for sale and I can buy the house. There's just one problem. I don't have the money. But I could do videotapes as I'm redoing the home and sell them, in Kmart."

In fact, Martha already owned the house and was simply angling for a way to get Kmart to pick up the tab.

But Barbara didn't know that, so she briefed Joe on Martha's proposal, and when the three met in Troy a few days later, Barbara told the new Kmart star to explain her idea to the boss.

"I want to buy this house," Martha began. "It's a restoration. If you give me a million dollars. I can buy the house and make the tapes and sell them."

But Joe wasn't interested. "We can't see doing it," he said, explaining to her that this wasn't something that would be appealing to Kmart customers.

Yet Barbara wondered if Joe had dismissed the idea too hastily, and that night she turned Martha's proposal around and around in her mind, trying to see what Kmart's vulnerabilities might be if the company didn't agree to cooperate. On one level, she knew that Antonini was right, and that a series of house restoration videotapes would likely turn out to be a dud, at least with Kmart shoppers. Kmart shoppers wouldn't be interested in home fixer-upper videotapes—that was Bob Vila stuff for *This Old House*. But if Martha were now to approach some rival retailer and get it to pick up the tab the arrangement would make Kmart look terrible. What if the company's new spokesperson, having been on the job barely three weeks, were to get a turndown for her proposal and wind up taking it instead to, say, Home Depot or Sears? Kmart would then be in the position of promoting a spokesperson who'd be selling her home renovation videotapes through a rival retailer—with Kmart getting none of the benefit from the star it had created.

Yet Martha's contract would not have prevented her from doing something like that. No one had even thought of such a ploy—no one, that is, but apparently Martha herself. Barbara began to wonder whether Martha wasn't a lot sharper and shrewder—and more ruthless—than she might ever have guessed.

A month earlier, Barbara Loren-Synder had figured she'd soon be dining on Martha under Glass. Now all of a sudden everything had been turned topsy-turvy, and it looked as if Martha was preparing to eat Kmart's lunch instead! Maybe that $200,000 price tag for Martha hadn't been such a bargain after all.

Night after night, Barbara worried over the situation, trying to find an escape hatch for Kmart that would enable the company to keep Martha in the fold while shedding the costs onto somebody else.

Finally, she hit on it, and picking up the phone, she dialed the Kmart wheel.

"Joe," she said, when he came on the line. "I think I have a way to get Martha what she wants and a free $14 million ad campaign [for Kmart]. It's a win, win, win situation for all."

"What do you mean?" asked Antonini, and Barbara set forth her idea: Kmart would develop a series of "At Home with Martha Stewart," ads and TV commercials, which would run for a year and focus on one aspect or another of Martha's renovation project. To pay for it, Kmart would round up a group of top-drawer housewares and renovations vendors, from General Electric (refrigerators and stoves) to Sherwin-Williams for paints. The vendors would participate in the project by contributing their merchandise and expertise, getting to film their commercials at the Adams House as the project progressed. Result: Kmart would get great advertising, nearly free of charge, as would the vendors—and Martha would get her house.

Antonini liked the idea. After all, Kmart's only exposure would apparently be for the $1 million that Martha had asked Kmart to give her to buy the Adams House in the first place. In return for that $1 million, Kmart would get to be associated with—and actually appear in—ads for some of the country's most prestigious consumer advertisers—a campaign that Barbara was estimating would probably top $14 million. This would be a priceless opportunity for a downmarket discount retailer like Kmart, which was struggling to upgrade its image in the market.

The deal was an obvious no-brainer, and Joe once again gave Barbara a thumbs-up—this time to help Martha buy a house that neither person knew Martha already owned.

From Martha's perspective, it was a home run, and scarcely had Barbara briefed her on the idea than she jotted off a handwritten note, on August 31, authorizing Barbara to go ahead and start soliciting vendors. By year's end, Barbara had lined up dozens of participants anxious to associate themselves with the radium hot new star of the American home, Martha Stewart, who had agreed to open and close each commercial personally—if the vendors would pay her directly for the privilege.*

---

*None even balked the following April when, with equipment about to be installed in the house, Martha insisted that the vendors supply *two* of each product being advertised—two stoves, two refrigerators, etcetera. As Martha explained it, one would be used for the Adams House project, whereas the other would be needed for free-standing "beauty shots" of the products for the ads. This Noah's Ark arrangement meant that, just as was the case with the house and all its equipment and contents, the second set of everything also became Martha's personal property.

Kathy knew none of this as she climbed into the back seat of Martha's chauffeured Mercedes for the ride from Westport into Manhattan to be paraded before the Kmart executives as Martha's director on the Adams House videotapes.

The car swung from the driveway and eased into the traffic. Minutes passed in silence, with Martha in the passenger seat, the chauffeur behind the wheel, and Kathy in the back. Suddenly and without warning—and without looking back—Martha took a sheaf of papers from her lap and tossed them over her shoulder at Kathy. They were Kathy's invoices for the second and third videos, and Martha was telling Kathy what she thought of them in exactly the way she had returned to Norma Collier (Martha's first business partner and one-time *Glamour* magazine modeling era friend) her various belongings when the partnership broke up: by throwing them in her face. In Norma's case, it had been through the door of a Madison Avenue boutique. A decade later, and it was now into the face of an employee in Martha's own chauffeured limo.

The papers were covered with circles and cross-marks. The screenwriting fees, $5,000 per video, had been simply eliminated. Travel expenses—expenses that Kathy had already incurred and paid for—had been chopped, as had other personal outlays. Kathy's director and producer fees were cut as well. The deductions went on and on, until Kathy's eyes fell to the bottom line, where the cuts were toted up, and $50,000 of expenses had become $15,000.

Kathy was in shock. "Martha, what is this?" she stammered. "How could you do this?" What about the expenses she'd already incurred? What about the $10,000 scriptwriter's fee for the first script, which Martha had already paid? Wasn't Kathy entitled to equivalent fees for the second script, and the third—especially since Martha had already agreed on the amount?

"You don't deserve it," said Martha, referring to the screenwriting fee. "You didn't write this, I did."

Kathy was horrified. She had spent weeks on those scripts, and on the shooting and editing that had followed . . . weeks during which Martha had mostly just showed up and fallen asleep.

"What do you think I've been doing all these months?" Kathy stammered.

"Well, you're being paid as a director," said Martha.

Kathy simply couldn't believe what was happening. Here she was, being insulted and chiseled all over again—this time on the way to meet a group of New York executives who were about to be told how talented she was. It was impossible. Surreal. Kathy wanted to jump from the car.

The next few hours were torture. In the company's Manhattan offices, Kathy met with Kmart executives and lawyers, as well as someone who was introduced to her as Barbara Loren-Snyder. Then the group adjourned to a nearby production studio to review Kathy's work. There was much discussion about videos and production costs, and Kathy was asked many questions, but it all had lost its interest to her.

Eventually the conversation swung around to Martha's contract with Kmart, and the things Martha had apparently decided she wanted changed. At one point, Martha got so animated that she began to jab her finger at a piece of paper and yell, demanding that she receive more payments under a certain clause of her contract. The Kmart executives were trying to remain calm and reason with her, but Martha's voice just grew louder as she said, "I don't care, I'll talk to my lawyer."

Then as abruptly as it began the meeting ended, as Martha rose and headed for the door. "We'll be in touch. You'll hear from us," Kathy heard the Kmart folks declare as she and Martha exited the room.

Martha had been pleasant and complimentary toward Kathy during the meeting, and on the way out, she whispered, "They love you."

But Kathy had bought the line one too many times already, and she wasn't going to buy it again. The return trip to Westport proceeded in silence. Once back at Turkey Hill, Kathy went to her room, packed up her things, and headed for her car . . . and like Andy Stewart before her, she pulled from the driveway, swung into the traffic, and never looked back.

About a year later, the phone rang at Kathy's house in Brookline. It was Martha on the other end. She was in Boston, working on some project, and wanted to talk to Kathy to rekindle old times.

"Hi," she said. "It's Martha."

"Martha?" Kathy paused. "To what do I owe this honor?"

"I'm in town," said Martha. "I thought we could get together and have lunch or something."

Kathy was beyond anger by now—and in fact, beyond Martha. A year had passed, and her nightmarish memories of Turkey Hill had begun to fade.

Seeing Martha and "getting together" was something she no longer had time for, and no longer ever would. *Get together?* Kathy answered with a single word—a word that spoke the anguish of a lifetime of trust betrayed. *Get together?*

"Why?"

"I thought it would be fun," replied the voice on the other end of the line.

"I don't," said Kathy, and hung up the phone.

Thus emerged one of Martha's basic business strategies—which she has used time and time again, sometimes as a result of happenstance, other times with seemingly calculated design: Get somebody else to pick up the tab. She has used it from the local hairdressers and merchants in Westport, to her personal friends and acquaintances, to the largest and mightiest of corporate giants, including Kmart and Time Warner.

One way or another, all have yearned, figuratively speaking, to take Martha Stewart to dinner—sometimes simply to be seen dining with a good-looking blonde, other times in hopes of sneaking some morsels from her plate. In the end, the bill—in terms of free advertising and marketing alone—has run far into the hundreds of millions with Martha herself as the ultimate beneficiary. That is because Martha's basic consumer product isn't magazines or merchandise, it is Martha herself—and her fame has long since been paid for by others.

People are still picking up the tab to be seen with Martha. In the summer of 2000, she took a television crew to the Alaskan Yukon, and the entire adventure was paid for largely by others. Airlines donated seats for the crew and waived the extra baggage charge for the camera equipment. An extra-plushed-out RV camper was prepared and donated by the Winnebago people, and driven to Juneau so that Martha would have a place to put her feet up between filming segments. Hotel rooms were provided free of charge, food came for free. It was as if the commercial enterprises of the country's largest and least populated state rose up as one to make the TV celebrity's stay a good thing . . . for free.

It was sometime in the summer of 1987, just around the time when Martha was signing her deal with Kmart and Andy was walking out on her, that the idea came to Martha to develop herself into a media business—"my own little publishing company," as she put it. This was, of course, what the husband who had just walked out on her was running: *his* own little publishing company.

Martha had no clear idea of exactly what she wanted her business to become, at least not initially, beginning instead with not much more than a list of books she still wanted to write in the wake of *Weddings*. She took the list to her publishers at Crown, naturally expecting them to jump at the idea since she was by now the biggest author they had going, with something approaching two million copies of her books by then in print as well as a whole series of videotapes about to begin flooding into stores.

To her surprise, Crown wasn't interested—partly one supposes, because she was more valuable to them the way things were. Why loosen the shackles on your prize author when, at least in financial terms, the status quo arrangement was as good as things could get? Besides, there was at least one other reason not to be embracing change at that moment: The economy was in trouble and no one knew how much worse things could become.

By mid-October, the stock market had grown increasingly jumpy after five years of relentless gains, and on October 19, 1987, the cloudburst finally came, with the Dow Industrial Average plunging 580 points, for the biggest one-day point loss of the century. The next day, the New York *Daily News* carried a single, one-word head-line—PANIC—that not only summed up the mood of the market but explained why, overnight, a decade of deal making screeched to a halt.

Yet so far as Martha was concerned, the collapse wasn't signifi-cant. Her deal with Kmart had already been signed, with its core provisions being built around a consulting arrangement whereby she would "design, create, critique, and oversee the manufacture of a line of bedding and bath products . . ." as well as visit manufacturers, make personal appearances on the company's behalf, and attend store openings. In return for all this, Kmart would give her a royalty on each Martha Stewart-branded item sold in its stores, while stim-ulating their sale by using her "name, image, biographical material, professional theories, and reputation" in promotional advertising of her Kmart-linked products.

By advertising her products, Kmart was simultaneously promot-ing Martha herself. What's more, scarcely had the ink dried on the contract than she had maneuvered the company into a situation in which she'd be making lots of money no matter whether anything with her name on it sold in their stores. That was thanks to the Adams House deal in which Kmart had unexpectedly—and com-pletely without being asked—agreed to (thanks to Barbara) put to-gether a Kmart-backed media campaign designed to capitalize on the renovation. It left Martha—who hadn't even asked for the ad campaign in the first place—in an unbelievably advantageous situation. She had, after all, insisted, from the moment she first began negotiating her deal with Kmart, on retaining all rights to her books and other publishing undertakings, either past or to come. Kmart had agreed, thereby effectively giving away any opportunity to share in these proceeds from any increase in her fame—for which they were paying the freight.

This meant that Martha could use her publisher, Crown, to market any number of books and tapes on the Adams House renovation, with 100 percent of all royalties accruing to Martha, with not a dime going to either Kmart or any of the advertisers. She had stumbled into a situation in which Kmart had agreed, in effect, to organize the most massive advertising campaign for a single author in the history of the publishing industry, with Martha and Crown not having to share a penny of the proceeds with the parties who were actually paying the bills.

So, though it is hardly any wonder that Crown would not have wanted to rock this gravy boat, it is equally no surprise that Martha would have wanted to find some way—any way—to set up a publishing operation on her own. With Kmart seemingly having committed itself to making her a national household name, she could become rich beyond dreaming if she could somehow just get control of the publishing system that marketed her words.

Thus, with still only a nebulous idea in mind for a business, Martha went to Time-Life Books, the in-house publishing arm of Time Inc. There she was initially met with a warm response, but an executive shuffle soon sidetracked the discussion, and Martha looked elsewhere. Her next stop was Si Newhouse, the perpetually scowling owner of Conde Nast Publishing. By now, Martha had moved beyond the idea of book publishing and begun to think about publishing a magazine, a field in which it was possible to make a lot more money anyway—especially if she didn't have to incur advertising and marketing costs.

Newhouse quickly saw how to do just that: Put Martha's face on the cover of each issue, thereby enabling the magazine to get a free ride on its brand identification with Martha herself. Newhouse got so excited about the idea that he authorized the company to develop a prototype. But soon he began to wonder how Conde Nast's other magazine editors—notably Anna Wintour, the newly appointed editor of Newhouse's revamped *House & Garden*—would take to the idea. Would Anna soon be asking to put *her* picture on the cover of *H&G* every month? After that, Newhouse started to fret about the audience. What was this magazine supposed to be anyway, if not a kind of fancied up *House & Garden*? He could wind up cannibalizing his own audience. The more he thought about it, the less comfortable he became with the idea, and eventually he abandoned it altogether, telling Martha that she could keep her prototype and try to sell it elsewhere if she liked.

So, Martha took it under her arm and went to Rupert Murdoch's magazine publishing operation, where she also got a turndown. Finally, with all options exhausted, she went back to Time Inc., which was now in the midst of a hugely expensive and distracting three-way merger struggle involving Paramount Communications and Warner Communications.

Time Inc.'s goal in the fight had been to complete a friendly merger initiated by the head of Warner—a one-time funeral parlor operator named Steven Ross—who had parlayed his Hollywood and Organized Crime connections into a perch at the top of the movie and music industries. But Ross' overtures to Time, headed then by an affable but weak executive named J. Richard Munro, simply whetted the appetite of Ross' arch rival, Martin Davis, the bilious head of Paramount Communications, who quickly lurched into the middle of the affair with an unsolicited offer for Time.

Paramount's bid forced Munro to switch from a "merger of equals" strategy with Warner into an outrageously expensive scheme to buy the Ross operation outright. This made the resulting company so big and debt-burdened that it prevented Paramount from devouring the combined businesses.

This strategy, which eventually heaped more than $13 billion of costs onto the combined companies, meant that the management of the new entity—named Time Warner, Inc.—now had to begin explaining the maneuver to its savaged shareholders. The rationale that Munro seized on was a Harvard B-school concept known as "synergy," which was based on a kind of "one plus one equals three" arithmetic. Theoretically, the cost of bringing together the two separate companies—one rooted in New York magazine publishing and the other grounded in Hollywood moviemaking and television— would be more than justified by the new revenues that would begin flowing once the executives of the combined companies got together and began cooking up movies based on magazine articles, and so on and so forth.

Thus, when Martha Stewart walked in the door of the Time & Life Building in Rockefeller Center, bearing a magazine prototype that somehow seemed to have the synergy concept written all over it, executives in the company's magazine development operation— known as Time Publishing Ventures—grabbed for it quickly. Here was a way for a group of men who were already feeling threatened and eclipsed by the more dynamic and forceful energies of Warner's world of movies and music to look relevant and on the cutting edge of the combined companies' future. At least it was a way to act as if they were listening to the company's chairman, Munro, as he ceaselessly talked up the opportunities of synergy in the Age of New Media.

The first executive to review Martha's offering was a trim Manhattanite named Christopher Meigher, who headed the Time Ventures operation. For the meeting, Meigher brought in an aging editor named Dick Stolley, one of the founding editors of *People* magazine. Because Stolley was thought to possess a kind of water dowser's knack for recognizing where to dig for publishing gold, Meigher had invited him to the meeting.

After pleasantries were exchanged, Meigher looked at the proto-type Martha had brought him. "It looks more like a book than a magazine," he thought, even down to the cover portrait of Martha, which suggested the dust jackets on most of her books. There also seemed to be an undercurrent of self-celebration in the prototype— in fact, in the entire concept—that troubled him. "Reg Brack won't like this," he thought, ruminating on how his boss, Brack, the head of Time Inc.'s, entire magazine publishing operation, might react. Would Reg welcome a magazine built around the idea of making its own editor into its main editorial topic? In another ten years, celebrity editors with magazines named after them would become a major publishing strategy. Martha made O, Oprah Winfrey's maga-zine, and *Rosie*, Rosie O'Donnell's magazine, possible—but at this point in time the idea simply seemed bizarre.

And Meigher knew something else: Time Inc. was a world of men, with an almost impenetrable glass ceiling blocking access to top management on both the editorial and business sides of the cor-poration. How would the men of Time Inc. take to the notion of a new magazine, celebrating so conflicted a theme as it own editor— when the editor happened to be a woman! And there was also the matter of her business involvement with Kmart. Would the maga-zine open Time to the charge of using its editorial voice to promote the image of a spokesperson for a downmarket discount retailer? The idea had trouble written all over it.

But in business if not in her personal life, Martha had been born under a lucky star. And just as she had lucked out with Barbara Loren-Snyder's idea to turn the Adams House into a national adver-tising campaign, Martha had also lucked out in turning up at Time's doorstep at precisely the moment when almost any new idea that seemed to bring together the multiplying worlds of the media was bound to be greeted warmly. Sure, the men might not like Martha Stewart personally, and many might have felt outright jealousy as well. And old-timer purists might even have recoiled at the thought of her involvement with Kmart.

But in Meigher's mind, Martha had one thing going for her that outweighed every such objection: Here was a woman who was already a mega-best-selling author with a super-high-visibility position in the media through her Kmart relationship. And in the wake of the merger, almost every utterance on corporate policy coming from Munro and his second-in-command, Gerald Levin, had emphasized "content extension"—from books to magazines, from magazines to movies . . . and anywhere else imaginable. If the deal with Warner were ever going to pay for itself, it would be through the active, aggressive, relentless pursuit of synergy in all its forms. And Martha Stewart was one of its forms.

"Come on," said Meigher. "Let's go upstairs and see Jerry Levin."

CONTROLLING THE STRESS LINES

T he departure of Andy left a hole in Martha's life that she seemed to fill with activity, anger, and money. The struggle left her rich and exhausted, and surrounded by the shallow, meaningless friendships of the celebrity world. But her efforts to show the world—and, most likely, Andy as well as herself—that she didn't really need him anyway also transformed her into one of the most successful, if least liked, business world celebrities in America.

Yet surprisingly, her initial major foray into the world of big business and media marketing did not get off to an encouraging start. While she was trying to promote her idea for a Martha Stewart publishing company to any corporate sponsor who would listen to her, Crown Publishing was already shipping copies of her soon-to-be-released videotape series, *Martha Stewart's Secrets for Entertaining*, to retail outlets around the country. Kathy Tatlock—the woman who actually produced the shows as well as wrote the scripts and directed the shooting—must have felt almost relieved that when the tapes were released and she discovered that Martha had usurped credit for them and took top billing for herself as principal producer and writer on the project. Reason: The reviews were awful, the first time Martha's work had been pilloried so extensively.

The first of the series, devoted to how to throw a buffet lunch-eon, went on sale in March 1988 at $24.95. *People* magazine reviewed the video and pronounced it controlling and even off-putting, say-ing, "Watching these tapes is like stepping into a Ralph Lauren ad and being told what to do once you're there. Not everyone is going to feel at home." The *Boston Globe* went further and pronounced it one of the "Ten Worst" video releases of the year.

Yet the tapes are memorable in at least one respect: They mark the last visual record of Martha before Andy walked out on her, and everything about her life—and her appearance—began to change. In the tapes—thanks to Kathy's artful filming—she is still seen as a lean and lovely woman, with shoulder-length blonde hair and—at least before the camera—an engaging, relaxed demeanor. There is even a scene in the tape in which one can catch a glimpse of Andy, laughing and talking as guests mingle and converse in the gardens of Turkey Hill. Thereafter, the face began to gather frown lines of stress as she raced to build a business while raging at her husband for deserting her when she needed him most—apparently never understanding why he'd left her in the first place: because she'd become impossible to live with.

Meanwhile, Martha's relations with Kmart had developed stress lines as well. To get her out before the public quickly, Kmart had come up with a kind of mini-introduction in the Kitchen Korner de-partments of some 400 of its stores in November 1987, to be followed by promoting her on the cover of its Christmas 1987 shopping cata-log, which would be mass-mailed to 10 million Kmart shoppers. But tension quickly developed over a cake recipe that Martha provided and that Kmart began distributing on flyers at its Kitchen Korner dis-play areas. The flyers brought thousands of complaints from shoppers who said the recipe didn't work as promised.

Martha may well have been right when she responded that the customers probably hadn't followed the instructions correctly. But maybe because Andy was no longer around as a lightning rod for her anger, an increasingly arrogant manner had begun to creep into her relations with others. When she dismissively told Barbara Loren-Snyder, "Oh, they didn't make it properly . . . ," it helped set the tone for an increasingly brittle relationship between Martha and Kmart.

By the start of 1989, Martha had begun making what Kmart viewed as disparaging public comments about the company. In fact, her comments were completely in harmony with what Kmart actually wanted her to say; the company just didn't like the way she was saying it—with an edgy, almost superior tone in her words. Thus, when Martha confessed to a reporter for the *Christian Science Monitor* in March 1988 that she hadn't actually been a Kmart shopper at all before signing her deal with the company—and, in fact, that even though she was now associated with the company as its most visible spokesperson, she had no intention of "changing the quality of what I do . . ."—she was saying exactly what Joe Antonini would have wanted her to say. Yet she was saying it in a manner that seemed both arrogant and self-absorbed, as if she were reassuring her fans, "Don't worry, Kmart is not going to ruin Martha Stewart."

The situation was particularly awkward for Barbara, who had been the person most directly responsible for bringing Martha to Kmart in the first place. Now, the woman in whom Kmart was investing so much hope—and money—was proving to be rigid, demanding, pushy, and aggressive—interested only, it seemed, in filling Kmart's aisles with the products her fans wanted regardless of their appeal to Kmart's existing customer base. As she told a reporter for the *Dallas Morning News*, "We have a major job with Kmart to get my kinds of things into the store. A major job. Is it going to take an attitude adjustment? For them, not me! I'm not adjusting anything."

Such comments only hardened the standoff, helping explain why the company felt it necessary, in January 1989, to send Martha a memo specifically detailing their concerns about her public attitude toward Kmart. The memo not only outlined what the company felt was appropriate for her to discuss publicly and what was not, but specifically instructed her to be more "positive" in her comments and less "negative," and to look to Jaclyn Smith, the company's other spokesperson, as a role model and example of how to handle herself in public.

More than anything else, Martha's condescending and dismissive attitude rankled the Kmart people, for when they focused on the substance of her contributions as opposed to her haughty demeanor, no one could deny that she was doing all they could have asked for. In fact, she was contributing more than they wanted—a lot more.

Martha's job didn't require her to become involved in the actual design of merchandise, just to consult on various concepts and proposals. At most, the brass had expected to see her at no more than a handful of meetings per year, smiling politely while asking the occasional intelligent-sounding but nonconfrontational question—then going out and pitching Kmart's products. That's what the deal was all about—at least as the Kmart executives understood things. What they really had expected was for Martha to be another Jaclyn Smith—affable, charming, ready to elevate a product's cachet and appeal by simply lending her name to it. That's how the celebrity endorsement game was played.

But it's not how Martha wanted to play it. Her name and her image were ultimately the most important assets she had, and she was certainly willing to let Kmart "rent" them for a high enough price. But she was not about to let the company do anything that she felt might threaten or even ruin them.

What Kmart did not expect—and was not prepared for—was a celebrity spokesperson who turned up at every meeting, determined to elbow and nudge her way into every decision made in her name, demanding information on the quality of every single product that would wind up bearing the Martha Stewart label—all the way down to demanding to know the thread-count per square inch in sheets and towels sold under her name.

At one meeting, she turned up bearing an elaborate presentation for an entire line of Martha Stewart stemware. "They're beautiful!" exclaimed Barbara when she saw them. But the Kmart people weren't looking for beautiful stemware designs from Martha; they had been expecting someone prepared to serve as a celebrity spokesperson and let it go at that. Yet Martha not only insisted on being involved in everything, she also wouldn't easily take "no" for an answer when her ideas were rejected.

On another occasion, she arrived with exact and detailed designs for a line of kitchen and dinnerware bowls in the shape of turkeys—her obvious idea being to capitalize on the spreading fame of her home, which by now was known everywhere simply as "Turkey Hill." To keep Martha happy, Kmart's purchasing department tried to find a manufacturer that could make the bowls at a low-enough cost for Kmart to sell them at a profit. But, though the designs were indisputably attractive, the market seemed a niche opportunity at best, and the company declined to go forward.

Yet Martha would not take no for an answer, and may not even have understood why her ideas were being rejected. It wasn't that they weren't any good—it was simply that they weren't any good for Kmart. "She didn't really understand what was appropriate merchandise for Kmart . . . and what was not," said Barbara later. In the sprawling corporate world of Kmart, Martha had become like the single out-of-step soldier in the army—yet week after week, month after month, she kept pushing to get the whole army to shift to her cadence.

By the end of 1989, Joe Antonini had about had it with his star. Her ideas and plans were certainly fine for Martha Stewart, but they often seemed inappropriate and even downright ridiculous for Kmart. The baffling thing was how Martha somehow had managed to upend and invert the whole relationship between Kmart and its spokesperson. Martha's job was to promote Kmart, but in some way that no one could quite figure out, Kmart had mostly wound up promoting Martha instead.

One of Martha's oddest proposals, as far as Kmart had been concerned, was her suggestion that the company become a backer of a magazine she wanted to publish—the exact same effort that wound up taking her eventually to the door of Time. But Kmart wasn't in the magazine publishing business, it was in the business of selling discount merchandise to working class shoppers.

In February 1990, matters finally came to a head when Martha insisted on a meeting not just with Barbara but with Joe and several others. Her goal: to convince them that Kmart should stock a line of Martha Stewart specialty foods including English butter cookies, jams, and fancy mustards, along with a companion line of gifts for cats such as catnip, toys, and expensive grooming tools.

Antonini was agog. In the two and one-half years since Barbara had brought Martha to him, Kmart had showered an absolute fortune on the woman. Her Adams House project alone had ballooned into a $20 million national ad campaign, with 37 different companies by now involved in it. There'd been 43 separate commercials, each featuring the background music of Corelli's "Suite for Strings," running almost nonstop on TV, with exposure on such high-impact programming as *Good Morning America* and *Today* in the mornings, and *L.A. Law* in prime time—and Martha had been in every one of them. There had been Sunday stuffer inserts for the newspapers. There'd been a consumer sweepstakes contest and nationwide radio spots. There'd been advertorials in *Better Homes & Gardens* and *Family Circle.* It went on endlessly, the most massive national advertising campaign in the company's history. In barely a year's time, it had transformed Martha Stewart from "caterer and author" into the best-known "lifestyle authority" in America—an inclusively nebulous branding that made her, in effect, the media's official, and ultimate, authority on every homemaking-related activity on earth.

And now, at the end of all that, she wanted even more? Now she wanted Kmart to begin selling Martha Stewart grooming tools for cats? And Martha Stewart designer mustard? It was insane. She was taking over the whole store. Here he was, Joe Antonini, supposedly running a $25 billion retailing business with more employees than the Pentagon. Yet somehow he'd wound up listening to this inexhaustible woman push yet another of her schemes on him. Attention Kmart Shoppers: Martha Stewart English butter cookies in aisle six. I don't think so.

"We'll look into it," he said. But as soon as Martha left the room, he leveled a withering stare at Barbara and declared, "This is a waste of my time!"

By pouring its millions into the development of Martha Stewart, Kmart hadn't simply been investing in a brand image like, say, Betty Crocker or Aunt Jemima, it had been investing in an actual human being, driven by needs, desires, and ambitions that the company was only now beginning to glimpse. And because the company lacked any ownership interest in the image itself, it had no way of sharing in the fruits of Martha's efforts.

Almost overnight, Kmart had elevated Martha's visibility to a huge national audience, creating a celebrity who actually owed the company very little and seemed much more interested in her own pursuits. In that sense, the Kmart ad campaign amounted to a slow pitch down the center of the plate that Martha knocked out of the park.

In October 1988, the first print ads began running for the Adams House renovation project, and within two months she was appearing on the *Today* show, introduced to the world as a "big-time caterer." Days later, the airwaves were drenched in network television commercials for the project. By July 1989, she was signing a deal with her publisher to bring out a book on the renovation— *Martha Stewart's New Old House*. Two weeks later still and she was back at Turkey Hill, filming a Christmas special to air on the Lifetime Cable Television Network. Since the filming was taking place in the hottest month of the summer, a Christmas feel was created by covering the grounds with plastic snow.

When the show finally aired on November 25, 1989, Martha's publisher had already shipped copies of a book entitled *Martha Stewart's Christmas* to stores, and it vaulted to the Number Two spot on the *New York Times* Advice Books Best Seller List. The book was a direct beneficiary of Kmart's investment in its author . . . an investment in which Martha was turning out to be the real winner.

With her newfound wealth, she began an acquisition binge that, over time, would have made Marie Antoinette blush. Within six months of Andy's departure, she had purchased a $1 million Manhattan co-op apartment on Fifth Avenue overlooking Central Park. Scarcely had her Christmas special aired on the Lifetime Cable Network, than she purchased a $1.6 million summer home in elegant East Hampton, on Long Island, down the street from media tycoon Mort Zuckerman and billionaire investor Ronald Perelman. This was followed by the purchase of a 29-acre, $1.25 million parcel of undeveloped residential real estate fifteen minutes from her Westport house, and eventually a second house in East Hampton. To all this, she later added an estate in Maine, a Manhattan loft in Tribeca, a 153-acre estate in Westchester, New York, two boats, a collection of antique noblemen's carriages, a stable of horses, and a helicopter.

Meanwhile, in December 1990, even as her buying binge was gaining steam, Kmart asked her to repay the interest-free loan she had finagled out of them supposedly to buy the Adams House, which, of course, she already owned.

Not wanting to part with the money, she told her lawyer, Jeffrey Stephens, to write to Kmart, telling them that she needed more time to repay . . . not telling them that the reason she didn't have the money was that she was now fixing up her place in East Hampton.

When a reporter for *USA Today* asked Martha how she was finding the time for all the activities in her hectic schedule, she answered, "I don't sleep and I'm tired lots of times . . ." a rare forthright response to the question, which she'd soon begin dismissing by saying that she really didn't need to sleep anyway.

The truth was, Martha had begun to divide into two different people: In her private life, she was an increasingly stressed and quick-tempered person; but to the world at large, she was Martha Stewart, the middle-aged Nancy Drew. As she liked to remind her assistants whenever it seemed appropriate: "Remember, I'm not Martha Stewart the person anymore, I'm Martha Stewart the lifestyle."

For Martha, her increasingly furious struggle to make all this happen—ultimately through the mechanisms of dominance and control—presented a bill of a different sort, as she began to morph into a real-life public caricature of the gentle creature inhabiting the pages of her books. Just as her father had ratcheted up his control over the inhabitants of Elm Place until they fled in horror from his abusive, domineering rages, Martha, too, eventually isolated herself from her husband and daughter, her neighbors, and many of her own business partners and employees, as she struggled to bring order to the world around her by using the techniques of dominance and control she had learned at Eddie's knee.

The unfulfilled promise in all this is acute, for by the late 1990s Martha had emerged from the early obscurity of a small-town caterer to become one of the best-known and wealthiest women in America. She was now perched at the pinnacle of an industry she had literally invented—"lifestyle consulting"—with her name in the newspapers more frequently than any other woman in the country except Hillary Clinton and Oprah Winfrey. Yet in 1997, just around the time when *Time* magazine was naming her one of America's 25 most influential people, Hallmark Cards conducted a survey to determine who Americans thought were the five "nicest" public figures in the country. Oprah Winfrey came in first: America's Queen of Nice, with six times as many votes as Martha, who came in last on the list.

Rarely has America produced a public figure who appears more tortured than Martha Stewart. The struggles seemingly centered in the depths of her soul have turned her public image, on one level, into one of the most potent and effective brands in the history of American marketing. It is suffused with irresistible messages of family traditions and home-centered self-reliance that have been stripped from American women over the past fifty years. Yet in many ways, creating and marketing the image of Martha Stewart has turned the real-life person behind it into the embodiment of all that seems least admirable in the world of big business and the ruthless men who run it. In the celebration of the American woman at her finest, Martha Stewart became the American businessman at his worst. Her impossible mission: To fill those two roles at once.

In Woody Allen's 1985 comedy classic, *Purple Rose of Cairo*, actor Jeff Daniels plays a matinee film idol who somehow develops the ability to move from the world of celluloid imagery into actual movie theater reality by literally stepping out from the screen and walking around among the startled audience. Something like that soon began happening to Martha's startled neighbors in Westport. For although Martha may have wanted to begin thinking of herself as a "lifestyle," her neighbors knew her as a real person. The tension between those two perceptions—aggravated enormously by the departure of Andy from her life—soon led to problems over the Adams House renovation, as a scandal erupted over whether she was attempting to swindle local residents into helping pay for her renovation with a bogus suggestion that their contributions would be tax deductible.

Beyond the world of Westport, the new and captivating celebrity who was emerging embodied the message that at century's end a woman could indeed move effectively and with grace between the worlds of business and the home. And many women could at least enjoy this message vicariously through Martha's public performance of herself, even if they had missed out on the opportunity in their own actual lives. "We've been fans of hers for years and love all of her books and videos," said a mother of two grown daughters as all three stood in line for Martha's autograph at a Virginia bookstore on a November day in 1991.

Added a lady named Alice Probst, who by the age of 45 was already a grandmother of two, and at the start of the 1990s was busily working to organize a Martha Stewart Fan Club. "I think what Martha Stewart tries to show is that you shouldn't be ashamed that after you get home from an office, or from driving a cab, that your house is important to you," said Ms. Probst. "If you want to cook a nice meal and be domestic, fine. You should not feel guilty about also wanting to be a housekeeper."

A Connecticut woman named Beverly Osgood professed to being such a fan that she had purchased four copies of a single Martha Stewart book the previous Christmas, adding, "When she's on TV, people call me up and say, 'Martha's on.'"

Martha herself was coming to appreciate the huge appeal of her image, though there is little to suggest that she was voicing a personal perspective when a reporter asked her to explain her appeal to women and she answered, "In the '60s and '70s, women went to work and the workplace became their priority. They forgot about their kids, and their home life got away."

But the closer one got to Turkey Hill, the more one came face-to-face with the reality of what it meant when work became the priority and one's home life "got away." Stories abounded of people who had seen Martha fly off the handle and begin yelling at someone or other—a neighbor, a local merchant—in public for no apparent reason. A neighbor who lived across the street said, "My son went to her door one day to sell Christmas wrapping paper for the Boy Scouts. He was 12 years old and in the sixth grade. He meant no harm to anyone. But he had apparently interrupted something when he rang the doorbell and she came running out, shrieking for him to get off her property or she'd call the police. He came back home in tears. It was awful." Another neighborhood child reported knocking on her door for Halloween trick or treat: "She opened the door a crack and threw some candy corn at me and told me to go away."

People told of pulling up to the drive-through window at the bank and having a certain blonde woman lean her head out the window of the car behind and begin honking the horn and yelling to hurry up because she was late for the airport. It was Martha. They saw her elbow her way to the head of the line at tag sales, heard her berate grocery store proprietors for not having copies of her magazine neatly racked up and ready for sale at the checkout counter. Martha seemed to be so deeply rehearsed in the politics of abuse that she had taken the script from which she had harangued her husband for twenty years and, in his absence, simply started reading from it to more and more people in the world at large.

The gossiping grew meaner and more shrill. People repeated tales of how Martha had gotten Greens Farms Academy—the country day school where Alexis had attended classes through the eighth grade—to provide the student choir as entertainment for one of her Christmas parties, only to leave the kids shivering outside in the cold. Similar stories were told—by the children themselves—of a group of youngsters who had been brought by their parents to Turkey Hill for a Thanksgiving party then left to stand outside because Martha hadn't wanted them to be seen in the scenes that were being taped for television inside. One of her ex-friends began telling people that she'd seen Martha purposefully run over a kitten.

Much of the gossip sounded petty and mean-spirited, but when it reached the ear of a local freelance reporter named Elizabeth Keyser, she decided to look into what was really going on behind the door at 48 Turkey Hill Road. Elizabeth was perfectly cast for the job, with unassuming good looks and a quiet demeanor that masked her fierce determination to get a story. Over the years, she had heard a lot about Martha from her mother, Rose Keyser, an attractive and engaging Westporter, who had been friends with Jill Robinson, the one-time best-selling author. She had been part of the Westport writers' set that had introduced Martha to Erica Jong back in the 1970s.

Soon, Elizabeth had penetrated the circle of Martha's friendships, and when she heard that the papers that Andy had long since filed in the divorce case could be viewed in the Bridgeport Superior Court, just up the coast from Westport, she dropped everything and drove to the courthouse to see for herself. It was a warm day in early May 1990, nearly three full years since Andy had walked out on Martha, and for the past two years the case file had simply sat there, unread by any reporter. Now the world at large would get a peek at what had been going on since Andy had walked out.

Bridgeport, Connecticut, is but a twenty-minute drive east from the genteel rolling lawns of Westport. But at the start of the 1990s, Bridgeport was part of another world, with gang and drug violence so out of control that whole sections of the city's downtown East End had been walled off with concrete barricades and concertina wire. People could move in and out through it only at police checkpoints. The city was also home to a large—and rapidly growing—immigrant population. Many of them were Brazilians and other Latinos who worked in Westport as day laborers and household domestics of one sort or another.

Elizabeth thus didn't feel terribly comfortable as she parked her car in the lot opposite the Connecticut State Courthouse building and headed inside. Perhaps her quiet voice and nonthreatening manner carried the day as she walked up to the Court Clerk's desk and tried to sound both matter-of-fact and entirely routine while asking, "May I please see the *Stewart v. Stewart* case file?"

The case file had in fact been sealed since the summer of 1988, but someone had apparently made unusually detailed entries on the public index to the sealed file—so detailed as to amount to an abstract of the papers that were supposedly to be kept from the prying eyes of the public. Yet two entire years had passed and no one but Elizabeth had thought to ask for the file.

"Is there someplace I can photocopy all this?" asked Elizabeth as the clerk handed her the folder.

When the clerk said no, Elizabeth began hand-copying the file. The entries ran back to about nine months after Andy had walked out. Though he had left the premises, the couple seemed to have still been seeing each other regularly—though hardly under conditions that Andy, the "plaintiff" in the case in which Martha was the "defendant," would have welcomed.

Under the date March 18, 1988, was an entry that read:

1.   On March 16, 1988, 4:30, the defendant came to the plaintiff's place of business at 740 Broadway and created a scene and disturbed the plaintiff's conduct of business by, among other things, ripping up the complaint she was served with and refused to leave when so requested by plaintiff.

2.   The defendant threatened to break a window in the plaintiff's office which is located on the 11th floor of an office building.

3.   This was the second time in the last three months that the defendant has engaged in such conduct.

4.   The plaintiff and defendant are separated and live in separate residences.

      The plaintiff requests that the defendant be restrained from entering upon the plaintiff's personal residence 25 West 76th Street, New York, N.Y., or office unless by written consent.

Elizabeth scribbled furiously.

A follow-up entry, under the same date, read:

Andrew Stewart requests dissolution of the marriage and equitable distribution of property. "The marriage has irretrievably broken down."

Three days later there was a stipulation that read:

1.   Neither party shall go to the other's business or home.

2.   Neither party shall harass or abuse the other party.

The entry said the stipulation bore the signatures of both Andy and Martha.

Under July 1988 were two more entries. One, which bore no date but was identified only as "Answer Counterclaim," read:

1. Plaintiff has on repeated occasions and continues to commit adultery.

2. Plaintiff willfully deserted defendant more than one year prior to date of this Answer with total neglect of his duty to the defendant.

On July 20, 1988, was another entry. It read:

Plaintiff says defendant has "physically grabbed him and screamed at him in public, sent letters to individuals known to the plaintiff in which she has made derogatory remarks and has made numerous telephone calls to plaintiff vilifying him.

Motion for Contempt of Court: Defendant broke order. "Went to plaintiff's residence without invitation and refused to leave."

A further entry under the same date stated:

Defendant requests that plaintiff cease harassment, telephone calls and insults. Plaintiff has taken girlfriend on vacations and holidays and physically abused defendant.

More entries followed month after month on down the page, as the two fought with each other over issue after issue, most of which seemed to boil down, in the end, to money and possessions, and who was going to get the most of both.

Elizabeth had read enough. She now knew she had a story—based on an irrefutable case record from a court showing that there may have been truth to the rumors she'd been hearing. And she knew exactly where she'd take her story to be published: a hard-hitting but entertaining and well-read alternative weekly known as the *Fairfield Advocate*—just the publication that wouldn't cave in to what she could already imagine would be a firestorm of protests from Martha to stop publication of her exposé.

12

No good deed goes unpunished

Luck usually turns out to be a coin with two sides, and just as Elizabeth Keyser was working on her story, she had a bit of good luck that for Martha, by contrast, turned out to be extraordinarily bad luck. By coincidence, Elizabeth's story broke in the midst of a local scandal that had erupted seemingly out of nowhere, automatically elevating interest in her reporting enormously since it seemed to confirm so much of what people had been saying about Martha all along.

Elizabeth's story—appearing, as it did, smack in the middle of a scandal that had begun swirling around Martha's business ethics—should have come as a warning that for all her talk about having been transformed by Kmart's publicity money from Martha the Person into Martha the Lifestyle, the public and private Marthas were still the same person. Perhaps it was Martha's discovery that she couldn't *force* people to view her personally as she had wanted to be seen publicly, that sent her fleeing in a seeming panic to Europe—or at least ducking calls on that excuse. Or maybe she had been planning the trip all along. In either case, she left at the absolute worst possible moment, as the two stories merged into one, creating a "Perfect Storm" of bad publicity.

The eye of the hurricane was the Adams House, which in some ways had been both the best and the worst stroke of luck she'd had since Andy had left her. On the plus side, it had been the fulcrum by which she had leveraged her association with Kmart into the instant and massive exposure that had transformed her from a writer of cookbooks into a kind of drama critic for the whole of American domestic life. Prior to the Adams House project, Martha's fame was limited mostly to the kitchen, the dining room, and weddings. After the Adams House, she was an authority on every aspect of the house, from the lawns and gardens on the outside, to the exterior maintenance, to decorations and renovations on the inside from the basement to the attic. The Adams House project made her ubiquitous.

But the project had also become a continuing bone of contention between Martha and Andy, whose names were both on the deed, as they fought to divide up the wealth of the Stewart estate. Finally, there was the sheer magnitude of the investment in the house itself, along with the complex tax issues involved. By Martha's own reckoning, the amount had been huge, running ultimately to more than $1.2 million, with $535,000 being the original purchase price, and more than $700,000 being poured in thereafter in renovations and capital improvements.

Much—maybe nearly all—of that $700,000 had come in the form of donated labor and material from Kmart's partners in the project, which ranged from corporate giants, all the way down to local tradesmen, carpenters, and landscapers. But since the house was owned by Andy and Martha jointly, the donated labor and material had to be treated as imputed taxable income by the couple on their annual tax returns. In effect, the estranged couple were joined at the hip in a speculative venture that was generating no income but producing large annual increases in their taxes.

The capital improvements did increase what accountants call their "capital basis" in the dwelling, meaning that they wouldn't face any capital gains taxes on the eventual sale of the dwelling unless the property were to sell for substantially more than $1.2 million.

But a sale at a price of much less than $1.2 million would have meant that the couple could have been left with little more than a tax loss to show for their trouble. As work drew to a close on the renovation, something like that seemed a distinct possibility. The economic recession of 1990/1991 accompanying the Gulf War spilled into the previously impregnable Westport housing market, raising questions as to whether the Adams House could ever be sold for the amount invested in it—a subject that became a matter of nonstop speculation among local real estate brokers and their friends.

At that point—with the project being watched closely, but quietly, by Westporters throughout town—Martha, seemingly unaware that the cumulative impact of the stories about her behavior had conditioned many townspeople to read the worst possible motives into most everything she did or said, took an apparently well-intentioned step that almost instantly blew up in her face.

In an attempt to make a charitable contribution to a worthy cause associated with a leading Westport public figure that might also help stop the carping and gossiping about her, she arranged for the Adams House, by then just about completely renovated, to be opened to the public for three weeks of tours at fifteen dollars per ticket. The proceeds would be donated to a well-known and much admired local charity.

That charity was an upstate Connecticut summer camp for severely ill children. Known as the "Hole in the Wall Gang Camp," the project had been the creation of Westport's best-known—and most widely admired—movie couple, Paul Newman and Joanne Woodward. They had named it after the hideout used by Butch Cassidy and the Sundance Kid in Newman's Oscar-winning movie of the same name, which had costarred Robert Redford, another sometime Westporter.

Paul Newman's philanthropic endeavors had received worldwide attention and praise over the years. He and another local celebrity, writer Aaron (A.E.) Hotchner—author of a 1966 best-seller, *Papa Hemingway*, which had been translated into twenty-six languages and published in thirty-six countries—had founded a not-for-profit salad oil company, Newman's Own, Inc., that donated its profits annually to charity. The company had ballooned into a wildly successful retail food conglomerate that eventually outgrossed Newman's films. Hotchner was married to an attractive blonde woman named Ursula, whom he had met when she was working as a photo researcher at *Time* magazine. Among Ursula's circle of friends was a woman named Evelyn Merrin. Evelyn also worked in *Time's* photo department and, in turn, had been friends with Elizabeth Keyser's mother, Rose Keyser, who worked there as well. In small town Westport, barely six degrees of separation divided nearly everyone in town, no matter what their relative levels of fame or wealth.

Both the Hotchners and the Newmans lived a few minutes' drive from Turkey Hill, and it was through Martha's connections with them, which traced back to an early catering job for the Newmans, that she hit on the idea of turning the Adams House project into a three-week charity promotion before actually putting the house up for sale. The Newman side welcomed the idea of a fundraiser for the camp, but to make sure that there could be no public confusion about the proceeds flowing to the Hole in the Wall Gang Camp and not Martha Stewart, the group told her that Martha's company should set up a separate account. That is at least what Martha later claimed through her sister-in-law as the press began clamoring for answers in what looked to be a distinctly fishy arrangement. Purchasers of tickets to the tour would make their checks payable to that account, which she called "Homestyles."

The account was not set up as what is known as a "not-for-profit entity" but was just a bookkeeping account in a company owned by Martha. This meant that the proceeds of the ticket sales would automatically become taxable income to Martha—income that would instantly become an offsetting charitable deduction for her the minute she turned the proceeds over to the Hole in the Wall Gang Camp. By contrast, the visitors who had purchased the tickets had made their payments not to the charity but to Martha's for-profit corporation, thereby losing the right to deduct the contributions on their own tax returns. They had, at least on paper, simply financed a tax deduction for Martha instead of themselves.

In Westport, one of the wealthiest communities in America, fifteen dollars was not a lot of money. But Westport was also filled with people who knew a lot about finance, and for many of them, the actual amount of money they contributed to charities each year was less important than how the contributions were handled. Just as people all across the nation flew into a rage when they discovered that charitable contributions they had made to the American Red Cross for victims of the September 11, 2001, terrorist attacks had been diverted by the Red Cross into its general purpose fund coffers, so, too, did Westporters get instantly riled when they discovered that their checks weren't to be written to the Hole in the Wall Gang Camp but were to be made payable to Martha's "Homestyles" instead.

The whole thing looked like a scam—a ploy by the town's increasingly resented superstar to shed some of the costs of her misguided foray into real estate development onto the backs of cancer-stricken children being cared for by Paul Newman. And the situation looked even worse when Martha organized a series of lecture presentations that coincided with the tour and were held in a church hall across the street. Tickets for the seminars were priced at three hundred dollars, and a great deal of confusion quickly developed over whether the purchase price was or was not also tax deductible. Three hundred dollars was, after all, a good deal more than fifteen dollars.

Publicity for the tour, dubbed "Martha Stewart's Showhouse," had begun as far back as January, and by the time the doors were thrown open to the public on May 1, Martha had assembled one of her typically spectacular presentations, headed by a blue-ribbon "Honorary Committee" of names like U.S. Senator Edward M. Kennedy Jr., of Massachusetts, and Connecticut Senator Christopher Dodd. Catering was provided by two of the swankiest restaurants in New York—La Caravelle, and "21," the midtown eatery where Barbara Loren-Snyder had three years earlier held the press conference that introduced Martha to the world as a Kmart consultant.

Yet scarcely had the crowds begun gathering to purchase tickets than muttering could be heard about why the checks that people were writing were not to be made out to the Hole in the Wall Gang Camp. Many of the noisiest complainers were Martha's own volunteers on the project, who seemed to feel that they'd been misled by the person they'd trusted most—Martha.

In the middle of all this, and even as the three-week tour was reaching its finale, Elizabeth Keyser's piece was rolling off the press. Much of the story was a straightforward profile of Martha and her life, pegged to the Adams House tour and featuring an interview with Martha as well as some color photos and quotes from one of her seminar presentations.

But the story contained three paragraphs toward the middle of the article that sent Martha into orbit. Grabbing the phone, she got Elizabeth on the line and began to rail and scream. "I want to know how you got your hands on my closed divorce file," she demanded. Elizabeth tried to explain that she'd simply gone to the courthouse and asked to see what was available, and they'd handed the file to her.

"It was really rotten," Martha spat. "You should be ashamed of yourself. I'm disgusted with you." The words began to tumble forth. "It's really neat to be an investigative reporter," she sneered. "It's really neat to investigate other people's private lives."

"It was a locked case," she yelled, "and I'm going to go to the courthouse today and find out." The rage was now pouring forth so furiously that Martha was becoming almost incoherent, and Elizabeth was having trouble keeping up with her note-taking. "And now it's going to be in papers all across the country . . . the divorce papers . . . it's very painful . . . you don't understand . . . it's all a game . . . you disgust me."

Next she got Elizabeth's editor at the paper on the phone and started all over again, virtually accusing Elizabeth of having bribed the court clerk officials to see the file. "It's really shoddy shit," she cried. "I don't know whether she bribed them or not. It was absolutely clear that it was confidential. It's very distressing. I'm very, very disturbed. It's really shoddy."

For Martha, it must have been as if all the hottest buttons in her life were being pushed at once, and she could do nothing about it except yell and scream at anyone she could reach. Here she was, at the crowning moment of her life as a single woman again, the self-made star of the American home . . . with possessions beyond counting, opportunities beyond reckoning, and admirers beyond numbering. All that and more had been accomplished by her alone— least of all with help from the louse who'd walked out on her when she'd needed his help most. And now, as the finale to her proof that she really hadn't needed him in the first place, some little no-account twit of a reporter had gone rummaging through the garbage of her past and dragged his despicable and twisted lies about her into full public view? It was unspeakable.

It was doubtless the roundhouse blow of Elizabeth's profile in the *Fairfield Advocate* that knocked Martha off-balance when the next story appeared—this one courtesy of a woman named Susan Malsch, whom Martha also telephoned and began berating and belittling in the wake of her story. Ms. Malsch wrote for the *Westport News*, the semiofficial newspaper of record for the town and had begun hounding the Hole in the Wall Gang Camp's lawyer, a fellow named Leo Nevas, for some answers on the disbursement of the event's funds. When weeks passed with no accounting, the *Westport News* published her story. Under a headline reading, "Some Eyebrows Raised Over Showhouse Receipts," it began with the lead:

> Calculators may still be computing, but there is no tally forthcoming on the amount raised by Martha Stewart to benefit the Hole In The Wall Gang Camp Fund during the three-week May 1–20 Homestyles showhouse, seminars and Gala Garden Champagne Party.

The camp's attorney, Nevas, only made the matter worse when he was quoted as saying that an accounting had not yet been completed, and that the camp fund would only receive the "net proceeds" of the affair, once the expenses had been deducted. Then Nevas said, "I don't think anyone out there is breathlessly awaiting the total. I have had a couple of calls from people asking why checks were made out to Homestyles, not the camp, but it's such a small amount. I can't imagine anyone being concerned."

He was wrong, for people were furious.

Said a volunteer on the project named Pauline Holder, who had sold tickets at the door. "They know exactly how many tickets they sold. We kept strict records, and I sold between 400 and 500 tickets at the showhouse in two Monday mornings alone. We were told the entire fifteen dollar donation would go entirely to the camp. That's why so many people came. I have never volunteered for anything where I have not known how much money was made. It raises some questions, and I know I'm not the only one."

The Malsch story quoted another volunteer on the project as saying, "I felt she was just using us and the Hole in the Wall Gang Camp for her own purposes. I would rather give my money straight to the Paul Newman camp."

Yet another said, "The people who worked so hard want to know how much we raised for charity. We have a special interest in cancer."

The story quickly spread to other newspapers that also began baying for answers. In the nearby town of Stamford, twenty miles west down the Connecticut coastline, a reporter for the Stamford *Advocate*, Joy Haenlein, picked up the ball and began phoning for interviews. She too came back with a story of disgruntlement and suspicion as to Martha's motives—as well as something else: an actual, on the record interview with Martha in her Turkey Hill home.

For Martha, the interview proved a disaster. She seemed alternately defiant and distraught—even near tears—over the firestorm that had suddenly engulfed her. The worst exchanges of all came when the reporter asked her if it might not be wise to simply answer the public's questions regarding the event's finances, and Martha defiantly answered that she had no intention of disclosing how much money had been raised or how it was being disbursed. As to whether the purchasers of the actual tickets had a right to know where their money went, Martha said, "I don't think we should give the dollar amount. They all got fifteen dollars worth of information out of that house. Think of it this way: It's like going to the movies."

When a reporter for yet another local newspaper—the Norwalk, Connecticut, *Hour*—saw the story the next morning in the *Advocate*, he leaped for the phone to get his own comment from Martha. But he got as far as a person named Rita Christiansen, who identified herself as Martha's finance manager and said that Martha had been "misquoted" and "misunderstood" in recent press stories, but that she couldn't come to the phone to speak for herself because she had left the day before on "a European lecture tour."

Rita Christiansen was indeed Martha's business and finance manager, but she was also something else: She was Martha's sister-in-law as well. Rita was married to Martha's brother, George, who had been so uncomfortable at the thought of going through life bearing his father's name of Kostyra that he had taken his wife's name of Christiansen. George had been promoted from Turkey Hill handyman to general contractor on the Adams House renovation—being paid for his work with the funds that Martha had been harvesting from Kmart on the project. Meanwhile, her sister-in-law—and George's wife—Rita, was busy keeping it all straight in the company's books and records, while simultaneously handling Martha's taxes as well as running backfield blocking for her in the press. In the small-town world of Westport, few family business circles were tighter than that.

But Rita's protestations accomplished nothing, for even as Martha was apparently escaping to Europe, the first really nasty and negative Martha Stewart story was going national, with both the *New York Times* and *Newsday* rushing to play catch-up. Said *Newsday* of Martha's stance, "The reason for a flap that has taken place in Westport, Connecticut, is simple enough: People want to know. The

problem is, Martha Stewart, who has written several books on entertaining, won't tell them." Newspapers everywhere now jumped
on the bandwagon. In her "let 'em eat cake" comment, the press had
found its new Marie Antoinette, and she had no one to blame for
her treatment but herself.

🍃

Toward the end of the summer of 1990, even as Martha was pre-
senting herself at the door of the Time & Life Building to interest
the company in her magazine idea, Elizabeth Keyser was knocking
on the door of New York-based *Spy* magazine downtown—an entertaining but often vicious magazine of satire and gossip—to interest
them in a story about Martha. The magazine's editor, Graydon
Carter, who went on to become editor of the *New York Observer* and
eventually *Vanity Fair,* liked the idea and gave her the assignment. But
scarcely had Elizabeth completed her story and a *Spy* researcher had
been assigned to fact-check it for accuracy, than Martha's lawyer,
Jeffrey Stephens—the same individual who had handled her Adams
House financing with Kmart—began bombarding Elizabeth, and
eventually the magazine, with threats of legal action.

Weeks passed and by and by *Spy* lost interest and moved on to
other topics—but not before Carter suggested to Elizabeth that she
talk to a media world friend of his named J. C. Suares, who might
just know a thing or two about Martha and Andy.

It turned out that J. C. did indeed know a thing or two about
Martha and Andy. In fact, he knew quite a lot. J. C. was a freelance
book designer and editor and had known Andy as far back as 1981
when he'd worked with him on various book projects. J. C. moved
in a world of celebrities, and as the 1980s progressed, he had
worked with Jackie Onassis on several books when she had been an
editor at Doubleday. At one point in the mid-1980s, these included
the autobiography of rock superstar Michael Jackson, which
brought about an odd get-together of J. C., Jackie O, and Martha at
the fashionable Ma Maison eatery in Los Angeles.

Fifteen years later, J. C. was still entertaining listeners with what happened at the table. Learning from Martha that she was planning to be in Los Angeles at exactly the time J. C. and Jackie expected to be there, J. C. invited Martha to join him for lunch and thereby meet the Doubleday supereditor—the reigning Queen Mother of American fashion. Martha jumped at the opportunity and agreed to meet the two at Ma Maison for lunch. But at the appointed hour, J. C. and Jackie were left twiddling their thumbs in the nearly deserted restaurant, waiting for Martha. Nearly an hour passed as the two sat at the table, trying to make small talk with each other, waiting for J. C.'s no-show guest.

Finally, Martha breezed in, sat down, and with neither an apology nor an excuse, simply joined in the conversation. Jackie said nothing of the rude behavior, but according to one of her biographers, Pamela Clark Keogh, made it a point never again to be able to remember Martha Stewart's name. Instead, she would feign forgetfulness and refer to her simply as, ". . . you know, that pretty woman." At other times she would muse aloud about what exactly Martha really did. Wasn't it obvious to serve food attractively, and to fill one's home with flowers?

As the 1980s progressed, J. C. urged Andy to leave Martha more than once, and by the time Andy finally did, he knew J. C. would be a sympathetic dinner companion. Thus, when Elizabeth finally got J. C. on the phone, he told her a story that simply confirmed what she had seen in the court files and had been hearing about Martha's behavior after the divorce. According to J. C., the two men went to dinner and Andy unburdened himself as to what it had been like toward the end. "She went nuts," J. C. said to Elizabeth, relaying what Andy had told him. "She chased him all over the place and treated him like shit. At one point she sent a letter to his girlfriend's parents in the Midwest, saying their daughter was a whore.* She would follow the girlfriend when she was out jogging, screaming obscenities from her car."

* The reference was to Robyn Fairclough.

Through such moments the secret world of Martha Stewart was unraveling. But as Ronald Reagan once observed, to get ahead in life, it helps to be lucky. And while so much about the Adams House was decidedly bad luck, ultimately it was a stroke of good luck of amazing proportions. Martha was the beneficiary of tremendous good fortune—from Barbara Loren-Snyder's initial phone call, to Kmart's agreement to the loan for the Adams House and, most importantly, to Kmart's agreement to line up more advertising for a single individual than a major corporation had ever done for any one person. To this was eventually added yet another stroke of luck regarding the renovation itself, as the advertising, the videotapes, and the book vaulted Martha to the attention of a whole new and rabid market—that of the home renovator. And home renovation was about to become a huge new booming business in the 1990s.

13

Time takes martha

In personal terms, the Adams House experience was a disaster for Martha, but in the rising tide of her business affairs, it simply vaulted her fame higher. The enormous promotional dollars that Kmart was spending on her annually had so completely branded her a national icon that almost nothing in her personal life could slow her rise. The symphonic promotions of her public image simply drowned out the discordant notes of her private life. The noisier and more off-key her private affairs became, the more she just cranked up the volume of her public performance—a spectacle that astonished everyone who beheld it as it began to seem as if Martha Stewart wasn't one person but twenty.

The next company after Kmart to get swept up in Martha's vortex was Time Warner, Inc. Having met with the company's then number three man, Gerald Levin, at the instigation of Chris Meigher, Martha made her presentation. Not long afterward, she was signing a Letter of Agreement with the company to produce two test issues of a national magazine to be titled *Martha Stewart Living*.

Almost no one at the company liked the idea of having Martha's face on the cover. People felt uncomfortable with the editorial conflicts it represented, to say nothing of the jealousies such an arrangement would arouse among other editors. What would one call it: a *me*-zine? One editor at *Life* magazine, Dan Okrent, was already going around quipping that Martha's magazine should really be titled *Why Is Martha Stewart Living?*

But Martha had a vision and was determined to do it the way she saw it. A *me*-zine is precisely what she wanted to create: a promotional publication devoted entirely and exclusively, like a colossal advertorial, to Martha herself. *Martha Stewart Living* wasn't supposed to be celebrating the Martha Stewart lifestyle, it was supposed to be celebrating the actual Martha Stewart; *she* would be the person embodying the Martha Stewart lifestyle, which meant that the magazine would write about *her*. In her emerging vision of what she could become, she had glimpsed the outlines of an entire world of media and marketing—magazines and books, radio and TV, and anything else that might come along . . . all radiating out from the center, distributing the Martha Stewart message, like rays from the sun, to the world of her admirers.

No more having to push her way into Kmart product meetings to argue with a room full of merchandise managers over what they proposed to put before the public in her name. If she were not only the editor of the magazine, but its subject matter as well, the result would be a closed system that would put her completely in control of the entire process, from creating the magazine's content by simply living her frenzied life, to interpreting and shaping it to the form that she wanted to present to the world. It would be life perfectly ordered and perfectly arranged. And she would be perfectly in control.

"She was a terrible pain in the ass," said Chris Meigher later, "And a potential egomaniac." She knew almost nothing about writing or editing, and her knowledge of magazine layout was rudimentary at best. But Martha knew her limitations in that regard, and, wanting to work with someone *she* was comfortable with, got Meigher to hire her former editor at Crown, a woman named Isolde Motley, to be the actual day-to-day editor of the magazine. For an art director, she lured away another Crown person she'd worked with over the years, Gael Towey, who'd done the layouts and designs for most of her books. Nor did Martha contribute much on the business and publishing sides of the effort. The Time Warner executive who had been assigned to serve as her publisher for the magazine, Eric Thorkilsen, would roll his eyes in dismay at her prima donna antics whenever she left the room.

But Martha brought something to the project that neither Isolde Motley nor Eric Thorkilsen, nor anyone else could hope to match: a loving, yearning, lifelong desire for a place of daffodil daydreams and tea in the afternoon, where all lips smile, all clothes are linen, all voices murmur, and all shades are pastel.

To the men at Time Warner, the first test issue—a November 1990 rollout of 500,000 copies for newsstands around the country—looked like a guaranteed crash-and-burn: 130 pages of Martha Stewart, cover-to-cover. The cover image was a photo of Martha. The text matter inside began with a "Letter from Martha," detailing how she came up with the idea for the magazine itself. There were pictures of Martha arranging flowers, wearing a sweater, selecting a Christmas tree. It was all Martha.

Yet to everyone's amazement, the test results were astounding—way above the newsstand and direct mail sales and response rates that had been projected. How could that be? Who could possibly have wanted to read such blather?

But Martha wasn't amazed. She'd known it would happen all along. She could tell from the crowds that seemed to grow larger at every book signing . . . from the women who wanted to talk to her and tell her their recipes . . . from the mothers who brought their daughters just so they could grow up to say they'd "seen Martha Stewart."

She had tapped into something deep and powerful, and she knew it; for the more she drilled, the more the gusher flowed. No, she wasn't surprised at all. She'd been confident of the outcome from the start.

Before she'd walked in the front door of Time Warner—after she'd been rejected by Conde Nast and Murdoch magazines, and Time & Life Books, and even Kmart . . . before she'd found a publisher and could even say she'd ever publish a magazine, she gave an interview to *House & Garden* and described the precise magazine she expected to publish. It was like watching Babe Ruth step to the plate, point his bat at the bleachers, and hit it into the stands.

She described a magazine ". . . with an initial circulation of one million, and growing from there . . ." It would be filled with the information that she herself craved, about how to make dining table ornamental wreaths and beeswax candles.

Said Martha, "I always write my books for me, not for anybody else." But that was only part of it, for not only did she always write "for" herself, but she also always wrote "about" herself—filling her pages with the dreams of the world as she had always wanted it to be . . . free of family conflict, with happy, smiling parents and children, and snow on the eaves and the sounds of sleigh bells in the lane.

What the November test showed—conclusively and beyond question—was that millions of people out there wanted the same thing . . . to inhabit the world in which Martha Stewart lived. Typically, in a successful test, the company could expect to sell out half the issues published. But with the *Martha Stewart Living* test, they got a 70 percent response rate, which was, basically speaking, off the charts. What's more, 100,000 subscription orders came back from a direct response mailing—and this for a magazine that the recipients of the mailing had not even seen. Ad sales had been fantastic too. The company had been shooting for twenty pages of ads, at a four-color price of $7,500 per page; they got twenty-five pages instead.

It stunned the Time Warner brass. For reasons that flummoxed every executive on the project, the world had gone mad for Martha Stewart. Now their view of putting her on the cover began to change. After all, you couldn't quarrel with the numbers. Time Warner itself could now see the appeal of Martha draped in a wicker chair, of Martha wielding a glue gun. They, too, could see the advertising dollars that might soon be flowing to them if they could get *Martha Stewart Living* to market. Now Time's brass wanted Martha to introduce them to the people at Kmart—to get some of those Martha Stewart ad dollars flowing into *Martha Stewart Living*. So what

Martha examining some coffee beans during her trip with Andy to visit Kathy and Chris Tatlock in Bogotá, Colombia, early 1970s. (*Photo credit:* Kathy Tatlock.)

Martha, towering over her husband, Andy, as Kathy took this shot of the couple during their excursion through the Colombian backcountry. (*Photo credit:* Kathy Tatlock.)

Martha poolside, Bogotá, Colombia. (*Photo credit*: Kathy Tatlock.)

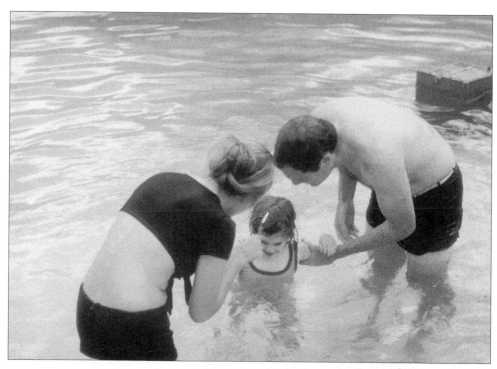

Martha, Alexis, and Andy Stewart, Bogotá, Colombia. (*Photo credit*: Kathy Tatlock.)

Poolside, Bogotá, Colombia. (*Photo credit:* Kathy Tatlock.)

Norma Collier, *Marie Claire*, early 1960s. (*Photo credit: Marie Claire* magazine. Reproduced with permission.)

Martha and Andy working at Turkey Hill, Westport, Connecticut, early 1970s. (*Photo credit:* Kathy Tatlock.)

Martha in her kitchen at Turkey Hill. (*Photo credit:* Kathy Tatlock.)

Martha, Westport, 1970s. (*Photo credit:* Kathy Tatlock.)

Martha with Kathy Tatlock and one of Martha's chow chows, at Turkey Hill. (*Photo credit:* Kathy Tatlock.)

Early Palais des Poulets (Palace of the Chickens), Turkey Hill.
(*Photo credit:* Kathy Tatlock.)

Robyn Fairclough, Martha's then assistant and Andy's future wife, Turkey Hill.
(*Photo credit:* Kathy Tatlock.)

In Westport in 1982, Martha and her friend and restaurant consultant, Ruth Leserman, of San Francisco, chop mushrooms while preparing dishes for a luncheon to celebrate the publication of Martha's new book, *Entertaining*. (*Photo credit:* AP/Wide World Photos.)

Martha and her daughter, Alexis, at "Avalon" premier, Metropolitan Museum, 1990. (*Photo credit:* Marina Garnier.)

Martha and *Time* magazine cover, early 1990s. (*Photo:* © Davis Factor/Corbis.)

Charlotte Beers, then chairman and CEO of advertising giant Ogilvy & Mather, in her office at the agency in New York in 1992. (*Photo credit:* AP/Wide World Photos.)

Charlie Rose and Martha celebrated his show going national at the Century Association, January 1993. (*Photo credit:* Marina Garnier.)

National Association of Television Program Executives (NATPE) Convention in Miami, January 1994. (*Photo:* © Savino Tony/Corbis Sygma.)

NATPE Convention in Miami with her producer, January 26, 1994.
(*Photo:* © Savino Tony/Corbis Sygma.)

Martha and real estate personality Mort Zuckerman at screening of
HBO film *Truman* in Sag Harbor, Long Island, August 1995.
(*Photo credit:* Marina Garnier.)

Martha and Sam Waksal celebrated the 100th anniversary of the Louis Vuitton monogram at the Mercer Hotel (then under construction) in New York, February 1996. (*Photo credit:* Marina Garnier.)

Martha and Time Warner publishing executive Don Logan met up at the Matrix Award lunch at the Waldorf Astoria, New York, April 1996. (*Photo credit:* Marina Garnier.)

Floyd Hall, then chairman and CEO of Kmart Corporation, chatted with Martha at Guild Hall in East Hampton, New York, prior to announcing a three-year alliance to design, market, and sell a line of bed and bath products, February 1997. (*Photo credit:* AP/Wide World Photos.)

Martha officially opened her new television studio and production facility at a media reception, April 1998, in Westport, Connecticut, as she posed with her two Chinese chow chows, Chin Chin and Paw Paw. (*Photo credit:* AP/Wide World Photos.)

Martha petted a hog while watching a 4-H show, August 1999, at the Iowa State Fair in Des Moines. (*Photo credit:* AP/Wide World Photos.)

Martha talked to an unidentified guest as they left a $5,000-a-person fund-raising lunch for seventy-five at the Long Island home of fashion designer Vera Wang, August 1999, in Southampton, New York. Proceeds from the lunch went to the U.S. Senate campaign of then First Lady Hillary Rodham Clinton of New York. (*Photo credit:* AP/Wide World Photos.)

Martha rang the opening bell to begin trading at the New York Stock Exchange, October 19, 1999. Joining Stewart on the bell podium were NYSE president William Johnston (left) and Martha Stewart Living Omnimedia president and chief operating officer, Sharon Patrick (right). The stock followed the market sharply higher in early trading. (*Photo credit:* Ray Abrams © AFP/Corbis.)

Martha laughed while talking with Specialist Barry Lyden (left) and Sharon Patrick (right) on the floor of the New York Stock Exchange at ceremonies held to mark the initial public offering of Martha Stewart Living Omnimedia shares. Lyden would trade the company's shares. (*Photo credit:* Peter Morgan, Reuters NewMedia Inc./Corbis.)

Martha and Susan Magrino attended the January 2000 antiques show at the Park Avenue Armory, New York City. (*Photo credit:* Marina Garnier.)

Martha and an unidentified friend at *All the Pretty Horses* premiere in New York City, December 2000. (*Photo credit:* © Pace Gregory/Corbis Sygma.)

Kmart's Angels, actress Jaclyn Smith (left), model Kathy Ireland (center), and Martha, pose for photographers at a Manhattan Kmart store where the company reintroduced the "Blue Light Special," April 2001. All three women have products sold under their names through Kmart. (*Photo credit:* AP/Wide World Photos.)

Martha leaves a book party for interior designer, Rose Tarlow, at the Four Seasons restaurant, New York, November 2001. (*Photo credit:* Marina Garnier.)

if she was a pain in the ass and an egomaniac. Who cared about that when she had shot the test numbers off the charts! The woman was gold.

When Martha had first sounded out Kmart with her magazine idea, she'd hit a brick wall. "I'm working on a magazine," she'd said at one point, suggesting that Kmart might have wanted to become a backer. "Uh oh," thought Barbara Loren-Snyder, with visions of Adams House II dancing before her, "I'd better alert Joe." She knew that they had to put a fast stop to this one.

Joe was emphatic. "The magazine cannot be a Kmart project," he had told her. They'd been down that road before, and he certainly didn't want Martha going to vendors like, say, Rubbermaid, and declaring, "I'm from Kmart, how about an ad?" As far as Joe was concerned, it had to be her magazine and only her magazine. Kmart was not going to be part of it.

But in the wake of the first test issue, everything changed. The numbers were too powerful, the audience too large. It was too good an opportunity to pass up. If Kmart couldn't be part of the deal, well, at least it could be an advertiser.

So, when Martha, Chris Meigher, and Isolde Motley caught a plane to Detroit in the wake of the market test for a get-together with Joe Antonini, he took one look at the presentation and said, "We'll take two spreads in every issue."

At a stroke, the synergy idea that Time Warner had used to justify its involvement with Martha had become more promising for Martha than it ever would be for either Time Warner or Kmart. She now had both her corporate backers fighting to drench her magazine with money, and the day would come when she'd buy the magazine back from Time Warner for $2 million of her own cash and sell it to Wall Street for $1 billion.

But all this activity represented only a small part of the frantic schedule that Martha was following. When she wasn't meeting with officials at Time Warner . . . or tossing off story ideas to Isolde

Motley . . ., or flying to Detroit to meet with Barbara Loren-Snyder and Joe Antonini, she was plugging her new magazine project on *Live with Regis & Kathie Lee* in New York . . . or opening a new Kmart on Long Island . . . or demonstrating how to marbleize Christmas ornaments in Detroit . . . or plugging her Christmas book before an audience in Cleveland . . . or hopping a flight for a Caribbean week in Saint Bart's.

By now, much of the work of actually running Turkey Hill was falling to others. She had been employing a Brazilian housekeeper from Bridgeport, named Necy Fernandes, for more than a decade. With the departure of Andy, who had done a lot of the draft mule work in her life from the start, she hired another Brazilian from Bridgeport—Renaldo Abreu—to replace him. Soon Renaldo was not only weeding in the garden but washing her cars, walking her dogs, and discharging all the other chores around the house that Andy had once performed. Meanwhile, Martha had her sister-in-law, Rita Christiansen, working as her bookkeeper and her mother, Martha Sr., as well as her baby sister, Laura, doing cooking, ironing, and other chores—a hidden, but growing, world of family members and immigrant retainers (whom she called her "maintainers") to free Martha from the chores of actually *being* the person she was claiming to be.

Of course, the work of putting on the *performance* of Martha Stewart had to be ten times more exhausting than actually being the real person, as tiring as even that had plainly been. Now came the speeches in Palm Beach and the appearances before the Junior League in San Francisco. There were the lectures, the signings, the filmings, the tapings. She had become one of the busiest, most hyperactive women in America.

At times, the energy level seemed almost frightening, as if motion alone was what mattered. She'd hop a plane to Anguilla for some sun, then decide after forty-five minutes on the ground that she "hated it" and hop over to Saint Bart's. Commenting on the frenzy became a kind of default-introduction for almost every public appearance she made. In December 1990, she appeared for the first time on *Live with Regis & Kathie Lee* and the show's host, Regis Philbin, introduced her this way, saying, "You must spend your whole day making, doing, buying, going through the woods, collecting filberts, and washing gravel. The woman never stops!" At that, the show's co-host, Kathie Lee Gifford, chirped in, "*She* is Martha Stewart, and you're not! And I'm not! And it makes me crazy!"

Thanks to Kmart and her ambitious drive, she had become one of the most recognized faces in America. She had gone way beyond weekly flyers and checkout counter handouts. Martha had moved on to TV commercials and talk show appearances. She had become ubiquitous, the face of the age. She had become so famous that, as the *New York Times* rightly pointed out, she no longer needed a last name. She had become simply "Martha"—a kind of Cher, or Madonna, or Jackie. In fact, she'd become more than that—not simply a one-word name, but a human adjective. Nobody would look at a sleazy, low-cut dress from Frederick's of Hollywood and say, "That's so Cher!" But just decorate a holiday centerpiece with gold-leaf pinecones and every woman at the table could be counted on to gaze admiringly on the display and declare, "Very Martha."

All the while, the angry and ugly streak in her nature—the Martha as Eddie Kostyra side of her, which until now had remained more or less hidden from the world at large—began almost inevitably to peek from behind the local curtain of Westport as she found herself increasingly in the public eye and the stress level mounted in the business of simply Being Martha.

People noticed when she snapped at waiters in restaurants or became abusive to someone in a department store or on an airplane. It had been one thing to snarl at the maître d' of a Chinese restaurant in the limited world of Westport, Connecticut, when she couldn't get a table. But it was another matter entirely to try to cut to the head of a movie line in New York and be instantly recognized by everyone else in the queue. Such "Martha sightings" eventually became standard grist for gossip columnists, and it was now that the gotcha-game began.

In December 1990, an observant, no-nonsense reporter for *New York* magazine, Jeannie Kasindorf, asked to fly to Cleveland with Martha for a profile on her exploding career. She had expected Martha to be on her best behavior during the trip because *New York* boasted an extremely high-impact readership in Manhattan media circles, where Martha had become one of the most closely watched people in the business. So Jeannie was astonished to behold, having scarcely boarded the flight at La Guardia airport, a side of Martha uncoil that no national journalist had ever before observed first-hand. Jeannie watched, transfixed, as the doyenne of domestic civility abruptly and furiously lashed into the man sitting next to her on the plane, who wouldn't move from his window seat so that Jeannie could sit next to her for the interview.

Martha's performance grew so disruptive that a stewardess intervened and arranged for the two women to move to other seats. As Martha rose to move, she declared loudly to the embarrassment of passengers all around her, "You know, in that crash [referring to a runway collision of two planes in Detroit the day before] . . . it was the people who were in the window seats who all died."

The Kasindorf article was an unwelcome watershed for Martha. Appearing as it did on the cover of *New York* magazine, with its author being a journalist who enjoyed a wide reputation for accuracy and thoroughness, the story introduced a new and permanently skeptical tone to press coverage of Martha as a person. She was portrayed as pushy, nasty, and self-absorbed, with a public relations minder named Susan Magrino, who was constantly getting her out of jams of one sort or another.

The story also set forth a version of Martha's life, courtesy of Martha herself, that she'd eventually come to regret and even attempt to rewrite. She described her work on Wall Street two decades earlier as "avant-garde" and "aggressive," and at the same time "very juvenile." Then oddly, while never referring to the troubles that her firm had stumbled into, she described herself as having been a "nervous wreck" by the time she departed Wall Street and confessed to actually waking up with hives from the stress of the situation.

She told of the arrival of Norma Collier in her life, offering a version of their relationship that Jeannie checked out with Norma, only to find that Norma had a completely different—and wholly less flattering—version of their relationship and why it ended.

In the profile, Martha came across as spiteful and angry at Andy as well, accusing him of timing his departure for its maximum disruption potential in her own life. She dismissed his postseparation request for a restraining order to keep her from going to his office as evidence that he was a "weak man . . . very weak," which contained an element of truth but sounded petty. The story even brought the couple's daughter, Alexis, on stage for the first time as a player in the drama, describing her as a "pouty, smart-ass version of Martha Stewart," who walked around in a cloud of permanent depression.

With the publication of the Kasindorf profile, it would no longer be possible for Martha to give a press interview almost anywhere without the resulting article making notice, one way or another, of the widening disconnect between the public image of Martha Stewart, and the private reality of the person who bore the name. Martha's response? To begin publishing her own version of the Martha Stewart Story, month after month, in the pages of the magazine she was preparing to launch, editing and reediting the facts of her life—as if they were nothing more than makeup on a fashion model—to suit the changing needs and expectations of the market over which she ruled.

14

Martha takes TV

In late February 1991, even as American troops were rolling through Kuwait in the Gulf War, copies of the second test issue of *Martha Stewart Living* were rolling off the presses and heading for newsstands. The purpose of the exercise: To reconfirm what Martha already knew—that demand for the Martha Stewart Message was all but insatiable. No one could quite nail down what the appeal of the magazine really was. Linda Jones, the marketing director of a home furnishings company, saw it this way: "warm feelings." The *Wall Street Journal* saw it as "fantasies for $3." The *New York Times* called it "the mauve-ing of America."

In fact, the sheer elusiveness of the answer identified the magazine's underlying appeal. This was more than just a fancy, four-color publication about arts and crafts in upscale American homes; this magazine somehow made women feel good about themselves—empowered them in some indefinable and encompassing way, to feel it was okay to be a woman. More than thirty years earlier, Hugh Hefner had launched a girlie magazine called *Playboy*, then spun an elaborate and windy series of essays around it that he called the "Playboy philosophy." Its purpose: to help men escape their guilt feelings about thumbing the pages of a magazine filled with subject matter in which they were genetically interested anyway.

But Martha wasn't about to be pinned down even to that. Her magazine wasn't just about warmth, or fantasies, or anything like that. Her magazine was about "demystification . . ." which meant "understanding," "knowledge," "power," and "control." These had been the words and the promise of the entire women's movement for the previous thirty years. Now, for the first time, these same words—and the same potent promise—were being wrapped around the images of femininity, domestic arts, and home life. Women everywhere were mesmerized by its appeal because *Martha Stewart Living* promised nothing less than the freedom to be themselves.

As expected, the second test was also a success, and in late May, Time Warner announced that it was signing a ten-year contract with Martha to publish her magazine. A company spokesman used the wheel-and-spokes concept that placed Martha at the center of the action—though the company wasn't prepared to let her drive solo. The spokesman said Time's own management team would be right there alongside Martha at the hub of the wheel.

But whether or not the Time Warner brass wanted to acknowledge it, Martha was already wriggling into the driver's seat. By July, she was making her first of six weekly appearances on the *Today* show, ostensibly to promote the magazine. And by the end of August, she was being renewed as a regular contributor on the show in her own right. "You do everything so well," sighed one of the show's cohosts, Faith Daniels, "If only I could be Martha Stewart in my next life."

Martha seemed to be living the lives of ten people already. Buying properties, undertaking renovations, she had begun darting back and forth from Westport to Long Island, often being flown in a private plane by the builder who had done the work on one of her projects—a fellow named Ben Krupinski. In the middle of all this, she paid $1.25 million for a 29.7-acre parcel of land ten minutes from her home on Turkey Hill Road, then constructed an enormous, forbidding stone wall that wrapped around much of the property.

Even as she was closing on the purchase of the property, yet another of her books came to market—*Martha Stewart's Gardening, Month by Month*—and she began an author's tour of signings, speeches, and appearances to promote it. Scarcely was that completed than she headed off for the Christmas holidays with her longtime PR person, Susan Magrino, who had by now left Crown Publishing to start her own firm. Days later, and she was back in East Hampton for a photography session. Scarcely was the camera crew packing up to leave than she was ushering in a painting crew to repaint the rooms. Next, she was jetting to Chicago for the thirtieth anniversary of the founding of Kmart, where she made yet more appearances, then headed for North Carolina to visit an open-air market. Then it was back to New York for an appearance at the Bronx Botanical Gardens.

Returning to Westport, Connecticut, she met with an editor from Crown to go over material for the print version of the Adams House renovation, which she was turning into a book under the title *Martha Stewart's New Old House*. After that came trips to Cleveland, to New York, to Houston, and elsewhere . . . in between which she squeezed in a tour of her gardens on Turkey Hill for forty local women. And none of that schedule includes numerous other junkets on Ben Krupinski's plane between Westport and East Hampton . . . or a planned trip to Shelter Island, New York, just for lunch . . . or television tapings and live-remotes from her home on Turkey Hill . . . or numerous appearances on the *Today* show . . . or an appearance on David Letterman's show in New York . . . or even one on *The Tonight Show* in California, for which she was paid only $1,138 (she turned up anyway because of the exposure it offered).

Many people would find it exhausting simply to hear about a schedule like the one Martha had begun to follow. But in fact, she was only getting warmed up. By the spring of 1993, Martha had burst free from the confines of the Time Life Building, where the magazine's staff had been housed, and had moved her activities to an office of her own on Forty-fourth Street. There she now shifted the entire operation into overdrive.

The magazine had already established itself as an enormous hit, with a circulation base that had jumped to 725,000 and continued to climb. But a magazine was only one of the spokes Martha wanted in her wheel, and now she began to turn her attention to the next one: a TV show of her own.

Though Time Warner didn't perceive what she was up to, she had already embarked on a plan that would take the millions in advertising and promotion that Time Warner and Kmart had showered on her over the years and turn it into a nationwide syndicated television show that would be hers alone. Once again, she was two steps ahead of the people she worked for, who never seemed to grasp that they weren't dealing with just another pretty face and a giant-sized ego. Behind the veneer of horse country gentility lurked a smart, success-obsessed, working-class street fighter from New Jersey. To the degree that her business partners were prepared to help her advance the success of Martha Stewart, she was prepared to work with them. To the degree they got in her way, she was willing to roll right over them.

Martha seemed to know little about the intricacies of finance. Nor had she shown herself to be a particularly adept money negotiator over the years, as evidenced by the way she'd walked straight into the pricing trap set by Barbara Loren-Snyder in their original talks over the compensation package Martha expected from Kmart. But she knew what she wanted from each business encounter—promotion for Martha Stewart—and she had no compunctions about cutting corners, throwing tantrums, and even tearing up contracts once she discovered that she could have gotten better terms. And because her value in the market always outweighed the personal frustration and pain that her business partners felt when encountering her lash, they—like most others in her life—kept coming back for more . . . and she kept getting her way.

The first media world executive who seems to have realized this about Martha, and used that insight to establish a smooth and profitable relationship with her, was a broadcasting executive named Richard Sheingold. At the start of the 1990s, Sheingold headed the television syndication business for Group W Inc., the one-time arm of Westinghouse Corporation that sold television programming to TV stations around the country. He presided over a chaotically cluttered suite of offices on Seventh Avenue, around the corner from the Time & Life Building and Rockefeller Center, and by a fluky set of circumstances, he looked up from his desk one day early in 1993 to find Martha Stewart staring back at him. She wanted Richard to market a TV show for her that would, of course, be about her as well.

Syndication of TV shows involved becoming, in effect, a sales agent for any number of TV production companies around the country. A TV company would produce a sample episode, or pilot, of a show, then the syndicator would try to line up TV stations across the country to broadcast the show for a certain number of episodes during the upcoming season. If enough stations could be lined up to reach a reasonably large audience of potential viewers, the syndicator would next try to round up advertisers for the program.

Under one desirable arrangement a "sponsor" would pick up a portion of the show's costs for the season. At the opposite extreme were so-called barter deals, in which the syndicator would have to give the local station a portion of the available commercial time in each episode just to get the station to carry it. There were almost limitless permutations on the two basic arrangements.

A television program that was being distributed in broadcast syndication was not as prestigious—or lucrative—a property as one being televised in the primetime evening hours between 8 P.M. and 11 P.M. on network TV. But it wasn't bad. Most non-news programming outside primetime hours was syndicated by outfits like Sheingold's Group W operation since local stations produced only limited amounts of programming on their own.

Over the years, the syndication market had produced huge hits. *The Price Is Right* had been a syndication blockbuster in earlier years. *Hollywood Squares* began as a syndicated offering. *Star Trek: The Next Generation* had been a syndie. So had *Geraldo Live*, which starred ABC newsman Geraldo Rivera. *Hard Copy*, *Jenny Jones*, *Baywatch*, and

Oprah were all syndies. There had also been many duds, forgotten the instant they went off the air.

This was the business in which Richard Sheingold worked. He made his living by signing up promising shows for syndication—and skipping the duds. If he passed on too many subsequent hits or wound up agreeing to promote too many duds, he would be looking for a new job, so he weighed his choices carefully and studied the opportunities in every deal. Group W syndication wasn't the biggest player in the game; at the start of the 1990s it was overshadowed by at least one major rival—Warner Brothers—but it was certainly a factor in the market. And as such, Sheingold looked at lots of deals and had a pretty good feel for what was being shopped around.

So it came as something of a surprise to him when one of his office employees came to him to say that a contact at Time Warner named Elizabeth McHaney wanted to meet with him to talk about an idea involving Time's new publishing superstar, Martha Stewart. "This ought to be interesting," thought Richard, "why not?"

At the meeting, Liz laid out a story that made Richard grow more intrigued with each new detail. It seemed that Time Warner, Inc.—by now the largest company in all of American media—had grown so large that it could no longer get out of its own way. Turf wars had broken out between the magazine side of the operation, headed by Time, and the TV syndication operation, which belonged to the Warner people. Was there an opportunity for Richard and Group W in all this? He listened intently as Liz told her tale.

Liz explained that she worked with Martha Stewart and that Martha wanted to do a weekly TV show based on her magazine, *Martha Stewart Living.* Unfortunately, said Liz, when the Time Inc. people took Martha's proposal to the Warner people, they were simply not interested even though the combined companies of Time and Warner were supposed to be paying for the merger through the very synergies that Martha's proposal represented.

Martha was apparently furious and had asked Liz to look around for another partner. Through a friend at Time Warner, Liz had gotten the name of Richard's associate at Group W, and now here she was.

Richard was interested, indeed. Competitive by nature, he could think of nothing better than to stick it to Time Warner, the big kahuna in the game, and snatch away a syndie deal from it. That the deal involved the hottest personality in all of magazine publishing—Martha Stewart—made it even better.

What's more, Richard was familiar with the syndication market for lifestyles and hearth-and-home programming because he had recently packaged a syndication deal for TV home-repair personality Bob Vila. Sears, Roebuck, which had already acquired Vila as a spokesperson, was now, thanks to Richard, sponsoring the show, titled *Bob Vila's Home Again*. Though Richard did not yet know much of anything about what Martha apparently had in mind, he was already considering whether the Vila deal might serve as a pattern for something involving Martha Stewart. Wasn't she a spokesperson for Kmart? If he handled things properly, this could develop into a Son of Vila/Sears!

"Sure," said Richard, "bring her over and let's have a chat," as he began to wonder just how big a deal this could actually become.

A few days later, Liz McHaney returned with Martha and the publisher of Martha's magazine, Eric Thorkilsen, for Martha to present her proposal to Richard Sheingold. Introductions were made, and Sheingold looked around for places for everyone to sit in the chaos of his office. Liz seemed a bit nervous about the situation, and Richard noticed a slight undercurrent of tension between Thorkilsen and Martha. But Martha herself seemed perfectly at ease—oblivious to the cluttered, messy surroundings, and interested only in the business she had come to discuss. She was, in a word, focused. Sheingold liked that.

Later, Sheingold learned just how contentious and brittle the relationship had become between Martha and her publisher, who seemed to resent her giant-sized ego and nonstop desire to position herself at the center of everything in the magazine. That may have been tolerable behavior within the Warner side of the organization, but the Time side had no tradition of working with stars on the payroll.

And Sheingold came to sense something else about the way Martha's colleagues handled her at Time: There was a slight but unmistakable—and ever-present—tone of condescension in their words, as if the members of the Time Inc. boys club wanted her to know that they still regarded her as nothing more than the fashion model she once had been, instead of the business executive she'd become.

In time, Sheingold invented a word for what they were doing to her. He didn't share the word with anybody, but it popped into his head every time he heard them belittling and dismissing her, in that certain way that would make Martha's jaw set and her face go cold. He'd hear them doing it—saying things like, "Martha's learning fast . . ." with Martha standing right there as if she were nothing but a piece of furniture, or "Martha knows we can't do that . . ." or "we've already discussed that with Martha . . ." as if she couldn't speak for herself. He'd hear that and he'd think, "They're chick-ing her again . . ." as in, "Martha's just some pain-in-the-ass chick we've got to put up with . . ." Chick-ing her. They didn't understand that "chick-ing" her was why Martha was now standing in Richard's office, trying to get her idea for a TV show based on a Time Warner magazine syndicated on TV by one of Time Warner's own competitors. Chick-ing Martha Stewart was a mistake.

Richard wasn't entirely sure who Martha really was—was she just some super Betty Crocker figure, or a kind of performance art creation like Madonna? Maybe she was a bit of both. Whatever she was, he could tell immediately that she was there to get answers to only one question: How could she get her show on the air?

She obviously didn't know the first thing about syndication, so Richard began to explain to her that the arithmetic worked against such a show . . . that to make a profit it would need to be cleared on lots of stations, reaching more than 70 percent of the TV viewing audience in the country. Also, the ad market was weak and the production costs in TV were high; and although Group W would be happy to distribute the show for a share of the revenues, it wouldn't be interested in helping to finance its production.

Even as he was talking, he began to realize what a long shot this really was. He thought, "We'll do everything exactly right, and get this on the air all over the country, and get advertisers and everything—and she'll *still* lose a fortune. This babe doesn't know what she's getting into . . ." But Martha cut him off.

"I don't care about that," she said. "That's not the point. The whole idea is cross-promotion to prop up the brand."

It was a concept Richard hadn't heard before, and it brought him up short. *I don't care about losing money?* That was a great attitude to bring to the game. In TV-land you could turn a big fortune into a small one in no time at all by thinking that way. TV shows were supposed to *make* money—or what was the point of putting them on the air? But here was this woman saying she didn't care whether it lost money, that the whole purpose of the exercise was to promote "the brand." The brand? What would that be? The magazine? Or would it be Martha instead? Now he was really confused.

There were other obstacles as well. He explained that it wasn't easy to get even a once-a-week show on the air these days because time slots were so scarce. About all that was left were the weekends, but even they were now disappearing because the stations were filling up their slots with hour after hour of paid "infomercial" programming—exercise machines, food preparation machines, self-improvement tapes. The stations loved them because they got paid to air them, so who cared whether the audience tuned in or not?

The advertising problem was significant, too. If the show didn't draw an audience, it was going to be hard to attract advertisers. And it was hard to get the audience if you couldn't get stations to put it on the air. "I just want you to understand the realities of the situation," Richard said. "This will not be that easy."

But Martha had her answer ready. "I'll sell my own ads," she said. "I don't need the help of Group W." She explained that she had a closer relationship with her advertisers than Group W would have because they were already advertising in her magazine, so she could get more money by selling both outlets at once.

The meeting ended with an agreement to continue the discussion. But in the days that followed, Richard turned Martha's words over and over in his mind, as he tried to zero in on what she was driving at. What was it that she was really after? The bit about not caring if the show lost money just didn't make sense. But she'd obviously given the matter plenty of thought, or else why would she have said that she'd be willing to sell her own ads? That could wind up losing her even more money!

Exactly when the lightbulb finally went on, Richard couldn't say. An hour later, a day later? He didn't know. All he knew was that at some point he got it. At some point, he realized what she was trying to do. She wasn't thinking of her TV show as a normal program at all. No, she was thinking of the whole thing as a kind of stealth infomercial . . . a half-hour show that was really a commercial in disguise.

It was brilliant; in fact, it was a stroke of genius. And from the moment he realized what she had in mind, that is exactly how he began thinking of her as well—as Martha Stewart the genius. It was so simple, and so obvious . . . and so *smart*. She intended to syndicate a half-hour commercial disguised as an actual program, and she was going to cut its cost of production by sticking commercials from her own advertisers right in the show. It was awesome! A commercial inside an infomercial. It was even better than that, for the infomercial would be promoting Martha . . . who would be cross-promoting the magazine . . . that would be carrying the ads . . . of the companies that would be advertising on the show! An arrangement like that could spiral right into outer space.

It blew Richard away. This woman was bringing him one of the most original and provocative marketing ideas he'd ever heard of—and why? Apparently because no one at Time Warner seemed to have the foggiest idea what she'd been talking about—either that, or they just hadn't wanted to listen. Well, Richard Sheingold wasn't going to make *that* mistake. He wasn't going to chick Martha Stewart; he was going to do a deal with her instead. He was going to make a lot of money from it, and then he was going to sit back and watch as the people at Time Warner squirmed. How would they explain that they'd let her get away? What would they say? That they'd chick-ed a genius right out the door?

On January 19, 1993, Group W Productions, Inc., announced that it had signed a deal with Martha Stewart and a subsidiary of Time Inc., called Martha Stewart Living Television, to syndicate a half-hour broadcast television series. The announcement had quoted the president of Group W Productions, Derk Zimmerman, in effusive praise of Martha, but the spark plug in the deal had been Richard Sheingold.

The series was described as offering viewers "a unique combination of inspiration and how-to information on entertaining, cooking, gardening, restoring, collecting, homekeeping, and decoration." Yet the real significance in the announcement was not the show's content but the promotional focus of the whole package. Just like Martha's magazine, the series was to be called *Martha Stewart Living*. And just like the magazine, it was to star Martha Stewart—described by Derk Zimmerman expansively, if somewhat vaguely, as "the foremost lifestyle authority."

Meanwhile, Martha left no doubt how she felt about the company that was financing the magazine and the TV production; within months of the Group W announcement, she had vacated the Time & Life Building and moved into her own offices on Forty-fourth Street. It was Martha's way of saying—to borrow the words of Richard Sheingold, and perhaps the petulance of a Richard Nixon—the men of Time Inc. weren't going to have Martha Stewart to chick around any more.

The company's most famous employee had simply walked out the door, leaving Time Warner with no choice but to keep financing her fame, the price of which would eventually include a chauffeur-driven Chevrolet Suburban, a $40,000 annual clothing allowance, a hair-and-makeup allowance, and, reportedly, even a $2 million loan to buy a second home in East Hampton, Long Island. No editor or writer in the history of the corporation had ever been treated so grandly. Her $400,000 base salary seemed like mere chicken scratchings when weighed against the millions annually that Time Warner was soon spending to celebrate her "personal perspective" on her life as a woman. On the other hand, no writer or editor in the history of Time Warner had ever before become an authentic super-star—the evidence of which Richard Sheingold of Group W was about to witness firsthand.

The occasion was the 1993 National Association of Television Programming Executives (NATPE) convention in San Francisco on January 26 and 27. These conventions are the high point of the year for the broadcast television industry, with every corporation in the business—from the largest broadcast networks to the most obscure and lightweight independent producers and agents—setting up exhibits on the convention floor. The exhibits range from small-time displays of little more than a few folding tables and some leaflet handouts to enormous miniconvention centers all by themselves, with more than 3,000 square feet of floor space, multiple interior offices and conference rooms, theaters, dining suites, and lots of assistants in miniskirts.

In these palaces within palaces, the exhibitors would put their stars on display, waiting to shake hands, make small talk, and have their pictures taken with any network or other industry executives who dropped by. Geraldo Rivera was a regular of the Tribune Corporation syndication service, which regarded him as a star and had been offering his series, *Geraldo Live*. Across the floor, visitors could get their photos taken with Jerry Seinfeld and the cast of his comedy blockbuster, *Seinfeld*. At the King World exhibit, you could meet Oprah Winfrey. There were *Baywatch* babes galore at the All American Television exhibit.

The mood of the 1993 convention was energized, upbeat, with signs of opulence and extravagance everywhere. The recession of the Gulf War was over, and people were wandering the floor looking to do deals. Advertising dollars were beginning to flow again, and executives were anxious to bring home the next breakout hit—to return from NATPE with the show that had "caught lightning."

Unfortunately, Richard Sheingold was in a funk. His company, Group W, had spent close to $2 million on its exhibit, and he wasn't at all sure how successful it would be. His big act was Vicki Lawrence, the former second banana on the *Carol Burnett Show*, who had spun off the character she'd played in the show—an amusingly smart-mouthed old lady named "Mama"—into a TV series of her own. Now she'd gotten Group W to syndicate a daytime talk show for her called simply *Vicki!*," and Sheingold, who didn't think she was very witty, but did think she had an attitude problem, was concerned about how well it would do. Group W also represented *Teenage Mutant Ninja Turtles* and *PM Magazine*—and he expected both to do well.

But Richard's big hope—at least on a personal basis—had rested with *Martha Stewart Living*. It was not until almost the very eve of the convention that he'd finally gotten a look at the pilot—the sample episode that any station executive would have to see before signing a deal. And now that Richard himself had finally seen it, he felt sick to his stomach.

Actually, it was even worse than that. "This thing is a loser," he said to himself as the scenes rolled past. The show was sappy, tedious, like a visit for grown women to *Mister Rogers' Neighborhood*. But there was something else; it seemed to conjure a world of fantasy satisfactions that no one actually experienced—at least no one

Richard knew. The worst segment of all showed Martha wandering in her gardens, advising viewers not to cut their roses at the height of the noon hour or the flowers would wilt. Instead, said Martha as she gently snipped the stems, you should cut them in the cool of the afternoon, when the first dew of evening glistens on the petals.

"What?" thought Richard. This was crazy. He had to sell this show to station managers in places like Cleveland and Detroit. *Don't cut your roses until there's dew on the petals.* They didn't even have gardens in those places!

Richard Sheingold fancied himself a competitive person, and he hated to lose. But maybe this had all been a great big mistake. In the ad game, they say you can lead a dog to the dog food, but you can't make him eat it. And that's what he was up against now. Who was going to eat thirty minutes of How to Cut Your Roses dog food in Detroit? This was a suicide mission. The next segment was something about how to make compost heaps, but by now Richard had stopped watching.

He turned to Martha. "I'm not sure I can sell this," he said. "I mean, maybe we can sell it, but I'm not sure we'll get renewals." A sense of desperation was creeping into his words as he said, "Martha, I mean, look, the people in the cities where we have to sell this show are in urban environments. They're working-class people. These people don't even *have* gardens."

Martha looked back at him. Her voice was even and cool, conveying the total confidence in her words as she said, "Yes, but they want them."

That night Richard felt fitful and restless, and he didn't sleep well. The next day was the start of the convention, and he had a couple of errands to run, which meant he was going to arrive late. Maybe if he ran a few more errands he wouldn't have to show up at all. He didn't know what to expect. Vicki Lawrence? Teenage

Mutant Ninja Turtles? The Group W exhibit could turn out to be the laughingstock of the convention.

It was midmorning when he finally arrived, and people were everywhere. Visitors were crowding the Columbia booth to meet the cast of the *Seinfeld* show, including Jerry himself. Talk show personality Ricki Lake was out there somewhere. So were Montel Williams, Jenny Jones, Rush Limbaugh, and many others. King World had even brought in Elton John. And what did Group W have? Mama and turtles and how to cut your roses. He sighed and continued on, through the mass of people, toward the Group W exhibit.

Then he noticed something . . . the thickening crowd. A few seconds more and he realized what was happening. The crowd . . . it was gathered around . . . the Group W exhibit! He couldn't believe it. What was this all about? Had something happened inside? But as he grew closer he realized . . . it was the crowd . . . there was something about them . . . they were . . . *all women!* There were hundreds of them, spilling out of the exhibit and onto the floor. All waiting to get inside. And as he pushed his way through, he saw why. There before him, at a desk, surrounded by dozens of women pressed up against her, was Martha. They wanted to talk to her, touch her, just somehow *communicate.* None of them wanted to leave. Richard looked around and his eyes fell on a security guard. The security guard looked back and smiled, then shrugged, as if to say, "Hey, what do you want from me?" And Richard thought, "Oh my God, this must be what it's like. I'm watching the birth of a star."

By May 1993, *Martha Stewart Living* had been sold to stations in 80 cities, covering 75 percent of the American television viewing audience, and the series was green-lighted for full production. By September, the show's coverage had been boosted to 82 percent of the nation, with 126 stations and the Lifetime Network on cable TV agreeing to carry the series. The show itself debuted to generally bad reviews, with critics zeroing in on exactly the things Richard Sheingold had feared. "This isn't living, it's working," carped one reviewer. "We'd say Martha's working, but the show is not," sniped another.

You could not have proved it by the numbers, though. By its fourth season, *Martha Stewart Living* had grown to 182 stations, in 185 markets, covering 97 percent of the country. By spring 1996, it was the most popular women's program on morning television, with one in ten of all television sets in use in the nation being tuned to Martha whenever she was on. That autumn, the show moved from a weekly half-hour format to a daily half-hour format. In defiance of critics who warned that Martha was growing so overexposed she was becoming almost a parody of herself, her popularity on TV soared even more. Within three months of debuting in its daily format, *Martha Stewart Living's* ratings jumped 10 percent over its ratings in the earlier weekly format, and by the end of 1998, 60 percent of the stations were repeating the show as soon as it ended, to fill up an entire hour of morning programming, so the show moved from a half-hour format to a full hour. From thirty minutes once a week, it had gone to sixty minutes five times a week, and *still* the ratings climbed.

It was as if Martha had become the video version of elevator music; as women all over America would get up, flip on the TV, and go about their mornings with the calming, enveloping words of Martha in the background. The tone was comforting, controlling; and the music of the show's composer Keb Mo, which opened and closed every scene, also set a peaceful and gentle mood, like the rustling of leaves in the high branches of a tree or the sound of waves lapping on the sand.

The show was built around themes—a cooking segment, an arts and crafts segment, a gardening segment. The message was inspirational: You can do this! You can strive for excellence in your life as a woman. You can have gardens like these . . . or set a dinner table like this one . . . or restore a breakfront to the elegance of these pieces.

But the tasks themselves were never threatening, and rarely even challenging. It was like watching *Sesame Street* for grown women. Here is Martha on her knees in her garden, patting the earth around some newly planted seeds. Here she is inside her house, tenderly placing bubble-wrap packaging around a boxed houseplant to prepare it for transport to a new home. You can do this! You can strive for excellence in your life as a woman. You can place bubble-wrap packaging around a houseplant and wind up with six acres of roses and regular guest appearances on David Letterman's show and *Today*. The effect was comforting, reassuring, almost hypnotic in the stress-free world it conjured forth.

And just as Richard Sheingold had expected, the men at Time Warner were soon freaking out over the money that was slipping through their fingers. They wanted *Martha Stewart Living* back, and Sheingold started sniffing out maneuvers and schemes to get her syndication deal back from Group W.

Sheingold would hear rumors of their plots at sales meetings and conferences. They were making promises to Martha that he feared would turn her head. By now, Martha was not simply a television superstar: She had such enormous name recognition and cachet that other superstars were dropping her name as someone they knew. Corporate CEOs started inviting her to their parties just to say she was coming. He wondered if Time Warner might flatter her so much that they'd actually lure her back. He knew that if the Time Warner people had been distributing her show they probably would have ruined it, by insisting that segments on compost heaps and rose cutting be dropped to make it more salable. Richard knew that, but did Martha?

He grew particularly concerned after the show had been on the air for two years and Martha asked him to arrange a breakfast meeting for her with his entire sales staff. The occasion was the 1995 NATPE convention, which this time was being held in Las Vegas, and Richard wasn't sure what to expect.

Things certainly didn't get off to a smooth start as the staff gathered for breakfast to discover that Martha had tapped the hotel's owner, Steve Wynn, to lay on a "Chinese breakfast" for the group. Richard and his staff sat down at the table to find themselves staring down, at 8 o'clock in the morning, at plates of steamed cabbage, rice, and various things in colloidal sauces that looked like mucus.

He felt instantly nauseous. He didn't want to be eating stuff like that for breakfast. Richard Sheingold was a big, beefy American male, who'd lifted weights in college and liked to suck in his stomach and look at himself sideways in the mirror. He wanted hash browns for breakfast, with a nice solid slice of grilled ham and some o.j. and coffee. He didn't want to be bellying up to a breakfast of green tea and something that looked like a bowl of snot.

Martha was seated next to him, and one by one she handed him plates as the various dishes circulated around the table. It all looked disgusting. Red food. Purple food. Richard didn't want to eat something purple or green when he was still trying to wake up. He wanted something made out of meat! A cup of coffee and a plate of meat and he was good to go. But this shit? It was going to wreck his whole day.

Finally, Martha handed him a plate with something that looked like it might at least have some meat *in* it—some egg roll-looking things with something that might have been sausages sticking out of the ends. He skewered one with his fork and put it on his plate, and passed the dish along. Martha eyed him disapprovingly and said, "It appears Richard only eats brown food . . ." and continued handing along the plates, and Richard thought, "Oh boy, here we go . . ."

But to his relief, the only thing on Martha's mind was that his staff should work harder . . . run faster . . . sign up more stations. That was the Martha Stewart he liked, was comfortable with, and knew how to relate to . . . the Martha Stewart who said, Okay, never mind about the food, let's just talk business. And apparently, she wasn't being won over by Time Warner.

In the company of women

A s the 1990s unfolded, Martha had become more than one of the most famous people in America, she was also an enormously successful businessperson. But her business had grown so rapidly, spreading out chaotically in so many different directions that it had become almost unmanageable. Martha was as famous as any Hollywood star, and already richer than most. But the nearest thing she had to an actual business manager was her sister-in-law, Rita, who handled her bookkeeping out of Martha's original catering offices in a rundown section of Westport near the train station.

Keeping track of Martha and her activities would have been a full-time job for an entire office of workers. And keeping accurate records of her whereabouts was important for two reasons. As a public figure who had built a business based on the activities of her private life, almost everything she did or said, and everywhere she went—almost every waking minute of her life—had potentially large and important tax implications, both positive and negative, depending on how one wanted to view those activities.

Moreover, much of Martha's carefully cultivated image as a supercompetent, self-actualized, can-do achiever was based on the presumed orderliness of her personal affairs. Her magazine even included a combined calendar of her personal and business commitments for the month ahead, as an example to her readers that if she could keep track of a schedule as complicated as hers, then they could certainly discipline themselves to do the same thing with theirs.

But just offstage, her personal records were so disorganized—and multiplying so rapidly—that not even her own business manager, Rita, could be sure where she was much of the time. For example, was Martha actually living—even temporarily—in her East Hampton home in early 1992? And if so, was it for business or personal purposes? No one really knew. Despite her public performance as a precisely organized person who made every minute count, Martha did not even keep an accurate day planner of her whereabouts. Far from being well organized, she seemed instead to be leading the life of a disorganized workaholic who rushed from one meeting to the next, leaving skid marks all over town.

When Martha received a questionnaire from the New York State Department of Taxation in May 1994, she had many more pressing matters to deal with, and simply handed it off to Rita to take care of as she continued with her ever more hectic schedule. It was not the last that she'd hear of the matter though, because her name had come to the attention of the Department as someone who might be owing New York State income taxes—a lot of taxes—as a nonresident taxpayer who was conducting much of her business in the state but not paying taxes on the proceeds. And once investigators discovered just how inadequate her records really were, they decided to probe further.

The disorganization in Martha's personal affairs simply mirrored a larger disorganization that loomed over her business as well. By autumn 1993, Martha was the editor of one of the most closely watched—and rapidly growing—magazines in America. She was the author of ten books, the star of her own hit TV show and six videotapes, and a regular guest on *Oprah*, David Letterman's show, and *Today*. She was a one-person media conglomerate, the largest cottage industry in America. But there was no structure to the business, no organizational plan or direction, just an amoebalike thing that kept moving out through the media in all directions. Some of her assets were tied up with her books and her contracts with Crown Publishing; others were wrapped up in her deal with Kmart. Part of her magazine business was under her own control and part was controlled by Time Warner, which also had an interest in her TV show, as for that matter did Group W. And every day, it grew more complicated, as more and more ideas seemed to fly out of her in all directions. She needed someone to help her pull it all together, give it a shape and a focus. Maybe she knew that if she could just get her arms about her own business, she could probably make it ten times bigger than it already was.

The person who wound up helping Martha do that was a former partner at the New York management consulting company of McKinsey & Company, the whitest of white-shoe management consulting firms, whose alumni, such as Lou Gerstner at IBM, often landed as CEOs of major corporations. This McKinsey alum, named Sharon Patrick, was the daughter of a middle-class family headed by a United Airlines sales manager, who had grown up in the opportunity-drenched sunshine of Southern California in the 1950s. She was voted "most likely to succeed" by her high school classmates, thereafter enrolling in Stanford University, from which she graduated in 1967, as the 1960s were reaching their final, convulsive blowout.

Her resume reads like a person possessed of a high sense of self-confidence, and mostly it seems to have been well-placed. Within three years of graduating college, she was leading a successful Title VII sex discrimination suit against the firm where she worked. From there, she moved briefly to a post in the Carter Administration, after which she earned an MBA at Harvard, then landed at McKinsey. She soon was made a partner, leaving the firm to become the chief operating officer (COO) of a cable TV programming company. She then stepped aside to start her own consulting firm, the Sharon Patrick Company.

There were two views on Sharon and her career. Some people regarded her as an opportunistic climber who couldn't hold a job. Others viewed her as smart, impatient, and ever on the lookout for the next mountain to climb. The facts of her career lent themselves to either interpretation, and perhaps both were partly true.

Sharon was a friend of a New York socialite named Sandra Pittman, the wife of Robert Pittman, a fast-rising media executive who was the founder of MTV.* Sandra, in turn, fancied herself something of an outdoorswoman, and had gathered around her a group of friends with similar interests. Among them was Martha, who had become part of the Pittman circle, and had begun turning up at the parties of another New York couple-around-town, the Kenneth and Katherine Lerers who were friends of the Pittmans. Through this set of associations, Sandy, Martha, Katherine, and Sharon all wound up getting together in September 1993 on an expedition organized by Sandy to climb Mount Kilimanjaro, the highest peak in Africa. Later, Sharon described her trek up the mountain as a bonding experience with Martha as the two women talked for six days almost uninterruptedly about Martha's plans for her company and her apparent confusion about how to bring them to fruition. Sharon had the answers.

Within three months of descending from the mountain, Sharon was counseling Martha on how to reorganize her business, and, eventually, helping her—in the best tradition of a McKinsey consultant—to rewrite her relationship with Time Warner. By the start of 1996, Sharon was rewriting the terms all over again, even as she was doing the same thing with Martha's Kmart deal. Sharon was, in fact,

---

*As a young man at the start of the 1980s, Bob Pittman had conceived an idea for a music-based programming service for cable TV. The service, which was dubbed "Music TV," and then eventually "MTV," played short video clips of rock stars lip-synching their songs. The clips were produced and distributed by record companies to promote their new releases, and cable TV operators seized on the service quickly, seeing it as a kind of Hamburger Helper programming to fill up unused channel space on their cable systems. The service became an instant hit with young people, giving Pittman clout as a man with a perceived golden touch in the infant industry of cable programming.

creating the business Martha eventually took public—Martha Stewart Living Omnimedia, Inc.—in a Wall Street IPO that would make Sharon a wealthy woman as well.

Sharon Patrick was a godsend to Martha in many ways because almost as soon as Sharon became involved in her life, Martha's business affairs began to shape up—particularly as they related to Time Warner. For the first time in her relationship with the company, the balance of power began to tilt sharply and decisively in her favor. Sharon showed her how to take control of the entire relationship, from beginning to end, then guided her through actually doing it.

Martha had felt for nearly a year that she should be getting more out of her relationship with Time Warner than she was. With perks on top of a base salary of $400,000, she was making $750,000 a year, and she wanted more than that—a lot more. And she also wanted to be taking less abuse from their belittling, jealous executives than she was—a lot less. She had even traced the pivotal "I've had it" moment in her mind to the previous New Year's Eve, December 31, 1993. She had been sitting alone in a friend's ski chalet in Aspen, Colorado, watching the snow fall outside, when the realization came to her that she simply couldn't take it anymore . . . that she had to do something about the situation with Time Warner.

As she saw it, her magazine was a huge success, and it was basically all her own doing because the people at Time hadn't been supportive of her from the start. It was the same with the TV show: big hit, no thanks to Time Warner. And yet those people were taking an enormous free ride on her labors when all they'd done (besides financing the projects) was put her down and mock her.

Well, she wasn't "just little Martha" anymore, was she? Now she was an out-and-out star, and she'd actually begun thinking and referring to herself as "a star." She wanted people around her who viewed her that way—people who looked up to her, instead of down at her like the men at Time Warner had done. Like that Eric Thorkilsen person she'd been forced to work with. How awful was he! Well, she shouldn't have had to be putting up with people like that. She wanted the negative forces out of the picture, not dragging along behind her wherever she went, trying to hold her back in everything she wanted to do. She wasn't "good old Martha" anymore.

The Time Warner people didn't fully grasp what she was trying to accomplish—to make herself bigger and bigger and eventually omnipresent in the media. They never got the point—that *she* was the message, *she* was the subject matter, *she* was the brand . . . with the magazine, with the TV show, with everything. Worse than that, when they finally did seem to sense where she was going, they began working to hold her back. Why should she have to put up with that? Didn't they see? She'd been right from Day One—they'd been totally and completely wrong—and frankly, five years had been plenty long enough time for them to have gotten the message. Why should she have to keep trying to educate them over and over again, year after year? They'd missed the boat, and she'd had it; it was simple as that.

The problem was, she hadn't known how to go about it—how to get control of the situation and make things happen . . . not *their* way but *her* way. She'd already talked about the situation with an influential female business leader in the media named Charlotte Beers. Martha had met Charlotte earlier in Chicago and had struck up a friendship with her. Charlotte had thereafter moved to New York to take over as head of the Ogilvy & Mather advertising agency and had spent much time as a houseguest in East Hampton. Thereafter, the two women had taken long, soulful walks along the East Hampton beach, past the imposing, multimillion-dollar beachfront "cottages" of business world figures like Ronald Perelman, the owner of Revlon Corporation, and his neighbor, Mortimer Zuckerman, a real estate developer who'd gained media world cache by acquiring *U.S. News & World Report* magazine and, eventually, the New York *Daily News*.*

Martha had found Charlotte a captivating personality—the first real business mentor she'd ever had. Charlotte had been able to zero in on Martha's core weaknesses, and at least get her to recognize them, if not actually fix them. Like a physician helping a patient to self-minister to her own afflictions, she was counseling Martha, in effect, on the first rule of the Hippocratic oath: At least do no harm. Martha needed to become a better communicator, or the standoff with the Time people would only get worse. Martha knew she needed help. In her dealings with people, she was too forceful and direct. Too blunt. In the world of business, that kind of approach just turned people off. Charlotte told Martha that to get what she was seeking from people, she needed to stop thinking in terms of what she wanted to *say* and to start thinking in terms of the response she wanted to *get*.

Sharon Patrick helped her figure out what that response was, and Sharon Patrick guided the negotiations that got the result. Sharon told her to sit down and write up an actual vision statement of where she wanted her company to go, and the role that Martha envisioned for herself in the process. Finally, Sharon sat down with her and helped her draft the actual document.

The statement amounted to a succinct summation of everything that the Time Warner brass found most detestable about Martha, from her arrogant and almost messianic ego to her controlling, authoritative personality as a self-defined "leader and teacher." But the statement also explicitly set forth the revolutionary vision of exactly what Martha sought to create: a company dedicated to marketing its

---

*Martha was eventually invited by Perelman to join the board of directors of Revlon Corp., which she did. She thereafter expressed bemusement to the author at the company's lax top management, reporting that on one occasion she attended a meeting of the Revlon board in the late 1990s as the company's fortunes deteriorated, only to learn that no one around the table except herself knew the name of Revlon's most popular lipstick shade that season.

own CEO as a living, breathing human brand. The goal: to reach all women everywhere, by manufacturing and distributing celebratory lifestyle messages about the CEO through every major media channel on earth—from print publishing to television, from multimedia to merchandizing.

Having people like Sharon and Charlotte in her camp gave Martha confidence that this could actually happen. They seemed to ratify her vision—to authenticate the idea that she could take the whole of American womanhood by the hand and lead it to a better, more fulfilling life of "family-oriented values," "excellent taste," and "quality ideas," in short, the value structure and lifestyle that she claimed as her own.

This is where Martha Stewart had been heading for the past fifty years—to a world where everything was elegant and gilded, where no one raised his voice in anger, where people drank from long-stem crystal goblets, and where no woman needed to feel inferior for not being a man. Two women who had already reached the top in business were telling her that she could take this mesmerizing vision, which had energized her whole life, and get to the top of the mountain as well. She could turn the celebration of herself into an entire corporation, with media messages in all channels of communication all the time: messages about herself that she could control. They'd be messages that would not only sell books and magazines but merchandise as well—and no longer for the benefit of Kmart, Time Warner, and Crown Publishing. Now the beneficiary of her marketing onslaught could become Martha herself.

The job of actually hammering out the details of a revised business contract with Time Warner fell to the third person on Martha's dream team, a gnomelike entertainment lawyer named Allen Grubman,* who was known as New York's "lawyer to the

---

*Eventually, Grubman would become known to the general public as the father of a nightclubbing young New York public relations personality named Elizabeth Grubman, who in July 2001 backed her father's Mercedes into a crowd of people waiting outside a Southampton, New York, discothèque, injuring 16 of them, then left the

stars." A graduate of Brooklyn Law School who had earned a reputation as a tenacious arguer as well as a deft handler of the tender
vanities of celebrity clients, Grubman had represented everyone
from Michael Jackson and Bruce Springsteen, to Billy Joel and
Madonna. As compensation, he typically took a 1 percent to 3 percent share in the proceeds of any contract he negotiated and was
so relentless in representing his clients' interests that he was said to
follow his adversaries into the men's room and continue arguing
with them through the closed door of a bathroom stall. His motto
was, "You don't ask, you don't get   "

One of Grubman's biggest coups—which instantly endeared him
to Martha—was his successful negotiation of a contract between
his pop music client Louise Ciccone (aka Madonna) and Warner
Records, Inc., a Time Warner operation. In the deal, Madonna went
from being just another Warner recording artist to becoming a 50/50
joint venture partner with Warner; she had her own record label,
music publishing business, and film production company. In a sense,
Madonna was the best example available as to what Martha was after,
and Allen Grubman seemed to be the man who could deliver the deal.

By the start of 1995, Martha had her contract—a complete re-
structuring of her relationship with Time Warner so that Martha
would now become the CEO of something to be called Martha
Stewart Enterprises—in effect a separate company within Time
Warner, with Martha at its head. There would be merchandizing
opportunities for consumer product spin-offs, as well as opportunities in the exploding new world of the Internet There would be
CDs, more TV, and on and on . . . and Time Warner would be paying the tab. A further part of the deal featured an offer for a so-
called phantom equity arrangement in which Martha could wind up

---

scene. The case gained instant attention worldwide as an example of the presumed
decadence of affluent and overindulged young people such as Elizabeth Grubman appeared to be. On September 12, 2001, a New York grand jury indicted her on 26 criminal counts, including assault and drunken driving. She pleaded not guilty, and at the
time this book went to press was awaiting trial.

receiving a cash payment, by one reckoning, of perhaps as much as $30 million by 2004; she rejected the offer as unacceptable.

Now even Time Warner was treating her like a star, with her clothing allowance, a car and driver, and even that reported $2 million loan with which to purchase her second house in East Hampton, to add to her growing collection of residences.

M artha's success in the marketplace now gave her the resources to surround herself with bright and talented people like Sharon Patrick and Allen Grubman, who could increasingly wrap her in a cocoon of supportive counseling while effectively managing her affairs. Martha's value as a marketing commodity was becoming so enormous that the people who gathered around her to enhance her worth were willing to give her needs their undivided attention because they stood to gain so much as well.

One of these Martha Minders was her public relations assistant, Susan Magrino. Like Martha and Sharon Patrick, she was a blonde with a freshly scrubbed, white-bread look. And like them, she pursued a highly visible gal-on-the-go schedule, darting from one see-and-be-seen meeting to the next.

Susan had worked as a book publicist at Crown Publishing for many years. But by 1992, the demands of their single biggest author, Martha, had grown so time-consuming that Susan left Crown and started her own agency, which enabled her to focus on all aspects of Martha's activities.

Since then, Susan had added a select list of other clients who, for one reason or another, wanted to have themselves shown in a certain way in the press. Unlike some public relations people, who measured their success by how often they could get a client's name in the press, Susan prided herself on how successfully she could control the spin of a client's coverage in the news or even, when necessary, keep the client out of the papers altogether. Her client list ranged from Martha herself, to the ultrafashionable and expensive Lutèce

Restaurant on Manhattan's East Side, and even the editor-in-chief of *Harper's Bazaar*, Elizabeth Tilberis.

Gossip columnists did not particularly like Susan Magrino, in no small part because she was skilled at controlling access to—and managing the facts about—her clients, typically with an incessantly positive and sunny response to every question reporters asked. "She's totally positive, and everything is always 'great' and 'wonderful,'" said one. She was also not above giving out subtle bribes in the form of freebie gifts and favors to help assure a columnist's cooperation. Free $250 salon treatments, free dinners at swanky restaurants, free books by her author clients—often the latest offering from Martha, with a note attached reading, "Martha wanted you to have this." Kill them with kindness was Susan's strategy, and she almost always bagged her prey.*

Eventually, as Susan's client list grew, gossip columnists began playing games among themselves to see who could be the first to spot Susan's fingerprints on a planted item in a colleague's column—and to guess what her next move might be in advancing her clients' interests.

One of Susan's clients was a New York based celebrity hairdresser named Frederick Fekkai, who also did Martha's hair (and who became famous when he began cutting Hillary Clinton's hair). Whenever Frederick received a mention in a gossip column by, say, Liz Smith or Cindy Adams, rival columnists would begin placing bets among themselves as to which of the two women would be the first to turn up next with an item from Susan—most likely an item about Martha. And no columnist would dare to write something critical about a Magrino client, as the wall of access for future items would come instantly crashing down. In this way, Susan kept the press on its toes, with its hand out for more.

---

*Susan was also the public relations representative for Victoria Gotti, daughter of Mafia figure John Gotti, and represented her on a book about her life as a daughter of a mob torpedo.

Whatever the press may have thought privately about Susan, the growing corps of journalists who were now writing about Martha regularly believed that Susan was, insofar as the press was concerned, Martha's single most important asset—a PR minder who could not only deny reportorial access to the hidden world of Martha's many secrets, but who could always also provide almost inexhaustible support and access for anyone who wanted to pursue a positive angle on her client. By controlling media access to the world behind the manicured hedges of Martha's public image, Susan could thus generate publicity that kept spreading the Martha message to a broader and broader audience.

To make sure that there were no breaches in the Maginot line of defenses she had constructed around her prized client, Susan traveled everywhere with Martha, on vacations and business trips alike, staying in the same hotels, dining in the same restaurants. "They even look alike," said one bemused columnist of their joined-at-the-hip public life.

However, there were some places, and some situations, in which Martha had to appear alone—and when she did, Susan's job was to make sure that the risks of revealing the Other Martha to the world were at an absolute minimum. Yet for Martha, the past was never very far behind, and no matter how far she traveled, or how fast she ran, her earliest years had an unnerving way of lurching dybbuk-like into her present moments, in the most unexpected of ways.

One such moment presented itself not long after the deal with Time Warner had been renegotiated, when Susan arranged for Martha to appear on the Public Television's popular interview and current affairs talk show, *Charlie Rose*, hosted by a tall and somewhat affectionately disheveled former CBS newsman of the same name, another of Susan's clients.

Though Charlie would sometimes dominate the interviews with his guests, asking questions and then answering them before the guests could offer their own opinions, his questions were interesting, and he was always well informed—sometimes even to the point of seeming to know more about the subjects under discussion than his guests did. What's more, the show's producers worked hard to line up guests who could discuss interesting and provocative topics, from the arts and music, to architecture, sports, and whatever might be happening in the economy or perhaps the Middle East.

It was rare to find a celebrity on *Charlie Rose* since those who appeared on his show were almost never permitted to get away with talking about themselves in the fatuous content-free ways that celebrities adopted to avoid discussing their personal lives. To appear on *Charlie Rose*, a guest had to have something interesting to say beyond when he'd next be appearing in Las Vegas or what he had been doing the night of the Oscars.

But Susan had gone ahead with Martha's appearance on the show anyway, since the risks of having the event backfire were minimal.

Charlie had undoubtedly been briefed carefully on what Martha could talk about, and what her interests were so he supposedly knew what to stay away from and what to bring up that would energize Martha on subjects that she wanted to discuss—like, say, the humiliating mauling her legal pit bull, Grubman, had just given Time Warner. Charlie was prepared to help Martha tell the story of her life in just the way Martha wanted it told: the triumph of America's own Nancy Drew, the little girl who grew up in humble but loving circumstances to become the Ur-woman for all America—1995's Everything Gal.

The trouble was, every time Charlie pitched her a fastball, high and inside, she not only hit it out of the park, she swung so hard she threw her bat right out after it.

Let's talk about your family, Charlie began: Tell me about growing up in New Jersey. And within barely a heartbeat Martha was onto the subject of Eddie, her father the "great gardener," the "artistic personality," the "beautiful man."

If Martha had simply taken a breath and said, "Okay, now let me tell you about mom," everything would have been fine. But she continued on with Eddie, and before anyone realized it, the audience was peeking behind the curtain at the real world of Elm Place, as she seemed to grow distant, saying, "A very artistic personality, a beautiful man, physically."

Charlie agreed. "Handsome," he said.

"Very, very handsome," she mused. "Talented." And then from nowhere came the truth—the negative, hovering resentful presence that had filled the household of Eddie Kostyra. Martha's father, Eddie: angry at the world, angry at his family, angry at himself. "Talented," she said, "but disappointed in his own life, and particularly so because . . ."

And now Eddie's daughter, Martha, entered the conversation, speaking back at him through the years—to the man who had been dead for over a decade and still hovered before her eyes . . . angry at what he had never appreciated about those he had gathered around him, whom he had brought into the world, and promised to love and cherish and provide for—and in the end had betrayed.

"Because," said Martha, ". . . *he had everything. I mean, he had everything. He had a great family, six kids . . .*"

Charlie threw some more chum in the water: "Yeah . . ." and Martha continued.

". . . a lovely wife. My mother is still a very active, personable, caring person . . ." She was growing almost incoherent now, beginning to lose her way in the feelings that seemed to be welling within her, saying, ". . . and he . . . yet . . . was not so satisfied with his lot in life . . . and I've tried to figure that . . . that one out."

Charlie seemed exhausted. The show had been underway for barely two minutes and look where the conversation had gone already. He moved to what he must have thought was safer ground: Martha in school, and after that her career on Wall Street, and after that life in the suburbs. But whichever way he turned the conversation, something odd and unexpected popped up to reveal a deeper truth—sometimes in subtle ways that seemed to escape even the interviewer.

When Charlie asked Martha to reminisce about her life as a stockbroker, she opened a window on what life in the Monness, Williams & Sidel brokerage firm had really been all about: life in an institutional bucket shop where the sales force was aggressively selling penny stocks, and where Martha wound up so agitated and stressed that she'd wake up in the morning with hives . . . a place that she'd finally had the good sense to quit before everything collapsed all around her. Now, on *Charlie Rose*, nearly thirty years later, she recalled it all, saying, "My father-in-law was a stockbroker, and he encouraged me to sort of gamble. I liked . . . I liked that little bit of life, too. And learned a lot about stocks. Went to work for a very interesting firm. No one was over 23 years old in my firm."

Charlie: "Yeah."

Martha [once again beginning to ramble]: "And we . . . we worked very hard. We started every day at zero. I learned a—how to really be competitive there. It was a tough, it was a tough environment, but . . . with just a microcosm of Wall Street. [And now the zinger]: *"The movie* Wall Street *had nothing on this firm."* Just so. *Wall Street* is a movie about a greed-inspired young man who trades on insider information while peddling junk stocks to the public in the blowout phase of a bull market. In Martha's mind, this was the place she really worked.

It went on and on like that. When Charlie asked her what it had been like to move from the fast track of life in Manhattan to the green fields of Connecticut, she once again answered more than had been asked, gratuitously informing him that, actually, she'd never broken out in hives in the first place—which certainly must have baffled him as the interviewer because he'd never asked her about it at all.

Martha was apparently still upset, five years later, over what she'd disclosed to reporter Jeannie Kasindorf in her 1990 profile interview for *New York* magazine—the only known place where her confession about having suffered hives from anxiety had found its way into print. Now she was trying to deny that she'd said it, without actually coming right out and saying so. But the manner of her denial simply dug her hole deeper, as she said, once again bringing up the mess she'd left behind on Wall Street, "I didn't wake up itching and, you know, nervous because of Wall Street and my clients and the ire that . . . that we aroused on Wall Street." What itching? What ire? Charlie hadn't asked.

At another point in the interview, Charlie turned the conversation to the happiness and pleasure that Martha was selling to women, and before anyone knew it Martha was talking instead about her divorce and having visited a psychiatrist—which she quickly recharacterized as a "psychologist"—to figure out why she'd let everything in her life "fall apart."

Then Martha asked herself a question: "Why did . . . you know . . . how did I mess up?"

And now she was on the thinnest ice of all: Why had all this happened to her? Where had these demons come from that had stalked her all these years? She was at an extraordinary moment. The ultimate Martha Moment of them all, right there on live TV . . . about to crash through the ice of a lifetime of denial, into the deep and eternal waters of self-knowledge and true growth.

Instead, the audience got this: "But that's not the point."

The point was, she had her work . . . and her business . . . and her one home that had now become four . . . and her TV shows and books and magazines. And so what if she was only sleeping three to four hours a night? Andy was behind her now (wasn't he?), and everything was turning out great. She said, "I just didn't roll up in a little ball and go under the quilts . . ." and Charlie said, "Yeah . . ." and waited for more.

At last, Charlie seemed to get what was really going on. Martha Stewart wasn't one person, she was two: Martha Stewart, a corporate empire-builder, living a life that bore no relationship whatsoever to the Other Martha that she was selling in the pages of her magazine. Could these be reconciled? Was there any way at all for Martha Stewart business supergal to snip roses in the afternoon?

Martha responded that others may have been baffled by the di-chotomies in her life, but she was having no trouble wearing both hats . . . or enjoying how well they both seemed to fit. So it was not without an evident sense of satisfaction that Martha chose to play the dragonslayer, magnanimous in her victory, when Charlie brought up the real reason she was on his show: her recent triumph over Time Warner.

Here was Charlie Rose, a one-time researcher in the dungeons of CBS, who'd fought for a quarter century to get the recognition he deserved, only to wind up no more visible—on the back end slope of his career—than as the host of a post-primetime talking heads show on New York public television. And there before him sat a di-vorced Connecticut housewife who seemed to have emerged from nowhere to dominate and outsmart every media mogul she shook hands with.

So in midinterview, Charlie said, "Everyone around here is talk-ing about how much fun it is to see the largest communication com-pany in the world being dragged around by the nose by a former caterer . . ."

And Martha responded, turning on the full force of her charm and grace, "Yeah, but I didn't concentrate on that, Charlie . . ." and switched the conversation to how to photograph a house.

SCHEMING TIMES

O nce Martha had signed her new agreement with Time Warner, Inc., at the start of 1995, relations between the company and its publishing superstar began to deteriorate again. Martha wanted more money, more power, more control. In fact, she wanted to be done with Time Warner, period. She'd had it, and she wanted out.

The latest problem was the new man she was having to deal with: a bear-sized good old boy from Alabama named Don Logan, who didn't seem to like her any more than she liked him although she would dutifully refer to him as a friend and mentor when questioned about their relationship.

When Martha first came to Time Warner in 1990, she'd dealt with Christopher Meigher, the natty Dartmouth man who had championed her magazine project with Time Warner's then third-in-command, Gerald Levin. Martha and Chris had gotten along fine—mainly because Chris had been able to disguise his dislike for her colossal ego and grating personality, and just help get her what she wanted.

But in 1992, Meigher had left Time Warner to start his own magazine publishing business—Meigher Communications, L.P.—and was soon publishing a *Martha Stewart Living* knockoff entitled *Garden Design*. The venture eventually foundered after Meigher spent more than a year desperately seeking financial support to keep it alive. In 2001, Meigher briefly resurfaced, making the rounds of the New

York publishing community with plans for a magazine to be distributed free of charge to hotels where "weary executives" could leaf its pages before falling sleep. The idea sounded like a snore, and failed to spark much interest.

Meigher's replacement at Time was a fellow named Robert Miller. Executives throughout the company watched closely to see if Martha and Miller would get along, and the general first impression was that Martha seemed wary of her new colleague. But as time passed, the two looked to have settled into a smooth working relationship, which basically meant that Martha got to have things her way. By and by, colleagues of the two began telling reporters that Martha "loved" Bob Miller, which seemed to be a good sign for everyone.

But in late 1995, Miller left the company as well, to found a magazine publishing business not unlike Meigher's. Thereafter, he acquired a magazine from Time Warner called *Vibe*, which had been started as a hip-hop publication by music composer Quincy Jones. Soon, Miller found himself in a wildly awkward situation when one of his top editors hired a man who had been charged, and then acquitted, of murdering the son of Gerald Levin, who by now had become chairman of the entire corporation. As had been the case with Meigher's magazines, Miller's publications ran into trouble and were put up for sale.

Only Martha seemed to have the golden touch. Yet here she was, presiding over the hottest magazine in the company—the only truly synergistic project Time Warner had produced in the nearly half a decade that had passed since the merger—and one after the next she was having to deal with men who kept insisting she didn't know what she was doing. But, once these same men got outside the elaborate support system of Time Warner, *they* turned out to be the ones who apparently didn't know what they were doing. Martha Stewart hadn't fallen on her face—*they had.*

Now, as 1995 drew to a close, she had to deal with the *next* Time Warner palooka—Logan—who promised to be the worst yet. Logan was the CEO of the entire Time Inc. magazine publishing operation, and Time Publishing Ventures was just one of his responsibilities. So long as he'd stayed safely at a distance from Martha, she'd been able to deal with the situation. But in the wake of Miller's departure, Logan had disbanded the entire Time Publishing Ventures operation and begun running its various activities himself directly. This meant that Martha had to deal with him all the time, and that was simply asking too much.

By year's end, Martha and Sharon were huddled almost nonstop at Martha's kitchen table in Turkey Hill, working on ways to design a company that could function independently of Time Warner. For Martha, nice-gal time was over. With Sharon's help, she was going to figure out how to get the money to buy back control of the business and start running it on her own—without the negative, counterproductive input from the men at Time Warner.

Yet in the worlds of big business and the media, things were never as simple as they seemed, as Martha had by now learned for herself. Although there was obviously no love lost between Martha and the Logan crowd, Time Warner was an enormous, sprawling bureaucracy, spanning every major media market on earth, and dominating many. Within the organization, there were departments and divisions with separate agendas, filled with executives who maneuvered among themselves, and with colleagues in other divisions, in a ceaseless struggle to enhance their power, prestige, and job security. Just as Count Otto von Bismarck had said of nineteenth-century European statecraft, "Anyone who speaks of Europe is wrong," so, too, was anyone wrong who figured he knew what Time Warner really thought or wanted to do about anything; there were simply too many conflicting voices within the company to generalize about any of them.

Even as Martha and Sharon were plotting their escape strategy from the world of Don Logan, a completely separate fiefdom within Time Warner was actively scheming to snatch back control of Martha's booming TV syndication business, which had escaped their grasp three years earlier. The goal: to claw the distribution of Martha's TV show away from Group W Syndication and drag it back into the Time Warner corporate fold. What none of the schemers could have imagined is that by trying to do so, the warring men of Time Warner would wind up making Martha five times as visible on television as she already was, even as they lost the battle to profit from her relentlessly surging fame.

Once again, the person responsible for Martha's good fortune was her admiring friend at Group W, Richard Sheingold. A capable, focused, and straight-ahead executive, Richard had done exactly what Martha had expected, and had successfully promoted the show in every market available. And because he had done his job so well, Martha had not interfered with his work and simply left him to continue in his efforts to bring her more fame. So they got along fine.

Richard had, in fact, promoted the show so successfully that jealousies among station managers were now almost commonplace. In the New York market, Richard had initially offered the show to the owned-and-operated flagship station of the NBC network, WNBC-TV. But the station had passed on it, claiming the show lacked appeal to viewers in a largely urban market like New York. So Richard had headed up the street to WCBS-TV—the owned and operated flagship station of NBC's arch rival broadcasting network, CBS—and successfully placed it there.

The CBS people not only had liked the show on its merits, but had welcomed it as a way to humiliate and embarrass their rivals at WNBC-TV. Like Time Warner, NBC was a sprawling corporate bureaucracy—as indeed was CBS—with innumerable executives all jockeying for power among themselves. Feuding at NBC was particularly intense between the executives who acquired and distributed programming for the NBC television network, and the executives who ran the company's owned-and-operated stations, of which WNBC-TV was the crown jewel. Neither group controlled the other, which created endless tension and bickering between them over whether each was being properly supportive of the other's interests.

The situation with Martha became yet another bone of contention. At the network level, NBC had been carrying Martha as a regular guest on the *Today* show since summer 1991. So, when the general manager of WNBC-TV, a man named Bill Bolster, chose not to pick up Martha's syndicated Group W show when Richard Sheingold brought it to market two years later, Bolster was making the calculated bet that not even Martha's rising visibility and popularity on NBC at the network level via the *Today* show would be enough to drive viewers to *Martha Stewart Living* as a syndicated show in the New York market.

But when Martha began appearing each morning on WCBS-TV, the miscalculation soon became obvious. The show proved to be an immediate hit, pulling female viewers from all other local New York stations to WCBS-TV the minute it came on the air after the *Today* show ended at 9 A.M.

When Bolster could stand it no longer, he phoned Sheingold to insist that *Martha Stewart Living* be switched from WCBS-TV to WNBC-TV. After all, explained Bolster, Martha was appearing constantly on NBC's own *Today* show at the network level, and it wasn't right for NBC to be promoting a CBS show.

But Richard sensed that Bolster wasn't really concerned about that at all. In Sheingold's view, what troubled Bolster was that he looked foolish within his own organization for not having signed up *Martha Stewart Living* when Sheingold had originally brought it to him, and now he wanted it back.

"Sorry," said Richard, relishing the moment. "You had your chance, and now she's with CBS."

But Bolster wouldn't take no for an answer and began fuming that if Sheingold didn't give him the show he'd see to it that Martha was removed from the *Today* show entirely.

Oh really? Richard was a straightforward guy, and what you saw was what you got: plain-speaking and honest communication. And one thing he didn't like was being threatened—especially when the threats involved Martha Stewart, for whom he felt great affection and admiration (even though she didn't like the fact that he only ate brown food). So the words came out evenly and with no tone of rancor, but as simply a statement of fact, as he said, "You don't have the juice . . ." and ended the conversation.

But WNBC-TV wasn't the only outfit that had missed its Martha Moment and now wanted a second chance. By summer 1995, Sheingold started hearing reports that Time Warner's television syndication operation, under the arm of Warner Brothers executives in Los Angeles, was telling station managers around the country that Warner Brothers would soon be unfurling a new syndication service that would offer *Martha Stewart Living*.

When a story on the plans actually turned up in *Daily Variety*— the bible of the Hollywood entertainment industry—in June 1995 and quoted a Time Warner executive in a way that suggested Time Warner had its eye on Martha, Richard grew alarmed. That story alone could make it impossible for Group W to sign another deal for *Martha Stewart Living* with anyone.

Richard instantly saw the pickle he was in. From here on out, every time one of his people made a sales call on a station, the general manager of the station would say, "Hey, didn't I read that Martha Stewart is going back to Time Warner . . . ?" and boom, the whole meeting would be wrecked.

Even if the salesman tried to explain otherwise, who was going to listen? The media business was boiling up on all fronts by now. The stock market was surging, advertising dollars were flowing everywhere, people just wanted to do deals. No one had time for details. The whole industry was running at Mach IV already, and the pace seemed to accelerate daily. Everyone was manic. No one was going to listen to some confusing explanation from a Group W salesman about an off-base story in *Daily Variety*. No one was probably even going to *remember* the story in *Daily Variety*. All they were going to remember was that they'd read something somewhere—about Martha Stewart maybe going back to Time Warner . . . and that's all they needed to know. The Group W salesman would be halfway into his "explaining" bit and the station executive would be fidgeting in his seat, saying, "Yeah, well that's all very interesting but I think we'll just wait until everything sorts itself out . . ." and start rummaging around for something on his desk to show that the meeting was over.

That one story could freeze up the entire market for *Martha Stewart Living*—just the way the market would freeze up when some upstart computer company would announce the launch of a new software package, and a giant like IBM or Microsoft would instantly wheel out its own announcement saying they were preparing to launch a software package that sounded like the exact same thing. At a stroke, the upstart's orders would evaporate as potential customers stood back to see what the industry leader planned to offer. In the computer software industry, the tactic was known as the "vaporware" ploy because the software that the big company announced almost never materialized; instead, the much-hyped software was quickly forgotten once the upstart had been driven out of business. In a word, the package was said to have vaporized.

That's what Richard figured he was up against now—a vaporware ploy to wreck his deal with Martha.

Richard knew that he had to do something fast because if that story were allowed to stand unchallenged, Group W would wind up at the NATPE convention, now only a few months away, without the ability to make a single convincing pitch to anyone. Somehow, he had to get a story out that Martha was still a Group W property.

Richard knew what he had to do, and it wouldn't be easy. He had to sign her up all over again and make a big, attention-getting splash in the process. He needed to show the world that Martha was still his girl.

But how? What could he offer Martha Stewart that was guaranteed to carry the day? He thought and thought. What was Martha's sweet tooth? What dish could he set before her that she simply couldn't resist? The answer was obvious, and once he saw it he acted quickly. What dish did Martha find irresistible? Well, duh—a dish of more Martha! If she agreed to re-up with Group W, Richard would agree to turn her once-a-week show into a daily offering, and thereby make her instantly five times more visible than she already was.

Richard still had plenty of time before the start of the NATPE convention when he set up a meeting with Martha and dropped by to see her at her office. He knew exactly what he wanted to say and how he wanted to say it. He knew that he wouldn't get anywhere if he started off by playing the loyalty card; that would simply put pressure on her and she'd stiffen up and back away. He also knew that if he played to her vanity too overtly, it would turn her off. It would be like telling her, "Martha, I've got your number, this whole thing is about fame, right?" Of course it was about fame, like it is with every celebrity who ever lived. The thing is, you just didn't want to come right out and say so. You'd be blowing their cover.

The safe way to approach it would be to get Richard and Martha together on the same side—focused on the enemy: Time Warner, Inc. The message needed to be: Richard and Martha, in this together, battling against the monster of all media, Time Warner.

Martha's office was a large, glass-enclosed space at the end of a floor of desks and chairs. There was a long, steel desk in the center, giving the place a cold, all-business—almost industrial—feel. At one end sat Martha, who rose to greet him. At the other end sat a woman he didn't know . . . a Sharon somebody, he recalled later. It was odd to see such an arrangement, this Sharon person sharing the desk of the head of the company. Yet there she sat, with the same shade of blonde hair that Martha had, and even the same solid-looking bone structure. It was almost like looking at Martha's doppelgänger; at one end of the desk sits Martha . . . then look to the other end of the desk and . . . there she is again: Martha II.

Richard was, in fact, looking at Sharon Patrick, who by now seemed to be as much a part of Martha's life as Martha herself. Peek through the window into the kitchen at Turkey Hill and there's Sharon at the kitchen table poring over numbers and strategy plans;

look through the glass partition of Martha's fishbowl-like office in New York, and there's Sharon all over again, doing the same thing.

Observing Martha and Sharon in action was a diverting pastime for Martha's staff—and easy, too, since all that one had to do was look through the floor-to-ceiling glass partition of the boss' office and there they both were. It was as if Martha's leadership role at the office had become mounted and enshrined in a kind of diorama exhibit for the employees: Martha Stewart and Assistant in Natural Business Habitat, ca. 1995.

Richard hadn't expected anything like this, and for a moment it threw him off. But he'd long since learned that to get what you want you've got to stay focused, which, frankly, was another thing he liked and admired about Martha. He had heard all the horror stories about her sharp tongue, and they didn't mean anything to him one way or the other. What mattered was simple: Martha was all business and Richard was all business, and as long as things stayed that way, everything always worked out fine.

So he began, saying, "Martha, I understand you're considering leaving us for Warner. I understand, because they're so powerful and they're the owner of your company. But I want to tell you why you should stay with us."

He had her attention now—focused and intense—as he said, "I would imagine they're telling you that they're going to open a new division and make you the flagship. But I know this business, so I want to tell you what I think they're *really* going to do. They're going to open a new division just like they're saying, and make you the flagship. But what they're *not* telling you is that they'll wind up using you as a way to clear other shows." Richard explained what he meant—that Martha's show would be used for bait to get stations to buy other, less appealing properties as well . . . as in, If you want to get *Martha Stewart Living*, then you're going to have to take *Mega Man* and *I Accuse*, or whatever.

You could see the lightbulbs going on in Martha's head, as if to say, "So that's how this game is played."

Richard continued. "Now here's what I have to offer. If you stay with me, you can create your own next *two* shows . . . and," Richard paused for emphasis, ". . . *and you can own them both.*"

He could see he had her now, so he came in with the clincher. He said, offering the faintest hint of a smile to reassure her that what he was about to add was just for fun, "And besides, you strike me as the kind of woman who leaves the dance with the guy who brought you . . ." and Martha smiled back at him and Richard thought, Yes!—from the half-court line and he'd sunk it with nothing but net!

Shortly thereafter, Group W issued a press release. It began, "Martha Stewart and Group W Productions have announced a long-term continuation of their television programming association. Group W Productions, which has been distributing the weekly *Martha Stewart Living* since its inception two and a half years ago, has been selected by Stewart to syndicate the series for the next five years." The release quoted some fawning praise for Martha from the president of Group W Productions, Derk Zimmerman, but buried deep in the release was a single sentence that told the truth of what had actually transpired, *and why.* The sentence read, "Richard Sheingold, executive vice president, Group W Productions, noted that there are plans to expand the Martha Stewart franchise in television, which will include new programming as early as September 1996."

The date was November 30, 1995, and Richard had made his deadline. Seven weeks before the start of the 1996 National Association of Television Programming Executives annual convention, he had put NATPE and everyone else on notice not to mess with his girl; Martha and Richard were leaving the dance together.

And Martha had got what she had wanted as well: More face-time on TV, as *Martha Stewart Living* not only shifted to a daily format beginning the following September, but her weekly show stayed on the air as well, meaning that Martha could now be seen in 97 percent of American homes fully *six* days a week.

As for Time Warner, well, it got basically nothing. Not only did the Warner syndication ploy backfire, increasing Martha's value in a way that did little for Time Warner, but in scarcely one more year Martha would be gone from the magazine side of the company as well. And when the baffled executives looked to see how she'd done it, about the only sign left to mark her passing would be the fading smile of their superstar Cheshire cat.

A TAXING SITUATION

I t is not easy for movie stars who are coddled and ego-stroked year after year to remember that their appeal to the public derives not from the content of their personal character, but from the success they achieve in portraying persons they are not. Not only is the public constantly confusing the two, but the stars' own public relations advisers work ceaselessly to augment the confusion, emphasizing admirable personal qualities the stars do not necessarily possess, while downplaying truthful information that sends an undesirable message.

For Martha Stewart, the dilemma was worse. Alone among celebrities, Martha claimed not only to know the meaning of lifestyle perfection, but to be actually living it as an example for women everywhere . . . a public pose that, in effect, denied the existence of her private life at all. Martha's books, her magazine writings, her appearances on television—all supported the message that from the most superficial and distant view, to the up-close examination of her most personal affairs, Martha was Martha, all the way through.

But she wasn't. Like everyone else, she was the product of her inherited genes and a lifetime of experiences that had affected them. The result was a person with good qualities and bad qualities, and still other qualities that seemed to occupy a kind of "work in progress" niche in between. Like everyone else, she had her flaws.

But her public image seemed to deny their existence. The subtext of the Martha Message had become "perfect table settings equal perfect person," and since everyone knew that was nonsense, she became easy prey for parodies and jokes. A parody of her magazine, entitled *Is Martha Stewart Living?* had been published, in September 1994, by two of her Westport neighbors. The magazine mocked the impossible lifestyle Martha claimed to be leading as the All American Everything Gal and contained articles with titles like, "Making Water: Impress guests at your next dinner party by serving them water you've made yourself or, better yet, by buying mine." Another article bore the title, "Relatives: Entertaining family members. This can be tricky, especially if they're from New Jersey." The magazine's send-up "calendar" of Martha's gal-on-the-go tasks included such items as "Thursday, Dec. 1st: Move outdoor gardens indoors . . ." and "Saturday, Dec. 3rd: Scrub north face of house with Borax . . ." and "Saturday, Jan. 20th: Stencil turnpike exit ramp."

In fact, the parody barely came close to capturing the wildly overextended, rush-every-which-way-at-once life that Martha was leading. A staff of assistants now managed her homes. But the free time that had been opened up by no longer having to tend to the affairs of her personal life had been filled up ten times over with the frantic self-promotion schedule she was now following to convince everyone she was the person she'd claimed to be.

Between the time when she'd wrapped up her Group W Productions deal in late November 1995 and had re-signed for a new five-year contract, and the twenty-first of December, when she left for the Christmas holidays—improbably for a trip to the Galápagos Islands off the coast of Peru—Martha's schedule included:

- The debut of her new weekly syndicated newspaper column, entitled "Ask Martha" (November 25).

- A luncheon and book-signing before 1,000 guests of the Lupus Foundation of America, in Buffalo, New York (December 1).

- The airing of her first appearance on CBS's *60 Minutes* (December 3).

- An appearance on the *Today* show (December 5).

- An appearance on *Larry King Live* (also December 5).

- Attendance at a celebrities-only film debut in New York (December 10).

- An appearance on the *Today* show (December 11).

- Airing of her first CBS primetime special, with then First Lady Hillary Clinton (December 12).

- Hostessing of a party attended by Frank and Kathie Lee Gifford (December 16).

- Demonstration of cooking toffee candies on the *Today* show (December 21).

In addition, during that period Martha appeared three times on her own syndicated TV show, *Martha Stewart Living*, for Group W, even as her name appeared 483 times in the American and Canadian press—more than any other woman in America except the then first lady of the United States, Hillary Clinton. Meanwhile, her latest book—*Martha Stewart Cookbook*—debuted at the number four slot on the *New York Times* best-seller list at the beginning of the period, and had climbed to the number three position by the end.

It was the latest high-water mark in a relentlessly rising tide of public adulation for the one-time housewife from Connecticut. All over America, people gawked in amazement at how she could keep it up. She was more visible, in more media channels, more of the time, than anyone else in the country. Yet her public would have been far *more* amazed, and maybe even a bit frightened, had they known of the other dramas in Martha's life that were unfolding just offstage and out of view—and of the toll her "perfect life" was beginning to take on the real Martha.

For one thing, the questionnaire that had showed up in her mailbox from the New York State Department of Taxation eighteen months earlier—which had sought information about her tax-related activities during 1991 and 1992, and which she had given to her sister-in-law Rita to answer and send back—hadn't satisfied the authorities at all. In fact, they'd found the responses so inadequate that they'd decided to probe further and had commenced a formal audit of her day-by-day whereabouts for the full two years.

This was a matter of concern. New York State regarded tax situations of nonresidents such as Martha, who lived in Connecticut but did a lot of tax-related work in New York, as usually fruitful cases to develop, and once a case was opened, the auditors rarely went away empty-handed.

Though Martha's representatives had succeeded in keeping the audit confined to just the 1992 calendar year, they hadn't killed it entirely. Worse, when Martha produced a collection of limousine invoices, expense reports, and various "itineraries" to show that she had not been physically present in New York during a number of days for which the auditors wanted explanations, the examiners reviewed the documents and pronounced them unsatisfactory to show where she'd actually been.

Much back-and-forthing had followed, and eventually the matters raised by the tax examiners also revealed questions about how Martha had handled the tax status of her East Hampton, New York, home on her federal tax returns for 1992 when she had been contending that the house had not been habitable for New York State tax purposes. Like someone who tugs on the loose end of a knitted wool sweater, the tax examiners kept pulling and pulling, and Martha's records for 1992 began to unravel into a mass of confusion.

Now it was eighteen months later, and the matter still hadn't been resolved. Yet more papers needed to be signed, this time so that her legal team could keep working through the material.

This was part of the background noise that buzzed constantly around her as she rushed from book-signings to TV tapings, from charity luncheons to black-tie dinners. It was another of those stress-filled Martha Moments—like the departure of Andy—that one could almost count on to bring out the worst and most unattractive side of her nature: the personality of the sharp-tongued scold. But this wasn't just a moment anymore, or even a day, or a week or a month. Frenzy and stress had now become her whole life.

The tongue-lashings and abusiveness, and the cruel and hurtful comments—the coping behavior that she had learned in Elm Place and that had once been confined to Andy and their daughter, Lexi . . . the behavior that she occasionally had later redirected onto her neighbors and friends once Andy left her—all of that was spilling from her lips onto those around her. She was no longer just the nasty lady in the big house at the top of Turkey Hill, she was now one of the most visible and closely watched figures in all of American public life. And there were some people she simply couldn't get away with abusing even once.

From time to time, hints at the hidden Martha would seep into print. In Buffalo, New York, a story appeared in the local newspaper, the *Buffalo News*, reporting that Martha had been the guest of honor at a luncheon book-signing for the Lupus Foundation of America. The guests had each paid $65 for lunch and a chance to have Martha autograph a copy of the *Martha Stewart Cookbook*, her latest book.

The event organizers had told Martha to expect a crowd of roughly 400, but her appeal was so strong that more than 1,000 people had actually showed up. So Martha signed all the books she could—about 400 according to the Lupus Foundation—then left for the airport. But the story quoted many women who hadn't gotten their books signed to the effect that they'd been cheated and that all Martha had wanted to do was sell copies of her book, pocket her speaking fee—which the paper pegged at $16,000—and skedaddle.

The wise course of action for Martha would have been to ask herself why she had created such animosity in her audience. She had, in fact, raised $60,000 for a worthy charity, and that at least should have counted for something. But the level of antipathy to her in the audience, and in the local press, had been such that the *Buffalo*

News had ignored that fact almost entirely, and focused instead on the bad taste she'd left in everyone's mouths. Why?

Charlotte Beers' counsel to Martha to develop better communications skills—in short, to focus on the response you want to *get* from people, and not just on what you want to say—seems to have been impossible for Martha to take to heart. Indeed, by the time the Lupus luncheon rolled around, she'd apparently forgotten it entirely, for once back in New York, and after learning of what had transpired in Buffalo after she'd left, she sat down and wrote a letter to the newspaper, beginning it: "I've been coming to Buffalo a long time, and I promise I'll think long and hard before I accept another invitation to your chilly and downright unfriendly city again." And what did the *Buffalo News* do? What else? . . . it printed excerpts of the letter in the next edition of the paper and made Martha look even worse.

Whatever Martha may have thought of her status and fame— and by the end of 1995 she obviously thought a lot—there was one woman on the scene whose fame and global stature kept every other woman on earth in permanent eclipse. In Hollywood, you had your Julia Roberts types and your Demi Moores and the others like them. In Washington, you had your Hillary Clintons and the rest. But in the global scheme of things—and on the ultimate mountain of fame—there was room at the top for only one woman. And in 1995, that woman was Lady Diana Frances Spencer, 34, the Princess of Wales.

The divorced wife of the future king of England, Princess Di had it all—the complete package: looks, wealth, class, image, everything. Even her divorce from Prince Charles hadn't really hurt; a momentary fillip on the cardiogram of world renown and it was gone, as she emerged from her trial more ethereal and graceful looking than ever—more vulnerable and at once more resilient and independent. Somehow she—and not her ex-husband—now seemed to wear the mantle of British royalty. She looked glorious, with the handsomest children on earth at her sides, associated with the best and most worthy charities . . . the Leprosy Mission International, the National AIDS Trust, the American Red Cross, and of course the International Campaign to Ban Landmines. As for Charles, he'd painted himself a boob and a cad, caught inflagrante in the midst of cell-phone sex with a woman who looked disturbingly like a horse.

Martha knew that she could never be Lady Di. But then again so did every other woman on earth. Lady Di was every woman's dream ride back to childhood, to the world of Prince Charming and happiness ever after, where nobody grew up to marry a man who yelled and drank, and money grew on lollipop trees *and everything was nice.* No one cared whether it was *really* that way for Lady Di; they just "knew" the truth even if there were facts to the contrary. Was it *really* true about the affair with the cavalry officer? Did anyone actually *see* it? Or the bulimia? Anyone actually *see* her throw up? Diana had something that made her unique. The entire world seemed to want to see only one side of her. The sunny side. And while the legions of Martha's fans either wanted to see only Martha's sunny side or didn't care about the other, the media certainly did care. Why was it different with Martha?

It was December 11, 1995, and the occasion was the Humanitarian Awards dinner of the United Cerebral Palsy Association at the New York Hilton Hotel. The distinguished recipient: Lady Di, the Princess of Wales.

It was the high point of the New York society season, the ultimate and most glamorous black-tie affair of the year. Over 1,000 of the most notable celebrities in America were there—in the media, in the arts, in the worlds of letters and public service. All the network news anchors were there, all the major political figures, all the most prominent people on Wall Street and in publishing and the law.

One of those in attendance was Robert Dilenschneider, the chairman of the influential and highly regarded public relations firm bearing his name. A member of the advisory board of the U.S. Japan

Business Council, the Center for Strategic and International Studies, the World Economic Forum, the Foreign Affairs Council, and numerous other transnational bodies, Dilenschneider thought big—so big, in fact, that he didn't often concern himself with pop-culture issues in the New York media market. He was going to the Princess Di dinner because that was the world he circulated in, and he figured he'd probably run into some friends.

Earlier in the day, his secretary had told him that a woman from the *New York Times* had telephoned to say she would be at his table and wanted to meet him, but the secretary had gotten only part of the name. So Dilenschneider had filed the partial name away and headed off to the Hilton. Moving through the crowd, he saw his friend Barbara Walters, and said hello, and met several other acquaintances, then headed toward his table, where he was a guest of the Versace family, still headed by fashion's most famous designer, Gianni Versace.

Dilenschneider took a seat and looked around. Up on the podium was General Colin Powell, still radiating glory from his triumph in Desert Storm, one of the most decisive victories in the history of American arms. Nearby was former Secretary of State, Henry Kissinger, now heading his own international political and economic consulting firm. Kissinger was there to bestow the Humanitarian of the Year award on the woman next to him, Lady Di, in a drop-dead little black dress reminiscent of Coco Chanel.

People were still milling about, and as Dilenschneider panned the room, his eyes fell on a woman sitting alone at the end of his table. She looked slightly downcast and ill at ease, as if she didn't know anyone and felt out of place. Dilenschneider thought, "What was the name of that woman from the *Times* . . . a "White" somebody? I wonder if that's her." So rising from his seat, he placed his napkin on the table and walked toward her. She didn't turn to look at him, so he cleared his throat and spoke.

He said, "Um, excuse me. Would you be Miss White from the *New York Times?*" and offered a sheepish grin.

It is impossible to know what Martha Stewart was thinking at that moment. She could have been thinking about the next issue of her magazine . . ., or her coming trip to the Galápagos Islands . . ., or her situation with Time Warner . . ., or how her latest cookbook was doing on the *New York Times* best-seller list . . . or any number of other things in her frenzied and complex life.

And she could also have been thinking about the woman seated not fifty feet away from her, who was about to be honored for her humanitarian efforts to ease suffering in the world . . . who looked like a fairy princess and lived like one, too . . . who had managed to dance through the raindrops of a traumatic divorce as if she were Ginger Rogers, and had emerged without a spot on her. And here at her feet sat Martha, a woman who'd worked a hundred times harder, and suffered more pain, and made herself famous, too . . . only she still didn't feel like a fairy princess. She still wasn't famous enough, like that woman up there. She still wasn't Princess Di.

It is impossible to know any of that because Martha hasn't said. But it is definitely possible to know, if not what Martha was thinking, then at least what she did—because Bob Dilenschneider will never forget it as long as he lives.

The woman looked at him and her face was a cold fury as she hissed, "You know who I am! I'm Martha Stewart!" and stared back in a rage.

Dilenschneider was shocked.

"Yes, of course," he said, and instinctively moved back a step.

But she wouldn't let it go.

"You know God-damn well who I am," she snarled.

A couple of people from nearby tables turned to look.

"I'm sorry," said Dilenschneider, "but really, I didn't."

"Don't tell me that," snarled Martha, her voice growing louder. "You did!"

Dilenschneider looked at her. "I didn't."

At which point, she said—as Dilenschneider later recalled— a line he never forgot, for it struck him as one of the most brutally arrogant, narcissistic, and self-absorbed insults he'd ever heard from anyone—and it was being hurled at him by a person he didn't know and had never spoken to until three seconds earlier.

She said, "Well, if you don't know who I am, then you don't deserve to be at this table! I'm Martha Stewart," and stared furiously at his face.

18

TIME TAKES A LICKING

Scarcely had Martha returned from her adventure vacation to the Galápagos Islands than the news broke that she was at loggerheads with Time Warner again and that she had hired entertainment lawyer Allen Grubman to get her more money from the company. The reporter who broke the story, Keith Kelly of *Advertising Age*, had become one of the best and most committed Martha watchers around. The rumors he'd been hearing told him that the situation was in flux and deteriorating—something that he knew from experience meant Martha would soon be on the warpath.

All over New York, the antennae of media industry executives were beginning to tingle. Everyone knew how bad relations were between Time Warner and its star editor. And everyone also knew what a gold mine *Martha Stewart Living* had become. Though Time Warner hadn't yet released any hard numbers on the matter, the magazine was believed to be generating $50 million per year in revenues by now—a sum that industry insiders could calculate relatively easily by simply adding up the number of advertisements in the magazine, then multiplying by a reasonable assumption for what Time Warner would charge per ad. They couldn't be totally precise about the estimate, but they could certainly get in the zone.

Magazine revenues were only part of it. In addition, Martha had the syndicated TV show and the books; and now a mail-order catalog called "Martha by Mail" had recently been market-tested by Time Warner with apparently excellent results.

Looking for reaction, Keith Kelly called up Steve Florio, the president of Samuel ("Si") Newhouse's Conde Nast publishing operation. Conde Nast was the first in the long list of media companies that had helped Martha on her way while letting the profits of her efforts slip between their fingers. Now Florio echoed Bill Bolster of WNBC-TV when he told Kelly, as if hoping to roll the tape backward for a second chance to dance with Martha, "If *Martha Stewart Living* ever went into play, we'd be very interested. It's more than a magazine, it's a media phenomenon . . ."

Indeed. Amazed at the success of the publication, Newhouse had already revived and relaunched *House & Garden*. Conde Nast had put the magazine on ice earlier in the decade, but Martha had demonstrated that a market for "nesting" publications really existed if editors simply provided readers the right content. In that sense, Conde Nast seemed just like Chris Meigher, who had come to the same conclusion and left Time Warner three years earlier to launch his own Martha knockoff magazine: *Garden Design*.

All over New York and throughout the worlds of publishing and the media, men of the American information industry who had either quarreled with Martha, or barely tolerated her—who had sneered among themselves and talked behind her back the minute she left the room—were falling all over themselves to mimic her success.

Martha's publisher at the magazine, Eric Thorkilsen, had escaped back into the comforting—and male-dominated—world of Time Inc. the very instant Sharon Patrick had arrived on the scene. On behalf of Time Warner, he had by now put together almost a mirror image of Martha's arrangements with Group W. Only instead of using Group W, Thorkilsen had worked out a deal with WGBH public television in Boston, producers of the *This Old House* PBS series that had starred Bob Vila. On the basis of Time Warner's presumed expertise in the cloning of Martha's magazine into a TV show (which Time Warner had actually resisted from the start), Thorkilsen was now able to nail down a licensing deal with WBGH to accomplish the same thing in reverse: cloning the WGBH television show into a Time Warner magazine to be called *This Old House*. Said the show's WGBH producer, Bruce Irving, reflecting the sales pitch that Time Warner had brought to Boston, "We don't want to 'Martha Stewart' ourselves. Martha Stewart is much ridiculed and her message is lost in her ubiquitous nature. We don't want to be that way." What way would that be? "We make shows about fixing houses," explained Irving. WGBH didn't want to get into the business of selling, as he put it, disdainfully, "children's blow-pops with 'This Old House' written on them."

Now Martha and Sharon were cooking up a plan to trump them all. What was happening just wasn't fair, and for the moment Martha's hands were tied. But not for much longer. Martha had invented a whole new approach to multimedia marketing, yet here she sat, shackled to the company that was holding her back while everybody in the media was starting to pile into her game. What could she do? How could she get free of them? Where could she get the money to buy back her business? Every time she and Sharon paid a visit to a bank or venture capital investment fund, the moneymen all wanted big chunks of equity in return for their cash. Raising money that way would just be switching one group of overlords for another. Martha wanted to call the shots herself, not be dependent on the whims of distant men who kept insisting that they knew how to run her company better than she did. Had *they* created the Martha Stewart phenomenon? Had *they* built it into a business?

Once again, the solution to her problem lay close at hand. And once again, it took McKinsey-trained Sharon Patrick to see the pattern in the puzzle, and start putting the pieces together. To raise the buyout capital for Martha's exit from Time Warner, Sharon and Martha didn't need to be running all over the place, talking to bankers. All the money they needed was right at their fingertips. It had been staring them in the face all along. All they needed to do was devise a strategy to reach out and grab it. They needed to figure out a way to get Kmart to finance their exit from Time Warner. After all, the entire phenomenon of Martha Stewart—the face of American womanhood—had begun with the money provided by Kmart. Wasn't it about time to go back to the well again?

To most observers, Martha's nine-year-old deal with Kmart seemed a beneficial arrangement for both. Martha got publicity, and Kmart sold merchandise. But in reality, the entire relationship had tilted heavily in Martha's favor from the beginning. Over the years, the relationship with Kmart had given Martha exposure of incalculable value in the consumer marketplace. In the year before her deal was announced in 1987, Martha's name had appeared in the American press a grand total of only forty times. In the year following, it appeared eighty-six times, then tripled in the year after that. By now she was receiving in excess of 5,000 mentions per year, and the number was *still* doubling annually.

But the arrangement hadn't done very much for Kmart, and probably shouldn't have been expected to either. In reality, Kmart was a company in the throes of long-term decline, with enough momentum behind that decline that almost no amount of celebrity endorsement hype was likely to turn things around. After ninety-two years—a longer time span than any consumer merchandise retailer except perhaps Sears—Kmart was becoming a company without a mission or, increasingly, even a market. Having begun life in 1899 as a five-and-dime store founded by a Michigan man named Sebastian Kresge, the company developed into a Midwest, and eventually nationwide, chain of discount department stores.

By 1976, it was the second-largest general merchandise retailer in the country after Sears. But management was ingrown and sleepy, inventory controls were poor, and the company failed to wake up to the threat presented by an upstart Arkansas discount retailer named Wal-Mart, whose stores had begun to spread rapidly throughout Kmart's markets. Wal-Mart was an efficient operation that emphasized low prices, courteous service, and computerized inventory controls. Instead of meeting the Wal-Mart threat head-on, the Kmart brass took an easy way out, hoping to create the illusion of quality and class to overcome what Wal-Mart was doing better. The device they chose was the celebrity endorsement ploy, first with Jaclyn Smith of *Charlie's Angels* fame, in 1984, and then with Martha, country music star Kenny Rogers, and even Indy 500 race car driver Mario Andretti. But nothing really worked, and for a simple reason: The company's stores were located in ex-urban and rural strip malls and rural magnet shopping centers, which meant that no matter how much the company spent to promote an upscale and quality-oriented image, the stores themselves were still going to attract only those people who lived nearby—basically the same people who had been shopping there all along.

Though Barbara Loren-Snyder later claimed that more than $1 billion worth of Martha-branded goods were moving through Kmart's checkout aisles by 1990, this represented no more than about 3 percent of the company's revenues, and soon thereafter the growth petered out anyway.

An obvious problem became "cannibalization"—referring to what happens when shoppers are induced by heavy promotions to switch from one line of products in the same store to a competing line. Sales of the promoted line may rise sharply, but overall sales often wind up going nowhere because sales in the promoted line are offset by weakening sales in the competing lines. Cannibalization: Good for Martha, bad for Kmart.

And there was another problem. As a discount retailer, Kmart didn't have very fat profit margins. The more that its customers were induced to migrate toward heavily promoted—and thus more costly—merchandise like Martha's, the more the company's profit margins were pressured. If a Kmart supplier sold a kitchenware item—a colander or strainer, say—to Kmart for 74 cents, Kmart might be able to mark it up to no more than $1 at retail before discovering that shoppers would simply go to a competitor like Wal-Mart and buy it for 99 cents.

Spread out over the company's entire merchandise line, this meant that Kmart had to operate with a mere 26 percent gross margin (revenues minus cost of goods sold), meaning that the whole rest of the company had to be run on just 26 percent of its sales revenues. That was about typical for the discount retailing sector (rival Wal-Mart operated with a 25 percent gross margin; a few others were higher). But the narrow operating margins meant that discounters had to be careful before spending promotional money on projects like celebrity endorsement campaigns because not much money was available to spend on the projects in the first place. It was a luxury that most discounters rightly felt they couldn't afford.

Not Kmart. As Kmart began moving more heavily into the celebrity promotion game, the company's spending on advertising reached something close to 2 percent of its sales revenues, meaning that it was spending $20 million on Martha's line alone, if not more than that. In addition, Martha was taking a licensing cut on all sales of her branded products, which reduced even more the amount that Kmart had left to pay its bills.

By the end of Martha's second year under contract as Kmart's lifestyle consultant, the business and trade press was growing openly critical of the entire campaign. In November 1989, the *Chicago Tribune* summed up the matter succinctly, with a story that began, "The Kmart Corp.'s effort to parlay Martha Stewart's flair for entertaining into a more stylish image for its 2,200 discount stores has been slow to produce results, the company concedes."

Nothing seemed to improve; by 1991, the company's top-line sales revenues had plateaued; and by 1993 the bottom line had slipped into the red. It was the company's first losing year in a decade, and it meant that Joe Antonini's days were numbered. In June 1995, he was replaced with a man named Floyd Hall, who faced the dilemma presented by what might be termed the Conundrum of Holes: When you're in one, do you stop digging, or dig even harder?

Hall chose the latter. Sitting in Martha's kitchen at Turkey Hill—a room that was developing into a kind of Decision Bunker for an assault on the mightiest forces in American media—Martha and Sharon saw their opening. In less than a year, Martha's contract with Kmart would be up for renewal, and Hall would be the man on the spot. So, with a new man in charge and Kmart's back to the wall, Martha could begin reviving and redefining her relationship with the company—this time in a way that would give her the capital to orchestrate a buyout from Time Warner.

Electricity filled the air, shimmering over everything like St. Elmo's fire: Bull market deal fever was spreading through the media. In August 1995, at just around the time Martha and Sharon were starting to draw up a plan for where they wanted Martha's company to be in five years' time, the blue chip Wall Street investment firm of Morgan Stanley Dean Witter took an obscure California company named Netscape Communications, Inc., public in a Wall Street stock offering, and the earth moved. The words "This Offering Involves a High Degree of Risk" were stamped boldly across the front cover of the prospectus, as well they should have been, for Morgan Stanley was trying to raise close to $150 million from the public by selling investors shares of stock in a company that hadn't even existed sixteen months earlier, and was losing money rapidly in a business that itself was barely a year old: Internet browsing on the World Wide Web.

In New York that summer, most people in the media and on Wall Street had only the vaguest of ideas what the World Wide Web even was, let alone what was meant by "browsing" it with the software program developed by Netscape. Martha was spending much of her time that summer darting between her *Today* show appearances, her home in East Hampton, her place on Turkey Hill, and parties in the South of France, where a high point of the season was a bash in Saint-Tropez featuring Prince Albert of Monaco, Barbra Streisand, and Martha.

But while the upper echelons of the media busied itself with its summer of preening, the volcano known as the dot.com revolution was boiling up beneath them. On August 9, the first spurts of steam and gas escaped, as Morgan Stanley's traders introduced Netscape's shares into the public market and active trading began—within minutes of which the share price of the stock had tripled. From a company with a $1 billion value in the market only minutes earlier, a fact that itself seemed rather astonishing, Netscape had become a nearly $3 billion company—and the company itself hadn't done anything except . . . Well, frankly, it hadn't done anything at all—just exist for three minutes; and in so doing, nearly $2 billion had been conjured out of thin air.

Gold rush stampedes don't erupt from a standing start. The word first has to get around that there is really gold out there to be found. The first hearty prospectors have to come back with their treasure and show it around the bar before others will follow and the stampede can begin.

By spring 1996, something like that was starting to happen. Investment firms all across Wall Street had been looking for their own fledging companies in the "Internet space" to take public in IPOs, and the offering prospectuses now began to flood across the corporate registration desk of the U.S. Securities & Exchange Commission.

They ranged from the prospectus for a California company called Wired Ventures, Inc., that published a monthly magazine called *Wired*, to something called Infoseek Corporation, to another company bearing the name Excite, Inc., to a company that sounded so torqued up with enthusiasm that it could barely contain itself: Yahoo!, Inc. Over the winter of 1995/1996, this was what Wall Street had become—a world of yahoos and excitement as underwriters rushed to tee up the "next Netscape."

Suddenly, any media company with an involvement in the online world, no matter how tenuous or uncertain, became a darling of Wall Street. A one-time Hollywood studio head named Barry Diller, who had failed several times to raise the capital needed to buy a major media asset in New York—thereafter winding up with a tacky-sounding TV service known as the Home Shopping Network—saw his shares jump 20 percent in value almost instantly on news that he was starting up a companion business to be called the Internet Shopping Network. The shares of Time Warner spurted nearly 50 percent on the promise of its own Internet-based service, which the company had recently started, called "Pathfinder." The shares of media financier Rupert Murdoch's News Corporation jumped 10 percent. The shares of CBS Corporation jumped, as did those of The Walt Disney Company.

Wherever one looked, and whichever way one turned, the men of Wall Street and big media were falling into each other's arms with an ardor not seen in a generation. Deals were being made, money was being raised, the value of everything in the media world was suddenly being marked up.

And in the midst of all this action stood Martha—the hottest marketing personality on television, with the hottest and most rapidly growing consumer magazine in America—chained to a company that was running away with her business. She simply had to get free of them. Soon.

People caught glimpses of her, and wondered what she was up to. Someone spots Martha heading through the offices of Conde Nast on the way to a meeting with the company's chairman, Si Newhouse, and the speculation starts. What could that be all about? Someone else hears that Martha is having talks with Chris Meigher, publisher of the *Garden Design* knockoff of *Martha Stewart Living*, and the speculation intensifies. There are rumors that Martha is launching an Internet service . . . that she's got a deal going with a network.

In fact, she was making demands on Time Warner that were perceived as so unreasonable and outrageous as to invite the Time side to let her leave simply to be done with her. A hint of the tactic appeared when a reporter for the *Wall Street Journal*, Patrick Reilly, published a story in April 1996 asserting that she had turned herself into a "world-class headache" for the men of Time Warner. Not only wasn't her $400,000 base salary with growing bonuses enough, nor her chauffeur and $40,000 clothing allowance, now she was apparently demanding 40 percent of the equity in the company itself.

The Time folks viewed the idea as preposterous. Here was this woman, asking them to put up all the money—and putting out her magazine cost a fortune because of the personnel and other resources needed to carry off every new idea she came up with—and all she was going to have to do was sit back and collect 40 percent of the resulting profits. They couldn't believe she was asking for that. It was completely over the top.

But that was the whole point, because Martha didn't just want 40 percent of the profits, she wanted 100 percent of the profits. And if she kept making more and more extreme demands, eventually they'd simply let her go away and she'd have what she wanted: 100 percent. "Allen handled it for me," she said later, referring to her lawyer in the negotiations, Allen Grubman. "Without him, I'd still be making $750,000 a year from those people."

The specific terms of the deal that Martha eventually managed to get Time Warner to accept were not disclosed. The Time side said nothing, while Martha's side issued a press release saying only that a new company, known as Martha Stewart Living Omnimedia LLC, had acquired a variety of media assets from Time Inc., including *Martha Stewart Living* magazine and a series of spin-off books called "The Best of Martha Stewart Living." The release, dated February 1997, contained the obligatory expression of best wishes from the Time Inc. man in charge, Don Logan (but no similar back-at-ya' sentiment from Martha). Instead, nearly the whole of the release was devoted to setting forth a new McKinsey-like organizational structure for the company: Publishing & Online; Television; Merchandizing; and "Corporate." At the top sat Martha, as chairman, with Sharon as her second-in-command CEO—a title that Martha took back from her and reassigned to herself once the buyout was complete.

But nobody wanted to read about organizational details and who was to be called what. What people in the media world wanted to know was this: Where had she gotten the money for the buyout? When Patrick Reilly, the reporter for the *Wall Street Journal*, snagged an interview and asked her, she answered, "internally generated capital," and turned to other matters. But *Martha Stewart Living* was by now a big magazine, with a circulation of well over two million copies monthly. The *New York Times* was already quoting sources as saying she'd paid $85 million, which certainly seemed on the low side considering the hyperactive state of the media market at the moment. But even at that, $85 million was still a lot of money, and frankly, something seemed baffling: $85 million—of *internally generated capital*? Was Martha really *that* rich?

Reporters at both *Fortune* and *Time* were soon burrowing into the matter, and the first glimmerings of the truth were not long in coming. Four months later, in June 1997, *Fortune* reported that according to informed sources, at least $16 million of the funds had come via a cash payment to Martha back in February, from none other than Kmart as a down payment on their new deal.

Nothing about the payment was mentioned at the time, by Martha or anyone else—least of all when, three weeks after the buyout, her attentive public relations aide, Susan Magrino, gathered a crowd of reporters to Martha's home on Lily Pond Lane in East Hampton to announce the whole new line of linens and other merchandise that Kmart was introducing. It was part of Martha's new-and-improved relationship with the retailer that she had been hammering out for months with Kmart's CEO, Floyd Hall.

Each of Martha's bedrooms was adorned with a different Kmart pattern. The bedding varied from room to room. One room centered around gingham while another boasted a floral theme. It all looked like the showroom of the Ralph Lauren Home collection; only once reporters touched the sheets they were reminded where they came from. They weren't as soft as Lauren's or Calvin Klein's, but they looked beautiful in Martha's multimillion-dollar home. Pillowcases, sheets, comforters, and coordinating towels and bath accessories were all on display. After that, the press dined on grilled salmon, cold asparagus, and risotto—a real Martha Moment.

As she explained things to the reporters, the arrangement with Kmart was proving especially gratifying because Kmart was now no longer treating her like a mere licensee but rather as a full-fledged "true partner"—so much so, that it would soon seem as if Kmart was not only helping her sell more merchandise than ever before, but was even helping her buy her way out of her entanglements with Time Warner.

Two and one-half years later, in the summer of 1999, when Martha and Sharon were at last gearing up to take Martha Stewart Living Omnimedia public in an IPO of their own—a deal in which they hoped to raise $130 million by valuing their company at $873 million, of which 83 percent would belong to Martha herself—the other shoe finally dropped, and it became possible to see what she had actually paid to get her company back out of the clutches of Time Warner.

The truth was astonishing. In actual cold cash, Martha hadn't paid the $85 million purchase price that the *New York Times* and others had suggested at all. In fact, she hadn't really paid much of anything. She'd signed a $30 million four-year loan; handed over $18 million in cash, some $16 million of which she'd apparently just gotten from Kmart; and issued Time Warner approximately 6.3 percent of unregistered shares in her new company's stock—that she quickly bought back with the proceeds of the IPO, while paying off the loan thereafter as well.

Thanks to the financial engineering arranged by Sharon Patrick, Martha had bought back her company for an actual, out-of-pocket cash outlay of approximately $2 million, which basically amounted to about three days' worth of the company's revenues. It was easily the greatest financial coup in the history of American publishing, and one of the most astounding in the whole history of Wall Street. And no one had to wait very long to see why, for when she finally took Martha Stewart Living Omnimedia public in her October 1999 IPO, the company's stock price nearly tripled during its first day of trading, giving the one-time Connecticut caterer a personal net worth of more than $1 billion . . . for which she had paid out of her own pocket a mere $2 million.

Few in American business had been smart enough—or nervy enough—to approach deal making by playing the needs of one corporation off the next to stage an end run around the normal and traditional sources of capital, namely the banks, particularly when the goal was to acquire huge amounts of money for a business designed expressly to celebrate its creator. Real estate financier Donald Trump played a version of that game in the casino industry and had gone broke once already. Moneyman Ronald Perelman played the game in cosmetics, and the stock of nearly every company he bought soon collapsed.

But no one had ever before even attempted to play this game in the media—least of all two women who plotted the whole thing from a suburban kitchen. The mediamen had never encountered anything like it, and in their befuddlement and confusion, Martha and Sharon took them by the heels and shook and shook until so much money fell out that all of American business simply stood back and gawked.

LABOR RELATIONS

Martha prided herself on being a detail-oriented, organized person. And on one level, her attention to detail was impressive. With a cell phone permanently at the ready, she glided effortlessly from one conversation to the next, jumping in and out of communications with friends, colleagues, and employees alike, on all manner of subjects. She could jump in quick succession from phone calls about what to feed her dogs—Paw Paw, Chin Chin, Zuzu, and Empress Wu, or her eight Himalayan cats (Teeny, Weeny, Mozart, Beethoven, Verdi, Vivaldi, Berlioz, and Bartók), or her six canaries (four white, two red, none named), or her various chinchillas, or even the innumerable barnyard animals on the grounds of Turkey Hill—then shift gears to a discussion about the best time of the year to go tarpon fishing in Boca Grande . . . and from that to the proper aquatic conditions for maintaining a year-round carp pond in Connecticut . . . then next to whether it was time yet to deadhead the peony bushes on her property in East Hampton.

But this frenetic activity—and its expression in her encyclopedic accumulation of eclectic, random knowledge—now seemed little more than an act, and a counterproductive one at that, since she was leading one of the most complicated lives on earth, of a scope that no one could conceivably micromanage. Yet the more challenging her life became, the more complex she sought to make it, as she filled up more and more of her days with the media-intense performance art that she alone could undertake—then heaped on more personal possessions, committed herself to more personal appearances, and dashed off on more adventure vacations to the furthest corners of the planet.

By February of 1997, Martha had left her NBC perch where she'd been appearing opposite *Today* show anchor Bryant Gumbel, who himself had only recently left the network. But whereas Gumbel had disappeared into a seeming kind of strange, early retirement, Martha simply hopped over to CBS and began appearing once a week, for more money, as the network's lifestyle authority on the CBS *This Morning* show, opposite *Today*.

Into this, she now injected a daily ninety-second syndicated radio broadcast show, "Ask Martha," even as her once-a-week TV show, *Martha Stewart Living*, ramped up to a daily half hour format, and soon thereafter to a full hour. In the middle of all this, she bought a sixty-one-acre estate on the coast of Maine from the estate of Edsel Ford, even though she already owned two homes in East Hampton, New York; two homes in Westport; and her apartment in New York.

When she made a pitstop appearance on *Larry King Live*, the incredulous King asked her whether she thought the frenzy in her life was all worth it—whether she ever woke up and said, "I don't like this anymore, who needs this!" To which, Martha answered, "I always think I need more time . . . a few more hours in the day." Weeks later, she was hiking up a mountain slope in Peru to view the ruins of Machu Picchu, an ancient Inca city; then it was off to Cuba for the arrival of Pope John Paul II; then it was destination Japan, for the Winter Olympics; then back to Turkey Hill for lunch with the President of the United States.

On one of Martha's returns to "home," a letter was waiting for her. The New York State Department of Taxation had served her with a delinquency, penalty, and interest bill that would eventually cost her a bundle because neither she nor anyone else in her life could prove whether she had been in Connecticut or New York for much of 1992.

By that time, a fat tax bill, even with a penalty, was hardly a financial burden for Martha. On the other hand, it underscored, as vividly as anyone could have asked for, that it simply was not possible to lead the life she was claiming to lead. Too many of the everyday details of living—both in her personal affairs and in business—were beginning to slip between the cracks of her ever-more energized schedule. And too many improbable claims and assertions were beginning to fall from her lips. These remarks seemed to tumble forth hastily and without reflection in the rush to do too much at once and wear too many different hats: media industry CEO, TV personality, radio commentator, newspaper columnist, world adventure traveler, mountain climber, gourmet cook, homemaker, housekeeper, and—enveloping everything and giving meaning to it all—her ultimate self-appointed job as role model for womankind.

One sensed that she needed to get offstage more, calm down a bit, and say less. But she couldn't. Instead, she had become like the Jim Carrey character in the hit 1998 movie, *The Truman Show*: Wherever she went, whatever she did, whatever she said, the whole world was watching and listening. And sometimes what she said just didn't hold up under scrutiny, as if she'd blurted out something without thinking it through . . . as if inspired by little more than the sense that it *ought* to be true.

In 1996, even as she was renegotiating her deal with Kmart, another high-profile personality, talk show host Kathie Lee Gifford, was coming under intense criticism in the press for her involvement with factories that employed low-paid workers in sweatshops to produce women's apparel under the Kathie Lee label. The spectacle featured Ms. Gifford at first denying indignantly that her garments were made under such conditions, then publicly reversing herself in a weeping press conference after she had discovered just how horrid the working conditions really were at the factories that manufactured her garments. Thereafter,

Gifford led what amounted to a public crusade to force retailers to investigate the conditions under which their goods were manufactured before offering them for sale.

The entire affair galvanized public attention on sweatshops and so-called slave-labor factories in the underdeveloped world. Perhaps this caused Martha to voluntarily announce at her East Hampton press conference in February 1997 that, because most of her product line would be coming from offshore suppliers in such countries as Peru, Mexico, Colombia, India, and Egypt, she would have representatives "inspecting every plant." Said Martha, "I don't want any problems with the manufacture of my products."

Neither did Kmart, which required its suppliers to sign statements that they did not employ child labor. But child labor was hardly the only problem with the labor practices of these places. An investigative *BusinessWeek* article on the world of Chinese sweatshops painted a picture of physical beatings of workers by factory guards, grossly inadequate wage levels, and other offenses. What's more, *BusinessWeek* revealed that factories had devised elaborate ruses to make their operations look strictly on the up-and-up whenever Western auditors came around; when they left, everything would revert to business as usual.

Interviews with its employees suggest that something similar was going on in at least one of the factories where goods with Martha's name were being made for sale through Kmart under her new arrangement. The factory, bearing the name Ceramics Co. Ltd., was located in the eastern Chinese city of Jiaozuo, some 1,000 miles from Hong Kong. Air quality in the city was so poor from industrial effluents that Jiaozuo was named by the World Resources Institute in 1999 as being one of the ten most heavily polluted cities on earth and likened the experience of children living there to be the medical equivalent of smoking two packs of cigarettes per day.

The factory, one of dozens in the city, made ceramics—in the case of Kmart, gray-colored coffee cups and large white plates bearing the "MSE" stamp for "Martha Stewart Everyday," the signature brand of her Kmart line.

The factory employed 6,000 workers, with females—many of them elderly—making up about half of the labor force. Three buildings formed the factory complex, which was merged together as a state-owned manufacturing enterprise in 1997. Previously, one of the three buildings had been a prison labor factory that made water pitchers. The building's corners were still adorned with guard towers.

Interviews with workers, obtained through the help of Human Rights Watch and pirate radio station operators, produced repeated and extensive charges of extortion and shakedowns of employees by the factory's bosses. Typical complaint: The bosses charged job applicants the equivalent of $1,000 to be hired, then made them pay the money out of wages that typically ranged between $15 and $40 per month.

For many people, the wages did not even cover food costs. For a person making $20 per month, a day's pay was less than the cost of a serving of pork. What's more, wages were reduced when workers failed to meet impossibly high output quotas, meaning that actual take-home pay was often almost nonexistent. Anyone who protested was fired, with the bosses keeping the money the worker had paid for the job in the first place, then reselling the job to the next person in line from the region's endless supply of cheap labor. Factory foremen and "team leaders" used gangs to enforce their will on the rank-and-file. There were no days off and no public holidays.

Martha's unsolicited claim that her representatives were visiting and inspecting the factories of all her suppliers didn't mean much, for abuses of the Jiaozuo sort were common throughout the underdeveloped world, and doubtless existed in other factories that supplied merchandise to Kmart under her name. The same assertion could be made for almost any other importer of consumer retail merchandise from Asia and Latin America. For Martha to say that she was inspecting every one of them for abuses just made her look silly and uninformed about her business.

Nor did Martha seem much more careful when talking or writing about her own family or her childhood in the pages of her magazine, which carried a popular column entitled "Remembering" on the last page of each issue. Increasingly, she described themes and facts that didn't line up with the public record or her own past articles—creating the impression that these writing obligations, too, were effectively being dashed off on the way to the airport.

In her first book, *Entertaining*, published in 1982, she claimed that she "went to Europe for the first time," "after college, when I married Andy." But sixteen years later, in a 1998 "Remembering" column, she stated that her first trip to Europe hadn't occurred with Andy at all, but four years earlier, in the summer of her freshman year of college—that is, in 1960—with her mother and sister instead.

In another "Remembering" column, she argued that material wealth and the accumulation of possessions is not important for a fulfilling life—and certainly not a motivational circumstance in her own life. She wrote, "The older I get and the more educated I become, the less interested I am in things and schemes and acquisition. I know deep inside that nature and people and light and peacefulness and pets and fresh air and good communication and beautiful colors are more important to me than living in a mansion or a palace." Two issues earlier, her magazine had contained a ten-page photo spread on her vast pink granite estate in Maine, "Skylands," and a birthday party she had thrown for herself inviting more than sixty of her "closest friends."

The impression was jarring. Visually, *Martha Stewart Living* magazine was superb and had already won numerous awards of one sort or another. Yet the least well-edited, and most internally inconsistent articles in it, month to month, were the ones that celebrated the name at the top of the masthead: "Editorial Director, Martha Stewart."

The accumulation of material possessions was becoming an obvious problem for Martha by now, taxing and exhausting her physically even as the desire to accumulate still more kept heaping new demands on her life. She coped with the pressures by insisting that it was the people around her who were causing her headaches, not herself—that jealous neighbors were forever trying to capitalize on her reflected fame by intruding themselves into her life and disrupting her affairs. She dealt with such problems the same way Eddie had attempted to cope with his frustrations—by yelling and vituperation, hoping, it would seem, to intimidate and thereby subdue the people who lay outside her circle of authority and control. Yet as her possessions reached grander and grander proportions—with more and more homes and estates now bearing her name on the deed—she kept colliding with more and more people she couldn't control, winding up in more and more fights and conflicts, which grew increasingly nasty, cranking up the stress in her life even more . . . stress that sought escape through the same relief valve: more yelling, more vituperative abuse.

One such situation involved her second home in East Hampton, which she had purchased for $2 million with the help of that reported $2 million loan from Time Warner, Inc., in the spring of 1995, even as she was starting to negotiate her exit from the company. The home, known locally as "the Bunshaft property," was a thirty-year-old contemporary designed by high-rise architect Gordon Bunshaft, creator of New York's Lever House. On Bunshaft's death in 1990, the dwelling had been donated to the Museum of Modern Art, which eventually put it up for sale.

The structure—constructed largely out of poured concrete and marble—was regarded as almost an eyesore by neighbors, with a cheerless road-front facade that suggested a cross between a military field bunker and a state highway department vehicle compound. But the building was located on East Hampton's Georgica Pond, the swankiest address in town, and far more prestigious than her other residence, a ten-minute drive away on Lily Pond Lane. Martha's Lily Pond neighbors may have included people like Mortimer Zuckerman and Ronald Perelman, but the lakeshore properties of Georgica Pond housed the likes of Steven Spielberg and Courtney Ross, which put the area at the very pinnacle of the East Hampton social pecking order.

Though the property had never been designated an official landmark, the Museum sold it on what amounted to a gentleman's agreement that it would not be altered without at least some unofficial input from the Museum. This apparently mollified neighbors for a time. But when Martha began making changes, adding a lap pool and various additions to the main structure, her neighbors were furious. Many were as wealthy as she was—and in at least one case, just as touchy and difficult to deal with.

That person was her next-door neighbor at the Bunshaft site, a wealthy New York City real estate developer named Harry Macklowe. Like Martha, Macklowe was accustomed to getting what he wanted and pursued an aggressive, elbows-out approach to get it. In 1985, he had shocked New Yorkers by ordering the late-night demolition of a welfare hotel in Manhattan without a permit to beat the approaching deadline of a new city ordinance that would have gone into effect the next day, halting the demolition of such structures. The contractor who followed his instructions was indicted in the case, but Macklowe himself escaped charges. That was the person Martha was soon to lock horns with.

One of the things Martha liked least about the Bunshaft property was that trees and brush had grown up over the years to block various views of Georgica Pond from the house itself, especially along one flank of the property that abutted the Macklowe land. But those trees were one of the things that Macklowe liked *best*: They blocked his view of the Bunshaft house.

Martha's frustration over the unwanted trees was much in evidence when, not long after acquiring the property, she attended a party at the home of yet another Georgica Pond neighbor—business promoter and founder of the Edison Schools, Christopher Whittle. Martha arrived in soiled gardening clothes because she had been working in her garden, and as the evening progressed, one curious neighbor watched her walk repeatedly to a window and stare intently in the direction of her own property further down the shore. Soon she walked down the lawn and began craning her neck this way and that, as if studying how other property owners had expanded their own views of the pond. (Martha apparently uses parties as research opportunities. In the fall of 2001 she was spotted at the home of a wealthy New York philanthropist unobtrusively taking photographs of rooms and accessories during a party.)

Not long after Whittle's party, landscapers arrived at the Bunshaft site and began cutting down trees, and almost immediately, Martha found herself at war with Macklowe, who insisted that Martha's pruning was ruining his privacy.

Macklowe retaliated by planting trees where Martha had cleared them. And this in turn caused Martha to accuse him of trespassing on her land. The issue was taken to the East Hampton Zoning Board of Appeals, where a foot-high stack of claims and counterclaims accumulated. After months of arguing and appeals, the zoning board ruled that Martha was the rightful owner of the land in question, which basically amounted to nothing more than a sliver of swampy marshland at the water's edge.

But Macklowe wasn't going to give up easily, and began a war of attrition through his lawyers, driving Martha's legal fees to $250,000, with no end in sight.

Finally, on November 8, 1996—at just about the moment her negotiations with Time Warner were reaching their final and most intense phase—the zoning board gave Martha permission to clear fourteen trees and shrubs that were growing along the border of her property and Macklowe's. Instantly, Macklowe filed a suit in the New York Supreme Court to have the permission rescinded, and the fighting began all over again. The Appellate Division of the Court issued a restraining order to block Martha from removing the vegetation, but Martha had beat Macklowe to the punch; her workmen had cut down the trees only a few hours earlier, echoing Macklowe's own scramble years earlier to demolish that New York City welfare hotel before the law could stop him.

Martha told the Zoning Board of Appeals that she planned to replant the strip of land with "indigenous wetlands species." But Macklowe wasn't buying it, and the fighting continued, week after week and then month after month. As time passed, the tedious documentation of the "Macklowe-Stewart feud" in the press turned the property into a bizarre local attraction, as people would take visitors to the site and say, "Can you believe it? This belongs to Martha Stewart!" With work having been long halted by injunctions from neighbors objecting to one thing or another, the place looked like an industrial construction site, with a chain-link fence across the roadway, and mounds of weed-covered dirt piled up on what had once been the lawn.

Against this backdrop, as the long Memorial Day weekend of May 1997 began, Martha arose from an early dinner with some friends at an East Hampton restaurant known as The Palm, and drove over to Georgica Pond to inspect her "Bunshaft" before heading home to Lily Pond Lane. As she approached, she noticed something she had not seen before: a six-foot-high chain-link fence newly erected along the boundary between her property and Macklowe's.

People can go crazy when fences are erected on—or even next to—their land, especially when the fence arrives as a kind of defiant "take that!" gesture from a neighbor with whom a fight has been raging for years. And Martha certainly seemed to do exactly that.

Spotting a workman in Macklowe's driveway who appeared to be loading equipment onto a truck, she wheeled her Suburban into the driveway and lurched to a halt in front of the man. The man was named Matthew Munnich, a landscaper employed by a local lawn care company known as Whitmore's Landscaping, and he was soon filing an affidavit in court as to what happened next.

As Munnich told his story, he was just finishing up reloading his equipment on the truck after a day of trimming bushes and mowing the lawn, when the headlights of the Surburban swiveled into the driveway.

"May I help you?" Munnich said to the driver when the car halted, not realizing, in the gathering darkness, who he was speaking to.

In his affidavit, filed with the East Hampton police two days later, Munnich said the driver demanded to know if he had built the fence. Munnich told the woman that he had not. And at that point, said Munnich in his affidavit, the woman started to shriek and scream and call him a "a fucking liar."

"All you Whitmore guys are fucking liars," she screamed. "You're all no good, the bunch of you. You and all your fucking illegal aliens are no good."

Then Martha threatened to call the police. Munnich told her to go ahead. Alarmed but still calm, Munnich said, "This is not really necessary to be talking like this. Don't talk about my guys like that." But Martha kept screaming.

"Don't you leave!" she ordered. "I'm calling the police and you're going to take that fence down."

It was at that point, says Munnich, that he finally recognized who the shrieking driver actually was: TV personality Martha Stewart.

Meanwhile, Martha had opened her cell phone and begun to punch in some numbers. Munnich started to walk away, but as he did, Martha started to back out of the driveway, the cell phone at her ear. Munnich quickly found himself trapped between Martha's side of the car and the nearby security entrance box, which operated Macklowe's electronic gate. The box was secured to the ground by a cement block. Martha was dialing the phone, putting up her window, and maneuvering out of the driveway backward, all at the same time. Suddenly, Munnich found himself stuck between the security box that wasn't about to budge and the mirror on the driver's side of the car.

"You're fucking crushing me," yelled Munnich. "Stop the car. Let me out." But, said Munnich in his affidavit, Martha just looked right at him and kept backing up. Then, as the car was pushing up against him, the mirror collapsed, opening a gap between himself and the moving vehicle and he was able to get free, leaping into nearby bushes to avoid being crushed. Martha continued to back out, and left without so much as another word.

In his affidavit, Munnich said his side was bruised black-and-blue, and that he went to a physician the next day. But the injury and his police testimony weren't evidence enough for a local judge, who ruled in a hearing eight weeks later that Martha Stewart would not be charged in the incident. Ruled the judge, "Both justice and common sense dictate that the confrontation between Ms. Stewart and Mr. Munnich, as objectionable as it may appear, does not warrant arrest and criminal prosecution."

News of the altercation had by then reached the local press, and from there the story of Martha's rage quickly spread to newspapers all over the country, as the fight with Macklowe now became a fight with his gardener as well. In September, Munnich requested that the governor of New York appoint a special prosecutor to investigate the case, but the request was never granted. The following May, Martha retorted, with a federal lawsuit against Munnich, accusing him of libel and extortion. But Munnich's lawyers fired back that the alleged $250,000 extortion claim was in fact a settlement offer put forth by Martha herself, and threatened to countersue for $6 million in compensatory and punitive damages.

The entire matter was resolved in an out-of-court settlement that was sealed with a gag order barring Munnich or anyone else from publicly discussing how much he had actually been paid to drop the case.

But the damage to Martha's reputation had been done: Martha's personal behavior became the elephant in the room that nobody wanted to discuss, even as they marveled at the astonishing conquests of her business career. In fact, more of both were still to come, as the elephant grew ever larger and the dimensions of her business success grew ever more amazing.

20

WHEN BEING IN THE PUBLIC EYE IS NOT A GOOD THING

Ten days after the incident in Macklowe's driveway, a bigger—and far more menacing—problem exploded in Martha's life. It was damaging enough to Martha's public image for newspaper readers all across the country to pick up their morning papers over the Memorial Day weekend and read an Associated Press wire service story that began, "East Hampton, New York, May 31, 1997: "Authorities in this summer playground of the well-to-do are looking into whether Martha Stewart, marketer of gracious living, injured her neighbor's landscaper by backing her car into him . . ."

But that was nothing compared with what happened next, as clerks in bookstores everywhere were already uncrating and shelving copies of a book-length exposé on Martha's life that seemed to confirm all the worst suspicions anyone ever had of her. The book, *Martha Stewart—Just Desserts, The Unauthorized Biography*, had been written by a *National Enquirer* reporter and celebrity biographer named Jerry Oppenheimer, and Martha had been dreading its publication for months. No doubt that was yet another reason she had behaved like such a loose cannon only days earlier in Macklowe's driveway. Martha had, after all, lived a life that had stayed largely hidden until now. But the veil of her public persona was about to be drawn back, and she knew it.

Martha and her public relations assistant, Susan Magrino, had been practicing preemptive damage control for nearly a year on the book, cajoling and pressuring friends and colleagues—and in particular, family members—not to cooperate with Oppenheimer or answer any of his questions. Foolishly, Martha had even taken to publicly attacking him in interviews months before he had finished writing the book, which simply stirred interest in it even more.

The book was everything she must have feared, and more, portraying her as a scheming, wicked person who had connived and lied her way out of the working-class row houses of New Jersey to become a Leona Helmsley-like figure in the world of business, dominating and tyrannizing all those around her.

One of the book's most devastating reports presented a woman of almost diabolical dishonesty: that she lied about her ex-husband, Andy—and in a most hurtful manner—to keep one of her own personal secrets hidden during an interview for a cover story in *McCall's* magazine. The question: Why had she never had more than one child? Martha's answer: It had all been Andy's fault, not hers. As the wheels of the interviewer's tape recorder turned slowly in front of her, Martha explained that although she had badly wanted to have more children, she had been unable to do so because Andy had been rendered sterile by cancer.

The news came as an astonishment, as well as an almost unbelievably excruciating public embarrassment, to Andy. By then he had been gone from Martha's life for more than a half decade and had married Robyn Fairclough and moved to Vermont. Astoundingly, even as he read the words, Andy's wife, Robyn, was five months pregnant with healthy and normally developing twins, which she eventually carried to term. They were his twins. He had never been rendered impotent at all, and Martha knew it. He had been stricken with cancer and beaten it, and now his ex-wife had smashed her way back into his affairs like some demonically possessed character out of a horror movie, to try to mortify him before the world with lies about a disease and his own masculinity.

After getting a blast of the truth from Andy, *McCall's* published a grudging retraction from Martha, who admitted in a subsequent "Letter to the Editor" that her ex-husband's health had had nothing to do with her decision not to have more children, which had been based entirely on "personal reasons."

Yet there was more to it even than that, and Oppenheimer revealed what the truth really was: Nearly fifteen years earlier, while Martha was still in her childbearing years and even before her career began to take off with the publication of *Entertaining*, she had decided not to have more children and had undergone a hysterectomy at least in part to prevent herself from becoming pregnant.

In the *McCall's* cover story, she had lied to the world about her ex-husband in a vicious and hurtful way, blaming him for a personal life-choice that she had made on her own and had now apparently come to regret—if indeed she regretted it at all and wasn't simply striking the pose to bolster her self-image as a paradigm of womanly virtue.

The publication of *Martha Stewart—Just Desserts* presented a whole new view of Martha, calling into question the accuracy and completeness of much of what she had said and written about herself over the years. How could a person write, in her own magazine, a paean to honesty and its importance in life—telling readers how comforting it is simply to tell the truth, even if the momentary pain may be severe, to escape the "sweat about the truth being discovered later"—then lie that way about Andy?

". . . a hideous piece of yellow journalism," was the best Martha could muster when she hosted a luncheon in Pasadena, California, several weeks later to discuss her TV show, *Martha Stewart Living*, which was to debut the following week as a daily thirty-minute show, up from its previous weekly format. "I try to ignore it because to me it's almost laughable that a person like Jerry Oppenheimer can make money off of my life, which has been a rather ordinary life."

Ordinary? She was grasping at straws. Rebutting the book was impossible, but ignoring it wasn't easy either. When a review in the *New York Times* labeled it "must summer reading," it leaped instantly onto the best-seller list and stayed there until Labor Day.

The weeks following publication of the Oppenheimer book were simply unbelievable for Martha. The book seemed the only thing people wanted to talk about. She'd turn up at a trade conference with media executives, and "the book" would come up. She'd appear on a TV interview and it would become the whole topic: Why are people after you, Martha? When are you going to answer back? *Why* don't you answer back? If you don't respond, it looks bad, Martha. Why don't you say something?

And when they weren't talking about the book, they were talking about the confrontation with Macklowe's gardener. The incident in Macklowe's driveway had occurred in May, but the publication of the Oppenheimer book kept the story alive. If Martha turned on the TV, there would be the Munnich man. "She pinned me against the wall with her car," he was saying . . . on TV stations in New York . . . in Portland . . . in Detroit . . . in Houston. He was on stations in Los Angeles, in San Diego, in Indianapolis, and in Boston. He was on the syndicated TV celebrity tabloid show, *Access Hollywood.* In Miami, a TV station began its Martha report this way: "Run down feeling: In New York a landscaper is suing Martha Stewart after she pinned him to a wall and almost crushed him." In a single day that September, more than forty different television stations around the country carried items about the incident. The next day came more. It was as if the entire world suddenly had begun to look at Martha all over again—differently.

On August 31, 1997, Princess Diana of Wales was killed in a Paris car crash, and celebrities the world over began appearing on television talk shows to pay homage to her passing. In Los Angeles, a couple of weeks later, Martha attended the forty-ninth annual television Emmy awards ceremony, then hopped the red-eye to New York, visited a fig nursery, met with her lawyers about the Oppenheimer book, attended a Yankees baseball game, worked out in her gym, then scurried to the Larry King show to express her own thoughts on Princess Di. But less than thirty seconds into the interview, Larry King had turned the conversation from Lady Di to Martha, asking, "Why do you think so many people seem after you?"

"Are you going to sue?" Larry asked. "Doesn't it look bad if you don't answer back?"

"I am not a litigious person," answered Martha, "no matter what you read in these silly stories. I have never sued anyone for anything."

"You've never filed a lawsuit?" King sounded incredulous.

"Never," said Martha.

The show took a break for a commercial, and then Larry King returned. Martha might have thought they'd now be shifting to other topics, but no such luck, as Larry said: "We're back with Martha Stewart. All right. When that book came out, it was a best-seller. That means a lot of people are interested in you. Why didn't you come right out against it?"

MARTHA: [sounding exasperated] Well, what good would it have done? It would only have made them go look at the book a little bit more closely. It's off the best-seller list now. It's a dead book.

LARRY: Did you read it?

MARTHA: No.

LARRY: Come on.

MARTHA: I didn't.

Larry kept boring in, question after question. She was reeling, on the ropes, flailing the air in front of her blindly. It was painful TV, but he stayed at it . . . quick, tight little shots to the body . . . rat tat tat: ". . . the parakeets, when they died, tell us about them. . . . People say you're a different person off camera than on . . . that you throw things . . . that you have a terrible temper . . . that you're tough to be around. How'd all that start? Where did that come from?"

MARTHA: I don't know. In that book . . . in that book, not one of my friends is quoted, not one friend is quoted.

LARRY: Not one?

MARTHA: Not one.

LARRY: But all these lies about you . . . they've got to do something to you, you're a human being, right?

MARTHA: Maybe one day I'm just going to drop dead, you know?

Martha staggered back to her corner and Larry turned to the camera: "We'll be right back with Martha Stewart. Don't go away."

Since she could not challenge the accuracy of the Oppenheimer book, Martha did the next best thing, and several weeks after her appearance on *Larry King Live,* she filed a $10 million libel suit against the *National Enquirer* newspaper, which had run an article over the Labor Day weekend under the headline, "Martha Stewart Is Mentally Ill."

In the article, two experts had stated, based on information in *Martha Stewart—Just Desserts,* that Martha Stewart was probably unstable. This, in turn, had given Martha's lawyers what looked like a chance to defend her reputation without arguing over the actual facts of her behavior.

In the article, Martha was said to have engaged in "self-mutilation" and to have "threatened suicide." But both of those facts, and many others like them, had already been published in *Martha Stewart—Just Desserts* and gone unchallenged. So the suit sought to sidestep that entire discussion by simply focusing on whether the *Enquirer* had defamed Martha by characterizing the testimony of the experts as evidence of actual mental illness instead of mere opinion on the matter.

On one level, the complaint amounted to a welcome time-out to let Martha catch her breath from the abuse she'd been taking in the press. Since few publications were likely to run stories on her personal life and emotional state until it was clear just how much of what was being said and written about her was actually true, the action at least halted the "piling on" stampede.

And the suit also invited expressions of support from voices in the celebrity world, where tabloid journalism was viewed as being on a par with child molestation. Celebrity columnist Liz Smith had already rushed to Martha's defense, pronouncing her a "strong, dynamic woman" who most certainly wasn't mentally ill—no more so, argued Liz, than was any "high-powered male executive who wants what he wants, when he wants it . . ."

But libel suits are never simple matters, and first amendment defense lawyers are adept at getting complaints dismissed on technical side issues that have nothing to do with the substance of the charges, thereby leaving plaintiffs looking worse than ever. It doesn't look good for the subject of a highly embarrassing and rough profile to paint the article as false and defamatory, only to have the case thrown out of court. People don't care about the reason for the dismissal; they only remember that the case was thrown out, concluding on the basis of that fact and nothing more that the story must have been true.

What's more, if and when a case eventually does get to trial, the defendant can always prevail, under the law, simply by showing that what he or she wrote was, in fact, the truth. With a public figure like Martha, the defense also will win if it can show that there was no reason to question the truth of what was presented. So, when Martha sued the *Enquirer* by claiming that its story falsely portrayed her as being mentally unbalanced, she was inviting the *Enquirer* to show that she did indeed have genuine mental health issues and that there was no reason to doubt the truthfulness of episodes and behavior patterns established in the Oppenheimer book. To that end, the newspaper hired the Washington, D.C., law firm of Williams & Connolly to defend it—the first step of which was to begin compiling a dossier—this time not with a reporter's notebook but with the deposition and subpoena power of the federal court. The purpose: to show that there were grounds to claim that Martha really was what her friend Liz Smith had insisted she was not: namely, "nuts."

Meanwhile, Martha's frenzied lifestyle continued to ramp up, as she abruptly found herself propelled, in a strange and somewhat dislocating way, into a supporting role in the precedent-setting state visit to Cuba by Pope John Paul II. The assignment was the end result of weeks of discussion in New York among executives at the CBS television network, where she was making regular weekly appearances as a "lifestyle" guest on the CBS *Morning Show* with hosts Jane Robelot and Mark McEwen.

Earlier in the year, Martha had been recruited away from NBC's *Today* by CBS, to become a weekly guest on their morning show as part of a drive to revive CBS's chronically weak showing against both NBC and ABC in the 7 A.M. to 9 A.M. time slots. The network constructed an elaborate kitchen on the set for Martha, which she used to demonstrate the food preparation activities that viewers found so mesmerizing.

The *Morning Show*'s rating quickly soared, creating an unexpected problem for the network when the CBS News Division, headed by Andrew Heyward, made plans to preempt the network's Entertainment Division programming with full start-to-finish coverage of the Pope's visit to Cuba. This would have knocked the *Morning Show* off the air, and Martha along with it, spoiling the ratings momentum she had helped build for the time slot. So CBS Network President Leslie Moonves hit on the idea of sticking Martha into the news coverage to do live reports on Cuba's lifestyle and cuisine to keep her growing legions of fans from deserting back to NBC once they discovered that she'd been preempted by Dan Rather standing at Havana Airport, saying, "The Pope's exiting the plane now . . . he's descending to the tarmac now . . ." and so on and so forth.

The News Division people loathed the idea because it seemed to dumb-down the idea of news into nothing more than prettified entertainment. What would be next, Martha Stewart as a coanchor with Dan Rather? Such an idea had actually been discussed but went nowhere when people realized the levels of ridicule they'd be inviting from such a move.

Even so, the "Martha Goes to Cuba" plan moved ahead, and on January 21, 1998, Martha found herself heading through the lobby of Cuba's Havana Liberty Hotel on her way to meet a local tour guide named Neil Joan, who was standing in the dazzling morning sunshine of Old Havana, just outside the hotel's front door, waiting for her. Behind Martha trailed her support staff: a camera crew, producer, and driver. Neil's job: to give Martha and her entourage a tour of the city so they could film segments for CBS about architecture and Cuban coffee.

The once-grand Havana Liberty Hotel—now home to journalists who had arrived from all over the world to cover the Pope's visit—had become a wreck during Castro's regime. But recently, the city had received a face-lift in preparation for the papal visit, and the hotel's crumbling facade of blue and white tiles, had been repaired tile by tile. But Martha hardly seemed to notice or to care as she exited the front doors at 8 A.M. and, looking straight ahead with a fixed, distant, and expressionless stare, climbed into a waiting white van belonging to the Cuban Ministry of Foreign Affairs. With Neil sitting in the seat behind her and her crew—fifteen people in all—following in a vehicle behind them, they headed off for the day.

For what seemed an eternity, Martha spoke to no one but simply stared silently ahead, looking at nothing as the caravan of cars snaked through the streets of the city.

Next to Neil sat Martha's producer, a tall, blonde woman named Kathleen Finch. She was the one who had hired Neil for the tour, obtaining him through a local company called Havana Tours. First impressions often count for a lot in life, and Neil had sensed that Kathleen was agitated from the moment she'd arrived in Havana. She'd seemed fretful, altogether too fearful of how Martha herself might react if Kathleen hadn't made all the arrangements just right. But why fuss so much? This was Havana, Cuba, after all—a city in which people still traveled around in 1951 DeSotos . . . a city that had just received its first coat of paint in thirty years . . . and here was this Kathleen Finch person, fluttering around as if she were a lady in waiting for the Queen of Siam.

"I won't be introducing you to Martha as a tour guide," said Kathleen. "Tour guides are sort of, you know, 'inferior.' So we'll make you a 'local historian.'"

The first stop on the tour was the Castillo de la Real Fuerza (Castle of the Royal Force), about fifteen minutes from the hotel. The oldest castle in Cuba and one of the oldest in the Americas, La Fuerza ("the force") was the first military facility on the island. But Martha wasn't interested in hearing about this. Instead, she wanted to take her camera and walk around pretending to film things while the rest of the crew would film her in the act of pretending. There was some hurried huddling among the producer and the camera people, who didn't like the idea, and then suddenly and without explanation, the whole group was heading back to the waiting vans, with Martha now seemingly in a snit. She hadn't gotten her way.

Martha's demeanor improved as the van headed toward the heart of Old Havana, where the city's reconstruction had begun in the early 1980s. Her face brightened and she began asking questions about the renovation plans. The politics and history of Cuba were leaving her cold, but architecture and the renovation of old buildings were obviously things that interested her.

Neil and Martha got out and began meandering down the charming Calle Obispo, while Neil talked about the city's restoration plans.

As the cameras rolled, the two headed into a small café. Since Martha apparently did not speak Spanish, Neil ordered coffee, and the two settled into an outdoor table for their international coffee moment— this curious encounter between a twenty-eight-year-old tour guide, who had been told to assume the role of being a "local historian" so as not to offend the class sensibilities of an American TV star . . . and of course, the TV star herself, whose life had developed into a parade of illusions, leading her finally to this communist café in a "classless society" where both she and her guide were now pretending to be what neither one actually was. Oh, my.

As the waiter departed, Neil looked around for objects of interest to point out and was about to speak when his eye fell on the man at the next table and his jaw dropped in surprise. It was American news anchor Tom Brokaw—yet another of the people who were suddenly stepping out of the TV and into Neil's life. Brokaw and Martha exchanged pleasantries, and Neil was about to join in when suddenly Brokaw got up and left.

Neil felt crushed. Brokaw was one of his heroes, and he'd barely even said hello to him, let alone gotten a chance to speak, when suddenly he was gone. Turning to Martha he told her of his admiration of Brokaw, and of how he himself had learned to speak English by pulling in the NBC network signal on a homemade antenna and listening to Brokaw speak.

Whether Martha was genuinely interested or irritated that her "guide" was talking about a rival celebrity instead of herself isn't known. But whatever her feelings at the new direction in the conversation, she nonetheless quickly managed to steer things back toward something that made her the center of events once again. She said, "I can buy you a satellite dish and send it to you."

Lunch had been booked at a well-known Havana restaurant called the Bodeguita del Medio. The crowd of fifteen, with Martha and Neil at the lead, headed into the restaurant. It was packed with foreigners. The group was led upstairs to a long table. Neil sat across from Martha and menus were passed around. The crowd was lively and talkative with numerous conversations unfolding at once. Eventually, one of the group ordered lunch for everyone. A variety of traditional dishes arrived, and the food was quickly devoured. But it wasn't until the dessert of Arroz con Leche was served that Martha pronounced judgment. And as she spoke, the room fell silent, waiting for her ruling on the restaurant's most famous dish— about which she declared, in a note of finality that invited no reply, "This is very bland, it's really tasteless."

The time was growing short. Pope John Paul II was due at the airport any minute, and that, of course, was the only reason the world, or the networks, or anyone else, was interested in what was going on in Havana that afternoon. But Martha seemed oblivious to that fact, and no one in her entourage seemed eager to point out that time was wasting. When he could stand it no longer, Neil rose and excused himself. "I've got to get to the airport," he said, and headed downstairs for the dash across town.

Whether Martha and her crew ever did go to the airport is something Neil doesn't know, but he certainly didn't see them there later that day. In fact, the last he ever saw of Martha Stewart was that afternoon in the restaurant, complete with its freeze-frame moment of her sampling its cuisine and pronouncing the food bland. But it certainly wasn't the last he ever thought about Martha Stewart for not only was he never paid for his services, but he never received his satellite dish either.

Very few individuals, men or women—public figures or private citizens—could have endured the emotional strain and pressure that Martha went through in the wake of *Martha Stewart—Just Desserts*. Wherever she went, whatever she did, whoever she saw, there was no way for her to know whether the people all around her were thinking the same thing: Is that the crazy lady who tries to run people down with her car? Isn't she the one . . . who did all those things?

Really bizarre and grotesque intrusions in her life began to take place, as people started trying to violate her personal space—like the London hippie who'd climbed up a drainpipe at Buckingham Palace and wandered around inside the Queen's bedroom chambers. It sounded crazy, but it was true. A trio of characters from New York's popular Z-100 rock music radio station drove to Westport one morning, and seemingly intent upon pulling off some goofy stunt like trying to broadcast from Martha's kitchen, talked themselves past the maid. The maid telephoned Martha, who was out somewhere, and Martha told her to call the police. Someone at the police station apparently tipped a reporter, and almost immediately there were wire service stories in newspapers from coast to coast.

Another time a limousine driver backed into the driveway of her estate in Maine by mistake, and Martha thought it was another trespasser so she called the police. Sample headline about the incident: "Martha Stewart Throws Away Welcome Mat."

After struggling much of her life to gain the public eye, she now found it impossible to escape public scrutiny. She was in the nearly unique position of being someone whom other people could turn into news by, in effect, simply walking up and touching her . . . or knocking on her door, or backing into her driveway. Thirty years ago, Martha had said to Norma Collier, "I'll do whatever it takes to get my name in the papers." Now she no longer had to do anything at all: just answer the door.

She appealed for her privacy, but the appeal had little meaning for she'd given her privacy away long ago. Her millions of supporters, who seemed to view her almost in evangelical terms, crowded closer as well. Her persecution seemed somehow to be their redemption. In May 1998, Martha appeared at an Ontario, Canada, department store to introduce a new line of Martha Stewart branded housewares. While making her presentation, she touched a bed ruffle. A woman in the crowd leaped forward, snatched the ruffle, and raced to the counter to buy it for $40—because Martha had touched it.

At the opposite extreme was her younger brother, Frank, a Vietnam War veteran, who disliked Martha intensely and had already been shopping around his version of her story to the tabloids. In the wake of *Martha Stewart—Just Desserts*, he began asking for five-figure sums to snitch on his sister.

It is hard to imagine more difficult circumstances than these in which to be the chairman and CEO of a supersuccessful, ultravisible, high-growth company—particularly when the company in question was in the male-dominated media industry and the person on the spot was a woman who had made monkeys out of some of the biggest egos in it . . . egos belonging to jealous men who made no secret of waiting to see her fall on her face.

But she was strong—possibly the strongest-willed CEO in all of American media except maybe Rupert Murdoch—and she had no intention whatsoever of falling on her face. She had figured out their game now, and she was going to beat them at it real good. Beat them until they bled . . . and then beat them some more. And frankly, she didn't care how rude or insulting or arrogant she sounded. Actually, she liked it. When a reporter asked her to comment on a new Time Warner offering, *Real Simple*, that looked like yet another knockoff of *Martha Stewart Living*, she said, "A real stupid move . . ." and nodded at the reporter's notebook. "Write that down." She was now obsessed with success, totally and completely absorbed with her business. Nothing else in her life appeared to matter.

Martha no longer acted as if she cared whether those around her liked her, particularly the men—if, indeed, she had ever cared at all. From time to time she was romantically linked with one man or another in the gossip columns. She and Mortimer Zuckerman, an East Hampton neighbor and owner of the New York *Daily News* and *U.S. News & World Report*, were once said to be an item; but friends said the relationship seemed to lack energy or purpose, existing simply so that the two could be seen together in public. For a time, she was linked as well with Charlie Rose, the PBS talk show host, but that relationship also seemed to wither and die. At lunch one day in a Japanese restaurant in Westport, a top assistant of Martha's turned to her as hibachi shrimps sizzled before them and said, "You know what? You'd be perfect with Charlie Rose!" and Martha answered as if she could hardly be bothered, "I've been there, he's boring." Once or twice, she turned up in the gossips as a companion of talk show personality John McLaughlin, then the sightings just sort of ended. Months would go by when Martha would have no published dates at all.

All in all, Martha's life seemed to have been pared down, by Martha herself, to four hours of sleep and twenty hours of work, seven days a week, with no room for anything except the obsessive, relentless struggle to make her business bigger and more encompassing. When social engagements had a business context to them, she would turn up—when they didn't, one rarely saw her. And when she did make an appearance, she seemed to go through the motions of civility with her mind a million miles away or use the opportunity to do some research.

In September, she attended the 1998 annual dinner, in Seattle, Washington, for the National Association of Broadcasters. Mel Karmazin, the head of CBS, was host of the affair, so a number of top CBS talent figures including Dan Rather and Charles Osgood, naturally attended, along with Martha.

The dinner, in the revolving restaurant atop the Seattle Space Needle overlooking Puget Sound, began with a cocktail hour and hors d'oeuvres, as everyone mingled, making pleasant conversation. Not Martha, who remained aloof and unapproachable.

Once the dinner started, the guests were treated to fresh Chilean sea bass with a potato bird's nest ensemble—a true Martha Stewart presentation.

After dinner was supposed to come the dessert. But when the meal was over, and the busboys cleared the dishes away, nothing happened. No dessert. The minutes passed. Tick, tick, tick . . . and no dessert.

Suddenly, there was a commotion at one of the tables—the sound of rising voices and the abrupt movement of a chair. Heads swiveled and necks craned. It was Martha. All watched as she rose from her seat and imperiously stormed out of the room. Minutes later, she stormed back in holding a tray of desserts, as waiters and servers followed along behind her with similarly loaded trays. With her face an icy mask, she served several of the guests, then sat herself down at her seat, served the woman next to her, and began eating her dessert in furious silence. Once she finished her own dessert, she rose from her seat and strode abruptly from the room. It was Martha's way of making a point that no one could mistake: Her time was more valuable than anyone else's in the room, including Mel Karmazin's—and actually, she was right.

By now, Martha's inner circle had been reduced to just a few individuals. One of them—her celebrity business chum Sam Waksal—was a nearly nonstop presence in her off-stage world, offering access to just about all that she had left of a life beyond the glare of global acclaim. And the same could be said for her Turkey Hill neighbor and confidante, Mariana Pasternak, who was likewise almost never seen with Martha in public. Instead, she hovered about her constantly in private, sometimes with Waksal and sometimes not, as they both orbited closer and closer the brighter Martha's flame blazed.

Lexi herself had long since tired of Waksal and his pretensions. Though the older man had showered her with rent money for her Madison Avenue apartment back in her Barnard College days, and had thereafter helped her launch a fitness club in the Hamptons, and even a diner, she'd grown increasingly uncomfortable at the thought of having him around—particularly when her mother was present.

"It was so obvious," said a woman who often witnessed the tension that flared between the two when Waksal appeared. "Martha was simply swept away by Waksal and his act. He had conquered the highest peaks that a New York social climber could scale, and

Martha seemed in out-and-out awe of what he had accomplished. So she kept pushing Lexi at him, over and over again, as if by doing so she could somehow relive the lost opportunities of her youth—back when she made her 'Andy Mistake.'" But the whole situation seemed to make Lexi increasingly uncomfortable, as it eventually began to look to some around them as if Martha was actually starting to compete with her daughter for Waksal's attentions.

"Frankly, it was downright sick," said a member of Martha's coterie, groping for some Electra-like analogy to the drama she'd watched unfold. But there was none—at least not in Greek tragedy—as this 1990s-era version of Anne Bancroft and Katherine Ross tussled over their aging Dustin Hoffman in a world of suburban pretense, where the secret word had been changed from "plastic" to "biotech."

Finally, Lexi could take it no longer and, as Martha eventually put it to a reporter for *Vanity Fair* magazine, "she threw him away"—apparently not realizing (or perhaps wanting to admit) that it may really have been the tension with her mother that Lexi had actually wanted to shed.

But this hardly fazed either Waksal or Martha since, with Lexi out of the way, the two now collapsed publicly into each other's arms. Soon enough they were squiring each other around, to charity functions, fund-raisers, and all the other places where the wealthy maneuver to see and be seen.

By 1995, the two had broken into the mainstream press with a *New York Times* story linking them among the 420 guests at the Pierre Hotel wedding of Manhattan power-lawyer Allen Grubman's daughter, Lizzy. This was followed, several months later, by a gossip column reporting that Martha had "fallen head over heels for her 30-year-old daughter's former lover . . ." identified as "Dr. Sam Waksal . . . a handsome immunologist and investor." By the turn of the decade, they had become a staple of the gossips and were regularly linked in stories involving celebrity and charity functions to which the two were even remotely connected.

In fact, the relationship between Martha and Sam was not only private, but operated on many levels—and one of them was financial. Sam himself had by now used his skill on the tennis courts—and his willingness to drop everything and appear on demand whenever summoned—to promote himself into the inner circle of his Easthampton neighbor, financier Carl Icahn.

Widely regarded as the reigning Sun King of New York moneymen, Icahn had a personal net worth that *Forbes* magazine estimated at something in excess of $6 billion by the late 1990s, and Waksal groveled before him shamelessly in an effort to gain access to his money.

Waksal's early three-year connection to Mount Sinai Hospital, where he took up as a researcher in 1982 after being asked to leave Tufts, also helped. Icahn's interest in health issues was widely known, and Waksal quickly began playing his Sinai card with the Sun King, as he encouraged Icahn to support research by the Center into trendy subject areas like genomics—then eagerly took credit for any donations Icahn made.

For his part, Icahn seemed the last person imaginable to let his head be turned by Waksal. Not only was he notoriously frugal in his personal habits, but he openly disdained the self-celebratory lifestyle that Waksal was working hard to perfect. What's more, he was a legendarily tough and skeptical negotiator in business deals, and was regarded by many as the inspiration for the character Gordon Gekko in Oliver Stone's 1990 hit movie, *Wall Street*.

It was surely a measure of Waksal's talent for flattery and biospeak that had Icahn soon handing over his money. Thereafter, Waksal began shopping deals to virtually anyone with money he had ever met, dropping the Sun King's name into his spiel as a credentialing device that he knew would prove irresistible. In the process, these Icahn-linked deals—many of which involved ImClone Systems itself—developed into the Wall Street equivalent of pet rocks that investors began buying for no other reason than that their friends and acquaintances were doing the same.

In the first of these promotions, Waksal beguiled Icahn and the Bristol-Myers Squibb Co. into jointly bankrolling a 1996 biotech startup named Cadus Pharmaceutical Corp., which operated for a time out of ImClone's own offices on Varick Street.

At the same time, Waksal talked Martha into becoming an investor as well, along with Mariana Pasternak's husband, Bart, and even Martha's friend and public relations biggie, Charlotte Beers. Foreshadowing worse to come, he even stuck his two daughters, Elana and Aliza, into the deal as well.

This was followed by more— and more exotic—promotions, as Waksal began positioning himself as nothing less than a kind of bantamweight Icahn, with deals that took on international dimensions. One of these—which went by the name Scientia Health Group— was set up by Waksal in the offshore tax haven country of Bermuda but was run day-to-day in New York, where Waksal used some rented floor space in ImClone's Varick Street headquarters.

Scientia's investors included many of the same names from the Cadus promotion, plus a number of new ones. In addition to Martha, Carl Icahn, and Mariana Pasternak's husband Bart, the Scientia investor list included Martha's celebrity-lawyer friend Allen Grubman, an Icahn friend from Wall Street named Leon Black, another Icahn pal from Wall Street named Nelson Peltz, and various society figures from New York's East Side and the Hamptons.

Meanwhile, Waksal was busy promoting himself as a society figure, and had taken to thowing lavish, attention-getting parties at his apartment, an enormous—and ultra-chic 7,000-square-foot artist's loft in a trendy section of Manhattan's lower West Side known as SoHo. In keeping with the eclectic mix of personalities in whose reflected fame he now sought to bask, Waksal's guests ran the gamut from aging British rock icon Mick Jagger to billionaire real estate developer (turned media figure) Mort Zuckerman, with countless leggy women half their age sprinkled about.

And when spring gave way to summer, and the society headed east to the Hamptons, so did Waksal, repeating his act with barbecues at his Easthampton digs. Sometimes Martha would make her entrance with her two chow-chow dogs on a leash, which was usually good for a line in the tabloid gossips. And when Allen Grubman's daughter Lizzy drove her car into a crowd of night clubbers outside a Hamptons' hotspot, Waksal leaped quickly to her defense, telling reporters the young woman was actually "a very nice, grounded individual."

Wherever Waksal went, whatever he did, whomever he met, and whatever he said, he never missed an opportunity to drop the sorts of names that would elevate his fame. When film director Sidney Lumet shot some footage for the movie *Family Business* at ImClone's offices, Waksal found a way to bring up the names of the film's stars, Sean Connery and Dustin Hoffman, during an interview with a reporter. From that he could segue effortlessly to the time he bought a meal for Joe DiMaggio, then pirouette into the mention of his "friend," and U.S. Supreme Court Justice Antonin Scalia.

He befriended politicians, then dropped their names as drawing cards to his parties. He invested in a movie that had Robert Downey Jr. under contract . . . in a magazine that had supermodel Helena Christensen on its masthead . . . in a restaurant linked to actress Mariel Hemingway—and all became chum in the water as he trolled ceaselessly for larger and more ambitious game.

A few saw through Waksal's act—some just in the nick of time. Yet rarely did anyone escape Waksal's clutches before he had managed to extract the exact bit of information regarding someone else higher up on the ladder of renown—a detail about an opportunity, let us say, or perhaps an interest in common—that would enable Waksal to trade up and move on. Through a society figure and writer named Lally Weymouth, he thus met and befriended one of Wall Street's true elder statesmen, Peter Peterson of the Blackstone Group investment firm, and convinced him to take a seat on ImClone's board. But Peterson developed an uneasy feeling about what he'd gotten into, and resigned from the board after attending his first meeting.

By contrast, Martha seemed hopelessly blinded by the con man in her midst, and had taken to waking him up at 5:30 in the morning for telephone chats about whatever was on her mind, as the two burrowed their way deeper and deeper into each other's lives.

In fact, in the summer of 1998, when Waksal's eldest daughter Elana married a corporate finance man named Jarrett Posner, Martha arranged for her magazine to cover the wedding, managing to leave out just about every noteworthy fact regarding both the affair and its backstory. Yet, it was the hidden backstory of the wedding that showed not only how Waksal himself operated, but revealed just how much Martha herself was now prepared to overlook as the one-time stockbroker in hot pants swooned over the world-class skills of a self-promoter.

In truth, the wedding was little more than a barbecue reunion for Waksal and Martha's circle of financier friends—and their outer rings of celebrity hangers-on—that Waksal had by now gathered together and was promoting as his own.

To begin with, his new son-in-law was hardly a stranger to any-one. Jarrett Posner was soon to begin moving his way up the ladder at a company run by a Carl Icahn investment world chum—and "Friend of Sam's"—named Nelson Peltz, chairman of Triarc Companies, Inc., who was by now an investor in several of Waksal's deals. From court documents and SEC filings, it appeared that Peltz was soon to begin using sweetheart loans from Triarc to help young Posner take a stake in Waksal's Bermuda-based Scientia Health Group promotion—in which Martha, Waksal, Icahn, and more than forty other New York society-set notables (and FOS, as in Friends of Sam) already held stakes.

Nor did Martha's magazine give even a hint of what was surely the largest irony of all in the situation—namely, that in an earlier day, Peltz and Icahn had both been clients of Drexel Burnham & Co.'s convicted junk bond swindler, Michael Milken, and so for that matter had Jarrett Posner's father and his grandfather—the leg-endary Wall Street cheat Victor Posner. And rounding out the sym-metry of the affair, the wedding itself took place on the palm-shaded Caribbean island of Nevis in the British West Indies, a notorious offshore tax haven long favored by individuals such as the two elder Posners, who had been barred by the Securities & Exchange Commission from holding positions as officers or directors of U.S. public companies.

🌿

Of such people—and their value structures—was Martha's private life now filling up. And the presence in that mix of her Turkey Hill neighbor and confidante, Mariana Pasternak, only added to the problems that were about to boil over.

Mariana, as well, continued to enjoy access to Martha's world, but only through her undivided and sometimes even suffocating loyalty to Martha, which had grown increasingly intense in the wake of Jerry Oppenheimer's unauthorized biography, *Just Desserts*.

As Mariana's marriage to Bart had crumbled, she had begun exploring breadwinning opportunities for herself in the Westport area, and at one point had worked as a colleague of Norma Collier's—Martha's early modeling world mentor—after Norma herself had taken a job at a Westport marketing company.

But the job hadn't lasted long, and by 1993 Mariana had gotten into the local real estate game and acquired a broker's license—an all-but-guaranteed route to money in Westport's ultra-expensive housing market. Then came the publication of *Just Desserts*, and Mariana—who'd managed to escape all but a passing mention in Oppenheimer's comprehensively researched narrative—was by now taking vacation trips with Martha, buying and selling property for her, and generally making herself available whenever Martha needed someone personal she could turn to in confidence.

It was a role—and a level of access—that Mariana certainly didn't want to put in jeopardy. So, when she and Norma ran into each other in a local food market and agreed to get together for lunch, Mariana soon had second thoughts. Reflecting on how it might seem if word got back to Martha that she was lunching with the much distrusted Norma Collier, she phoned Norma and cancelled. "Boy, you're really under Martha's thumb," said Norma as the conversation drew to an end. But Mariana let it go; after all, 10,000 luncheons with Norma Collier would never be equal to one real estate transaction on behalf of Westport's wealthiest resident.

Mariana had effectively all-but-transformed her own life into a shadow of Martha's. By mid-decade she had begun vacationing with Martha, and in 1995 left Bart at home while taking their two teenage daughters with her to join Martha and Martha's brother, George, and his children, for the Christmas holidays in the Galápagos Islands.

The trip had been organized by Martha with all the military precision for which she was famous. Each person was assigned to bring a specific list of garments, to be packed in one duffle bag and one backpack per person. In a set of marching orders reminiscent of the days of Eddie and Elm Place, each child was instructed to keep a diary every day; to eat everything he or she was served; to study the native flora, fauna, and weather; and to be polite, courteous, and considerate. In Martha's words, the trip was a "success." How Mariana felt privately about it isn't known.

It would be five more years before all these elements—Martha, Mariana, Bart, Sam Waksal, a Christmas trip to a holiday in the sun, and the stockbroker they all shared, Peter Bacanovic—would finally collide in a single cell phone call by Martha that would change the lives of all involved, and make headlines around the world.

By that time, working for Martha had become out-and-out hell, as the sheer pressure of running her company found release in the way Martha always let off steam: by attacking those around her. She had so many things on her mind—so many plates in the air—that remembering what was happening from minute to minute seemed overwhelming. Yet still she piled on more. In addition to everything else she was doing, Martha added the following to her calendar as 1998 began:

- A trip to Nagano, Japan, to deliver lifestyle reports for CBS during the Winter Olympics.

- ❧ The negotiation and signing of a marketing contract with Sears, in addition to the Kmart deal she already had.
- ❧ The official opening of a new television studio for *Martha Stewart Living* TV productions.
- ❧ The hosting of a $5,000-per-plate Democratic fund-raising luncheon starring President Bill Clinton.

Meanwhile, her five-times-per-week, half-hour show had gone to a full hour, and she had signed up Ford Motor Company as a sponsor. What's more, she would soon be filling in as coanchor for the CBS *Morning Show,* even as *Fortune* magazine would name her one of the 50 most powerful women in America.

It is hard to think of any CEO in the America media, or even many in the whole of business, who kept a schedule to match the one Martha was now following every day. But the pressure had to escape somehow, and it did, as common courtesy—which had never been her strong suit—now morphed into outright hostility toward anyone, or anything, that slowed her down or got in her way.

Anyone who interrupted her—for almost any reason at all—ran the risk of a tongue-lashing.

She answered her phone with a single barked question: "What?" When she'd said what she had to say, she wouldn't say goodbye, she'd simply hang up.

She never addressed her own business manager by his proper name. To Martha, he was known simply as "What is it?" He would approach her office, and she'd look at him and say his name: "What is it?"

At night, she slept only fitfully and would wake up at odd hours and phone up her employees for bizarre reasons. One morning, she called her director of technology in the predawn hours to berate him because a sophisticated multiline telephone he had just installed in her house wasn't working; she was calling him from that very phone.

Some of her employees lived in fear of encountering her in the halls. By the start of 1998, she had outfitted an elaborate Westport television studio not far from her home, for her TV tapings, and had equipped it with an enormous, industrial-size kitchen to prepare various dishes for her cooking segments. The studio contained a smaller kitchen as well—an exact replica of the kitchen at Turkey Hill. Other studio sets suggested the look and feel of cozy Colonial-type New York settings. There was an enormous arts and crafts room, with floor-to-ceiling bins of different kinds of paper, glue, stenciling materials, and whatnot for use on her shows. There was even a fitness room, with her own personal trainer always on call.

The facilities were first-rate, and the spaces were clean and orderly—all in all, an attractive and comfortable place to work.

Yet many of the employees seemed to scurry about in a state of unrelenting panic at the thought of actually encountering Martha in the halls. Some had even developed an early warning system and would pass the word throughout the building whenever she left her office. Instantly, people would vanish behind their desks and bury themselves in their work.

One group of people dealt with answering viewer mail. Much of the mail concerned products that didn't work, or arts and crafts segments that were too hard to follow. Other mail—which was invariably positive and even adulatory—came from a segment of the population among which Martha had developed a huge following that no one wanted to bring to her attention, so these letters were not shown to Martha: her fan mail from male prison inmates.

In the TV production department, people reached states of near hysteria as taping days approached for various segments on her shows. No one wanted to make decisions, to take responsibility for almost anything that would eventually reach the eye of Martha. As a result, simple three- and four-minute scripts for various segments would be labored over for hours, sometimes days, as producers and their colleagues debated endlessly about the placement of mere commas in sentences.

Sometimes when she showed up on the set, she would be pleasant, and other times she would scream at people and berate them in public. No one knew what to expect.

When she scolded people, her language was often foul. "I was shocked—I mean really shocked," said a producer on her show. "She had the worst potty-mouth I ever heard . . . on anybody." During her first day as an employee, one staffer watched Martha's Jekyll-and-Hyde behavior unfold during a summer barbecue scene being taped outside on the studio grounds. When the cameras were rolling, Martha was at her genteel best. When the cameras were switched off, she erupted in a lava flow of barked commands and foul language. Typical instruction from Martha: "Get me a drink, it's so fucking hot out here!"

On another occasion, the source watched a segment being taped in which Martha was supposed to demonstrate how to prepare poached pears in wine. The segment went badly, and finally Martha exploded at everyone and roared, "Shit, we have to fucking do this over again." Then she looked at three opened bottles of wine in front of her on the countertop and cried, "How many bottles of this do we need! Do you think I'm made of money?"

Fidgeting and anxiety reached fever pitch on the day before the actual segments were to be taped, as producers would phone up guests with elaborate instructions on how to handle Martha. "You'll have to guide her," instructed one producer to a guest. "We've got a script all prepared for her, but she might not have read it. Sometimes she doesn't know what the segment is about, so you've got to be prepared to help her get through it."

Martha's instructions for how the scripts were to be prepared were elaborate, intricate, and rigidly enforced. The scripts had to be typed on specific weight bond paper, to specific margins, with a single staple, placed horizontally, in the upper left-hand corner, then labeled with a black-on-white Brother P-Touch labeler.

And the scripts had to be waiting for her at a specifically assigned location so that they would always be within easy reach when she arrived at the studio. Sometimes she would arrive in the predawn hours. Sometimes she would arrive at midmorning. But whenever she arrived, she expected the scripts to be there waiting for her, in their precisely assigned location—on the wash basin next to the toilet in her private CEO's bathroom—a facility that no one else in the organization was permitted to use.

Yet rarely did she seem to have studied her carefully prepared executive reading matter, and segments often had to be retaped over and over again, until Martha finally figured out what the segment was supposed to be about. Those were the Martha Moments that the public never saw.

21

FROM WALL STREET TO MAIN STREET

Exactly when Martha decided to sell stock in her company to the public is not clear. But it was certainly on her mind since the days of the Time Warner buyout, when she first began talking about the matter publicly in interviews, and probably even earlier than that. Sharon Patrick also undoubtedly played a big part, having been trained at both the Harvard Business School and, later, the McKinsey & Company management consulting firm, which often became involved in helping companies raise capital on Wall Street.

But assuredly the biggest factor of all was the market for initial public offerings—so-called IPOs—which were changing the economy, the culture, and how Americans defined success in the world and even their own worth as human beings. At every stage of her life and career—from the go-go 1960s on Wall Street, to the hearth-and-home nesting of the 1970s, to the yuppie self-indulgence of the 1980s, to, at last, the world of Wall Street megawealth in the 1990s—Martha had invariably been where she should be, at exactly the right time. Now she would reap the ultimate reward, becoming an overnight billionaire—and the richest self-made woman in America—at the absolute zenith of the biggest bull market in the history of Wall Street.

Stocks had been rising, almost without interruption, since 1982—the longest such advance the stock market had ever known, and every year the pace had inched up. By the mid-1990s, when dot.com fever began to spread through the market, gains of 20 percent annually in stock portfolios were beginning to seem almost ordinary to investors, especially as more and more IPOs in the dot.com sector were flooding onto the exchanges and instantly leaping to unheard-of prices.

Between the start of 1997, when Martha finally got free of Time Warner, and the start of 1999, when she began actively working to put together an IPO, stocks in the Nasdaq Composite Index soared an unprecedented 80 percent in value—and that number masked the vastly larger gains being racked up by the individual dot.com IPOs within the Index itself. In the spring of 1997, at almost exactly the moment when Martha was backing her car against her next-door neighbor's gardener in East Hampton, and Martha the Wild Woman began to make headlines, a second-tier investment firm underwriter on Wall Street named Deutsch Morgan Grenfell, Inc., was placing shares with investors for an IPO offering in an Internet-based book retailer named Amazon.com. By the time Martha was packing her bags for a Christmas adventure-vacation up the Amazon River nineteen months later, the value of Amazon.com had soared 5,239 percent in value, and looked to be heading even higher still.

And Amazon.com was by no means the only such performer, or even the most spectacular one. On a single day, November 13, 1998, an underwriter named Bear Stearns & Company sold stock in a dot.com IPO called the Globe.com, Inc., which had been started by two Cornell University undergraduates. The shares leaped 900 percent in value on their very first trade in the public market. Had trading in the company continued at that pace for the rest of the week, the market value of the company would have exceeded the entire market value of all stocks on Wall Street. Another week more of such trading, and the company would have been worth $338 quadrillion, or more than the known financial value of all assets on earth.

Speculative fever like that had never been seen before on Wall Street, and people completely lost their heads over it. A top official at Boston University quit his job to become a day trader from his den and made close to $1 million in profits, at least on paper, in barely a week. The CEO of one of the nation's largest and most prestigious management consulting firms, Andersen Consulting (now Accenture Ltd.), resigned to become the chairman of a dot.com start-up in the grocery delivery business, and made $123 million in stock options profits almost instantly. The president of AT&T became the face on a dot.com start-up; the former heads of HBO and Universal Studios became players in the dot.com sector too. So did the former co-chairman of Time Warner, Inc.

Wherever one looked, the "old economy"—and especially the leaders in "old media"—began stampeding into the mesmerizing new world of the dot.com sector. The pull of the money was too strong to resist. A CEO could make the value of his company double, and even triple, by selling stock and then issuing press releases about his big new plans in the dot.com space. A Scandinavian hotel operator with a stock worth 17 cents per share began issuing press releases announcing that he was getting out of the hotel game and into the dot.com business, and his stock soared to $105—a record-breaking run-up of more than 60,000 percent.

Martha wanted to be part of the action, and said so to friends. And if anyone deserved it, she was the one. She had actually created the business structure that media giants like Time Warner had been trying to mimic for a decade. She had a true, cross-platform, multi-media business, and no one else really did. With the launch of her company's retailing website—MarthaStewart.com—in September 1997, she was able to take any product she could dream up, from a dessert recipe to the dinnerware to serve it on, from imported flower bouquets to the vases to display them, from bed linens and com-forters to porcelain figurines, and market her wares in every major media channel in the country. And millions of her fans would snap them up.

She could publish an article in the pages of *Martha Stewart Living* on ingenious techniques for wrapping a holiday gift box—just as her "Martha by Mail" shop-at-home catalog would be arriving in mailboxes, complete with a spread on wrapping paper and ribbons. She could then demonstrate the wrapping techniques on her TV shows and talk about it on the radio, while her website billboarded a wrapping paper and ribbons promotion on its home page. She had put together something unique in the media: an information company in which everything existed to cross-promote everything else. She was what the New Media was all about; in all markets everywhere, able to market almost anything imaginable, by simply attaching her name to it and pushing the brand identification with Martha out through the big Martha Stewart marketing machine. Why shouldn't she go public! Why shouldn't she get a "dot.com multiple" on her company!

By the start of 1999, Sharon Patrick was hard at work to improve the company's financials for an IPO. Employees at the company's corporate headquarters in New York would look up from their desks to see Martha and Sharon in their fishbowl office, with papers and printouts blanketing the desk between them. They were preparing budgets, with the idea being to pull into 1999 as much advertising revenue as possible, while cutting costs to the bone—all to show the maximum possible growth in operating margins and profitability over the previous year.

At one such meeting, the company's executives assembled in the fishbowl. In attendance: Martha, Sharon, the company's business manager, one of the TV department executives, and some others. The issue: whether to move forward with a proposal to start a Martha Stewart Television Network. The TV executive wanted to pursue the idea, but Sharon did not; it wasn't the right time, not with the IPO coming up.

The discussion continued, and soon everyone was talking at once and voices were rising. A minute more and what had begun as a civil discussion had escalated into a nasty argument.

"You're getting nothing," Sharon finally shouted, as those out-side thought, Uh oh, here it comes. . . . They had seen more than one such meeting in Martha's office escalate this way as pressures in-tensified over the IPO. One recent encounter had ended with Martha throwing a coffee cup against the wall, and shouting, "How come everyone is so stupid around here?" Sharon—who had discov-ered that the best way to deal with Martha was give it right back—replied with a volley of fucks and shits . . . those being the preferred expletives by which Martha and her top aides now increasingly communicated their feelings.

There was plenty of reason to be confident that the IPO would go off without a hitch. The market was not only unbelievably hot, but the company's financials looked fantastic—even without the spit-shine Sharon was giving them. As the market soared higher and higher, almost every kind of dot.com company imaginable was being taken public—for online drugstores, online telephone com-panies, and e-mail companies, even ones for flower and pizza deliv-ery services and an Internet company in the pet food business. Almost none of these companies had produced any profits, and some had been in business for only a few months.

Against such competition, Martha Stewart Living Omnimedia, Inc., looked like an investment in Fort Knox. The company was gen-erating more than $222 million in annualized revenues, which themselves were growing at a nearly 30 percent annual clip. And best of all, the company was actually making huge amounts of money: nearly $30 million on an annualized basis. And the profits were actual cash money. There were no weird and twisted account-ing tricks in the company's financials—no depreciation for good-will, no off-balance-sheet liabilities or derivatives . . . just a solid, straight-ahead presentation that any investor or money manager could read and understand in thirty seconds.

Martha also had one of the most powerful Wall Street forces working for her: her co-underwriter on the deal, Morgan Stanley &

Co. On a personal level, that fact alone brought her great satisfaction since, thirty years earlier, she had applied for a job at Morgan and been turned down, winding up at the glorified penny stock shop of Perlberg, Monness. Now here she was, three decades later, hiring Morgan to work for *her*. Talk about a dish eaten cold.

But there was another, and more immediately practical, reason for satisfaction at having Morgan in her corner. Morgan was one of the two most prestigious investment firms on Wall Street, and was constantly vying with its key rival, Goldman Sachs & Company, to serve as lead, or at least top co-underwriter on all the best offerings. Because Morgan had a highly skilled and aggressive trading desk, it could almost always make the shares of its underwriting clients "pop" in the after-market, which meant, in turn, that a Morgan-underwritten deal all but guaranteed success.

That success had spilled over onto one of its technology stock analysts, a woman named Mary Meeker, who had been part of the Morgan team that had brought Netscape Communications—the IPO that started the dot.com craze—to market in 1995. Thereafter, a recommendation by Meeker came to be seen as a kind of dot.com seal of approval that sent almost any offering quickly soaring to astronomical heights.

The combination of Morgan's trading desk and Mary Meeker's reputation meant that any dot.com IPO from Morgan was marked up with a "Meeker multiple" even before it was sold to the public. It was the Meeker multiple that Martha was hoping to profit from, as the extra sweetener from a Morgan-backed underwriting, when her company finally went to market.

Best of all, being linked with Morgan meant that others wanted part of the Martha Stewart action, too, and this added to the buzz forming around the IPO. The key players in that regard were at a West Coast venture capitalist group named Kleiner Perkins Caufield & Byers, which had long and close ties to Morgan Stanley. The Kleiner Perkins fund had gotten in early on the dot.com game, and held big start-up stakes in a whole range of Internet darlings, including the @Home, Inc., cable modem service, Amazon.com, and many others.

One of the firm's superstars was a fellow named John Doerr, who had joined Kleiner Perkins in 1980 and had risen to a position of enormous power and influence in the field of high-tech investing. Doerr had become a director on the boards of numerous ultra-successful technology companies, which meant that his name—like Mary Meeker's—was something that investors automatically looked for when hunting for promising IPOs that would soon be coming to market.

So, when Doerr's name turned up as a new member of Martha's board, in July 1999, no one on Wall Street had any doubt that the Martha Stewart Living Omnimedia IPO was drawing near and that it was going to be a huge hit.

It was easy enough to see why Kleiner Perkins wanted in on the deal: The terms offered the fund were too juicy to resist. In the deal, Kleiner Perkins paid Martha's company $25 million in cash to retire all the existing debt on Martha's balance sheet, receiving back two million shares of stock in her company. This in effect meant that Kleiner Perkins was getting stock in Martha's company at a premarket price of $12 per share when the shares themselves were almost certain to be priced much higher in the IPO.

How much higher? It depended in part on how charming Martha herself could be when she and her underwriters went on a nationwide and European marketing trip to drum up support for her shares among institutional investors. She was now only one or two steps away from grabbing the ultimate brass ring of American business. The girl who had fled a collapsing penny stock firm at the start of the longest bear market since the Depression was now ready to return to Wall Street, thirty years later—escorted by the swankiest and most powerful firm on the Street—to be anointed America's first self-made, female, stock market billionaire, at the pinnacle of the longest bull market the country had ever known. Timing? The lady was about to retire the cup.

But the company first had to be promoted to the underwriters' own institutional investor clients—the well-heeled hedge funds, mutual funds, and money management companies that would buy the shares at their offering price, then turn around and often resell them to individual investors once actual trading began in the public market.

This promotion process was known on Wall Street as the "road show." Typically, the underwriter would take the company's CEO and one or two other top officials on a multicity tour where they would make presentations to the executives of their largest institutional clients to impress them with the company's bright business prospects and its dynamic, visionary CEO.

Most such events were tedious, time-consuming, and generally regarded as a waste of time by everyone involved. The market was by now so hot—and the quality of the IPO offerings so poor—that institutions were signing up for big blocks of stock without even bothering to "inspect the merchandise." They knew it would be threadbare and basically worthless, but they also knew they'd be able to resell it for a quick killing, so it was hard to justify wasting a morning at a road-show presentation.

With Martha it was different. People wanted to meet her and listen to her talk whether they were going to buy her stock or not. She had become an authentic star, radiating the charismatic appeal that made people just want to get near her, crowd up close, and listen and touch. Because Morgan Stanley had major institutional clients in Europe, the road show included stops in London and on the Continent, and there were presentations in cities across the United States as well. The wealthiest clients with the most capital to invest got one-on-one treatment, with Martha and her crew of seven turning up personally in the client's offices to make forty-five-minute presentations; less wealthy clients were simply herded together for luncheons in hotel conference rooms.

But there was a side to Martha's life that she was determined to keep hidden from Wall Street at all costs, especially now, on the eve of her IPO. It was the side that dealt with her personal behavior—the fits of depression and the threats of suicide and even an event of self-mutilation . . . her abusive treatment of the people around her . . . the mercurial and explosive temper . . . the foul language.

The entire flip side of the one-eyed Jack known as Martha Stewart had been coming into focus, slowly but relentlessly, for nearly twenty years . . . in the early profiles in *New York* and *Working Woman* magazines . . . in the local newspaper stories by the reporters she'd insulted and belittled . . . in the mistreatment that she'd heaped on her husband, and the anger and resentment she'd stirred up among her neighbors.

Here she was, on the brink of going public in a stock offering that could make her rich beyond fathoming, and unknown to the world at large, her past was coming back to haunt her again. When she'd filed that $10 million libel and defamation action against the *National Enquirer* nearly two years earlier for calling her mentally ill, the newspaper hadn't simply rolled over and played dead. It had hired the best law firm it could find to defend it, and the firm had immediately set out to prove that there was a sound factual basis for the tabloid to carry the story—that she was mentally ill.

To that end, the Williams & Connolly's legal team, headed by an aggressive First Amendment defense lawyer named Gerson Zweifach, had gone through *Martha Stewart—Just Desserts* page by page, line by line, word by word, and traced back the assertions and statements and incidents in the book's pages to the original sources for each of them. Then one after the next, they had put people interviewed in the book under oath and interviewed them all over again.

And each and every one they questioned—three dozen witnesses in all—had said the same thing: The book accurately reflected what they had told the author. Said Martha's college era friend, George McCully, who had been a regular and frequent weekend guest at Turkey Hill after the Stewarts had left New York, "I would say it [the book] is very nearly totally accurate . . . on the whole, a very accurate book."

Even Martha herself had been put under oath and deposed. Guests at the mid-June 1999 wedding on Long Island of CNBC cable television personality Maria Bartiromo to the son of Wall Street financier Saul Steinberg had no idea what awaited Martha, as the queen of domestic perfection moved among them, her face a mask of cool resolve. Four days later, she would be raising her right hand in a rented room in a Norwalk, Connecticut, Doubletree Inn and swearing to tell the truth to lawyers who were determined to show that their client had the right to publish an article saying that she was mentally ill.

The resulting testimony ran to more than eighty-five pages, but almost nothing of what she said was ever made public. She testified that she had tried to stop publication of *Martha Stewart—Just Desserts* before its publication and had actually telephoned the president of William Morrow & Company to ask him to help stop publication. She acknowledged as well that she had tried to stop her friends from returning Oppenheimer's calls when he was writing the book and telephoning around for interviews.

But what else she said may never be known, for her lawyers filed her deposition under seal, and the full testimony quickly sank from public view, as the smothering silence of court-ordered confidentiality enveloped the case. The lady who had gone to court to show the world that she was not mentally ill, now didn't want the world to see her own sworn testimony any more than anyone else's on that very subject.

As to why, there seemed little doubt. After all, how would it look to be making the rounds of Wall Street in search of $130 million worth of public money for her company while the state of her mental health was being debated in the pages of every newspaper in America? The stress of the situation must have been almost unbearable: After a lifetime of struggle, from the working-class suburbs of New Jersey to the lawn-apron'd estates of East Hampton and the coast of Maine, she was about to rise from the power circles of international stardom into the rarified air atop the highest financial peak of all: She was about to become, at century's end, a Wall Street billionaire . . . if the tabloids just didn't start rehashing what the *National Enquirer* had published years before.

In the midst of all this, something odd occurred. For reasons that may be best explained by the tug of the moon and the tides within our genes, or maybe left simply unexplained, Martha dropped everything, and with her TV production crew in tow, headed for the Iowa State Fair in Des Moines. Her purpose: to tape a segment for an upcoming broadcast of her show. The objective: to show her feeding hogs, tasting pies, and examining quilts . . . all in a way that would remind people—including no doubt her underwriters on Wall Street—that the heartland values of America were what Martha was really all about.

And so, under the cloudless sky of a late August in the corn country, the 975,000 visitors to the 141st Iowa State Fair were able to watch not just a tractor-pulling competition, or a lady riding a unicycle, or someone carving a scene from the Last Supper out of a mountain of Iowa butter. Beyond all that, they could behold, most compellingly of all, the inestimably famous Martha Stewart being taped by her production crew—just as had been done in Havana, Cuba, the year before—as she went about her performance of Just Being Martha.

The farther one got from Iowa, the cornier the whole event seemed, with the attitude of bemused superiority being perfectly captured by a headline atop a story on Martha's appearance that ran in the *Spokane-Review* newspaper in Spokane, Washington: "The Happy Homebody Hogs Space at State Fair." But no one in Iowa viewed her appearance as hogging anything—and that was the message that America's bicoastal media elites had missed about Martha Stewart from Day One. In fly-over America, her appeal was simply indescribable. In the working world of the American heartland, where women by the millions toiled in Norman Rockwell's silent rituals of life and death and yearned for something more, Martha Stewart had become the American Evita, draped not in jewels looted from the national treasury but in the faux finery of her ruby slipper dreams.

The potency of her appeal was undeniable as she strode through the exhibits, followed by her entourage, and crowds as large as those at the 2002 Winter Olympics simply parted to let her pass, to murmurs as ceaseless as the wind through the cornfields: "That's Martha Stewart . . . over there . . . here she comes now . . . Martha Stewart. Hush." Said a 13-year-old girl named Andrea Kemp, who had been preparing for months to enter her prize Yorkshire hog in the 4H Club competition, "She came over and watched. I had to concentrate and keep my eye on the judge, but if I had the chance I would look at Martha."

A few hours more and Martha was heading back to the airport to prepare for the debut, in New York, of yet another cloning of her ubiquitous media messages—this time as a TV series entitled *From Martha's Kitchen*, to begin airing in September on the cable television Food Network. But had she simply slowed down even slightly, and diverted her caravan 76 miles to the east for a brief visit to the town of Ladora, Iowa (pop. 308), she would have come face-to-face, in the ripeness of her life, with the ghosts of much of what made her what she was . . . and what she had become . . . and what she now represented to the women of America. For it was from the dusty streets of Ladora—back at a time when ragtime was played slow and folks hung bunting on the porch at the Fourth of July—that a young woman much like Martha Stewart had yearned to escape.

It was a yearning that took the young woman first to college, and then, like Martha Stewart, to New York and the writing of books. And, like Martha Stewart, her output was prodigious, eventually dwarfing that of most any other female writer of the twentieth century, with almost 150 books to her name, and millions of copies of them in print. And, like Martha, her career reached its fullest flowering late in life as, well into middle age, she became a global adventuress, piloting her own plane to the ends of the earth, stopping perhaps just long enough to scale the peak of some mountain, or explore some ruin from the ancient world.

Her name was Mildred Benson but the world knew her better by her nom de plume of Carolyn Keene, the original writer of the series of children's books that had set fire to Martha's imagination nearly a half century earlier, with her character creation of the self-confident, ambitious, self-reliant, quick-witted teenage girl who was the match for any man. For here in Ladora, in the corn country of the American heartland, was the birthplace and hometown of the young girl who grew up to pen the Nancy Drew detective series that Martha has never acknowledged in her writings as having read at all—but which her childhood friends from Nutley, New Jersey, say she simply couldn't put down. Here in Ladora were the ruby slippers that Martha clicked at the heels three times and discovered that she suddenly wasn't in Elm Place anymore. And she never paid a visit, and she probably never knew.

By mid-October there were but a handful of days left before the company's shares were due to be "priced" and sold to the public—and *still* the world knew nothing of the legal drama unfolding just offstage. Meanwhile, preparations quickened for the crowning Martha Moment. At 9:30 A.M., on October 19, she would step to the balcony overlooking the main trading floor of the New York Stock Exchange, and with a banner reading "Martha Stewart Living Omnimedia" stretched against the wall behind her, and NYSE chairman Richard Grasso at her side, she'd pick up a mallet and strike the opening bell to signal the commencement of trading. In a lifetime of finest hours, it would be the finest one of all . . . *if.*

And through it all, she never broke a sweat in public—not the slightest hint of the tension mounting within her . . . at least until now. Which headline would she wake up to first: Martha Stewart Billionaire? Or Martha Stewart Nut?

In midmonth, the road show took its performance to San Francisco, and paid a visit on the offices of R.S. Investments, a Morgan Stanley institutional client group that managed some $7 billion in funds for investors interested in the stock of small- to mid-size, high-growth companies—companies exactly like Martha's. But by now, the strain was starting to show. The group—Martha, Sharon, and assorted salespeople and bankers from Morgan—arrived in midmorning and were escorted to the conference room. With them, they brought large pastel canvas bags containing sample magazines, hats, hand soaps of one kind or another, dishware, and whatnot—and began passing the items around. Then presentation handouts of the company's financial projections were distributed, and the team went into its spiel: Martha spoke for fifteen minutes, then Sharon, then a third woman, identified as the CFO, and finally one of the men from Morgan Stanley.

Martha came off well informed on the basics, with a "good grasp of the business," as one of the R.S. men in the room put it. But it was odd. There was something missing, a lack of energy maybe, or excitement—*something*. The R.S. man couldn't quite put his finger on what it was. The Morgan reps just stood there like bozos, the way they always did on road shows. Which was okay because the main attraction was supposed to be Martha. Yet she, too, seemed a bit distracted, as if she had her mind on other things. "We asked questions about how the company was going to get to its goals," said the R.S. man, "how were they going to hit their EBITDA numbers (earnings before interest, taxes, depreciation, and amortization—a measure of cash profitability) and that sort of thing. But none of them could really say. They seemed to be having trouble explaining. It was strange."

The most dislocating moment of all came when one of the R.S. people asked a question and one of the Morgan people began to answer—in the middle of which Sharon Patrick flipped open her cell phone and began making a phone call without first excusing herself from the room. Her conversation continued, with her voice loud and almost braying, even as the R.S. people began to shoot glances back and forth among themselves, as if to say, "Who *is* this person?"

Forty-five minutes later, the group was heading for the door. Next stop: somewhere else in town, where they'd do the same sell routine all over again . . . and then maybe again and again after that. It was the end of the road show and everyone was tired. A few more days and it would be all over. The end was in sight.

Or was it? On the day before the IPO was to take place and the shares were to begin trading in the public market, something happened in the U.S. District Courthouse in Los Angeles, where the case known as *Martha Stewart v. National Enquirer et al.* was proceeding apace. Nearly two full years had now passed since Martha had filed her suit, and the procedural maneuvers of the two sides had finally reached what is known as an argument over a Motion for Summary Judgment—in this case a request by the *National Enquirer* that Martha's libel action be thrown out by the court because Martha had failed to produce evidence to support her case that was worthy of proceeding to trial.

Often, summary judgment motions are simply a way station on the road to trial, and it is unusual to find the plaintiffs in a case, having come this far, not want to see things through and actually get to trial on the merits on the case. But something unusual was about to happen. On Monday, October 18, 1999, exactly twenty-four hours before the IPO was to take place 3,000 miles away in New York, Martha's lawyers stepped to the bench and requested that the presiding judge in the case, the Hon. Mariana R. Pfaelzer, grant a continuance in the case. The judge agreed, ordering opposing counsel to return to her courtroom in a week.

No explanation was ever publicly forthcoming as to why Martha's lawyers requested that continuance. Nor was there any explanation as to what discussions—if any—may have followed thereafter before the two sides returned to court on the morning of October 25. There was only rumor and gossip—and one incontrovertible fact: Martha had started the suit, and now she was agreeing to drop it without any further fighting. Why? Only Martha and her lawyers knew, and her side wasn't talking.

Meanwhile, the IPO went off without a hitch. After handing out orange juice and brioche breakfast snacks to floor traders, Martha moved upstairs to the balcony to ring the opening bell. The deal had been priced to the investors of the underwriters at $18 per share, which meant that Martha, who had been set up to own 70.4 percent of the stock as well as hold 96 percent of the voting power on the board of directors, stood to be worth—at least on paper—a minimum of $614.7 million the instant the stock went public.

But by the morning of the IPO, interest in the deal had reached such a level of intensity that the stock actually began trading not at $18 but at $37.25. Result: Martha's net worth soared instantly from $614.7 million to $1.27 *billion*. She had, in a word, made it. From the daughter of a working-class drunkard and a mom in a housedress, she had climbed and clawed—in six decades of furious struggle— around, over, and sometimes straight through, every obstacle, human or otherwise, she had ever encountered. For much of that time, she had had no clear idea of where she was going, she had just been going *somewhere*—and now at last she was there. At the end of the twentieth century, there was simply no place else to go.

Four years earlier, during the summer of 1995, Martha had given an interview to the American Academy of Achievement in Williamsburg, Virginia. By that time, she was already enormously wealthy, with estates from Maine to Long Island, and in that interview one could glimpse the frustration she seemed to feel as the pace of her life quickened and the material it was spawning began to gather at her feet. When the subject turned to the meaning of "the American dream," she answered by saying, "Monetary success is not what it's all about," and "serenity about life" is the key.

But was that really how she felt? Or did she simply *think* she felt that way—or think perhaps that she *ought* to feel that way? And if so, for how long would the feeling last?

For lunch on the day of the IPO, Martha was invited to the Manhattan home of then *Talk* magazine editor Tina Brown, who had gathered together a salon of notables, including ABC television personality Diane Sawyer, fashion figure Diane von Furstenberg, and Martha's friend from PBS, Charlie Rose.

Thirty years earlier, Tina Brown had been a talented young magazine writer looking to make a name for herself in London magazine circles. Since then, she had, like Martha, honed the blade of her sword to its sharpest edge and carved her way to the top to become arguably the best-known magazine editor in America.

But as she rose to answer the door, she knew that the person standing outside now wore that crown. The reigning empress of magazine publishing was no longer Tina Brown, it was Martha Kostyra Stewart . . . who was something else as well.

"How are you doing," asked Tina as she greeted her fashionably late guest, who answered with two words that summed up a lot.

She said, "I'm rich," and walked in to see her friends.

22

To THE ENDS OF THE EARTH

Martha eventually returned to my life as subject matter for a book. I hadn't planned to write such a book. But an editor at John Wiley & Sons named Pamela van Giessen, whom I'd known for almost a decade, telephoned one day with an idea for a book that she was excited about: the business success story of Martha Stewart, which Pam saw as having been largely untold and underappreciated. Pam had recalled my favorable column in the *New York Observer* about the IPO and decided to see if I was still interested in the company.

I told Pam that it sounded like a good idea but there was a potential complication, as well as an offsetting potential advantage: I actually knew Martha personally—she and I had been neighbors for thirty years—and if she were willing to cooperate, we could wind up with uncommonly good access to an inside business story. It would be ideal to have Martha as a source.

"So ask her," said Pam, and I e-mailed a note to Martha explaining what Wiley wanted to do—a story on "how Martha Stewart built and runs a public company"—and the next day I got back her answer: "dear chris—sounds like a great idea, but i have been writing the book for years! i have a title and everything, just don't have the time. we'll talk over the phone."

I told Pam that it looked like Martha wanted to cooperate, but that she could always change her mind and that she might well do so if she and I wound up disagreeing over the course of the book. Pam said that risks like that were part of undertaking any such biography, and that she and the publisher wanted to go ahead anyway. Although having the subject under research available as a source is an added bonus, it's not necessary. Biographers of dead people obviously can't call on their subjects as sources, and many corporations refuse to cooperate with corporate biographies. So contracts were signed, and I began pulling together research. But repeated requests to sit down with Martha got nowhere, as if suddenly, with a book actually now a real prospect instead of simply something to talk about, she was having second thoughts.

Weeks passed, then more than a month. By and by, the snow-covered landscapes of Connecticut blossomed with the forsythias and crocuses of spring. When we finally spoke again, an edge had crept into her words. Gone was the chatty and personal warmth I had earlier known. Now she was all brusque business, the Martha everyone else knew—and that I was now seeing, close up and personal.

It seemed that what Martha had meant by agreeing to cooperate with a book about her life was not what I had meant. I had meant this: She tells me her story, then I go out and conduct independent research and interviews, and write up the results *my* way. She had meant: She tells me her story, and then I write it up *her* way. What she hadn't said in so many words, but what she had most surely meant, was that I ghostwrite her autobiography—in essence, write up the latest version of her remembered past, the way Betsy Weinstock had written up its first version in the pages of *Entertaining* nearly twenty years earlier.

"No deal," I said to her on the phone after it became clear what she was after. "I told Wiley I'm going to write a book about you and your company and that's it. You either cooperate or not, it's your choice."

But Martha wouldn't let it go and began a series of maneuvers to try to derail the project. When that didn't work, she began telling people not to answer questions about her, quickly turning what had been a cordial and friendly relationship between us into an intense standoff. Her last words to me were, "My life belongs to me, and no one can tell it *but* me."

Almost immediately afterward, she issued a press release announcing that she had at long last decided to publish the story of her life. This time, she said, she was going to tell it "warts and all"—the full story of Martha Stewart, to be called *Martha, Really and Truly* . . . the story that until now had not been told by anyone. But why now . . . why at this exact and unexpected moment, when her life was busier and more overloaded than ever before? Why suddenly decide to draw back the curtain on the hidden world of Martha Stewart now? "Because the time is right," Martha answered, and let it go at that.

But the story of Martha Stewart had already been told, not just once but a hundred times, in a dozen different ways. She had become the most closely watched woman in American public life, with her every movement and public utterance chronicled in hundreds of newspapers daily, in every town and city in America. For more than twenty years, every succeeding year had been her Elvis Year, with more and more fame and notoriety enveloping her. By 2001, she had surpassed Oprah Winfrey to become the most written-about woman on earth except for Queen Elizabeth of Great Britain—and, of course, a lot of the writng "about" Martha had actually been done by her.

How would Martha reconcile all those conflicted accounts of her past? And why should readers believe yet another version of her life story when as recently as November 2001, she was telling the press in articles that ran in the *Arizona Republic* and the *Chicago Tribune* that her father had been a pharmacist? Eddie Kostyra had a number of jobs over the years—physical education teacher, salesman, even pharmaceutical salesman. But he had never been a pharmacist and did not have a degree in pharmacy, nor possess a pharmacist's license. So why call him a pharmacist? In a late 2001 issue of *Martha Stewart Living*, she referred to her family as "middle class" but had previously described their circumstances as "meager." Which is it? More to the point, which version, past, present, or future, should we take as the "really and truly" right version?

Because Martha's inner life—the secret garden of her desires and dreams—was what really mattered, she had erected around herself and her past a perimeter of Potemkin village defenses more elaborate than those of any figure in American public life since Frank Sinatra. The false fronts of her life appeared in her magazine columns and her interviews, in the pages of her books, and on TV. When someone asked her aunt in Nutley, New Jersey, why Martha seemed to exaggerate and distort so much of her past, the aunt answered forthrightly, "It makes a better story." Her ex-husband Andy said much the same thing, but from a different perspective, when he and Norma Collier together watched Martha on an episode of Robin Leach's *Lifestyles of the Rich and Famous* long after Martha had become both. At the end of the show, Andy simply shook his head sadly and said, "I don't understand why the truth was never good enough."

Was she now going to answer that question in the pages of *Martha, Really and Truly*? The friction of her struggle to reconcile her view of life with the views of others seemed to be popping up all over. Her own neighbors in Westport—the town from which her fame had blossomed—had by now thoroughly wearied of their "Martha problem." Many wealthy and famous people lived in Westport, but only one seemed to be having trouble simply getting along. So bad had relations with her neighbors gotten that she had long since constructed an enormous castlelike stone wall in front of her house—to which her neighbors had responded by constructing walls of their own, turning Turkey Hill Road into something that looked like a demilitarized zone between warring armies.

In this environment, no one could ever be sure what fusillade would be fired from the windows of Martha's house next. One day in the spring of 2000, Susan Magrino went to lunch with a friend at a midtown Manhattan restaurant called Michael's, a popular watering hole for executives in publishing and the media. As it happened, Martha had returned to the news in recent days in a pose as a spoiled, petulant, nobody-loves-me brat. And since everyone knew Susan was her public relations assistant, the diners at nearby tables all listened carefully to see if they could pick up a tidbit or two about the backstory to Martha's latest tantrum.

They watched and listened furtively as Susan shook her head in dismay and said to her companion, "Well, she wrote that article and we're not so sure how it's going to be received."

Susan was referring to a column that Martha had written and that had been published only a few days earlier in the Sunday edition of the *New York Times*. The article sought to explain to her neighbors, via an announcement to the entire world, why she had come regretfully to the conclusion to "leave Westport." Her reason? Well, that was just it. What her reason was—or indeed why she thought it needed to be spelled out in the Sunday edition of America's newspaper of record—was somewhat perplexing.

The column—at once whining and angry, pathetic and imperious—rambled from point to point almost incoherently, as if the whole thing had been written in a late-night bout of solitary self-pity. The complaints were ho-hum and recited a litany of criticisms about changes in Westport that were not unlike changes that had taken place in any town over almost thirty years. She complained that Westport's downtown shopping district had changed and that the rents were now too high. She complained that parking had become "a nightmare" . . . that independent movie theaters had closed and been replaced by "impersonal multiplexes," . . . that her favorite coffee bar had closed . . . that the town's "really good greengrocer" had gone out of business.

But mixed in with these superficial complaints were other more personal frustrations, for which she also blamed the town. She complained that her divorce had cost her many friends. She complained that "entertaining just wasn't the same" anymore . . . that her "bold attempts" to keep up traditions, like "open house at Christmas," had gone unappreciated, and that tours of her gardens by the local historical society no longer brought her "new local friendships" or "dinner invitations." She complained, oddly, that telephone poles and wires now blocked her view of the sky . . . that traveling from Westport to New York for meetings now made her feel "exhausted."

The column ended this way: "Most likely I'll end up living in Manhattan full time, or perhaps I'll move to another town that's closer to the city. But wherever I end up, I'm sure that my current feelings of frustration about Westport will eventually mellow to a fond liking."

It was sad, pathetic even, for here was a woman who should have had happiness radiating from her in all directions. She had climbed the highest mountain that life had presented her, and now she stood alone at the top, complaining that telephone poles blocked her view of the sky.

Ultimately, she never left town at all . . . just began renovating another estate—this one on 153 acres of land in Westchester County north of New York, where she promptly fell to fighting with her neighbors over various improvements. It was the same old story: Martha buys home, neighbors complain, fighting begins. Westport, Norwalk, Fairfield, East Hampton, Westchester. Couldn't she get along, with *anyone*?*

Fantasy escapism, it seemed, was by now driving Martha literally to the ends of the earth. At one moment it's bird-watching in Tierra del Fuego, the next minute it's off to Newfoundland for sea

---

*Nearly two years later, on the eve of publication of this book, Martha attempted to disavow her letter to the *New York Times*, claiming in a speech sponsored by the Westport YMCA that the article had been edited in a way that distorted its meaning and that the end result "wasn't my article." For all that, she could only cite as examples of the alleged poor editing the fact that the *Times* had not used a title she had supplied with the story, or a photograph of herself. For this she said she felt "tarred and feathered," and declared of the newspaper, "I will not be working for them in the future." All in all, a performance that came off as petty and whining as her original letter.

kayaking in the North Atlantic. Then it's back on the plane for Alaska—this time with a *Martha Stewart Living* television production crew in tow—to film her in the act of scaling a glacier, mushing a dog sled, and panning for gold.

The episodes—shot to fill up a week of programming on her TV show—showed Martha at her Gal on the Go best. Here she is "ice walking" across a stretch of Mendenhall Glacier. In another scene, we find her scaling the actual face of the glacier, crampons digging into the face of the ice. It was all so savage, so exhilarating, so raw.

But was this escapist entertainment just for her viewers, or was it more basically, escapism for Martha? On another occasion, the entourage motored in a caravan of campers to a streambed outside Fairbanks to film Martha in the act of "panning for gold." The day before, a local tourism official had gone out to the site and placed two gold nuggets in a carefully selected location on the stream's bank. Then when the group arrived the next day and began panning, what should pop up but "Gold!"

Later, she and her crew had been flown in four pontoon-planes to a fishing lodge on the remote Arctic shores of a place called Tincup Lake. And even there—ninety minutes by air west of the Canadian town called Whitehorse—her fame had preceded her.

It was the ultimate frontier heading north, and still she was "Martha." Last year, it had been as far as she could go southward, to the Land of Fire, Tierra del Fuego; now it was as far as she could go in the opposite direction, to the land of the midnight sun; if she went a little farther northward, she'd be heading back down the opposite side of the earth.

Her squadron of planes—all to get Martha and her film crew to Tincup Lake for a couple of hours of on-location filming—settled onto the lake like a flock of migrating ducks, and one by one motored to the dock.

There to greet them was the lodge's chief cook and all around bottle-washer, a lady named José Janssen. José knew all about Martha, and she had been in a state of high excitement for days.

Over the years, she had seen Martha on TV in Whitehorse and Fairbanks, and other places besides. She'd seen her ripping plants from the ground with those honest-to-God hands, pruning bushes and cutting back vines of ivy. Martha was José's idol, and she could hardly wait to meet her.

José wondered how Martha would view Tincup Lodge and the surrounding countryside, where nothing had been pruned or cultivated, ever. It was totally wild, raw, and basic. Except for the lodge, it could have been 50,000 B.C. How would she react? What would she think?

But scarcely had Martha stepped from the plane than José could see that she was completely enthralled with the place . . . the clear air, the majestic peaks of the St. Elias Mountains in the distance, perfectly framed in the mirrorlike stillness of the lake. Martha looked about, smiled, and followed José up a rocky path to the lodge where a buffet lunch was waiting. "This is marvelous," she exclaimed. "It's beautiful."

Once inside, Martha called to the crew: "Check this out!"

José had prepared a banquet for them, with a table that groaned under a spread of sandwiches, salads, vegetables, and drinks.

After lunch, Martha selected a "walking stick," and as the crew filmed her every move, walked around using it. After that, the procession headed to the lakeside, where Martha threw in a line and caught a fish.

Then as fast as she had arrived, she climbed back aboard her plane, pulled the door shut behind her, and the plane took off, followed by the three others.

That was it. Four planes, a twelve-member production crew, and a lodge worker who'd cooked for days—all for a noontime photo-op lifestyle Martha Moment. But she wasn't through yet.

Here she was, at the top of her game, at the top of the world. Beneath her, the Alaskan wilderness stretched out in glorious, crystalline splendor. Four time zones behind her, and a continent away, the men and women of Wall Street and Main Street were heading homeward, to their ordinary lives, in their ordinary homes, with their ordinary families.

She hated ordinary; perhaps it reminded her of so much she wanted to forget. Yet thanks to them—although mostly, thanks to herself—there she was, above them all, in splendid isolation, at the top of the world . . . for the moment at least, the richest self-made woman on earth, a large portion of which now lay literally at her feet.

Next to her, in the pilot's seat of the single-engine DeHavilland Beaver, sat the plane's pilot, Larry Nagy, owner of the lodge, which had supplied all four aircraft to transport her northward on this, her latest expression of what it means to be able to buy anything you want—even an experience—whenever you want it.

Only days earlier she'd been sitting in Connecticut, deciding what to do next in a life of infinite possibilities. And now she was actually doing it—the ultimate lifestyle performance in the age of instant gratification: Neither time nor distance nor expense could halt or even delay her appointments with the destiny of simply being herself.

She could have whatever she wanted, whenever she wanted it, however she wanted to receive or experience it, by simply saying so. A mile high in the blue Alaskan sky, Martha Stewart had arrived.

Or had she?

We are not given to know, in the moments of our greatest fantasy, just when it is—or even why—that the eternal tug of entropy will begin pulling us earthward again, to drench us in the nightlong sweats of our earliest memories, as we struggle, scheme, and reach for the stars, hoping to escape the memories of a past that never leaves.

Which is why, in the thin air over Tincup Lake, in the vast Alaskan interior beyond Juneau, Martha Stewart—probably the richest, and certainly one of the most influential and powerful women in America, who numbered among her possessions seven palatial homes; a media empire that celebrated nothing so much as the very life she had chosen to live for herself, and that included boats, cars, horses, dogs, cats, and canaries; who could have literally anything on earth that she desired, simply by expressing the desire to have it—turned to the pilot next to her, and in a moment of un-thinking abandon, told another of the impulsive little lies that had consumed her life.

She said, "I've got a pilot's license, you know."

"Want to fly it?" he asked.

"Sure," she answered—and as had been the case on so many other occasions, at so many other times, and in so many places—she reached out and took control.

Two years later, after purchase of her latest estate and her temper tantrum in the *New York Times*, she was still living in Westport, in the big house on Turkey Hill. But Martha sightings became less fre-quent now, as if the most visible woman of her time had become a recluse in her own hometown. To see her now, you had to get up early, the way she did, at four or five o'clock in the morning, and drive down to the beach, which is not far from Turkey Hill, and ac-tually never was.

You can park your car at the end of the point, where the British landed in 1777, or further down the street, where the local farmers came out to stop them and fired a few musket shots from behind a stone wall and then ran away . . . where there now stands a cast bronze war memorial to mark where the blood had been shed . . . across the street from where an abandoned farmhouse had once stood, where I played as a child . . . where Scott and Zelda fought one summer before I was born and he drank away his pain with Scotch and screaming all night, which you can catch glimmerings of in a book of his writings called *The Crack Up*. And if you were to do all that, and wait in the dark, you might find her there, where Scott said we always return, in the deep dark night of the soul, at quarter to four in the morning.

EPILOGUE

The new millennium did not begin well for the CEOs of American business. The more visible and celebrated they had been in the 1990s, the more vulnerable to criticism they became as the new decade began. With the economy at last starting to roll over from the longest bull market expansion in the nation's history, many of the grandest business triumphs of the 1990s began one after the next to collapse. And almost inevitably, Martha Stewart became a target of blame.

The hunt for a scapegoat had begun with the collapse of the dot.com stocks, which had fallen from their perch in March of 2000 like oxygen-starved canaries in some collapsed coal mine. After the dot.coms came the collapse of the telecom stocks, the collapse of the biotech stocks, and eventually the collapse of just about every remaining tech-sector stock on Wall Street. And from the Nasdaq, the collapse spread thereafter to the Dow Industrials, as investors stamped "paid" to the end of an era—the longest of its kind on record—when opportunity had beckoned at every turn, and nothing seemed impossible, and all an investor had to do was buy his ticket at the corner of Broad and Wall, then hurry to the check-in gate for that red-eye flight to Eldorado.

Of course, it had all been a dream, as bull market fantasies always are, and when the nation at last awoke from it, some $3 trillion worth of stock market value—representing more than half the retirement savings of the American people—had simply vanished. Meanwhile, the line outside the congressional hearing rooms had begun to form.

Most of the action centered on a congressional subcommittee bearing the unwieldy name of Subcommittee on Oversight & Investigations of the House Energy & Commerce Committee. The Committee, one of the most powerful and feared in Congress, held long-standing authority to investigate almost anything that was even remotely connected with federal law, and when public interest began to swing toward abuses on Wall Street in the wake of the market's collapse, investigators quickly pounced on the issue. The immediate focus of the Committee's concern was a Houston-based "energy and financial services" company called Enron Corp., which had plunged from $80 to less than $5 on reports of pervasive accounting irregularities. By the end of 2001, Enron was bankrupt, its auditors at Arthur Andersen faced felony fraud charges, and the American people had a whole new set of enemies to blame for their woes, both real or imagined.

For five years in a row, *Fortune* magazine had named Enron "America's Most Innovative Company," with the highest "quality of management" in all of American business. Yet on examination, America's Most Innovative Company turned out to have been conducting its affairs through the same sorts of off-shore tax haven banks and shell companies favored by drug dealers, money launderers, and, it seemed, the same individuals who were financing world terrorism.

The revelations that tumbled forth during the waning months of 2001 were so astounding—and at the same time complex and confusing—that they soon blurred into a vague and encompassing fog of corporate evil that seemed to have spread across all of American business.

For starters, there was the abrupt resignation of the company's CEO, Jeffrey Skilling, that August—though only after quietly cashing in $25 million worth of his Enron stock. Eight weeks later, the company announced a $1 billion third-quarter write-off, after which it was only a matter of time—and not very much time at that—before the stock collapsed to nothing, a Hail Mary merger with a rival energy trading firm had come apart, and the company was filing for bankruptcy . . . at which point the whole horrid story of Enron's finances tumbled forth, complete with corporate whistler-blowers, shredding machines, and the company and its accountants both pointing the finger of blame at each other.

Soon it began to seem as if Washington itself would be dragged into the affair, as the press began to run stories reminding readers that Enron had been one of the largest congressional campaign contributors on record.

The White House seemed no cleaner. How could the president sign (or veto) any eventual legislation in financial and accounting reform when one of his top sources of campaign dollars had been Enron's own auditors at Arthur Andersen? And what about his then top economic advisor, Lawrence Lindsay, who turned out to be a former Enron consultant? The president's trade representative, Robert Zoellick, had been an Enron advisor. His key political advisor, Karl Rove, had been a big holder of Enron stock. So was Under Secretary of State Charlotte Beers, who had been appointed to the post by Bush at exactly the time Kenneth Lay was lobbying the administration for secret bailout help.

In short, the Enron scandal had gotten so big and encompassing, so quickly, spreading out to involve so many individuals and institutions, that it was becoming almost impossible to follow. As Captain Ahab railed in *Moby Dick*, "Who's to doom when God himself is dragged to the bar?"

To do its job, the Committee didn't need to document a thousand—or even a hundred—crimes by what President Bush was soon calling America's new class of "corporate evil-doers." What was needed was a CEO and a scandal that *personalized* the greed and wrongdoing, reducing it to manageable human scale—a single, simple, easy-to-understand offense like, say, insider trading.

In Martha Stewart and her involvement with Sam Waksal and ImClone Systems, the Committee found what it needed, and from the moment Committee investigators began probing press reports of insider trading in the shares of Waksal's company, Martha's fate was sealed.

Points of connection could even be found between Martha and Enron. All three companies—Enron, ImClone, and Martha Stewart Living Omnimedia, Inc.—shared a common auditing firm in Arthur Andersen. All three had boards of directors linked by common friendships and even board members. One of ImClone 's board members, John Mendelsohn, was also a member of the board of directors of Enron, with a seat on its all-important audit committee. And one of Martha's board members, Charlotte Beers, who owned blocks of stock in all three companies, even offered a link to the Bush administration, having been appointed earlier that year to the post of Under Secretary of State for Public Diplomacy and Public Affairs.

As the Committee's work unfolded, none of those links developed into much more than intriguing coincidences that helped position Martha in the world of her suddenly awkward friendships. What's more, by the time the paperback edition of *Martha Inc.* went to press in January 2003, a full year had passed since the committee began its probe, and no government case had yet been filed against Martha by any governmental body.

Yet, it really didn't matter, because once it became clear late in the spring of 2002 that Martha's activities with Waksal had been a matter of interest to subcommittee investigators for weeks and maybe even months, the rumors of wrongdoing quickly engulfed her, sending her stock—and her reputation—into a tailspin from which neither have yet recovered.

The subcommittee's interest in ImClone was triggered by press disclosures at the start of January 2002 suggesting that Waksal may have been involved in apparent insider selling in ImClone 's stock only weeks earlier, in the days leading up to a Federal Drug Administration announcement that ImClone would not be permitted to bring its Erbitux anticancer drug to market.

In the wake of the stories, subcommittee investigators began looking into the matter. Almost simultaneously, officials at Merrill Lynch & Co.—where Waksal maintained an account—advised the Securities & Exchange Commission (SEC) of an apparently improper request from Waksal that he be permitted to transfer nearly $5 million worth of unregistered ImClone stock held in his name from his own account into his father's account and sell it even as the insider trading mushroomed. In reaction, investigators from the SEC's Enforcement Division opened a probe of their own.

Not long afterward, subcommittee investigators asked ImClone to turn over any and all books and records relating to Waksal's trading activities, and in the documents they received was Waksal's secretary's telephone log entries for December 27—the day before the FDA issued its letter declaring that the cancer drug Erbitux could not be brought to market. On the log were a number of names—some well known, some less so—that investigators eventually linked to Waksal's circle of friends. At 11:05 A.M. Carl Icahn had called. Fifteen minutes later the socialite ex-wife of Ronald Perelman, Patricia Duff, had rung up.

Then at 1:43 P.M., a person with the most recognizable name of them all—Martha Stewart—had phoned. And the notation on the phone log indicated that she had wanted to learn the same thing from Waksal that investigators themselves were now probing: what was up with ImClone 's stock, which had already tumbled 10 percent that day on seven times the previous day's volume.

Martha's ultra-high-visibility name—and the context in which it had suddenly surfaced—led federal prosecutors into the case as well, and in April they asked for an explanation as to why she had placed the call, what specifically she had wanted to know, and why she had simultaneously sold every share of ImClone she then owed—some 4,000 shares worth approximately $223,000.

Martha's answers to those questions, which she subsequently repeated in press statements and through lawyers once her name had surfaced in the affair, became the anvil against which the media and the subcommittee smashed her credibility to bits.

Instead of simply answering that she had telephoned Waksal to ask why ImClone's shares were falling, she produced a confusing—and as of this writing unsupported—story involving a "prior agreement" with her broker to sell the shares when they fell to $60.

Unfortunately, neither Martha nor anyone else was subsequently able to produce evidence that such an agreement existed. And as skeptical press aides at the subcommittee began expressing their doubts to reporters, Martha's entire hidden world of involvement with Waksal began to tumble forth.

It quickly developed, for example, that Waksal's stockbroker at Merrill Lynch was also Martha's stockbroker. And that person turned out to be none other than Peter Bacanovic, the same individual whom J. C. Suares had met at a Turkey Hill party some 15 years earlier. At the time, Bacanovic was still a young man, and having just graduated from Columbia, he represented exactly the sort of individual Martha had wanted Lexi to pursue—a handsome young scion of a wealthy Manhattan family.

Waksal had spotted Bacanovic's value too, and had hired him to work as a finance man at ImClone Systems, where he toiled from 1990 to 1992. After that, he moved on to Merrill Lynch, where he developed a clientele of wealthy East Side dowagers and became known in society circles as New York's stockbroker to the celebs.

And it also soon developed that two hitherto unknown figures from Martha's inner circle of friends—a Westport neighbor named Mariana Pasternak and her exhusband Bart—were also figures in the drama. Martha, it turned out, had made her fateful phone call to Waksal from her private jet during a refueling stopover in San Antonio, Texas, while she was en route to a Christmas holidays vacation at the San Jose del Cabo resort at the southern tip of Mexico's Baja, California, peninsula. And, it turned out, Mariana had been on the plane with her.

Mariana's presence on the plane in turn raised speculation in the press, which prosecutors hardly tried to discourage, that Martha had passed along whatever she had learned from Waksal, and that Mariana had relayed the information on to her exhusband Bart, who was said to be providing her with child support payments and, it now developed, had sold $600,000 worth of his own ImClone stock the next day.

When reporters began looking into Bart's background, it was easy enough to discover that he'd been a deeply involved investor in Waksal companies for years, beginning with Cadus Pharmaceutical and Scientia, and now ImClone.

Nor did it end there. As information began to pour forth from the subcommittee, it developed that there hadn't just been one ImClone-related phone call involving Martha on the 27th, but several, beginning shortly after Bacanovic received instructions from Waksal's daughter, Aliza, for whom he also managed an account, to sell 40,000 shares of ImClone at the market price, or roughly $2.5 million.

No sooner had Bacanovic's office processed the order than he picked up the phone and called Martha. But since she was already airborne and headed for her holiday with Mariana, he left a message with Martha's secretary to have Martha phone him when she touched down. The secretary's log note read, "Peter Bacanovic thinks ImClone is going to start trending down."

When Martha's plane touched down in San Antonio at 1:30 P.M., she phoned her office for messages, learned of the call from Bacanovic, and immediately placed a call to him at his Merrill Lynch office. But Bacanovic was himself on vacation, in Miami, and his assistant—a young man named Douglas Fanouil—took the call and began processing her instructions to sell out all her remaining ImClone stock. Then, and only then, did Martha loop back to Waksal and place the call that brought the roof down on her.

As the facts thus emerged, the likelihood that Martha had engaged in actual insider trading seemed less and less clearcut. Nothing had surfaced anywhere to show that she had issued her sell order after learning anything improper from Waksal or anyone else. But it seemed equally clear that she hadn't been fully forthcoming when investigators had interviewed her back in the spring, since nothing had surfaced to support her claim of a "$60-and-out" stop-loss order. Indeed, the very fact that she herself had placed the order, and that the sale had taken place at an average price of less than $58.50, seemed to argue that no such agreement in fact ever existed.

This now shifted the focus of the case away from insider trading and toward questions of possible obstruction of justice and lying to government agents, both of which were also federal felonies—and, under the law, easier to prove. Yet the case had trouble gaining traction on this basis too. By August, Waksal had pleaded guilty to nine felony counts related to insider trading, and none had involved Martha. And though Bacanovic and Fanouil were both dismissed from their positions at Merrill Lynch, and Fanouil wound up pleading to a misdemeanor offense in return for his testimony against others including, presumably, Martha, nothing developed on that front either.

By September, the subcommittee had pretty much exhausted the public relations value of "Martha-gate," and shortly after Labor Day the lawmakers washed their hands of the matter entirely, handing the case file to the Justice Department and moving on to other concerns.

As the year drew to close, reports occasionally surfaced suggesting that the story was about to flare back to life. In October, a number of newspapers cited unnamed sources as saying that a "Wells Notice" had been served on Martha by the Securities & Exchange Commission. Such a notice effectively informs the target of an SEC investigation that he or she is going to be served with civil charges, thereby giving them opportunity to reply or negotiate a settlement.

But the stories died away and, by year's end, the news had moved on to escalating tensions in Iraq and the deteriorating economy at home, leaving questions about the "CEO Crime Wave" that had swept across Wall Street in the 1990s increasingly ignored. For

Martha, however, the legacy was ever-present, in her ruined stock price and her tarnished reputation, and the obvious question of whether she could ever lift herself, or her company, back to the heights from which they'd tumbled in barely a year's time. What's more, the subject had an eerie way of returning unexpectedly to the headlines at odd moments. At year's end, the press began reporting, for example, that the case against Martha wasn't dead at all, and that prosecutors were re-interviewing key witnesses in the matter. Among those named: the Merrill Lynch brokerage assistant, Douglas Faneuil, who had dealt with Martha on the day of her ImClone trade. And there was speculation that Mariana Pasternak was also being re-interviewed—though she wasn't identified in the stories by name.

In fact, so deeply had the scandal burned itself into the public consciousness that simply mentioning Martha's name—even to defend her—seemed to have the opposite effect. Nonetheless, supporters did begin to rally to her cause. In its January 2003 issue, *Worth* magazine published a cover story entitled "The Case for Martha," reminding readers that she hadn't actually been convicted—or even formally accused—of anything. And a good-hearted TV commentator, Larry Kudlow, rarely missed an opportunity to say the same thing whenever Martha's name came up on the daily talk show he hosted with his entertainingly out-of-control co-anchor, James Cramer, on CNBC cable TV. Martha's problem was, of course, that every time anyone rose to her defense, the whole subject of what she did or didn't do got ventilated all over again. It had become the permanently affixed asterisk on her name, and it raised questions as to whether she'd ever be able to make it go away.

In many ways, the IPO for Martha Stewart Living Omnimedia, Inc., was thus the high water mark for both the company and its principal stockholder, Martha Stewart. It was Martha's singular good fortune—as well as bad luck—to go public with her stock offering at almost the absolute top of the greatest bull market in American history. This bit of timing meant while she immediately became a billionaire on paper, the stock would likely drift down with the rest of the market, so that, financially speaking at least, she basically had no where to go but down as well.

Not only was she unable to translate the initial phenomenal paper gains into cash, but there were other—and more troublesome—questions clouding the company's future, even without the added menace of a criminal investigation involving the activities of the chairman and CEO.

One question had been hovering over the company from the day it went public: What would happen to the shares if Martha herself— who held more of them than anyone else—were to meet an untimely end? Now investors had the answer for in every sense that really mattered, the eruption of the ImClone scandal had been the functional equivalent of the company having been sideswiped by a truck.

At the start of 2002, the market value of Martha Stewart Living Omnimedia, Inc., stood at roughly $1 billion, and it rested on the ability of the company's chairman to bolt from bed each morning and begin pursuing one of the most demanding schedules of any public figure on earth. A year later and Martha was still bolting from bed each morning, but there was a lot less applause for the performance, and the value of the company had plunged by 50 percent over the course of the year.

And there was another problem that abruptly moved from the realm of the theoretical to the real: Would Martha's company be able to survive looming problems besetting its most lucrative business partner, Kmart Corp.? The entire matter became real, immediate, and suddenly urgent in January 2002 when Kmart, having lost the confidence of investors and lenders in the wake of a disastrous holiday retailing season, filed for bankruptcy protection from its creditors.

A year later and every problem Kmart faced had grown worse than ever. Nearly 13 percent of the company's stores had been closed, and at year's end the company said it expected to close even more stores early in 2003. Two weeks into the new year and the company announced plans to close 326 additional stores, bringing the total to 609, or 28 percent of the total operating at the time of bankruptcy, thus confirming predictions made in the hardcover edition of *Martha Inc.* Kmart faced the likelihood of having to close perhaps as many as a third of its stores if it was to have any real chance of surviving on a long-term basis.

The company tried to put a positive spin on the January 2003 announcement, saying that the closures were coming with $2 billion in fresh loans so that the company could emerge from bankruptcy as early as March of 2003. But the new loans simply replaced a $2 billion "debtor-in-possession" loan package that would have expired anyway. Nor was the company's claim that it had finally turned profitable over the Christmas 2002 holiday season very convincing. The assertion made sense only if the company didn't count interest on nearly $800 million of borrowings from its debtor-in-possession package to finance its Christmas inventory. In any case, investors didn't seem much impressed and knocked another 34 percent off Kmart's relentlessly shrinking stock price as soon as the news of the store closings was released. The stock had already tumbled from $6 per share at the start of 2002, to 35 cents per share by year's end, when it was de-listed after eighty-four years of trading on the New York Stock Exchange, and tossed into the functional equivalent of Wall Street's gutter, where they began being quoted in the so-called over-the-counter "pink sheets." Now, they'd been knocked down further still and were beginning 2003 at barely 17 cents per share.

The entire ordeal refocused Wall Street's attention on Kmart's most high-profile business partner—Martha Stewart—from an angle at which neither she nor her company had been viewed before: Just how dependent were both on the Kmart relationship in the first place? The disturbing and unexpected answer turned out to be "very," as the troubles at Kmart put a lid on the ability of Martha Stewart's own stock to recover in any meaningful way from the scandal that had savaged it earlier in this year—and this in spite of the fact that the scandal had increasingly faded from view by year's end.

Both these sets of concerns had begun to manifest themselves slowly, but relentlessly, in the company's stock price, almost from the moment of the Martha Stewart Living Omnimedia IPO. Though the price had touched an intraday high of $49.50 per share on its first day as a public company, the shares quickly began to weaken—as was the case with nearly all IPOs at around that time—and thereafter traded irregularly downward for the following two years until they reached barely $16 per share by the end of 2001.

The decline, which accompanied the plunge in the stock market itself, and the collapse of advertising through the entire media sector, made the company worth less in the after-market than it had been valued at to insider investors even at the time it went public— what is known on Wall Street as a "busted IPO." This in turn meant that all the company's original backers, had they stayed with the stock from the time of the IPO onward, or at least through February 2002, would have wound up losing money on their investments; it was not Martha's fault, it was simply the reality of the market and the economy.

In a sense, even Martha was a loser because, as the company's namesake and largest shareholder, it was difficult for her to sell any of her own stock in the company without raising questions among investors as to whether she had confidence in the company's future. Yet by 2001 she too had become a seller—though not in large amounts—unloading roughly 450,000 shares of her stock, or about 1 percent of her publicly tradable shares, for about $8.5 million.

Then, in early 2002—mere days, in fact, before the Kmart bankruptcy announcement—Martha stunned the investment world by selling three million more shares, or roughly 9 percent of her public stock, at $15, for $45 million more. Though it's not uncommon for entrepreneurs to turn a little of their stock into cash as a kind of reward for their hard work once the company becomes publicly traded, the size of the sale seemed unusually large, raising obvious questions—which quickly spread through Wall Street—as to whether the company's weakening stock price reflected deeper problems than had previously been thought. Surprisingly, the broker on the transaction was not any of the white shoe firms that had taken her public in the IPO, but her old friend Andy Monness, who had hired her on Wall Street more than 30 years earlier, and was now running a firm bearing the name Monness, Crespi, Hardt & Co.

Martha tried to contain the damage by issuing a press release that stated she was selling "for diversification and estate planning purposes." Though she still owned 60 percent—which amounted to absolute control—the sale had nonetheless cut her position measurably, from the 70 percent stake she held upon the completion of the IPO. In other words, in barely two years time, she had peeled off and sold more than 10 percent of her stake in the company that bore her name—not a good harbinger, in the minds of investors, for what might lie ahead.

Worries simply intensified as Sharon Patrick, the McKinsey & Co. consultant who had assembled the company's financial profile in preparation for the IPO, also emerged as a heavy seller in the stock. Obviously concluding that a dollar of cash was worth more than a dollar of Martha Stewart Living Omnimedia, Patrick as well became a very substantial post-IPO seller of MSO stock, shedding close to one third of her holdings by the end of 2001, for close to $14 million. In fact, her selling continued right on into the spring of 2002, and even as prosecutors and investigators from both the SEC and Congress were circling the company, she sold another $3 million worth of shares, lifting her total take to some $17 million.

Whether Martha was selling stock to buy a new home (Martha-watchers claimed to have seen her house shopping in Marin County, California, at around that time), or she was selling for diversification purposes or otherwise, there was evidence aplenty that *Martha Stewart Living* magazine—the presumed heart of the business—had begun to mature. In 1999, when the company went public, *Martha Stewart Living* magazine was published 10 times per year.

The following year, the company published an eleventh issue, and in the year 2001, a twelfth issue, which is to say, a 20 percent increase in the number of issues published in 36 months. Those two additional issues accounted for nearly all revenue growth for the entire publishing segment. Circulation also appears to have stabilized around 2.1 million, and by mid-2001 was actually slipping slightly.

The same trends continued in 2002 and were inevitably aggravated by Martha's legal problems involving ImClone and Waksal. In September, a spokesman for a company under contract to produce a new line of so-called "Martha Stewart Signature" furniture said sales were going far better than expected. But on October 31, 2002, Martha Stewart Living Omnimedia released its own financial results for the period and they acknowledged that furniture sales were weak and outlook for the entire company had darkened.

Under a section of the report entitled, "Trends and Uncertainties," the company declared that, thanks to the combined impact of the investigations by prosecutors and the SEC into Martha's ImClone stock sale, the business had now begun to experience "some negative impact."

It was as if the very name "Martha Stewart"—one of the most recognizable brand names on earth, had suddenly and dreadfully acquired a whole new negative meaning. From "Martha" the positive adjective, as in "That's so Martha . . . !" the word had somehow morphed into a verb with cynically negative connotations, as in "Don't Martha me . . . !"

One clear sign of that came when the DaimlerChrysler Corporation announced, at the start of 2003, that it was dropping an advertising campaign it had earlier signed with Martha Stewart Living Omnimedia and replacing it with a campaign built around singer Celine Dion.

And certainly the best evidence of all came when Martha Stewart Living Omnimedia introduced its first new magazine since the scandal erupted. It turned out to be the first product offering by the company that didn't use Martha's name in the title. The magazine, devoted to quick-and-easy meal preparation, was simply titled, *Everyday Food.*

The company said that although it was difficult to be precise about the matter, it seemed pretty clear that distribution of the *Martha Stewart Living* syndicated TV show was suffering, that magazine circulation was being pressured, that ad sales were being squeezed, that the catalog business was being hit, and that the furniture business was starting to hurt. What's more, the company said it was becoming harder to find new partners for future deals.

Through the downturn, the company's flagship property— *Martha Stewart Living*—appears nonetheless to have held up reasonably well, with advertising revenues actually increasing about 4 percent over the year-earlier period, though much of the gain looks to have come from the publication of special issues as well as discounting on the rates charged per page. Even so, the magazine remains extraordinarily profitable, as well, with a 36 percent operating margin that is by far the best in the business—twice, for example, that of Meredith Corp., publisher of *Ladies' Home Journal.*

There are various explanations for this among financial analysts—one being that the magazine is so profitable because Martha runs a tight ship. The other explanation involves the belief, which has somehow taken root on Wall Street and among media analysts, that the magazine is unusually profitable because it has very low marketing and promotion costs.

The latter point is thought to be buttressed by the fact that *Martha Stewart Living* does not appear, in any formal sense of the term, to be an obvious and aggressive advertiser of itself in the way that, say *Time* or *Newsweek* are. You just don't seem to see lots of ads around for Martha's magazine, anywhere.

One reason for that is, of course, that Martha is a living, breathing advertising juggernaut all by herself. One might properly argue, in fact, that the nearly $2.7 million in salary and bonuses Martha received in the year 2001, was really the heart of the magazine's advertising budget for the year.

Viewed slightly differently, one could likewise argue that the whole of her presence on television—indeed, all her interviews in newspapers and magazines, all her newspaper columns and radio shows, in fact everything she does or says anywhere on earth— amount to a nonstop, multimedia advertorial campaign to promote the magazine. It is the collective impact of those messages—in 240 newspapers, on 285 radio stations, on cable TV's the Food Network, on CBS's *Morning Show*, and most especially via her one-hour daily broadcast TV show, *Martha Stewart Living*—that appears to be the only marketing the company actually does for the magazine.

The syndicated TV show alone, if viewed as a promotional vehicle for the magazine, is almost incalculably valuable, reaching 88 percent of the American TV viewing audience with what amounts to a daily sixty-minute infomercial for the magazine. Using as a benchmark the $32 million in advertising revenue that flowed to Martha Stewart Living Omnimedia from commercials purchased by local advertisers on her show during 2000, one might reasonably argue that that the entire show—if priced as an actual infomercial— would have an equivalent revenue-value of $240 million per year, or about 25 percent more than the entire TV advertising budget of either General Electric or Kmart.

Yet in spite of the relentless Martha Messages that pour into the media without letup, her magazine, *Martha Stewart Living*, is hardly getting a free ride. In reality, the magazine appears to have been extremely aggressively marketed all along, right from the very first stages of its development within Time Warner. The evidence is hard to ferret out because the costs remain scattered throughout the whole of the Martha Stewart business, and prior to 1997 the details are skimpy. But it's there nonetheless for anyone who wants to dig it out.

For most of 1995, for example, Martha's catalog business, Martha By Mail, did not exist, and nor, for that matter, did her newspaper column. Even her TV shows were a once-a-week thirty-minute affair that generated relatively little revenue. Aside from her merchandizing deal with Kmart, and her magazine, which was at that time still owned by Time Warner, and was estimated to be generating $50 million per year in revenues by that time, the only other significant revenue stream she enjoyed was roughly $3.6 million per year in book publishing royalties.

In 1996, the nonmagazine revenues began to grow sharply as money started to flow from by her catalog operation and, thereafter, a website, and her TV show. But even as late as the end of 1997, the sum of all nonmagazine revenues for her company totaled only $24 million, of which roughly $7 million were her licensing fees from Kmart. In other words, only about $17 million of the company's revenues were coming from her nonmagazine media endeavors, and the total was certainly much less in 1996.

In spite of all that, financial filings with the Securities & Exchange Commission show that in 1996, the company spent $24.5 million in marketing and promotion—this during a year when *Martha Stewart Living* seems to have been generating something less than $80 million per year in revenues. In other words, the magazine was apparently the only undertaking of any significance that the money *could* have been spent on because Martha really had no other projects of note under way at that time.

This is all supposition, of course, because the company has not shared the facts publicly. But it is entirely possible that in 1996 perhaps as much as a third of the revenues for *Martha Stewart Living* were being consumed by simply promoting the magazine in the market and to readers—a pretty good reason, we may assume, why Time Warner was willing to sell the whole business at the start of 1997 for $80 million, or roughly one-time its revenues. Maybe the Time Warner brass knew that the magazine really wasn't worth much more than its revenues because the cost of acquiring those revenues was so steep as to be eating up all the profits.

The year after that, 1997, the picture becomes clearer as a result of historical financial information contained in the company's IPO filings. The data show that marketing and promotion costs jumped 30 percent, to roughly $32 million for the company as a whole, and that nearly 100 percent of the increase, or $7.5 million, was accounted for by what the company called "increased subscription acquisition spending and advertising sales costs to support higher advertising revenues." That's another way of saying, "We had to spend more money to get more subscribers so we could charge more for our ads."

Filings with the SEC show that in 1998, marketing and promotion costs for the magazines rose another $1.3 million, In 1999 they increased $2.6 million more, and in the year 2000, they rose by yet another $5 million, suggesting that by the beginning of 2001, marketing and promotion costs for the company's publishing group stood at close to $41 million annually, or about 22 percent of revenues.

There is no way to tell whether that $41 million sum is included in the operating costs of the company's publishing group, or scattered elsewhere throughout the cost structure of the entire business. But there is no question that it represents a very substantial burden on the company's overall ability to generate profits.

In 2002, the company was not only hamstrung by the ImClone scandal but was financially burdened by it as well. A good indication of just how much Martha's stockholders had to pay to defend their investment in Martha in the ImClone scandal came late in the year when the company announced that it had run up $2 million in expenses in the June to September 2002 period alone for "legal, corporate communications, and other expenses" related to the scandal. Those costs accounted for nearly 100 percent of the company's decline in net income during the period, from $5.2 million in the 2001 quarter to $2.9 in the comparable 2002 period.

The company's other big problem was Kmart. But it was not until the discount retailer went bankrupt in January of 2002 that investors began to realize where the real profits of Martha's business were coming from: not the publishing group, nor the company's website operation, nor its catalog business, but from its merchandizing deal with Kmart itself.

By the beginning of 2002, the business that had begun 19 years earlier with the publication of a single cookbook—*Entertaining*—had evolved into an extraordinary media and marketing enterprise, with activities that reached literally around the world. Thanks to Sharon Patrick and her McKinsey-rooted organizational skills, the company had been grouped into four business segments—publishing, television, merchandizing, and direct marketing, with activities that included the following and were expanding all the time:

- A regular monthly magazine—*Martha Stewart Living*—with a two million-plus circulation.

- A regular quarterly magazine—*Martha Stewart Weddings*—with a circulation of 650,000 per issue.

- Test issues of yet another quarterly magazine: *Martha Stewart Baby*.

- Some 34 different books, 20 of which are under the "Martha Stewart Living" rubric and amount to the recycling of editorial material from the pages of her magazines, and 14 being books authored by Martha herself.

- Two separate weekly newspaper columns—askMartha and askMartha Weddings—that are also presumably authored directly by Martha and are syndicated by the *New York Times* syndication service to 240 newspapers in the United States and Canada. The columns reach approximately 40 million readers per week.

- An askMartha broadcast radio program, which is carried on 285 radio stations reaching 93 percent of the U.S. market. The programs are distributed by the Westwod One syndication service.

- Two different mood music CDs, distributed by Rhino Entetainment Co.

- A one-hour television program—*Martha Stewart Living*—that is syndicated by King World Productions, plus a once-a-week

"best of the week" re-edit of the shows, to be aired on the
weekends.

- 🍃 A half hour daily program, *From Martha's Kitchen*, that is aired
  twice daily, seven days a week, on the cable television Food
  Network.

- 🍃 Regular weekly appearances by Martha personally as a
  "lifestyle correspondent" on the CBS *The Early Show*, for
  which the company received free 30-second commercial
  spots on the program. (This program has been cancelled.)

- 🍃 Distribution of Martha Stewart-branded television programming, via satellite, to Canada, Brazil, and Japan.

- 🍃 Merchandizing deals with Kmart, the Sherwin-Williams
  Co., the Hudson's Bay Co., Sears, Jo-Ann Fabrics, and many
  specialty stores.

- 🍃 A catalog and direct marketing business, via the World Wide
  Web, for yet more Martha Stewart-branded merchandise.

Yet of all this activity, in all these various markets and media,
only one—the Kmart merchandizing deal—really generated any
significant bottomline cash for the business. Fifteen years after Barbara Loren-Snyder got the bright idea to introduce Martha to Joe
Antonini as a fresh new face to promote Kmart to the world, the resulting relationship was still benefiting Martha far more than Kmart.
Having invaded the company's aisles with Martha Stewart-branded
merchandise that now included not just kitchenwares but 2,400 different products, in 27 different categories, from linens to garden
tools, barbacue grills, plants, fertilizers, kitchen utensils, and on
and on and on, Martha had turned Kmart into the most important
distribution channel in America for merchandise that carried her
brand name.

Through the top-line revenues flowing to Martha Stewart
Living Omnimedia from the Kmart deal were relatively modest,
amounting to roughly 10 percent of her company's total revenues,

the costs of acquiring those revenues was small, with the result that the bulk of the revenues fell all the way down to the bottom line as profits for her company. By 2001, those revenues may have been accounting for as much as 100 percent all the company's operating profits, suggesting that the entire rest of the business was running at barely break-even.

There is simply no way to be certain about the exact percentages because the company has never disclosed the allocation to its various segments of the overhead, but the general observation would appear indisputable: the Kmart relationship—and not the company's publishing, or television, or catalog marketing efforts—are the heart of the business.

Viewed from a different perspective, if you were to take out the merchandizing revenue and just look at the company as if the Kmart deal didn't exist, Martha Stewart Living Omnimedia, Inc., would have shown a 5.6 percent pretax profit margin in 1997. But that would have declined to a 4.5 percent margin by the year 2000, then slumped to a 1.5 percent margin for the first nine months of 2001, falling finally into negative territory by the third quarter of 2001 as advertising continued to dry up throughout the whole of the media. The red ink would have continued to flow throughout 2002 as well.

As a result of its own current troubles, Kmart is thus almost certain to try to renegotiate its deal with Martha on terms that are more favorable to Kmart in 2003—assuming of course that it survives and doesn't simply liquidate the business. Sensing the disadvantage at which her company would thus find itself, Martha quickly began dropping hints in interviews, almost the minute Kmart filed for Chapter 11, that she was in talks with other merchandisers.

This in turn led immediately to speculation that she might sign a deal and move to Sears or maybe Target Stores instead. But nothing ever came of the hints, making obvious enough that shifting to a new retailer wouldn't be anywhere as easy as she had let on. And scarcely had the dust settled on the bankruptcy announcement than Sharon Patrick and Martha were both clarifying things with statements that

they were actually sticking with the bankrupt Kmart for the foresee-
able future. Then came the ImClone fiasco, damaging the very brand
name she had been trying to shop elsewhere, making it clear enough
that any new deal in the future would be on far less favorable terms
than Kmart had given her.

To be sure, it is possible that Martha could get an even better
deal from a reorganized Kmart in the end anyway—or that there
will be a scramble by Sears, J.C. Penny, Target, Kohl's, or some
other retailer to capture the prize if Kmart shuts down. Martha's entire history in business has been of emerging the winner while others have lost out. But for how much longer will her winning streak
hold? Even Joe DiMaggio failed to get on base eventually.

Of one other thing there can be little doubt: Without Martha
Stewart herself, her company will lose the uniquely vigorous
marketing and promotional energies of the person who has infused
every aspect of its corporate culture. Company officials speak
bravely of efforts said to be underway to plan for the orderly transi-
tion of the company to the period when Martha no longer has the
capacity—or the appeal—to inspire millions upon millions of American women with her Everything Gal message.

Yet it is hard to take comfort in the assurances in light of the
events of 2002, when the company's problems seemed to multiply
by the day—and all traced directly to the one person who could not
be replaced, Martha Stewart. In fact, as its troubles mounted, the
company hired an outside public relations firm, the Brunswick
group, with a reputation for adroit management of corporate crises,
to try to put some distance between Martha as a person and Martha
Stewart Omnimedia, Inc., as a corporation. But the effort got no
where because, as it quickly became clear, it was impossible to talk,
or even think, about one without the other.

As a business executive, Martha would hardly have been missed
within the organization at all, with many of her employees almost

certainly breathing a sigh of relief at the thought that she would no longer be stalking the halls in search of underlings to scold. But as the human embodiment of an abstract marketing message, she was simply irreplaceable, making all the company's public relations protesting to the contrary simply wasted effort. If ever there was a time when Martha needed to step aside, it came in 2002, but she hung on.

And it should have been clear from the start that this exactly what she'd do. When the question of "corporate succession" came up with a group of San Francisco investment bankers during the Martha Stewart Living Omnimedia IPO road-show, she responded, almost dismissively, that the magazine had stockpiled thousands upon thousands of never-before-seen photographs of her, and that it could thus doubtless go on publishing monthly issues for many years before anyone would even miss her. But it is absurd to think her death would go unnoticed. Not even Chairman Mao got away with that one.

Aside from being a flip and unworthy response to a legitimate question, her response also missed the true vulnerability of the entire enterprise: the mortality of Martha herself, who personally supports, like the point on an upside down pyramid, the entire corporate superstructure that has been constructed in her name.

Martha is the living, breathing person whom people tune in to watch every morning on her television show. She is the person who is presumed to write the newspaper columns that appear under her byline. Hers is the voice on the "Ask Martha" spots on the radio each day. Remove Martha Stewart from the equation and the "omni" part of "Omnimedia" disappears. The radio spots go away and the television shows vanish. Even if the newspaper columns are salvaged, every electronic media appearance by Martha is gone. How long will her fans tune into reruns? Her fans just don't want to know how to get wine stains out of tablecloths—they want to have Martha herself tell them, live on TV, how it's done. When Martha can no longer communicate the message, how many of her fans will stick around?

Take Martha out of the picture and what's left? A money-losing website, some merchandizing royalties from a foundering retailer, the residual royalty streams on her books, and a magazine that will need a huge infusion of promotional and marketing money to stay in business.

How huge? Well, the people at Meredith Corp. run a pretty tight ship, and as of this writing their operating margins are only 15 percent, so why should those for *Martha Stewart Living* be much different?

Using Meredith Corp. as a model, publishing group marketing and promotion would probably have to double, meaning that operating income from publishing would probably drop by roughly 50 percent, to $32 million. What's more, without Martha, television income would plunge as well—which is what began to happen the minute she walked off the set of the CBS *The Early Show* and her harrowing interview with Jane Clayson—never to return—at least so far.

In December 2002, the company's TV programming distributor, King World Productions, issued a rather half-hearted press release declaring that Martha's syndicated TV show *Martha Stewart Living* would be appearing on stations reaching 70 percent of the American television viewing audience in the September 2003 season. But that was down from her peak penetration level of 97 percent five years earlier. More importantly, the shows were being pushed by station managers to less attractive time slots, thus reducing advertising revenue. In the autumn quarter of 2002, when the costs of the scandal were really starting to bite, the company's syndicated TV revenues tumbled 12 percent from what were already depressed year earlier levels.

In other words, with TV revenues slumping, and the company having to make up the loss through increased marketing and promotional spending, the entire business could easily implode unless its money-losing Internet site were shut down and millions were trimmed from corporate overhead.

In fact, even without the Internet and direct marketing operation, net income would still drop by about 40 percent, to about $8 million. Assuming a super-generous price-earnings multiple of about 30, which is what Meredith Corp now supports, the entire company would thus have a market value of no more than $7 per share . . . and that, of course, assumes the merchandizing royalties don't disappear, in which case the company would arguably be worth next to nothing.

Looming over everything is the biggest question of all: What would happen to the stock price of a company whose only significant asset is a magazine celebrating the life of a woman who could, at any minute, succumb to the fate that awaits us all—namely, death.

There is a precedent for the answer, and it is not a comforting one. Would people continue to subscribe to *Martha Stewart Living* when Martha herself no longer is (living)? Probably in the same numbers that people continued to subscribe to *George* magazine, another publication that was intimately and inescapably linked to a celebrity founder who met a tragic end: John F. Kennedy Jr.

When JFK Jr. died in a plane crash off Hyannis, Massachusetts, in 1999, the Hachette Filipacchi publishing house spoke of continuing to publish his four-year-old magazine, which had already begun to gain traction as a popular read at the crossroads of pop-culture and politics. A new and talented editor, Frank Lalli, was brought in to continue JFK Jr.'s efforts, and the editorial output seemed, in many respects, seamless from what had gone before.

But the sad truth was, without JFK Jr. as the living, breathing presence that made the magazine a "must read" simply by being associated with it, *George* lost all reason for existing, and within nine months Hachette had shut it down. It is frankly hard to imagine *Martha Stewart Living* escaping the same fate . . . and along with it, the company that bears her name.

This is a completely different situation from, say, the passing of Walt Disney. Although Disney set a tone and a standard for the entertainment properties that emerged from his company, his personal creative involvement in crafting those products had long since ceased to be important by the time of his death in 1966. He did not need to be involved in any aspect of his business for it to run smoothly, any more than a member of the Ford family has needed to be involved in the design, manufacture, and marketing of Ford Motor Co. automobiles. Most importantly, neither Ford nor Disney was, or is now, selling products that celebrate the personal life—whether real or imagined—of the company's founder. In that Martha Stewart is unique. Where Walt Disney planned for his passing (so obsessively, in fact, that he had his corpse frozen cryogenically, to be thawed out whenever medical science thinks it is ready to bring him back to life), Martha seems determined to ignore the inevitability of her death—at least so far as her company is concerned.

In the end, it may mean that Martha Stewart Living Omnimedia, Inc., is not really an institution so much as a kind of colossal one-woman band that is destined to fall silent when the musician stops playing.

But what music she played—and how we all listened!

The late twentieth century formed the stage for one of the most extraordinary business careers in American history. All the stars lined up just right, and the desperate dreams of a working class girl from Nutley, New Jersey, came true, astounding not just herself but the world. Yet the cruel calculus of Wall Street leaves no room for sentimentality, and in the end, the Schumperterian winds of creative destruction inevitably sweep away yesterday's dreams, no matter who may have dreamed them, or how urgent they may still seem to some, to make way for dreams—and dreamers—to come.

ACKNOWLEDGMENTS

No book of this sort is ever the work of one person. On-the-record interviews were conducted with roughly fifty individuals, many of whom are cited in the source notes. Background interviews were conducted with an equal number more. Martha Stewart did not cooperate and, in fact, discouraged cooperation by others. Yet many of her present and former friends and associates spoke anyway, though not all wished to be identified. In addition, the enormous public record of Martha's life—much of it from her own hand—provided further, and exhaustive, primary source documentation regarding her business and personal activities. Readers are invited to review the source notes for details as to where various information came from, how it was interpreted, and why.

This is a book about a woman in a man's world, and I could not have written it without the contributions of four extraordinary women in my world. Without their involvement, I would have never been able to write almost anything about a person so complex and many-faceted as Martha Stewart.

The idea for this book did not originate with me, it came from a long-time friend of mine, Pamela van Giessen, executive editor of trade books at John Wiley & Sons, Inc. Pam was smart enough to see the richness in the life of Martha Stewart that I had never imagined, and without her insight and continued editorial guidance, this book would never even have gotten started, let alone been finished.

I can say the same for my agent, Joni Evans of the William Morris Agency, who has saved me from myself on this book more times than I can list.

And I particularly want to stress the enormous contribution made by my researcher on this project, Bridget Samburg, who helped gather and organize what ultimately totaled more than one million words of interviews, newspaper and magazine articles, court records, deeds, tax documents, import invoices, and other such materials. Bridget not only did all that, but also helped interview sources in Hong Kong, Alaska, Cuba, and Africa, as we worked to reconstruct the global reach of Martha Stewart's extraordinary life.

Finally, I want to thank the true hero of this book, my wife Maria Byron, who shared the research chores with Bridget—and had the singular misfortune of having to do it at the desk next to mine, where she has sat with a smile for fifteen years, letting me take credit for all her insights and humor. She's just the best, and I'm very blessed.

SOURCE NOTES

Prologue

Page 1   "It was 5:30 A.M. . . ." Details regarding Martha's appearance on the CBS *The Early Show* June 25, 2002, came from interviews with past and present employees and officials of both the CBS *The Early Show* and *CBS News,* autumn 2002.

Page 6   "The focus of all this . . ." Details regarding the government case against Sam Waksal can be found in *United States of America vs. Samuel Waksal* Indictment, U.S. District Court, Southern District of NY, and in Securities and Exchange Commission against Samuel Waksal, U.S. District Court, Southern District of NY, both filed June 12, 2002.

Page 8   "As 2001 drew to a close . . ." Details about the leak of the FDA letter and associated events can be found in "the House Committee on Energy and Commerce; An Inquiry into the ImClone Cancer-Drug Story," June 13, 2002.

Page 15   "Blonde and trim, . . ." Interview with an eyewitness.

Page 29   "Neighbors on Turkey Hill . . ." Interviews with neighborhood sources.

Page 29   "A working-class housewife . . ." Interview with source at Martha Stewart Living Omnimedia, Inc., summer 2001.

Page 29   "In Vermont . . ." Interview, Larry Faillace, owner of Three Shepherd Farm.

Page 29   "One time I ran into . . ." Party given by Mr. and Ms. Kenneth Lerer, NYC, 1991. See Chapter 15.

Chapter 1

All information on Martha Stewart's early years, including the characterizations of her parents, is drawn from primary sources such as hospital birth records, school records, and interviews—some previously published and some for this book—with relatives, neighbors, and classmates. An exhaustively detailed profile of Martha Stewart's early years, including background information about Andy Stewart and his family, is to be found in Jerry Oppenheimer, *Martha Stewart—Just Desserts* (William Morrow, 1997). The book is discussed at length in Chapter 20 and figured prominently in a 1997 libel case brought by Martha Stewart against the *National Enquirer*, which published excerpts from and commentary about it. No factual errors involving anything in the book or excerpts were ever established in the suit, and the case was eventually settled out of court. Additional valuable information was derived from Martha Stewart's own first-hand writings. Most of those writings appeared in her monthly "Remembering" columns, which have been published continuously in the pages of her magazine, *Martha Stewart Living*. At the time of this book's writing, ninety-five such columns had been published. Copies of all were obtained and digested for this book. Additional material on Martha's early years can be found in her books, most notably, *Entertaining* (Clarkson Potter, 1982), *Martha Stewart's Christmas* (Clarkson Potter, 1989), and *Martha Stewart Weddings* (Clarkson Potter, 1987).

Page 33   "Martha Stewart was born . . ." New Jersey Department of Health and Senior Services, Bureau of Vital Statistics.

Page 34   "There are early pictures of . . ." Martha Stewart, "Remembering," *Martha Stewart Living*, April/May 1992.

Page 35   "And when she wasn't doing that . . ." The recollection of her mother sitting at the kitchen table, a cigarette dangling from her lips, was apparently a strong one for Martha, for she has evoked the image at least twice in her "Remembering" columns. See Martha Stewart, "Remembering," *Martha Stewart Living*, February 1998 and February 2002.

Page 35   "Rather than the syrupy, . . ." The show ran live, on CBS tel-
            evision, from 1949 to 1956.

Page 36   "The Kostyra home, . . ." Nutley, New Jersey, Township Tax
            Assessor's Office.

Page 36   "The house had a single full bath . . ." The crowded living
            conditions and lack of personal privacy at 86 Elm Place
            plainly bothered Martha, for she discussed the matter more
            than once in her "Remembering" columns. A column in the
            February/March 1993 issue of the magazine carried this
            headline: "For a Family of Eight, One Bathroom Was Never
            Enough. How We All Got In and Out Is Still a Mystery." See
            as well, seven years later, Martha Stewart, "Remembering,"
            Martha Stewart Living, May 2000, wherein she complains, "The
            eight of us slept in three and one-half bedrooms and shared
            one bathroom and two half bathrooms; one of the half bath-
            rooms was a toilet and sink off the kitchen—that was really
            Dad's private domain, and the other was a toilet in a wain-
            scoted closet in the basement."

Page 36   "Eventually, eight people occupied the dwelling . . ." Martha
            Stewart, "Remembering," *Martha Stewart Living,* May 1997.

Page 36   "In Martha's columns . . ." Martha Stewart, "Remembering,"
            Martha Stewart Living, May 2000.

Page 36   "Eventually, the controlling . . ." Eddie Kostyra's intrusive
            and controlling "intercom" system also seems to have made
            quite an impression on Martha. She refers to its "staticky
            speakers" jarring her awake each morning in a "Remember-
            ing" column in *Martha Stewart Living,* June 1999, and again in
            May 2000.

Page 37   "Once assembled in the kitchen . . ." Martha Stewart, "Re-
            membering," *Martha Stewart Living,* May 2000.

Page 37   "In her columns, Martha has tried . . ." Reading her columns,
            one cannot help but be struck by the conflicted feelings
            Martha seems to have held, even decades later, toward her fa-
            ther. He is described time and again as "handsome," and "beau-
            tiful," and "artistic" and a "perfectionist," but when his character
            and behavior and mannerisms are evoked, he comes across as
            someone the writer regards as a negative, confrontational,

provocative, and even defiant person. See, for example, when Martha's mother instructs her children during a summer outing to the Jersey shore, to "wear your hats, keep your shirts on, and cover your knees . . ." and Eddie is described in the next sentence this way: "Dad immediately removed his shirt, his shoes, and his socks . . ." Martha Stewart, "Remembering," *Martha Stewart Living*, June 2001.

Page 37   "There'll be no housedresses . . ." Martha Stewart, "Remembering," *Martha Stewart Living*, May 2000.

Page 37   "Some fifty-three children . . ." Interviews, neighborhood sources.

Page 38   "When she was as young as nine years old . . ." Martha Stewart, "Remembering," *Martha Stewart Living*, October/November 1993.

Page 38   "According to Martha," Martha Stewart, "Remembering," *Martha Stewart Living*, September 1997.

Page 38   "Though Eddie had promised his wife . . ." Martha Stewart, "Remembering," *Martha Stewart Living*, September 1996.

Page 39   "On the other hand, he . . ." Martha Stewart, "Remembering," *Martha Stewart Living*, October 1997.

Page 39   "In one column, she . . ." Martha Stewart, "Remembering," *Martha Stewart Living*, April 1998.

Page 39   "In another column, she . . ." Martha Stewart, "Remembering," *Martha Stewart Living*, December 1998/January 1999. Similar complaints about her family's stressed finances can be found in other columns as well. She complains about her neighbors, the Allegris, who had a "luxuriously carpeted living room" and who had put a television in their "finished basement" for their children; Martha herself was "depressed" that in 1950 the Kostyras still did not have a TV of their own. Martha Stewart, "Remembering," *Martha Stewart Living*, September 1997.

Page 39   "On still another occasion, Martha recounted . . ." Martha Stewart, "Remembering," *Martha Stewart Living*, June 2001.

Page 39   "The overcompensation in reaction . . ." Interviews with visitors to Turkey Hill.

Page 40   "Eventually her search . . ." Anstruther, *Old Polish Legends*, Hippocrene Books, 1991.

Page 40 "In later years, Martha recalled . . ." Martha Stewart, "Remembering," *Martha Stewart Living*, February 1997.

Page 40 "In fact, Eddie Kostyra . . ." In an interview on Martha's relationship with her father, her ex-husband Andy recalled her as having been "hugely embarrassed" by Eddie, with deep feelings of anger toward him mixed together with equally deep feelings of love.

Page 42 "Martha's world still . . ." See Clarke, Tupperware, *The Promise of Plastic in 1950's America*, Smithsonian Institution Press, 1999.

Page 42 "Tupperware was big in the Kostyra household . . ." Martha Stewart, "Remembering," *Martha Stewart Living*, April 2001.

Page 43 "We were a close-knit . . ." Interviews with classmates.

Page 44 "The Nancy Drew character . . ." Carolyn Keene, *The Clue in the Diary* (Grosset & Dunlap, Inc., 1932).

Page 45 "I can almost bend steel with my mind . . ." O, September 2000.

Chapter 2

Page 47 "Yet, almost overnight . . ." Martha Stewart's career in modeling has been frequently discussed in print, and by Martha herself in numerous interviews. Yet oddly she has never devoted a column in her magazine to the subject, though she has written extensively in "Remembering" columns about almost every other aspect of her life. There is considerable confusion as to when her career in modeling actually began, and how long it lasted. See for example, Martha Stewart, "Remembering," *Martha Stewart Living*, October 1999, which says Martha Stewart began modeling for *Glamour* in 1954 at the age of 13. But, her first widely known appearance in the magazine was not until 1961.

Page 49 "Later in her career, she looked back on the job . . ." Kasindorf, "Living with Martha," *New York*, January 28, 1991.

Page 50 "Such were the circumstances . . ." Versions of how and where Martha and Andy met, courted, and eventually married have been published in many places. There are snippets in many of Martha Stewart's columns, as well as discussions in several magazine profiles and in *Weddings*. Interviews with people who knew Martha at the time fleshed out the picture presented here.

Page 51   "One time I went to the Stewart apartment . . ." Interview, Kathy Tatlock, summer 2001.

Page 52   "One obvious reason . . ." The information on Martha's selection as a *Glamour* model comes from several extended interviews with Norma Collier as well as others. Norma was a principal source as well for the relationship of the two women in their Connecticut catering business, and the business' eventual and acrimonious breakup. See Chapter 5.

Page 54   "Said Richard Avedon of . . ." Strodder, *Swin' Chicks of the '60s*, Cedco Publishing, Co. 2000.

Page 55   "By comparison, Martha Stewart . . ." Assignments and day rates for Norma Collier and Martha Kostyra are from the Plaza Five modeling agency client book for the period.

Page 55   "It is impossible to assay . . ." Martha and Andy Stewart both have separate and complex relationships with their daughter, Alexis (Lexi), whose own complex personality seems to have been shaped in part at least out of the conflicts between her parents over how to manage their own independent relationships with her. In the same way that Eddie sought to control Martha and his other children, Martha in turn sought on many occasions to use the techniques of domination and control in raising Alexis. When Lexi, at the age of six, was sent by her parents for a month to a sleep-away summer camp in Massachusetts during their first year of living in Connecticut, the child wrote letters to which Martha responded like an officious schoolmarm by correcting her spelling and grammar. Worst of all, Martha sent her sheaves of prestamped envelopes, addressed to people the six-year-old barely knew, with instructions to send them letters about her summer in sleep-away camp—a controlling gesture that Alexis seethed over and still hadn't forgotten decades later. (See Martha Stewart, "Remembering," *Martha Stewart Living*, June 1998.)

One of Martha's most revealing columns regarding Alexis appeared in the September 2000 issue of *Martha Stewart Living* magazine. The column represents an effort on

Martha's part to convince the reader that Alexis, like her mom, is a "born decorator." In fact, the column actually says far more about the stern, domineering influence Martha continued to have on Alexis even after she graduated prep school and began life as a college student, like Martha, at Barnard. The column is graceless in its writing and displays an obvious lack of sensitivity on the writer's part regarding the use of language, describing her reaction upon entering Alexis's freshman dorm room at Barnard—one-half having been decorated by Alexis and the other half by her roommate—as being "hilarious . . . like entering the brain of a split personality . . ." The column describes the roommate's side of the room as having been cluttered with "posters and souvenirs and dolls and stuffed animals," whereas the side of the room belonging to Alexis (the "born decorator") is described approvingly as "white bare-bones minimalism, [with] everything stored in plain rectangular boxes stacked evenly and perfectly," with utterly nothing in view to suggest Alexis's actual abilities of self-expression except "a pencil and pen and a typewriter." The bedsheets, observed Martha, were tucked so tautly as to suggest that the room were about to be inspected by "an army sergeant." Martha apparently failed to realize that she herself was the "army sergeant," for whose inspection Alexis had been preparing.

Page 56   "Decades later in 1996 . . ." See notes Chapter 20.

Page 56   "Kathy's office studio . . ." The picture presented here of Martha Stewart and Kathy Tatlock's relationship in New York, and again in Bogotá, Colombia (see Chapter 4), derives from several extended interviews with Ms. Tatlock in Boston during the summer and autumn of 2001.

Chapter 3

Martha's career as a stockbroker on Wall Street has been variously reported to have spanned as much as ten years. But the actual period began, according to the employment records of the New York Stock Exchange, on August 14, 1968. The NYSE has no records indicating her termination of employment as a stockbroker, but from interviews and Martha's columns and other writings, her career on Wall Street had ended by the summer of 1973.

Page 64   "Martha had interviewed at . . ." Martha Stewart discussed her job search on Wall Street with the author. The chain of events by which she wound up at Perlberg, Monness were supplied in an interview with Andrew Stewart, winter 2001.

Page 65   "So Martha took . . ." Martha's most detailed discussion of her life as a stockbroker is found in Martha Stewart, "Remembering," *Martha Stewart Living*, October 1999, the publication of which coincided with the stock offering for Martha Stewart Living Omnimedia, Inc.

Page 66   "In a 1999 biography . . ." Wooten, *Martha Stewart, America's Lifestyle Expert*, Blackbirch Press, 1999.

Page 66   "One of Martha's . . ." Interview, Greg Gilbert, summer 2001.

Page 66   "A good measure of just . . ." See Kasindorf, "Living With Martha," *New York*, January 28, 1991, where Martha is quoted as giving her salary at "about $135,000" at that time.

Page 67   "Perlberg himself has said that when Martha arrived . . ." Interview, Edward Perlberg, summer 2001.

Page 67   "When it came to closing a deal . . ." Interview, Greg Gilbert.

Page 67   "But what junk they were . . ." Interviews with firm clients.

Page 67   "When Andy Monness . . ." *New York Post*, October 2, 2000.

Page 67   "When Frank Williams . . ." Profile of Williams in *Financial World*, October 17, 1984.

Page 68   "Now Martha began . . ." Interview with Norma Collier, autumn 2001.

Page 69   "Andy Stewart—timid by nature . . ." Interview with Andy Stewart, summer 2001. Andy Stewart could not recall his exact words in his warning to Martha to "be careful" of the firm, but he was insistent that his warning to her had been "strong." He said he was particularly concerned once he began to sense, from conversations with Martha, that research being conducted at the firm regarding various investments the firm was recommending, were not being shared with the firm's customers. Andy said he believed Martha took his warning seriously, which may have contributed to her eventual decision to leave the firm. He said that shortly after she resigned from the firm, he telephoned Andy Monness to find out exactly what Martha had been doing for the firm, but Monness was extremely uncooperative and wouldn't answer any of his questions.

Page 70   "For Norma Collier . . ." Interview with Norma Collier, autumn 2001.

Page 70   "By the start of . . ." Kasindorf, *New York*, January 28, 1991.

Page 70   "Adding a mordant note to the proceedings, Gary Levitz . . ." *Atlanta Journal and Constitution*, March 16, 1986.

Page 71   "Ralph's wife, Jacqueline, then . . ." Ibid.

Page 71   "During the five years . . ." CNN, November 26, 1995.

Page 71   "One of the firm's . . ." *Orange County Register*, March 2, 1998; *Los Angeles Times*, December 21, 1997.

Page 72   "Andy Monness was soon . . ." See United States of America Before the Securities and Exchange Commission, Release No. 7334, September 23, 1996.

Page 72   "Ed Perlberg, the founding . . ." NASD CRD File, National Association of Securities Dealers; *New York Law Journal*, December 19, 2000; the *Times* (London) March 18, 1989.

Page 73   "Says Andrew Monness . . ." Interview with Monness, summer 2001.

Page 73   "But as far as . . ." Interview with George McCully, summer 2001.

Chapter 4

Page 75   "But it was not an auspicious beginning . . ." Interview, Andy Stewart.

Page 75   "In her columns . . ." Over the years, Martha has discussed various aspects of renovating and improving the property at Turkey Hill (see for example her columns in *Martha Stewart Living* of October 1996, February 1999, March 1999, and March 2000), but, not discussed the reasons for the move, except in her 1982 best-seller, *Entertaining*.

Page 76   "Not quite . . ." Interview with Andy Stewart, summer 2001.

Page 77   On the other hand, even . . ." Westport Town Hall, deed and field card land records, #48 Turkey Hill Road South, Westport, Connecticut.

Page 77   "He was constantly . . ." Martha Stewart, "Remembering," *Martha Stewart Living*, July/August 2000.

Page 78   "Such a guest arrived . . ." Interview of individual in the event described.

Page 79   "I'm not going to say anything negative . . ." Interview, Andy Monness.

Chapter 5

Page 88   "Said Martha to Kathy . . ." Interview, Kathy Tatlock.

Page 88   "One day in early 1974 . . ." Interview, Norma Collier. The Norma Collier relationship with Martha Stewart has been recounted in at least two places—*New York* and *Martha Stewart—Just Desserts*—without significant discrepancies. The version presented here, and throughout this chapter, comes directly from Norma Collier.

Page 90   "The idea: To start . . ." Martha's version of the start of her catering business is found in *Entertaining*. By contrast, on March 14, 2001, she gave a speech at Harvard University and was reported by the *Harvard Gazette* to have claimed that she actually started her catering business two years earlier, in 1972, when she would still have been employed on Wall Street.

Page 96   "One local resident . . ." Personal knowledge of the author.

Page 96   "Demand grew so rapidly . . ." Interview with Lee Papageorge.

Page 96   "To do that, she . . ." *Westport News*, January 28, 1977.

Page 97   "Eventually, Martha opened her . . ." Aspetuck Valley Health Inspections office.

Page 98   "Since the town also . . ." The first notable appearance of a Martha Stewart profile in the *New York Times* was May 8, 1977, describing her "Market Basket" business. The story contains the first known reference in print to her career as a stockbroker, which is erroneously said to have lasted "seven years." The story also references her work as a live-in domestic for two elderly women on Fifth Avenue, with Martha describing the work vaguely as being that of "cooking."

Page 98   "Meanwhile, Martha had incorporated herself . . ." *The Hour,* December 17, 1996.

Chapter 6

Page 99   "During the firm's salad days . . ." Martha clearly enjoyed the effect she had on men, and had no qualms about making use of, and later acknowledging, her charm and sex appeal as part of her repertoire of Wall Street business tactics. Martha's first public acknowledgment that her stockbroker's wardrobe included hot pants appeared in the August 5, 1996, issue of *Fortune,* where she was quoted as saying in a roundtable discussion that included her friend and confidante Charlotte Beers, "When I was a stockbroker, I was outrageous. I wore hot pants. I was one of the few women on Wall Street. I thought the way of dressing there was just stupid. I had beautiful long legs. I wore brown velvet hot pants with brown stockings and high heels."

Page 100   "The two were inseparable . . ." Interview, Sandy Greene.

Page 101   "At one of the couple's early Christmas parties . . ." Interview, Norma Collier and additional source.

Page 102   "Meanwhile, Andy caught his . . ." Interview, Andy Stewart.

Page 103   "Meanwhile, Andy struggled not only . . ." Martha's first known public discussion of Andy's cancer appeared in *McCall's,* October 1996. There is an elaborate discussion of Andy and his illness in *Martha Stewart—Just Desserts.* Other instances of cancer in the Martha Stewart circle of friendships are all drawn from interviews with surviving spouses, or from newspaper and magazine articles.

Page 105   "By the late 1970s . . ." Interview Andy Stewart.

Page 105   "Instead, she turned him into something approximating . . ." Interview with Cary Pierce.

Page 105   "The house and grounds . . ." Westport Town Hall, deed and land records, Westport, Connecticut.

Page 107   "By the end of the 1970s . . ." *Washington Post*, December 11, 1978.

Chapter 7

Page 110   "While attending the *Gnomes* launch party . . ." Interview with Andy Stewart.

Page 110   "Yet it hardly put . . ." *New York Times*, October 11, 1981; *People*, August 9, 1982.

Page 111   "I prefer big parties . . ." *New York Times*, September 23, 1981.

Page 111   "At the same time . . ." Ibid.

Page 113   "A reviewer for *Newsweek* . . ." *Newsweek*, December 1, 1986.

Page 113   "In fact, women accounted ultimately . . ." United States Census Bureau. What Rose Monroe (aka Rosie the Riveter) came to represent, through the propaganda films and posters of the War Manpower Commission, was the first stirrings of a developing sense of unfairness in social policy and employment law that would lead, twenty years later, to the creation by the administration of John F. Kennedy in 1961, of the nation's first Presidential Commission on the Status of Women, and thereafter, to the passage of the Equal Pay Act (1963), the publication of Betty Friedan's best-selling book *The Feminine Mystique* in 1963, Title VII of the Civil Rights Act in 1964, and the signing by Lyndon Johnson in 1965 of Executive Order 11246, mandating affirmative action in hiring practices to overcome employment discrimination.

But the role that American women played in World War II has been marginalized by history to not much more than a footnote though, in economic terms, their impact on the outcome of the war itself was at least as great as that of the men in America's uniformed forces.

At the outbreak of World War II, America's entire civilian labor force numbered about fifty-two million. Of them, barely 15 percent were females. But by 1942, so many men had been drafted into the uniformed forces that acute labor shortages had developed throughout the whole of American

industry. To fill the gap, the newly established War Occu-
pations Commission began a vast propaganda effort to re-
cruit women into the workforce. Women took jobs as
welders, lumberjacks, riveters, security guards, steelwork-
ers, taxi drivers.

By 1945, the female labor force in America had grown by
50 percent, with women eventually accounting for close to
40 percent of all workers. Some facilities were staffed almost
entirely by women.

Then, almost as quickly as it had begun, the war effort
began winding down. As early as 1943, the *New York Times* declared that "real women" would be happy to tie back on those
aprons and get back to scrubbing and dusting once the war
ended. More than four million women got a chance to do
exactly that following V-E day, as war production plants all
across the country began shutting down.

How did women feel as a result of all this—women who
were suddenly and bluntly being told by the government to
return to the "womanly" world that Pearl Harbor had demanded they leave behind? Many were no doubt glad to be
rid of the whole world of assembly lines and rivet guns. One
poll, taken in 1936 by *Fortune* when the nation was still mired
in the Depression and jobs were scarce, reported that 79 percent of women themselves were opposed to married females
in the labor force. But a government survey of more than
13,000 women in war-related jobs in 1944–1945 showed just
how much the war had changed women's opinions on the
matter. The survey found that 75 percent of those questioned expected to remain employed at the end of the war,
while half of all those who gave their prewar occupation as
"housewife" said they wanted to continue working following
the war. Said President Roosevelt's Secretary of the Interior,
Harold Ickes, to the *Saturday Evening Post*, in a comment on
the matter even as fighting raged in Europe, "I think this is as
good time as any to warn men that when the war is over, the
going will be a lot tougher, because they will have to compete with women whose eyes have been opened to their
greatest economic potentialities."

Page 115   "Wrote one social critic of the era . . ." Bruce J. Schulman, *The Seventies, The Great Shift in American Culture, Society, and Politics*, The Free Press, 2001.

Page 116   "These were the women whom Martha Stewart reached . . ." *People*, December 13, 1999.

Page 119   "And in the midst of all that . . ." Martha Stewart, *Martha Stewart's Quick Cook*, Clarkson Potter, 1983.

Page 120   "By 1985, she and Andy . . ." Stewart, *Martha Stewart's Pies & Tarts*, Clarkson Potter, 1985.

Page 121   "Typical of the extravaganzas . . ." *New York Times*, December 19, 1982.

Page 121   "She was very efficient and businesslike . . ." Interview, Pamela Barnett.

Page 123   "Said Martha as she turned . . ." Interview, witness.

Page 123   "This approach to human relations . . ." *New York Times*, July 30, 1995.

Page 124   "Not yet accustomed to handling themselves . . ." *People*, April 14, 1980.

Page 124   "In December 1981, he took Alexis . . ." Martha Stewart, "Remembering," *Martha Stewart Living*, December 1996/January 1997.

Page 124   "But the following December . . ." *New York Times*, December 19, 1982.

Page 125   "In fact, though . . ." Details of Martha's relationship with the Pasternaks came from another interview with informed sources. Details regarding the involvement of the Suares family came from extended interviews with J.C. Suares.

Page 127   "Oddly, Bart hardly . . ." Details regarding Bart Pasternak's and Sam Waksal's investment activities in ImClone come from informed eyewitnesses.

Chapter 8

Page 133   "Yet of all the things that . . ." The presentation of Martha's relationship and dealings with Kmart Corp. in this and subsequent chapters derived from numerous extended interviews with Barbara Loren-Snyder, in the summer, autumn, and winter of 2001. Where appropriate, Ms. Loren-Snyder refreshed her memory of events by reviewing her files and handwritten notes of various events. Further comment was provided on various matters from Kmart corporate spokesmen.

Page 133   "Yet of all the things . . ." In January 2002, Kmart Corp. filed for bankruptcy protection from its creditors, creating major business uncertainties for the future of Martha Stewart Living Omnimedia, Inc. See Epilogue.

Page 134   "Antonini, a first-generation . . ." Many of those who worked with Joe Antonini at Kmart referred to him as a likable, jovial man, overflowing with energy. But not everyone shared that view. A 1994 profile of Kmart in *Forbes* characterized Antonini in terms that might as easily have applied to Martha Stewart: a chip-on-the-shoulder personality, often bullying and abusive, who would publicly berate his executive teams with epithets like "stupid," "jerk," and "inept." At Kmart they were known as "beat-'em-up sessions." *Forbes,* January 3, 1994.

Page 144   "The oddest character of them all . . ." The most complete biography of Sam Waksal appeared in the *Wall Street Journal,* Sept. 27, 2002. These facts are drawn from that story. See also, *Barron's,* June 28, 1993, for his brother, Harlan's, drug problems.

Page 146   "The Butterball turkey company . . ." PR Newswire, November 10, 1986.

Page 147   "The show featured . . ." *Christian Science Monitor,* November 5, 1986.

Page 147   "Stomachs began to growl . . ." *Christian Science Monitor* and Interview, Kathy Tatlock.

Page 147   "A month or so later . . ." Interview, Kathy Tatlock.

Chapter 9

Page 155   "In the weeks that followed . . ." Interview, Barbara Loren-Snyder.

Page 156   "Last year Martha Stewart had 42,569 people to dinner . . ." *Family Circle,* November 1987.

Page 156 "Many strange combinations . . ." *New York Times,* August 23, 1987.

Page 157 "She wanted to make videotapes of herself . . ." Interview, Barbara Loren-Snyder.

Page 162 "But now it seemed Martha had . . ." Interview, Kathy Tatlock.

Page 162 "Martha's sister, Laura, was present and accounted for . . ." Interview, Kathy Tatlock.

Page 164 "Since the start of 1979 . . ." *Boston Herald,* December 18, 1996.

Page 165 "Martha had been coveting . . ." *Family Circle,* February 1, 1989.

Page 165 "Her offer of $535,000 was accepted . . ." Westport Town Hall, deed and land records, Westport, Connecticut.

Page 165 "The date was June 19, 1987 . . ." Interview, Kathy Tatlock.

Page 169 "Martha began calling Andy on the phone . . ." Interview, Kathy Tatlock.

Page 170 "The maître d' at the Chinese restaurant . . ." Interview, witness.

Page 170 "Meanwhile, her physical appearance began to deteriorate . . ." Interview, Kathy Tatlock.

Page 170 "When Kathy and Dick began . . ." Interview, Kathy Tatlock.

Chapter 10

Page 173 "On November 10, 1987, . . ." Interview, Kathy Tatlock.

Page 173 "Through what plainly looks to have been . . ." Interview, Barbara Loren-Snyder. See also Westport Town Hall, land and deed records for the Adams House property, which bears a deed signature of Ruth Adams as the seller, and the names of Andrew and Martha Stewart as the buyers, on July 1, 1987. See also the deed and land records of 48 Turkey Hill Road South, through which Kmart's financing for the Adams House property was thereafter filtered, beginning with a home equity loan on the property from a local Westport bank, on November 5, 1987, in the amount of $350,000 at 10.25 percent, followed on February 3, 1988, with a Kmart open-ended mortgage loan in the amount of $400,000 (75 percent of which being interest free), on the Adams House property, on which Martha alone is the signator.

Page 174   "A month earlier still . . ." Westport Town Hall deed for 91 Long Lots Road, Book 895, Page 053, dated July 1, 1987.

Page 174   "Ten days later . . ." Interview, Kathy Tatlock.

Page 174   "Thus in late August . . ." Interview, Barbara Loren-Snyder.

Page 175   "Yet Martha's contract . . ." Interview, Barbara Loren-Snyder.

Page 176   "After all, Kmart's only exposure . . ." Interview, Barbara Loren-Snyder.

Page 177   "Suddenly and without warning . . ." Interview, Kathy Tatlock.

Page 180   "Airlines donated seats . . ." Interview, Informed source.

Page 180   "Sometime in the summer of 1987 . . ." Kasindorf, *New York*, January 28, 1991.

Page 181   "The next day, the New York *Daily News* . . ." *Associated Press*, October 20, 1987.

Page 181   "Yet so far as Martha was concerned . . ." Description of Martha's Kmart consulting contract appears in State of New York, Division of Tax Appeals, *In the Matter of the Petition of Martha Stewart*, January 13, 2000.

Page 183   "After that, Newhouse started to fret . . ." Kasindorf, *New York*, January 28, 1991.

Page 184   "This strategy, which eventually heaped . . ." Detailed histories of the Time Inc., Warner Communications merger have been published in many places. A good overview of the issues and personalities in the fight can be found in Richard M. Clurman, *To the End of Time, the Seduction and Conquest of a Media Empire*, Simon & Schuster, 1992.

Page 184   "The first executive to review . . ." Kasindorf, *New York*, January 28, 1991. Also, interview with Christopher Meigher.

Chapter 11

Page 188   "*People* magazine reviewed the . . ." *People*, June 27, 1988.

Page 188   "The *Boston Globe* went further . . ." *Boston Globe*, December 24, 1989.

Page 188   "To get her out before the public quickly . . ." Interview, Barbara Loren-Snyder.

Page 189   "Thus, when Martha confessed to a reporter . . ." *Christian Science Monitor,* March 25, 1988.

Page 189   "As she told a reporter . . ." *Dallas Morning News,* December 6, 1989.

Page 192   "There'd been 43 separate . . ." *New York Times,* July 7, 1988.

Page 193   "By pouring its millions . . ." Martha has often been compared to Betty Crocker as a marketing device. But the comparison is flawed in one respect. Betty Crocker never actually existed as a person. Instead, both the name and image were created in 1921 to promote Gold Medal flour. An actress, playing Betty, hosted a radio program on cooking in the mid-1920s, and various other actresses continued the tradition, first on radio, and then on television, until the mid-1970s. There were Betty Crocker cookbooks, and Betty Crocker cake mix, but no actual Betty Crocker, just like there was no Marlboro Man or Energizer Bunny, or Pillsbury Doughboy.

Similarly, there was never an actual Aunt Jemima, another ubiquitous marketing image of the American kitchen that is also often compared to Martha Stewart. According to *Advertising Age,* the idea of Aunt Jemima was the invention of a late nineteenth century newspaperman named Chris Rutt, who needed a brand name for a pancake product that he and a friend had developed and wanted to market. Rutt attended a vaudeville show and saw a performer in Black-face wearing an apron and bandana sing a song called "Aunt Jemima," and Rutt took the name and image for his product.

Page 193   "In October 1988, the first print ads . . ." February 25, 1989.

Page 193   "Two weeks later still . . ." *USA Today,* December 18, 1989.

Page 194   "Scarcely had her Christmas special . . ." East Hampton, New York Town Assessor.

Page 194   "This was followed by the purchase of a 29-acre . . ." Town Hall, Fairfield, Connecticut, land and deed records.

Page 194   "To all this, she later added . . ." *New York Post,* August 3, 2001.

Page 194   "Meanwhile, in December 1990 . . ." Interview Barbara Loren-Snyder.

Page 194   "When a reporter for . . ." *USA Today*, December 18, 1989.

Page 195   "As she liked to remind her assistants . . ." *USA Today*, December 18, 1989.

Page 195   "Yet, in 1997, just around the time . . ." *Time*, June 17, 1996; *Adweek*, April 28, 1997.

Page 197   "Added a lady named . . ." *Washington Post*, November 28, 1991. After the appearance of this article, Alice Probst became an increasingly visible fan of Martha Stewart's and appeared on the Oprah Winfrey television show in 1994, and was thereafter quoted in *People* in 1995 in support of Martha.

Page 197   "A Connecticut woman . . ." *Chicago Tribune*, October 24, 1991.

Page 197   "A neighbor who lived . . ." Interviews with informed sources.

Page 198   "People told of . . ." The gossip, which became incessant by the start of the 1990s, is gathered and presented from the author's experiences as a local resident, Westport, Connecticut.

Page 198   "Much of the gossip . . ." How Elizabeth Keyser became interested in the Martha Stewart story, and her reporting on it thereafter, comes from several extended interviews with Ms. Keyser.

Page 200   "1. On March 16 . . ." from Ms. Keyser's notes, supplied to the author.

Chapter 12

Page 204   "Much—maybe nearly all . . ." E. Keyser interview notes with Martha Stewart and others, supplied to the author.

Page 206   "The Newman side welcomed . . ." See "Stewart Sets the Record Straight," *Westport News*, June 26, 1990.

Page 207   "Publicity for the tour . . ." Details are contained in "Homestyles, Trends & Traditions," a 120-page booklet, with advertising, that was handed out to visitors at the event.

Page 208   "In the middle of all . . ." Keyser, "Taste's Great, Catering Star Martha Stewart's Empire Stretches from Show Houses in Westport to the Aisles of Kmart" the *Fairfield County Advocate*, May 28, 1990.

Page 208 "It was really rotten . . ." From E. Keyser's handwritten notes of the phone conversation, supplied to the author.

Page 208 "Next she got . . ." Interview with E. Keyser and quotes from her handwritten notes.

Page 209 "When weeks passed . . ." *Westport News,* June 1990.

Page 210 "The story quickly . . ." *Stamford Advocate,* June 21, 1990.

Page 211 "When a reporter . . ." *The Hour,* June 22, 1990.

Page 211 "Said *Newsday* of . . ." *Newsday,* June 26, 1990.

Page 212 "But scarcely had . . ." From E. Keyser's research file, including Attorney Stephens' letter to *Spy* magazine. Interestingly, Stephens was later to sue Martha in a Connecticut court over a claim that he was entitled to a share of her business on the basis of a promise he alleged that she had made to him. The suit was settled out of court under terms that were never disclosed.

Page 212 "Weeks passed and . . ." Interview with E. Keyser.

Page 212 "It turned out that . . ." The incident at Ma Maison restaurant is detailed in Keogh, *JackieStyle,* Harper Collins, 2001.

Page 212 "J. C. moved in . . ." From E. Keyser's handwritten notes of the interview with Suarez.

Chapter 13

Page 215 "The next company . . ." Interviews with C. Meigher and other Time Warner officials.

Page 215 "One editor at . . ." *Folio's Publishing News,* October 15, 1991.

Page 217 "To the men . . ." *Folio's Publishing News,* October 15, 1991, and interviews.

Page 218 She described a . . ." *H&G,* May, 1990.

Page 218 "Typically in a successful . . ." *Folio's Publishing News,* October 15, 1991, and interviews.

Page 219 "When Martha had first . . ." Interview with Barbara Loren-Snyder.

Page 219 "So, when Martha . . ." Interview with source.

Page 219   "When she wasn't meeting . . ." This itinerary comes from Kasindorf, *New York,* January 28, 1991, and is typical of the schedule Martha had begun following by that time.

Page 220   "By now, much of the work . . ." Necy Fernandes, Martha's housekeeper, also appeared at this time as a "Contributing Editor" on the masthead of *Martha Stewart Living* magazine. Her handyman/gardener, Renaldo Abreu eventually wound up in an acrimonious legal fight with her when she refused to pay him overtime. Martha won on the argument that Abreu was an agricultural employee and thus did not need to be paid overtime. Martha was represented in the case by Attorney Jeffrey Stephens, who himself eventually wound up in a lawsuit with her over a claim for compensation in an unrelated matter. (See Chapter 12, p. 186; "But scarcely had . . ."). Rita Christiansen is identified as her bookkeeper in State of New York, Division of Tax Appeals, *In The Matter of the Petition of Martha Stewart,* January 13, 2000. The phrase "maintainers" appears in an interview Martha gave *Bookpage* monthly, April 1992. In the article, she describes herself, at another point in her career—referring to her time on Wall Street—as a "speculator."

Page 220   "She'd hop a plane . . ." *H&G,* May 1990.

Page 221   She had become ubiquitous . . ." *Chicago Tribune,* April 28, 1991.

Page 221   "Such 'Martha sightings' . . ." The gossip-hungry publications of the New York media market were particularly adept at ferreting out "gotcha" items on Martha. One of the classics of its kind appeared in a 2001 issue of *New York,* which reported that Martha had cut to the head of a half-block long queue of moviegoers waiting to get inside for a screening of *The Golden Bowl* at New York's Paris Theater across the street from the Plaza Hotel.

The item quoted Martha as telling an usher, "I need to come inside right now. It's too windy."

Denied entry, Martha reportedly began to argue, saying, "I can't stand outside anymore. I just can't do it . . ." as if waiting for the usher to recognize who she was.

Getting nowhere with the usher, she returned to her place in line, muttering, "Fine. Fine." Then, when finally permitted entry along with the rest of the audience, she passed the usher and snapped, "Oh, now I can come in, I suppose."

When a *New York* reporter called Martha for a comment, she got this from Martha's dutiful press aide: Martha had just wanted to use the Ladies' Room. The story was quickly picked up nationwide. See *Ottawa Citizen*, June 9, 2001.

Chapter 14

Page 225   "The *Wall Street Journal* . . ." *Wall Street Journal*, March 28, 1991.

Page 225   "The *New York Times* . . ." *New York Times*, March 17, 1991.

Page 226   "As expected, the second test . . ." *New York Times*, May 27, 1991. The story referred to Martha as the "Fred Astaire of home entertainment," and gave readers a brief summary update of her prodigious output to date: "Books: *"Entertaining, Martha Stewart's Quick Cook, Martha Stewart's Hors D'Oeuvres, Martha Stewart's Pies and Tarts, Martha Stewart's Weddings, The Wedding Partner, Martha Stewart's Quick Cook Menus,* and *Martha Stewart's Christmas."* Videos: "Martha Stewart's Secrets for Entertaining," "A Buffet for Family and Friends," "A Formal Dinner Party," "An Antipasto Party," "A Holiday Feast for Thanksgiving and Other Festive Occasions." Note that the video series on entertainment closely track the recommendations of Kathy Tatlock (see Chapter 9).

Page 226   "You do everything . . ." *Newsday*, September 19, 1991.

Page 226   "In the middle of all this . . ." *Connecticut Post*, October 6, 2000.

Page 226   "Scarcely was that completed . . ." See Kasindorf, *New York*, January 28, 1991, which quotes Martha as claiming that she is taking flying lessons in her contractor's private plane. See also Martha's tax case, State of New York, Division of Tax Appeals, *In The Matter of the Petition of Martha Stewart*, January 13, 2000, reveals that Krupinski was the builder on the renovations for her East Hampton home, for which she paid $1,304,296.86 during the 13-month period of March 1990 through April 1991. In June of 2000, an electrical fire erupted in the basement of Martha's Lily Pond home, and the East Hampton Fire Department was called. A photograph taken by *Hamptons Journal* gossip and lifestyle columnist Stephen Gaines shows Krupinski approaching the house and being greeted by Martha as firemen pack up to leave after extinguishing the fire. A caption on the photo, published on the *Hamptons Journal* website, describes Krupinski as "builder-to-the-stars" and Martha's close friend.

Page 227   "Days later, and . . ." The itinerary presented here is derived principally from State of New York, Division of Tax Appeals, *In The Matter of the Petition of Martha Stewart*, January 13, 2000.

Page 227   "Scarcely was the camera crew . . ." Ibid.

Page 227   "Next she was jetting . . ." Ibid.

Page 228   "The first media world executive . . ." The portion of Martha Stewart's career related to Group W Productions was derived from two extensive interviews with Richard Sheingold. Information was checked against relevant public record documents.

Page 230   "Turf wars had . . ." All the Warner Communications entertainment properties, including syndication, were held by Time Warner Inc. in a separate, majority-controlled asset known as Time Warner Entertainment.

Page 236   "The company's most . . ." *Wall Street Journal*, April 10, 1996.

Page 239   "By May 1993, *Martha Stewart Living* had been sold to stations in 80 cities . . ." *Electronic Media*, May 3, 1993.

Page 240   "This isn't living, it's working . . ." *Inside Media*, January 19, 1994.

Page 240   "By its fourth season . . ." *Electronic Media*, August 26, 1996.

Chapter 15

Page 244   "When Martha received a questionnaire . . ." State of New York, Division of Tax Appeals, *In The Matter of the Petition of Martha Stewart*, January 13, 2000.

Page 245   "This McKinsey alum, named Sharon Patrick . . ." *More*, February 2001.

Page 245   "Within three years of graduating college . . ." *More*, February 2001.

Page 246   "Later, Sharon described her trek . . ." *More,* February 2001.
            Martha's climb up Mount Kilimanjaro has been reported on
            extensively. Martha's version of what happened appears in her
            "Remembering" columns in *Martha Stewart Living,* December/
            January 1993/1994. A more interesting version appeared in
            Forbes, October 23, 1995, by Sharon King Hoge, who was on
            the climb. Hoge sets out a version of events in which the
            other climbers reached the summit without Martha, who
            stayed behind and thereafter "simply went on by herself,
            reaching the summit alone." Martha's version of the climb sug-
            gests, though not explicitly, that the climbers all reached the
            summit together.

Page 247   "With perks on top of a base salary . . ." *Orange County Register,*
            April 11, 1996. Martha's salary at Time Warner was never
            publicly stated, but Keith Kelly, a leading journalist covering
            Martha's activities on a day-to-day basis during the mid-
            1990s, estimated her salary and perks to be in the range of
            $750,000 per year by 1995. *Advertising Age* (December 18,
            1995) and similar numbers were published subsequently in
            the *Wall Street Journal* (April 10, 1996).

Page 247   "She had been sitting alone in a friend's ski chalet . . ." Kasin-
            dorf, *Working Woman,* December 1995. Ms. Kasindorf's story,
            a four-year-later follow-up to her *New York* story of 1991,
            once again presented a full profile of Martha's emerging busi-
            ness empire, capturing Martha's developing view of herself in
            a number of self-admiring quotes. Thereafter, Kasindorf
            never returned to the subject.

Page 247   "Well, she wasn't 'just little Martha' . . ." Kasindorf, *Working
            Woman,* December 1995.

Page 248   "She'd already talked about . . ." *Tampa Tribune,* June 21, 1995.
            See also Kasindorf, *Working Woman,* December 1995. Char-
            lotte Beers eventually became a member of the board of di-
            rectors of Martha's company, Martha Stewart Living
            Omnimedia, Inc., where she served on the company's audit
            committee, which appointed the Arthur Andersen account-
            ing firm as the company's financial auditor. In October of
            2001, Ms. Beers, a Texan by birth, left the private sector to
            become Under Secretary of State for Public Diplomacy and

Public Affairs in the administration of President George W. Bush. Thereafter, she briefly surfaced in the Enron Corp. scandal as one of the two largest shareholders of Enron stock in the Bush Administration. See Center for Public Integrity, Washington, D.C., "Fourteen Top Bush Officials Owned Stock in Enron," January 11, 2002.

Page 248   "Charlotte had thereafter . . ." Kasindorf, *Working Woman*, December 1995.

Page 249   "Charlotte had been able to zero in . . ." Ibid.

Page 249   "The statement amounted to a . . ." *New York Observer*, February 6, 1995.

Page 250   "The job of actually hammering out . . ." Kasindorf, *Working Woman*, December 1995. Grubman lives across the street from Martha in East Hampton.

Page 251   "As compensation, he typically took . . ." *Forbes*, April 29, 1991.

Page 251   "His motto was . . ." Ibid.

Page 251   "One of Grubman's . . ." The Madonna negotiations were specifically mentioned in comments by Martha to the author as evidence of Grubman's prowess in handling Time Warner, Inc.

Page 251   "By the start of 1995, Martha had her contract . . ." Kasindorf, *Working Woman*, December 1995.

Page 251   "A further part of the deal . . ." *Wall Street Journal*, April 10, 1996.

Page 252   "Now even Time Warner was . . ." *Orange County Register*, April 11, 1996. Time Warner has never confirmed the granting of a $2 million loan to Martha to buy a second home in East Hampton, but the existence of such a loan was widely gossiped about within the company, and it was reported as a fact in the *Wall Street Journal*, April 10, 1996.

Page 253   "She's totally positive . . ." Interview, Informed source.

Page 253   "Eventually, as Susan's client list grew . . ." Interview, Informed source.

Page 254   "Whatever the press may have thought . . ." Interview, Informed source.

Page 254   "They even look alike, . . ." Interview, Informed source.

Page 255   "Let's talk about your family . . ." *Charlie Rose*, July 26, 1995.

Page 257   "Martha was apparently still upset . . ." *New York*, January 28, 1991.

Page 258   "I didn't wake up itching . . ." *Charlie Rose*, July 26, 1995.

Chapter 16

Page 261   "In 2001, Meigher briefly resurfaced . . ." *Advertising Age*, September 10, 2001.

Page 262   "But in late 1995, Miller as well left the company . . ." *Forbes*, January 27, 1997.

Page 264   "Richard had, in fact, promoted the show . . ." Interview with Richard Sheingold.

Page 264   "At the network level . . ." *New York Times*, June 18, 1991.

Page 265   "So, when the general manager of WNBC-TV . . ." Interview with Richard Sheingold.

Page 265   "When Bolster could stand it no longer . . ." Ibid.

Page 266   "When a story on the plans . . ." *Daily Variety*, June 14, 1995.

Page 266   "From here on out every time one of his people . . ." Richard Sheingold interview.

Page 268   "Martha's office was a large . . ." Interviews, past and present employees.

Page 269   "Observing Martha and Sharon in action . . ." Interviews, past and present employees.

Page 270   "It began, 'Martha Stewart and Group W Productions . . .'" PR Newswire, November 30, 1995.

Chapter 17

Page 275   "Meanwhile, her latest book—*The Martha Stewart Cookbook* . . ." *New York Times*, November 26, 1995.

Page 277   "In Buffalo, New York, a story appeared . . ." *Buffalo News*, December 5, 1995.

Page 278   "Indeed, by the time the Lupus luncheon . . ." *Buffalo News*, December 20, 1995.

Page 279   "It was December 11, 1995 . . ." *New York Times*, December 12, 1995.

Page 279   "One of those in attendance . . ." The scene and characterizations, and Martha's quoted words, and Dilenscheider's quotes and reactions, come from a detailed interview with Dilenschneider on the event.

Chapter 18

Page 283   "Scarcely had Martha returned . . ." *Crain's New York Business*, January 1, 1996.

Page 283   "Everyone knew how bad relations were . . ." *Crain's New York Business*, January 1, 1996.

Page 284   "Only instead of using . . ." Rifkin, "How WGBH Markets Its Brand," *Strategy*, December 6, 2001.

Page 285   "Said the show's WGBH producer . . ." Ibid.

Page 287   "Though Barbara Loren-Snyder later claimed . . ." Interview, Barbara Loren-Snyder.

Page 288   "Spread out over the company's entire . . ." All numbers regarding Kmart Corp's financials are either quoted from, or derived from, public filings by the company with the Securities & Exchange Commission.

Page 288   "The Kmart Corp.'s effort to parlay . . ." *Chicago Tribune*, November 5, 1989.

Page 288   "In June 1995, he was replaced with a man named Floyd Hall . . ." *Chicago Tribune*, June 18, 1995.

Page 289   "In August 1995, at just around . . ." *New York Times*, August 9, 1995.

Page 289   "The words 'This Offering Involves a High Degree of Risk' . . ." *Financial Times* (of London), August 12, 1995.

Page 289   "Martha was spending much of her time . . ." *USA Today*, July 26, 1995.

Page 292   "A hint of the tactic appeared . . ." *Wall Street Journal*, April 10, 1996.

Page 292 "Allen handled it for me . . ." Comment to author by Martha Stewart.

Page 293 "The *New York Times* was already quoting . . ." *New York Times*, February 8, 1998.

Page 293 "Four months later, in June 1997, . . ." *Fortune*, June 23, 1997.

Page 293 "Nothing about the payment was . . ." *Roanoke Times*, February 21, 1997.

Page 294 "After that, the press dined on grilled salmon . . ." *Los Angeles Times*, February 20, 1997.

Page 294 "Two and one-half years . . ." All numbers are derived from the company's 1999 IPO prospectus.

Chapter 19

All information concerning Martha Stewart-branded merchandise as it relates to labor and working conditions in China was developed by author's researcher, Bridget Samburg, for this book. None of this information has ever before been published in any form anywhere. To develop this information, in July and August of 2001, Samburg purchased Martha Stewart-branded merchandise from Kmart stores in Boston, Massachusetts, containing the Federal Drug Administration labeling code "41T002." Among the items marked with that code was a set of four white dinner plates, which had been boxed and wrapped in cellophane. The outside of the box contained the FDA label. Samburg gave this code to the FDA's Center for Food Safety and Applied Nutrition in the Division of Enforcement and Programs in Washington, D.C., on August 17, 2001, and received back the corresponding factory names on August 22, 2001. Through contacts at Washington, D.C., based Human Rights Watch, Samburg and the author obtained the cooperation of a dissident Chinese in Hong Kong, and through this source Samburg was able to gain contact with employees at the Jiaozuo General Ceramic Factory No. 46, Gongzi Road, Jiaozuo, Henan, China, which produces ceramic tableware bearing the stamp MSE for "Martha

Stewart Everyday," the brand name of the Martha Stewart product line at Kmart Corp. Samburg, through her contacts in Hong Kong, obtained extensive interviews, with the factory's employees, in Chinese, and had the interviews translated into English.

Page 298 "Into this, she now injected . . ." *Desert News,* September 10, 1997 and, "she bought a 61-acre estate . . ." *Portland Press Herald,* September 26, 1997.

Page 298 "To which, Martha answered . . ." *Larry King Live,* September 16, 1997.

Page 298 "The New York State Department of Taxation had served her . . ." See State of New York, Division of Tax Appeals, *In The Matter of the Petition of Martha Stewart,* January 13, 2000. The tax bill came to $221,677. Susan Magrino attempted to contain the PR damage by telling reporters that Martha planned to appeal, but to no avail, for press stories quickly erupted everywhere regarding Martha and her taxes. The *New York Post* published one under the headline, "She's a Dough Nut" (February 28, 2000). The *Chicago Tribune* carried one by a *Boston Globe* columnist that began, "Many people, my wife among them, see Martha Stewart as a role model for how to do everything from baking a cake to fixing up a room, to stacking firewood. But the dominatrix of domesticity showed recently that she's no role model for the ideal relationship with a tax preparer." [The columnist was referring to an excuse Martha Stewart advanced in her defense, which the Court quickly rejected, that the problems weren't her fault but had been caused by her tax preparer.] *Chicago Tribune,* March 20, 2000.

Martha's vulnerability in the case derived, in part, from her own published words in the pages of *Martha Stewart Living* magazine, which were used by the tax auditors to impeach her testimony. In certain instances, various issues of the magazine contained photographs and text conflicting with Martha's testimony that her property in East Hampton had not been inhabited during the tax audit period in question.

Page 299 "In 1996, even as she was renegotiating . . ." *New York Times,* June 27, 1996.

Page 300   "Perhaps this caused Martha to . . ." *East Hampton Star*, August 24, 1998.

Page 300   "Neither did Kmart, which . . ." Interview with Kmart public relations spokesman.

Page 300   "An investigative *Business Week* article . . ." *Business Week*, October 2, 2000.

Page 300   "Interviews with its employees . . ." Interviews, factory workers.

Page 300   "Air quality in the city was so poor . . ." *World Disease Weekly Plus*, February 8, 1999.

Page 301   "The factory employed 6,000 workers . . ." Interviews, factory workers.

Page 302   "But sixteen years later . . ." Martha Stewart, "Remembering," *Martha Stewart Living*, March 1998.

Page 302   "In another 'Remembering' . . ." Martha Stewart, "Remembering," *Martha Stewart Living*, September 2001.

Page 302   "Two issues earlier, her magazine had contained a ten-page photo spread . . ." Martha Stewart, "Remembering," *Martha Stewart Living*, July 2001.

Page 302   "Yet the least well-edited . . ." One official who worked for Martha in the mid-through-late 1990s says her columns were almost always turned in by Martha late, and always needed editing, but no one wanted to incur Martha's wrath by pointing out problems. Typical example: A column, in September 1997, that discusses some of Martha's favorite TV shows from 1950, then says, "Probably the most memorable event in those days was the appearance of Fidel Castro on *The Tonight Show* with Jack Paar." In reality, that appearance did not occur until nearly a decade after the events discussed in the previous sentences, and in any event was certainly less noteworthy or significant than the Army/McCarthy hearings, which were contemporaneous with the era described in the column, and are generally regarded as a watershed in news programming on television.

    Over the years, Martha's "Rememberings" columns have accumulated enough inconsistencies and factual misstatements as to make one wonder just how carefully researched and fact-checked the columns are, if at all. In a July/August 1998 column, "Lessons of the Sea," Martha describes her father's boat as a "wooden skiff, approximately eighteen feet long." Three years later, in a June 2001 column, "Crabbing at the Jersey Shore," she describes what appears to be the same boat as "Dad's sixteen-foot wooden skiff." A minor detail? Unquestionably, and certainly not one that Martha herself should have been expected to remember. But picking such nits is what magazine fact-checking is all about—especially when the articles in question are authored by the top person on the masthead. One source at the magazine said assistants are simply too fearful of bringing such discrepancies to Martha's attention.

Similarly, in an April 2001 column, "Exploring Close to Home," she fondly evokes memories of trips and outings she took with her family as a child. She cites one such favorite jaunt of the Kostyra family as having been trips in the family car to watch the construction of the Verazzano Narrows Bridge—at the time the longest suspension bridge in the world, connecting Staten Island, New York, to Brooklyn. Yet for Martha to have beheld the bridge's construction as a child, with or without her family, would have been quite a feat: Construction of the bridge did not begin until after she was in college.

In the January 2002 issue of *Martha Stewart Living*, Martha wrote a "Remembering" column that clearly entangled her business interests with the magazine's editorial voice in a way that helped neither—and no editor at the magazine was either willing or able, or perhaps even much concerned, to prevent it. On the cover appeared a photograph of a birthday cake, and inside, was the revelation that the cake was baked by Martha, using a recipe provided by her daughter, Alexis, as a surprise fortieth birthday party for Chuck Conaway, the CEO of Kmart. The text fails to point out that at the time the article was published, Kmart was not only facing bankruptcy but was Martha Stewart Living Omnimedia, Inc.'s most important business partner and owed it more than $13 million. Besides the poor editorial judgment reflected by publishing a story that amounted to a brown-nosing effort on Martha's part, the magazine also clumsily edited Martha's column in a way that made it seem as if she had decided, in the manner of a clairvoyant, to throw the birthday party for Conaway months before he even came to work at Kmart. The effort did her no good in any case because two months later Conaway "resigned" and left the company in a management shake up.

Page 303   "One such situation involved her second home in East Hampton, which she had purchased . . ." Assessor's Office, East Hampton, New York.

Page 303   "On Bunshaft's death . . ." *New York Times*, February 23, 1995.

Page 304   "In 1985, he had shocked New Yorkers . . ." *New York Times*, December 27, 1985.

Page 304   "But those trees were one of . . ." Interview, Informed source.

Page 304   "Martha's frustration over the unwanted trees . . ." Interview, Informed source.

Page 305   "Macklowe retaliated by planting trees . . ." *Newsday*, April 14, 1996.

Page 305   "Finally, on November 8, 1996 . . ." *Newsday*, November 9, 1996.

Page 305   "Instantly, Macklowe filed a suit in the New York Supreme Court . . ." *New York Times*, January 26, 1997.

Page 306   "Martha told the Zoning Board of Appeals . . ." *New York Times*, January 26, 1997.

Page 306   "Against this backdrop, as the long . . ." *Daily News*, June 8, 1997.

Page 306   "Spotting a workman . . ." Easthampton, New York police report.

Page 306   "As Munnich told his story . . ." Munnich's claims are set forth in a signed affidavit, which he filed with the East Hampton, New York, police. The quotes are drawn from the affidavit.

Page 308   "But the injury and his police testimony . . ." Suffolk County District Attorney press release, July 25, 1997.

Page 308   "In September, Munnich requested that the governor of New York . . ." *Newsday*, September 12, 1997.

Page 308   "The following May, Martha retorted, with a federal lawsuit . . ." *Newsday*, May 7, 1998.

Chapter 20

Page 309   "It was damaging enough . . ." *Associated Press*, May 31, 1997.

Page 310   "Foolishly, Martha had even taken to publicly . . ." Martha Stewart, during interview with Charlie Rose, 92nd Street YM-YWHA lecture series, Manhattan, March 26, 1996.

Page 310   "One of the book's most devastating . . ." Three documents relating to the matter of Andy's cancer and the fact that Martha Stewart never had more than one child merit attention. In the October 1996 issue of *McCall's*, Martha was quoted as saying, "The only regret I have in my entire life is that I don't have more children. That is a very serious regret. My husband had cancer that precluded him from having more children. And I didn't want to adopt. It was stupid. I'd give anything to have a son now."

Three months later, in the January issue of the magazine, *McCall's* published what seems, on the plain meaning of the words, a clear enough retraction, by Martha, of her statement that Andy's cancer had "precluded him" from having more children. Her statement read, "I would like to clarify that my former husband, Andrew Stewart, and I did not have more than one child for personal reasons, not because of any medical disability on Mr. Stewart's part. As far as I am aware, there is no such medical disability." Leaving no doubt as to what Martha was "clarifying" and to emphasize that it was not the reporter's mistake, the editors followed her statement with an italics statement of their own, which read, "Martha Stewart told writer Gail Collins in a taped interview that she hadn't had more children *because of her husband's cancer* [emphasis added].

Nonetheless, when the subject of the *McCall's* statement and Andy's cancer came up in a court deposition in June of 1999, Martha reversed herself with a confused explanation that seemed once again to blame Andy. At one point in the deposition she said that the "personal reasons" she referred to in her *McCall's* statement did relate to Andy's cancer, including his sperm count. Then she continued on to assert that she had been informed at the time by doctors, which discussions she said took place in front of her husband, that "it would be inadvisable to have children, they might have deformities or something." That statement would appear to be irreconcilable with her previous statement, in the January 1997 issue of *McCall's*, that she was unaware of any medical reason why Andy could not have more children.

In interviews for this book, Andy Stewart said Martha's hysterectomy occurred while she was still in her child-bearing years, but couldn't be precise as to the date. Norma Collier was more specific. She recalled being told personally by Martha at about the time the two women were operating The Uncatered Affair that she (Martha) intended to undergo a partial hysterectomy.

Page 311 "After getting a blast of the truth . . ." *McCall's*, January 1997.

Page 311 "How could a person write, in her own magazine . . ." Martha Stewart, "Remembering," *Martha Stewart Living*, June 1992.

Page 311 ". . . a hideous piece of yellow journalism, . . ." *Denver Post*, July 14, 1997.

Page 311 "I try to ignore it . . ." *Tampa Tribune*, September 6, 1997.

Page 312 "In Los Angeles, a couple of weeks later . . ." *Daily Variety*, September 16, 1997.

Page 313 "But less than thirty seconds into the interview . . ." *Larry King Live*, September 16, 1997.

Page 314 "Since she could not challenge . . ." Copley News Service, November 20, 1997.

Page 314 "In the article, two experts . . ." *Associated Press*, November 22, 1997.

Page 315 "Celebrity columnist Liz Smith had already . . ." *Newsday*, September 3, 1997.

Page 316 "The network constructed an elaborate kitchen . . ." *USA Today*, February 10, 1997. A CBS correspondent, interviewed for this book, said staff people on the show lived in constant dread of using or even touching anything in Martha's kitchen. Large handwritten signs were displayed, reading, "Do Not Use," and "Stay Out."

Page 316   "So CBS Network President Leslie Moonves . . ." *Columbus Dispatch*, January 15, 1998.

Page 317   "Even so, the 'Martha Goes to Cuba' plan . . ." The information, itinerary, and characterization of Martha's travels through Havana, Cuba, come from interviews with her guide, Neil Joan.

Page 321   "A trio of characters from . . ." *Daily News*, December 17, 1997.

Page 321   "Another time, a limousine driver backed . . ." *Chicago Sun Times*, August 27, 2000.

Page 321   "In May 1998, Martha appeared at an Ontario . . ." *Report on Business*, July 1998.

Page 322   "At the opposite extreme . . ." See *New York*, January 20, 1997. The quoted price for an interview for this book was $10,000, which was declined.

Page 322   "When a reporter asked her to comment . . ." *Advertising Age*, October 16, 2000.

Page 322   "At lunch one day in a Japanese restaurant . . ." Informed source.

Page 323   "The dinner, in the revolving restaurant . . ." The description of the dinner at the Seattle Space Needle comes from a source who attended the dinner and witnessed the events described.

Page 327   "In the first of these . . ." Details regarding Scientia Health Group, Cadus Pharmaceuticals, and Triarc Companies, Inc., come from Securities and Exchange Commission filings. A copy of the Scientia Health Group investor list was obtained by the author.

Page 327   "Meanwhile, Waksal was busy . . ." See *Vanity Fair* magazine, June 2002.

Page 331   "By mid-decade . . ." "Remembering," *Martha Stewart Living*, December/January 1997/1998.

Page 332   "Meanwhile, her five-times-per-week, . . ." *Automotive News*, September 7, 1998.

Page 332   "What's more, she would soon . . ." *Fortune*, October 12, 1998.

Page 332   "She answered her phone with a single . . ." Multiple sources.

Page 332   "One morning, she called her director of technology . . ." Informed source.

Page 333   "Other mail—which was invariably positive and . . ." Informed source.

Page 334   "When she scolded people . . ." Informed source.

Page 334   "Fidgeting and anxiety reached fever pitch . . ." Experience of author when being prepped for appearance on Martha Stewart's show.

Page 334   "But whenever she arrived, she expected . . ." Informed source. Though it sounds petty in the extreme, the requirement was in fact rigidly enforced. The source told of the panic that erupted on the set when executives at the studio were giving a tour of the facilities to some visiting dignitaries and discovered, upon entering Martha's private office, that the bathroom was at that moment being used by one of the show's producers. For yet more of how staffers lived in fear of encroaching on Martha's personal spaces, see p. 290 "The network constructed . . ." regarding the specially built kitchen for her use on the set of the CBS *The Early Show*.

Chapter 21

Page 337   "Sharon Patrick also undoubtedly . . ." *More*, February 2001.

Page 338   "On a single day, November 13, 1998, . . ." *Associated Press*, November 29, 1998.

Page 339   "A top official at Boston University quit his job . . ." Interview with author.

Page 340   "Employees at the company's corporate headquarters . . ." The working conditions and prevailing mood, and specific instances of events occurring at the company's headquarters come from company employees who worked in the office as well as outsiders who visited Martha there.

Page 341   "The company was generating more than $222 million . . ." *Fortune*, May 14, 2001.

Page 342   "The key players in that regard . . ." *Venture Capital Journal*, December 1, 1999.

Page 343   "In the deal, Kleiner Perkins paid Martha's company $25 million . . ." Martha Stewart Living Omnimedia, Inc., IPO prospectus.

Page 344   "With Martha it was different. . . ." Interview with those whose attended the road show for R.S. Investments.

Page 344   "The wealthiest clients with the most capital . . ." Ibid.

Page 346   "Even Martha herself had been put under oath . . ." Case file. *Martha Stewart vs. National Enquirer, Inc.* Case No. 97-8531, United States District Court, Central District of California.

Page 346   "Guests at the mid-June 1999 wedding on Long Island . . ." *USA Today*, June 16, 1999.

Page 346   "Four days later, she would be raising her right hand in a rented room . . ." Deposition of Martha Stewart. *Martha Stewart vs. National Enquirer, Inc.* Case No. 97-8531, United States District Court, Central District of California.

Page 346   "The resulting testimony . . ." Ibid.

Page 349   "At 9:30 A.M., on October 19, she would step . . ." *Denver Post*, October 20, 1999.

Page 350   "In midmonth the road show . . ." Sources in road show at R.S. Investments, San Francisco.

Page 350   "Martha came off well informed . . ." Ibid.

Page 350   "The most dislocating moment of all came . . ." Ibid.

Page 352   "After handing out orange juice . . ." *Good Morning America*, October 20, 1999.

Page 353   "For lunch on the day of the IPO . . ." *New York Times*, October 20, 1999, *Talk*, jointly published by Hearst Corp. and Miramax Films, was launched by Ms. Brown with much fanfare in the summer of 1999, but succumbed to mounting losses in the weakening advertising market of 2001. It ceased publication in January of 2002.

Chapter 22

Page 357   "But Martha wouldn't let it . . ." Martha's efforts to control the content of this book were blatant but not unusual.

Among other things, they included having her lawyer, Allen Grubman, approach the author's literary agency, the William Morris Agency, with an offer to hire the author as a "writer for hire" to obtain control of the book; and having her company legal counsel write to the publisher in an effort to examine and influence the book's content.

This sort of behavior is typical of her efforts to control and shape independent public commentary about her life, even though it is she and no one else who has sought to make her life public. She disparaged Jerry Oppenheimer's book, *Martha Stewart—Just Desserts*, as "stupid" even before it was published. In her deposition in the *National Enquirer* libel suit, she acknowledged under questioning that she had approached the president of the William Morrow and Company publishing house, publisher of the hardcover edition of the book, in an unsuccessful effort to stop publication. She also acknowledged doing "whatever I could" to discourage people from talking to Oppenheimer.

Later, when the Arts & Entertainment cable television network undertook a biography of Martha Stewart, she successfully controlled access to every person interviewed for the program. Said a producer for the show, "We had to clear every single interview, in advance, through Susan Magrino. Every single thing about the documentary was hard, Martha was hard all the way. She behaved as if she were the coproducer of the show. She censored a lot of the people we wanted to talk to. George Christiansen [her brother, the Turkey Hill carpenter] had wanted to talk to us but she stopped it. She totally controlled our access to people who knew her." The source explained that Martha would give the show unlimited freedom to talk to her friends, but whatever the producers asked in interviews would get back to Martha immediately, and if she didn't like the line of questioning, months would go by before they could get anyone at all to talk with them again. In this way, a highly favorable biographical portrait emerged that the producers privately agreed was a wholly incomplete picture.

This type of "access control" is a favored tactic of nearly all celebrities in dealing with the media. For an entertaining discussion of the process in action elsewhere in the media, see Jeanette Walls, *Dish: The Inside Story on the World of Gossip*, Avon Books, 2000.

Page 358   "When someone asked her aunt . . ." Interview, Informed source.

Page 358   "One day in the spring of 2000, Susan Magrino went to lunch . . ." Informed source within earshot.

Page 359   "The article sought to explain to her neighbors . . ." *New York Times*, April 9, 2000.

Page 360   "Ultimately, she never left town at all . . ." Interview, Informed source and *New York Post*, August 3, 2001. As of publication date for this book, the town board of Bedford, New York, where the property is located, had made several onsite inspections of the premises and finally voted 3-to-2 to issue building permits to allow her to make various improvements to the premises.

Page 360   "Nearly two years . . ." *Westport News*, February 15, 2002. At one point in her speech, Martha mistakenly said she had paid $49,000 for her Turkey Hill home and moved to Westport in 1972. In reality, she had paid $33,750 and moved to Westport a year earlier, in 1971. See Chapter 4.

Page 361   "On another occasion, the entourage motored . . ." Interview, Buckwheat Donoghue.

Page 361   "Her squadron of planes . . ." Interview, Larry Nagy.

Page 361   "José knew all about Martha . . ." Interview, José Janssen.

Page 364   "She said, 'I've got a . . .'" Like the teen adventuress Nancy Drew, Martha is fascinated by airplanes and has models of numbers of them displayed in her studio offices in Connecticut. But several searches of Federal Aviation Administration records in Oklahoma City, Oklahoma, during 2001 by researcher Bridget Samburg, established that Martha did not, and never did, possess an FAA-issued pilot's license of any sort, either student or otherwise. The searches were conducted using her legal name as well as all reasonable alternative spellings of it, as well as her maiden name, and all turned up negative results.

Epilogue

Page 366   "The immediate focus . . ." See MSNBC.com Jan. 20, 2002.

Page 369   "In the wake of the stories . . ." The best continuing coverage of the " ImClone/Martha scandal was done by Charles Gasparino of the *Wall Street Journal,* Constance Hays of the *New York Times,* and Lauren Barach of the *New York Post.* The narrative events of the epilogue are drawn from their numerous stories on the matter.

Page 374   "At the start of 2002 . . ." Financial information regarding Martha Stewart Living Omnimedia, Inc., is from the companies' own publicly filed financial reports with the Securities and Exchange Commission.

Financial information regarding Meredith Corp. and Kmart Corp. are similarly drawn from annual and quarterly statements (Forms 10K) supplied to the SEC by these companies.

INDEX

Abrams, Harry, 102

Abrams Publishing, 102–103, 107, 109, 121, 124

Abreu, Renaldo, 220, 413

Adam, Eleanor, 44

Adams, Ruth, 158, 408

Adams House renovation project, 165, 168, 214, 408
    Kmart and, 181–182, 192, 194, 204, 212
    magnitude of investment in, 204–212
    print version, 227
    purchase price, 165
    scandal involving, 196, 203–212

A&E biography, 430

Alaska, Tincup Lake, 361–362, 363

Allegri, Thomas, 78, 79

Antonini, Joseph, 142, 157, 174–176, 189, 191–193, 219, 220
    characterization of, 407
    Loren-Snyder and, 133–137, 142, 150, 153, 407
    replaced at Kmart, 288–289

Avedon, Richard, 54

Bacanovic, Peter, 130–131, 331, 370

Bangor Punta Corporation, 76, 77, 102, 109

Barnard College for Women, 47, 49

Barnett, Pamela, 122, 406

Bass, Michael, 2, 5, 16

Bayles, Daphne, 75, 76–77

Beers, Charlotte, 248–249, 270, 327, 416–417

Benson, Mildred (Carolyn Keene), 349

"Best Dressed College Girls" (*Glamour* magazine, 1961), 47, 52–53, 59

"Betty Crocker," 232, 410

Biographies of Martha Stewart:
    A&E television, 430
    autobiography, plans for (*Martha, Really and Truly*), 357
    Oppenheimer (*Martha Stewart—Just Desserts, The Unauthorized Biography*), 319–322, 345–346, 394, 430
    Wooten (*Martha Stewart, America's Lifestyle Expert*), 66

Black, Leon, 327

Bogotá:
    Stewarts vacation to, 82–85, 150, 166, 399
    Tatlocks moving to, 63, 80–85

Bolster, Bill, 265, 284

Bonwit Teller, 47, 49

Books by Martha Stewart, 109–125, 412
    Entertaining, 76, 90–93, 102–103, 119, 123, 145, 149–150, 302, 356, 372
    Hors D'Oeuvres, 118
    Martha Stewart Cookbook, 275
    Martha Stewart's Christmas, 194
    Martha Stewart's Gardening, Month by Month, 226
    Martha Stewart's New Old House, 193, 227
    Pies & Tarts, 118, 146

Books by Martha Stewart (*Continued*)
  *Quick Cook, Two Hundred Easy and
    Elegant Recipes*, 118, 119–120,
    146
  Weddings, 118, 146, 157, 180
Brack, Reg, 185
Brokaw, Tom, 319
Brown, Tina, 353, 429
Broyard, Anatole, 89
Bunshaft, Gordon, 303
Business names:
  Market Basket, The, 95–98, 103,
    106, 120, 402
  Martha Stewart, Inc. (1977), 98
  Martha Stewart Enterprises, 251
  Uncatered Affair, The, 92, 93, 97,
    101, 106, 111
Butler, Marion, 43

Capasso, Andrew, 71
Carter, Graydon, 212
Catalog and direct marketing, 340,
  368, 372
Catering business, 90, 91, 120–121,
  402
CBS television network:
  The Early Show, 1, 3
  Martha Stewart Living TV show, 264,
    265
  morning show, 298, 316, 332, 428
  primetime special, 275
  Winter Olympics, 332
Ceramics Co. Ltd. (Chinese city of
  Jiaozuo), 300–301
"Chick-ing," 232, 236
Child, Julia, 100, 110
Chinese factory conditions, 300–301
Christiansen, Rita, 211, 222, 243, 276,
  413
Christiansen (Kostyra), George, 104,
  120, 144, 162, 211, 430
Christmas special, 193–194
Christmas trips, 25, 124–125
Ciccone, Louise (Madonna), 251, 417

Cina, Vinny, 43
Clarkson Potter imprint, Crown
  Publishing, 110. *See also* Crown
  Publishing
Clayson, Jane, 2, 3, 5, 14–20
Clinton, Bill/Hillary, 195, 253, 275,
  278, 332
Collier, Norma:
  catering business partnership with
    Martha, 87–95, 111, 398
  Glamour magazine, best dressed
    college girl list, 52–53
  Levitz stock, 68, 70, 87, 93–94
  on Martha's/Andy's relationship,
    78–79, 100–101
  modeling career, 55, 56, 398
  recollections of Martha, 78, 88, 93,
    121, 223, 321, 358, 403
  split with Martha, 93–95, 177, 223
Collier, Wolf, 104
Collins, Gail, 425
Common Market, The, 95–98
Conaway, Chuck, 423–424
Conde Nast Publishing, 182–183, 217,
  284, 291
Cramer, James, 373
Crespi, Neil, 72
Cronkite, Walter, 4
Crown Publishing, 118–119, 180–181,
  182, 245, 250
  editors, 216, 227
  Entertaining, 102, 109–110, 118
  Magrino and, 227, 252
  videotapes, 149, 163, 166, 187
Cuba, 316–320, 427

DaimlerChrysler Corporation, 378
Daniels, Faith, 226
Davis, Martin, 183
Debtor-in-possession, 375
Dennehy, Brian, 66
Diana, Princess, 278–279, 281,
  312–313
Dilenschneider, Robert, 279–282

Dion, Celine, 378
Diller, Barry, 291
Disney, Walt, 389–390
Doerr, John, 343
Dowd, Maureen, 123
Durshkin, Mikki, 91

Edelman, Asher, 72
Eisenstein, Ruth, 103
Elfenbein Studio, 56–58
Enron, 366, 417
Everyday Food, 379

Faillace, Larry, 393
Fairclough, Robyn, 143, 163, 213, 310
Fairfield Advocate, 201, 209
Faneuil, Douglas, 373
Fans, 196–197, 320–321, 333, 411
Fast, Jonathan, 90
Fekkai, Frederick, 253
Feminism and women in society, 48,
    54, 65, 114–115, 404–405
Fernandes, Necy, 220, 413
Finch, Kathleen, 318
Flemming, Olivia, 43
Florio, Steve, 284
Flying lessons/pilot's license, 364,
    414–415, 431
Ford Motor Company, 332, 390
Foster-Ferguson Group, 48–49
Friend, Larry H., 71

Gabel, Hortense, 71
Galápagos Islands, 274, 281, 283
George magazine, 389
Gifford, Kathie Lee, 221, 275, 99–300
Gilbert, Greg, 66, 67–68
Glamour magazine ("Best Dressed
    College Girls"), 47, 52 53, 59
Gnomes, 103, 107, 109, 110, 118, 121
Gottlieb von Lehndorff, Vera, 54–55
Gotti, Victoria, 253
Grasso, Richard, 9, 349
Greene, Sandy, 66, 99–100

Green Farms Academy, 198
Group W. Syndication, 228–242, 245,
    263–271, 274, 275, 284
Grubman, Allen, 24, 250–251, 252,
    255, 283, 292, 327, 417, 430
Grubman, Elizabeth, 250
Gumbel, Bryant, 3, 11, 298

Hachette Filipacchi publishing house,
    389
Haenlein, Joy, 210–211
Hall, Floyd, 288–289, 293
Hallmark Cards survey ("nicest
    women"), 195
Hayford, Pamela, 44
Hefner, Hugh, 225
Herbert, Kim, 104
Heyward, Andrew, 2, 10, 316
Hoge, Sharon King, 416
Holder, Pauline, 210
Hole in the Wall Gang camp, 205–212
Home Shopping Network, 291
Homestyles, 207
Hotchner, Aaron (A. E.), 205–206
Houses/homes of Martha Stewart, 194,
    302–303, 307, 360, 414–415
    Bunshaft site (Macklowe feud),
        303–308, 319–320, 321, 424
    Turkey Hill farmhouse, 9, 39–40,
        75–85, 120, 153–154
Human Rights Watch, 301, 420

Icahn, Carl, 326–327, 329, 369
Ickes, Harold, 105
ImClone Systems, Inc., 6–9, 127,
    326–328, 367–372
Internet explosion, 289–290
Iowa State Fair, 347–349
Is Martha Stewart Living? (parody), 274

Jackson, Linda, 43
Janssen, José, 361
Joan, Neil, 317–318, 427
John Wiley & Sons, 355–356

Johnson & Johnson's, 57, 58
Jones, Linda, 225
Jones, Quincy, 262
Jong, Erica, 25, 90, 91, 117–118, 198

Karmazin, Mel, 323, 324
Kasindorf, Jeannie, 222–223, 257–258, 416
Keene, Carolyn (Mildred Benson), 349
Kelly, Keith, 284, 416
Kelly, Pat, 135
Kennedy, Jackie, 52, 212–213
Kennedy, John F., Jr., 389
Keogh, Pamela Clark, 213
Keyser, Elizabeth, 198–201, 203–204, 206, 208–209, 212, 411–412
Keyser, Rose, 198, 206
King, Billie Jean, 114
King, Larry, 275, 298, 313–314
Kleiner Perkins Caufield & Byers, 342–343
Kmart Corporation. *See also* Antonini, Joseph; Loren-Snyder, Barbara:
  and Adams House project, 176–178, 181, 204, 211, 214
  bankruptcy of (2002), 365–366, 370–374, 407, 423, 432
  benefits to Martha of deal with, 193–194, 286–289, 370, 374
  celebrity promotion, 287, 288
  contract with Martha, 133–154, 155–157, 161, 165, 168–169, 182, 228, 245
  operating details, 287–288, 375
  rejection of magazine deal, 217–218
  renegotiation with, 245, 246, 250, 293–294, 299
  stress in relationship with Martha, 187–193
  sweatshop labor, 299–300, 420
  thirtieth anniversary of, 227
  Time Warner and, 185, 286, 293–294

Kostyra, Eddie, 33–51
  Andy and, 54, 99
  death of, 107
  Martha's characterizations/
    remembrances of, 255–256, 355–356, 394
  Martha's controlling personality
    based on, 41, 50, 77–78, 93, 101, 122, 195, 303, 396, 398
  and Martha's modeling career
    as teenager, 48
  in Westport, 104–105, 106–107
Kostyra, Eric, 34
Kostyra, Frank, 48, 322
Kostyra (Christiansen), George, 104, 120, 144, 162, 211, 389
Kostyra, Laura, 104, 144, 162, 220
Kostyra, Martha. *See* Stewart, Martha
Kostyra, Martha (mother), 34–35, 50, 395
  cooking show appearance, 105
  Martha's description of (on *Charlie Rose* show), 256
  in Westport, 106–107, 146, 162–163, 220
Kresge, Sebastian, 286
Krupinski, Ben, 226, 414–415
Kudlow, Larry, 373

Labor/factory working conditions, 299–302, 420–421
Lalli, Frank, 389
Lang, Jennifer, 139–140, 143
Lawrence, Vicki, 237, 238
Lerer, Kenneth and Katherine, 246, 393
Levin, Gerald, 186, 261, 262
Levitz, Gary, 70–71
Levitz, Jacqueline, 71
Levitz, Leon, 70
Levitz, Ralph, 71
Levitz Furniture stock, 67–71, 87, 93–94

Logan, Don, 261, 262–263, 292
Loren-Snyder, Barbara, 133–144
    Antonini and, 133–144, 150–154,
        156–157, 161
    Kmart, bringing Martha together
        with, 136–144, 150–154,
        156–157, 161, 178, 214, 228,
        374, 406–407
    Kmart and Adams House deal,
        173–178, 181, 185
    magazine project, 219, 220
    and stress in Kmart/Martha
        relationship, 189, 191, 192
Lumet, Sidney, 328
Lupus Foundation book-signing/
    luncheon, 274, 277–278

Macklowe, Harry, 304–308, 319–320,
    312, 424
Madonna, 251
Magazine project (*Martha Stewart
    Living*), 215–223, 225–226,
    227–228, 368–370, 377, 379
Magrino, Susan, 146, 227, 252–253,
    293, 358, 421
    A&E biography and, 430
    damage control, 222, 310, 358–359
    in Kasindorf article, 222
Malsch, Susan, 209, 210
Market Basket, The, 95–98, 103, 106,
    120, 402
Martha Inc., 375
Martha Stewart, America's Lifestyle Expert
    (by Sara McIntosh Wooten), 66
Martha Stewart. *See* Stewart, Martha
MarthaStewart.com, 339
*Martha Stewart—Just Desserts, The
    Unauthorized Biography* (by Jerry
    Oppenheimer), 312–322,
    345–346, 394, 402, 425, 430
Martha Stewart Living Omnimedia,
    Inc.:
    activities of, 370–371
    advertising dropped, 378

    Beers on audit committee of,
        416–417
    business segments (four), 372
    catalog and direct marketing, 340,
        370
    current status and future of,
        365–376
    financial data (SEC filings), 370,
        371, 432
    importance of Martha herself to,
        386–388
    initial public offering (IPO),
        122–123, 246–247, 290, 294,
        335–352, 365, 371, 376, 429,
        431
    stock price decline, 9, 366
    Time Warner deal and, 292–293
McCall's, 310, 311, 425–426
McCully, George, 68, 73, 78, 80, 101,
    118, 346
McHaney, Elizabeth, 230–231
McLaughlin, John, 223
McMurran, Kristin, 124
Meeker, Mary, 342, 343
Meigher, Christopher, 184–186,
    215–216, 218, 261–262, 284, 291
Menegus, Joyce, 44, 49
Meredith Corporation, 369, 388–389,
    432
Merrill Lynch, 373
Merrin, Evelyn, 206
Milken, Michael, 329
Miller, Robert, 262, 263
Mirken, Alan, 110, 163, 166
Mo, Keb, 240
Modeling career, 47–62, 397, 398
Monness, Andy, 64–67, 72, 73, 79,
    367, 377, 401
Monness, Crespi & Hardt, 72
Monness, Williams & Sidel brokerage
    firm, 69, 71, 257
Monroe, Rose (Rosie the Riveter),
    404–405
Moonves, Leslie, 11–12, 316

Morgan Stanley & Co., 289–290, 341–342, 344, 350
Motley, Isolde, 217, 218, 219–220
Mountain climbing (Mount Kilimanjaro, September 1993), 246, 416
Munnich, Matthew, 306–308, 312, 424
Munro, J. Richard, 183, 184, 186
Murdoch, Rupert, 183, 217, 291, 322
Myerson, Bess, 71

Nagy, Larry, 363–364
"Nancy Drew," 44–45, 119, 195, 255, 349, 431
National Enquirer libel case, 309, 314–315, 345–351, 394, 429, 430
NATPE convention, 236–237, 267–268, 270
NBC network, 264–265, 275, 298
Negrin, Vicky, 97
Netscape Communications, Inc., 289–290, 342
Nevas, Leo, 209–210
Newhouse, Si, 182–185, 284, 291
Newman, Paul, 27, 205–206, 207, 210
New York State Department of Taxation, 244, 275–276, 298–299, 421

Ober, Eric, 10
Okrent, Dan, 215–216
Onassis, Jackie Kennedy, 52, 212–213
Oppenheimer, Jerry (*Martha Stewart— Just Desserts, The Unauthorized Biography*), 319–322, 330, 346, 394, 430
Orr, Patricia, 91
Osgood, Beverly, 197
Osgood, Charles, 323
Otis, Beverly, 44

Pantelioni, Michael, 64
Papageorge, Lee, 96
Paramount Communications, 183–184

Parody (*Is Martha Stewart Living?*), 274
Pasternak, Bart and Mariana, 125–128, 327, 330, 373
Patrick, Sharon, 245–250, 252, 263, 268–269, 377, 383
    initial public offering (IPO) and, 337, 340, 341, 350–351
    organizing business, 372
    meeting, 245–247
    selling stock, 367–368
    Time Warner coup and, 284, 285, 289, 293, 294–295
PBS project, 146–149, 157–158, 159
Peltz, Nelson, 327, 329
Pennybacker, Miles, 96
People profile, 124
Perelman, Ronald, 194, 248–249, 295, 303
Perlberg, Ed, 64–65, 66, 67, 72
Perlberg, Monness brokerage firm, 99, 112, 400
Peterson, Peter, 328
Pfaelzer, Mariana R., 351
Philbin, Regis, 221
Pierce, Cary, 105–106
Pilot's license/flying lessons, 364, 414–415, 431–432
Pittman, Robert, 246
Pittman, Sandra, 246
Pope's Cuban visit, 316–320
Posner, Jarrett, 329
Posner, Victor, 329
Probst, Alice, 197, 411

Quick Cook, Two Hundred Easy and Elegant Recipes, 118, 119–120, 146

Radio ("Ask Martha"), 298, 372
Rather, Dan, 317, 323
Reilly, Patrick, 292, 293
"Remembering" columns, 37, 44–45, 80, 302, 394–396, 422–424
Revlon, 249
Riggs, Bobby, 114

Rivera, Geraldo, 229–230, 236–237
Road show, 344–345
Roberts, Dick, 162, 163, 165–166, 170
Robinson, Jill, 89, 118, 198
Rose, Charlie, 254–259, 322–323, 353
"Rosie the Riveter," 404–406
Ross, Steven, 183–184
R.S. Investments, 350–351
Rutt, Chris, 410

Samburg, Bridget, 420–421
Satter, Robert, 123–124
Sawyer, Diane, 353
Schlafly, Phyllis, 115
Schulman, Bruce J., 115
Scripts, 334–335, 428
Sears, 332
Seattle Space needle dinner, 427
Severeid, Eric, 4
Sheingold, Richard, 228–242, 264–271
Siebert, Muriel, 65
Smith, Jaclyn, 129, 137, 140, 141, 154,
     190, 287
Smith, Liz, 315, 316
Spy magazine, 214
St. John, Jill, 140–141
Staff/employees, Martha's relationship
     with, 121–122, 332–335,
     340–341, 428
Stephens, Jeffrey, 194, 212, 413
Sterling Vineyards, 149
Stewart, Alexis (daughter):
   as baby, 57–58, 60–61, 62, 84
   birth, 55–56
   boyfriends, 104, 323
   as child, 88, 91, 198, 398–399
   in column by Martha (2000),
     398–399
   in Entertaining (1982), 110
   in Kasindorf article (1990), 223
   relationship with parents, 277,
     398–399
   schools/classes, 91, 104, 144, 146, 198
   Turkey Hill apartment, 104, 160–161

Stewart, Andy (ex-husband):
   Adams house, 165, 174
   cancer, 98, 103–104, 310, 403,
     425–426
   career, 26, 54, 61, 76, 99–107, 212
   college/law school, 26, 50, 53, 54
   Entertaining, 110, 145
   Gnomes, 102–103, 107, 109, 110, 117,
     121
   Kmart deal and, 150–153, 155
   leaving Martha and divorce, 143,
     164–169, 179, 180, 194, 196,
     223, 276
   her behavior after, 169, 213–214
   Stewart v. Stewart case file, 199–201,
     208–209
   on Martha's career as stockbroker,
     69, 399–400
   on Martha's depression after Levitz
     debacle, 87–88
   on Martha's embarrassment over
     Eddie, 397
   Martha's father and, 101
   other women and, 109, 117–118,
     143
   People profile, 124
   public interest in, 146
   relationship with Martha and her
     treatment of him, 50, 76, 78–80,
     91, 99–107, 124, 160, 277
     leaving Martha alone at Christmas,
     25, 124–125
     meeting Martha, 50, 397–398
     newlywed year, 53–54
     serving as employee/stage prop,
     98, 120, 164, 165
     wedding, 50
Stewart, Ethel (Andy's mother), 51, 120
Stewart, George (Andy's father), 50–51
Stewart, Martha:
   author's relationship with, 26–27,
     355–357, 430
   catering business, 90, 91, 120–121,
     402

Stewart, Martha (*Continued*)
    childhood/family background,
        33–45, 394–397
    college years, 47, 49, 52–53, 59
    companies (*see* Business names;
        Martha Stewart Living
        Omnimedia, Inc.)
    controlling nature of personality, 41,
        49, 50, 59, 77–78, 80, 93, 101,
        122, 195, 303, 362, 394,
        396–397, 419–420
    dichotomy of public image vs.
        private reality, 26, 30–31,
        195–196, 223, 258–259,
        273–274, 277, 333–334, 345
    disorganization of personal records,
        243–244
    frenzied schedule, 226, 316,
        331–332
    hands, condition of, 153–154
    high school class of 1959 (Nutley
        High School), 41, 43–45
    hives incident, 257–258
    hysterectomy, 55
    job as live-in domestic, 49–50
    marital breakup/divorce, 143,
        164–169, 179, 180, 194, 196,
        199, 201, 208–209, 213–214,
        223, 258, 276
    modeling career, 47–62
    on money, 350–351
    as mother (*see* Stewart, Alexis
        (daughter))
    negative stories/gossip about, 198,
        203–204, 221–222, 319–324,
        331–335, 414, 426–429
    on not having more children, 55,
        310–311
    parents (*see* Kostyra, Eddie (father);
        Kostyra, Martha (mother))
    people skills/staff relationship,
        121–122, 277, 331–335,
        340–341, 428, 429
    pets, 297
    privacy, appeal for (1998), 321
    stockbroker career, 63–73, 80,
        99–100, 222–223, 256–257,
        398–400, 401, 416
    strategy of getting others to pay,
        173–186
    trips, 25, 246, 274, 281, 283, 302,
        353–362, 416, 419, 431–432
    on wanting publicity, 121
Stewart, Tabori and Chang, 151
Stewart v. Stewart (divorce case file),
    199–201
Stockbroker career. *See* Wall Street
    career
Stock market eras/milestones, 88–89,
    159–160, 181, 289–290, 338–339,
    344
Stolley, Dick, 184
Suares, J. C., 128–132, 212–213,
    370
Syndication market, 229–230

Tatlock, Alison, 61, 62, 84
Tatlock, Chris, 58, 60, 61, 63, 80–85,
    104, 148, 166
Tatlock, Kathy, 56–62, 87, 88, 143,
    147–149, 365, 407–409
    Bogotá move, 61–63, 80–85
    early friendship with Martha, 56–62,
        90
    final break with Martha, 179
    hosting Stewarts in Bogotá,
        80–85
    marital breakup, 104, 166
    pregnancy/children, 60–61
    talking with Andy about Erica Jong,
        118
    video projects, 147–150, 157–172,
        173, 177–179, 415
Taxation questionnaire, 244, 275–276,
    298–299, 422
Television appearances/shows,
    225–242, 263–264, 332, 340,
    358–359, 367